Using BBC BASIC

Using BBC BASIC

P. J. Cockerell
University of Kent at Canterbury

JOHN WILEY & SONS

Chichester · New York · Brisbane · Toronto · Singapore

Library of Congress Cataloging in Publication Data:

Cockerell, P. J. (Pete J.) 1962–
　　Using BBC BASIC.

　　Bibliography: p.
　　Includes index.
　　1. BBC Microcomputer—Programming.　2. Basic (Computer
program language)　I. Title.　II. Title: Using B.B.C.
B.A.S.I.C.
QA76.8.B35C6　1983　　　001.64′24　　　83-10607
ISBN 0 471 90242 X

British Library Cataloguing in Publication Data:

Cockerell, P.J.
　　Using BBC BASIC
　　1.BBC Microcomputer—Programming
　　2.Basic (Computer program language)
　　I. Title
　　001.64′24　　QA76.8.B3

　　ISBN 0 471 90242 X

Typeset by Pintail Studios Ltd., Ringwood, Hampshire.
Printed in Great Britain by Pitman Press Ltd., Bath, Avon.

Dedication

Working on the assumption that this might be the only chance I get to dedicate a book, I'd like to make the most of the page allocated. So, this book is dedicated:

To my project group:
    Francesca (who promised me a kiss if I mentioned her),
    Pete, Richard and Mohammed (who promised NOT to kiss me if I mentioned them)

To my friends:
    D, Neale, Pete (again), Russell, Ray and the others

To my sister and brothers:
    Denise, Andy, Paul, Martin, Steve and Kevin

To my parents:
    Mummy and Daddy

Last, and most,
    To Deborah, for being.

Contents

Preface

By now it is a well established fact that the BBC Micro is a very powerful computer, and that its BASIC is a very fast and useful version of the language. Unfortunately this very sophistication can make programming the machine a daunting task, even for users who are relatively knowledgeable of BASIC. The size of the User Guide is a testament to the complexity of the computer.

The aim of this book is to address a subset of the facilities which can be used from BASIC and Assembly language. The idea is to foster the reader's interest in the subjects covered, so that he has some kind of grounding on which he can base further reading of the more specialised books. The choice of topics covered has been dictated by space, time, and my personal interests. Hopefully there is some degree of correspondence between mine and the reader's.

The first two chapters cover the "stuff" of programming, data and control structures. Chapter two, in particular, tries to emphasise the importance of planning and structuring programs when they are of a significant length. BBC BASIC provides some of the tools for writing readable and reliable programs; you should take every possible advantage of these.

Chapter three has two aims. Firstly to encourage the use of special "robust" input routines, which improves the reliability of programs to be used by "dumb" users (anyone but you), and also to provide a grounding for Chapter four, which covers BBC Graphics. A single chapter could not hope to cover exhaustively all the possible uses of the BBC Computer's graphics facilities. Instead I touch on several important techniques and point you in the general direction of the bibliography for further reading.

Finally, Chapter five covers the use of the BASIC Assembly, but does not try to teach assembly language. The method here is to bombard the reader with examples to illustrate the various techniques. There is no reason, of course, why the programs cannot be used by non-assembly language programmers. Accuracy in keying-in is probably a more important requirement than a knowledge of assembler.

There are clearly many topics which aren't covered and which deserve to be. The filing system, the MOS and sound are examples. This deficiency may be rectified in future volumes, dependent upon the sales of the current book (so stop browsing and get your cheque book out). Some omissions were forced upon me by, for example, lack of anything but MOS 0.1, and I apologise in advance to any MOS 1.0 and above users for any differences which I failed to take account of.

The ideal reader of this book would have read the User Guide, and understood some of it. He (I use "he" to denote he/she and ?? throughout the text) would also have a fair knowledge of BASIC, as gleaned through reading Cryer & Cryer, or owning a Spectrum etc. for a few weeks. This isn't a text book, so rather than discuss every technique in detail I have opted for using them in programs which (I hope) are well laid-out, and leave you to work-out what's going on. If this method leaves you totally confused, I apologise, but ask you to imagine the satisfaction you get when (if) the penny finally drops.

I am anxious to receive any comments/criticisms/large cash donations you would like to make, with a view to improving future products. Please write either c/o the publisher, or direct to me at:

63 Quorn Gardens,
Leigh-on-Sea
ESSEX SS9 2TA

Thanks.

Canterbury   PETE COCKERELL

Since this book was completed two new ROMs have become available for the BBC Micro from Acorn. The purpose of this note is to explain how possession of these ROMs will affect your use of the book.

The first new ROM is the long-awaited Series One operating system (i.e. MOS 1.2). It turns out that it was worth the wait in gold, as there are many features in this version that aren't even mentioned in the new User Guide. There is one change from MOS 0.1, however, that might affect the operation of some of this book's programs, though I have tried to amend these wherever possible. The change is that after a VDU 5 statement (print at the graphics cursor), you can no longer use PRINT TAB(x,y), or its equivalent VDU 31,x,y to position text on the screen – MOVE has to be used instead. The relationship between the co-ordinates given after TAB and those given after MOVE varies depending on the number of text columns in the current mode, but in general PRINT TAB(x,y) becomes MOVE fact*x,1020-32*y where fact is 16 for MODE 0, 32 for MODEs 1 and 4, and 64 for MODEs 2 and 5.

The second ROM contains the so-called Level II BASIC. This is BBC BASIC minus a few bugs (e.g. the ON . . . GOTO . . . ELSE one mentioned in Chapter 2) plus a few new features. Although it was intended primarily for the Acorn Electron ("out soon"), some BBC Micros are also being fitted with it. The unfortunate effect of this is that the machine code programs of Chapter 5 which reference internal BASIC routines (as opposed to operating system routines) will not work if you have Level II BASIC. The way to tell is by pressing BREAK, then typing REPORT. If the message thus obtained has "(C)1982" in it, then you have Level II. Level I (the version used in this book) says "(C)1981". It must be stressed that only the machine code routines won't work under Level II; the programs in the other four chapters will produce exactly the same results under both versions of the language.

Acknowledgements

Although I can claim that the main graft of thinking up the words and typing them in (to my trusty BBC Computer) was "all my own work", there are several people who deserve a mention for the role they played in making this tome a possibility.

I would like to thank Peter Brown for initiating the whole process when he, lazily, asked me to write to Wiley on his behalf. Once it became clear that the Publishers were going to be foolish enough to offer me a contract, I decided I should really get hold of a BBC Micro. Cynthia Britten of BL Marketing has my gratitude for expediting the delivery of my machine by a good six months.

The bulk of the text was written during the summer vacation of 1982. Thanks are due to my parents and my brother Andy for bearing with me during that time, and to my girlfriend Deborah for baring with me during that time. Long hours of typing seemed to go quicker when I was listening to music. White Heat and Lindisfarne deserve thanks for the albums "In the Zero Hour" and "Lonely Nights" respectively, which kept me sane but didn't do much for my concentration.

I am grateful to David Turner for his permission to use the quoted strings problem of chapter two and for teaching me to look at solutions to problems in terms of recursion when this is feasible. I hope his influence on me is transferred at least partially to the reader.

Finally, I would like to say thank you to the Publishers for not sending round the MAS (manuscript acquisition squad) when I didn't quite meet the deadline.

Chapter One

Dealing with Data

The most important of elements of most programming languages are the data manipulation and program structuring facilities. The first two chapters of this book cover those two topics with respect to the BBC version of BASIC. This chapter deals with the way data, e.g. numbers and strings, can be processed and chapter two is concerned with the language facilities provided in BBC BASIC to do this processing. Since the procedures used in manipulating data can be closely dependent on the "structure" of the data, these first two chapters cover some common ground.

As I am assuming a familiarity with "standard" BASIC, I also assume that you know about numbers and the simple arithmetic operations which BASIC provides, and also about strings and their related functions. Just to get us on a common ground, though, the first section of this chapter covers the three principal types of data object in BBC BASIC – integers, reals and strings. This will pave the way for the next two sections, which deal with arrays and the indirection operators respectively.

1.1 Simple Data Types

As mentioned above, the building blocks of any language are the "objects" it lets the programmer manipulate and the commands it provides for this manipulation. The different data objects usually have a "type" associated with them. Programming languages are said to be strongly or weakly typed, depending on how easily the programmer may differentiate between different sorts of data. In one extreme there is BCPL, a language used for writing operating systems and compilers for other languages. This has only one type: the bit pattern or word. This is just a set of between 16 and 36 binary digits (depending on the computer being used) which can be used to represent any "object" the programmer desires. For example, he may choose to view a particular pattern as a number. On the other hand, the bit pattern of a variable may stand for an address in the computer's memory, or a truth value (TRUE or FALSE). The language itself makes no distinction between these different uses, and treats all values in the same way. This puts a responsibility on the programmer to ensure that he does sensible things with his bit patterns. It would be silly, for example, to take the average of a list of machine addresses. BCPL, however, would not mind a bit.

The opposite view taken is that as programmers use the computer's underlying bit patterns to represent different real-life objects, the various types should be clearly separated, and the programmer should be given the opportunity to create his own types if none of the built-in ones are suitable for his needs. This process is known as data abstraction, and is exemplified by the Pascal programming language. This language has several built-in types – characters, real numbers, integers, and boolean values, and provides for "structured" types – records, sets, arrays and files. Furthermore, the programmer can make-up his own types. For example, if the BBC Computer's graphics were being used in Pascal, it would be possible to define a type called "plot_mode". Variables of this type could have any of the values "store", "or", "and", "xor" or "invert". (See Chapter 4.) The Pascal programmer would give this list of values at the start of the program, a process known as enumerating the type. He could then have variables of type plot_mode, just as we have variables of type string in BASIC.

Where does BASIC appear in this range of typing? Predictably, somewhere in the middle, but probably nearer the BCPL end. BBC BASIC has the two principal data types – numbers and strings – with the common extension that numbers can be real (with fractional parts) or integer. Unlike many BASICs which have this distinction, BBC BASIC actually provides special facilities for dealing with integers. A lot of micro BASICs have a so-called integer type, but throw away the resultant advantages (speed and reduced storage requirements) by dealing with them internally exactly as reals. In addition to the normal structuring facility of arrays, BBC BASIC provides various extras with the existence of the indirection operators (see 1.3).

1.1.1 Integers

Originally all numbers in BASIC were treated as reals, quantities with a fractional part. These are stored in a form known as floating-point, and have the advantage that a wide range of numbers can be stored fairly accurately. However, careful consideration of many problems which are solved on computers reveals that very often numbers are used to represent quantities which aren't strictly numerical at all: the plotting modes cited above is a good example, and there are many others, such as the type of seats allocated in an airline booking system. Other quantities might only be able to have a whole value, such as a memory address in the computer or a telephone number. Representing all these values as real numbers is wasteful of both time and space. Any arithmetic performed on numbers stored in a floating-point form is slower than the equivalent on a similar integer, and floating-point representations often take more bytes of memory (in BBC BASIC, for example, integers and reals are stored as four and five bytes respectively).

Integer variables in BBC BASIC are denoted by the presence of a % sign after their names, e.g. a%, time_taken% etc. As they are stored in four bytes, or 32 bits, they can represent a total of 2^{32} values. Integers in BBC BASIC are interpreted as two's complement numbers, which means that the range of numbers is divided into two halves of minus and plus values. There are 2^{31} of each, which means that

BBC integers can have any value between $-2,147,483,648$ and $2,147,483,647$. The important points to remember are that an integer variable can take any WHOLE value in the above range, and that as long as the calculation stays within the range, it will be totally accurate. This differs from real numbers which are prone to such things as rounding errors.

Another way of accessing four-byte integers is with the "pling" operator, "!". This is one of the three indirection operators, another of which is "?", which can also access numbers. The idea of ! is to give the integer whose four bytes are at the address given after it. For example "!&20E" would give an integer whose four bytes are at locations &20E, &20F, &210 and &211. These are stored in increasing order of significance, so that &20E would contain the byte which determines the first 256 values of the number, &20F would hold the byte responsible for the components 256 to 32768 (2^8 to 2^15 respectively) and so on. In this particular case the four bytes would be interpreted as two 2-byte addresses, as they are the indirection vectors for two operating system routines (see Chapter 5).

The ? operator only accesses one byte at a time and is equivalent to PEEK function (and the POKE statement) on other micros. Values obtained using ? are always in the range 0–255. These two operators are covered in greater detail later on.

What can we do with integers that we can't do with reals? Firstly there are the special arithmetic operators DIV and MOD. These provide integer division (which is faster than real division with /) and the remainder when two integers are divided. A typical use of DIV and MOD would be in base conversion: converting number from one base to another. The function below returns a string which is the representation of n% in base base%.

```
1000 DEF FNconvert_base(n%, base%)
1010    REM  Converts n% to base base%
1020    REM  Return a zero for n%=0
1030    IF n%=0 THEN ="0"
1040    REM  Otherwise convert the upper digits
1050    REM  and return the lowest one
1060 =FNconvert_base(n% DIV base%,base%)+FNdigit(n% MOD base%)
1070
2000 DEF FNdigit(d%)
2010    REM  IF 0<=d%<=9 THEN returns "0" to "9" else
2020    REM  returns "A" for 10, "B" for 11 etc.
2030    IF 0<=d% AND d%<=9 THEN =STR$(d%)
2040 =CHR$(ASC("A")+d%-10)
```

The function is very simple; if n% is zero, it returns the string "0", as 0 is the same in any base. Otherwise it uses itself to convert the upper digits (given by n% DIV base%) and appends to this the character representation of the least significant digit, given by n% MOD base%. The function FNdigit is used to return a letter character if the "digit" required is greater than nine. In hex (base 16) for example, the digit-values 10 to 15 are represented by the letters "A" to "F" respectively. FNconvert_base is an example of a recursive function, more of which in Chapter two.

MOD and DIV can also be used to examine the individual bits of a number. The expression "n% DIV 2^bit%" is equivalent to "shifting" all the bits in n% bit% places to the right. Thus we can define a function FNbit which returns the state of bit bit% (counting from zero) of n%:

```
1000 DEF FNbit(n%, bit%) = (n% DIV 2^bit%) MOD 2
```

This is really just a special case of the base conversion function. The same function can be written a little more efficiently using one of the logical operators discussed below.

Another use of MOD is to force an expression into a particular range. For example, if a program accepts some input which increments a value, it might be desirable to reset the value back to zero if it exceeds some upper limit, rather than give an error. Note that clocks work using "modulo" arithmetic; after 23:59:59 comes 00:00:00. In this case, the seconds and minutes are counted MOD 60 and the hours MOD 24. The program below prints a menu with an inverted cursor to select the current item. Pressing any key while an item is inverted will cause that item to be chosen. It could be used in programs designed for disabled people who can only make an indiscriminate stab at the keyboard (thanks Neale):

```
100 PROCinit
110 choice%=FNselect(1,5)
120 PRINTTAB(0,24);menu$(choice%);"?"
130 REM and so on
140 END
150
160
200 DEF PROCinit
210    DIM menu$(5)
220    menu$(1)="Choice no. one"
230    menu$(2)="Choice two"
240    menu$(3)="Here's the third one"
250    menu$(4)="Number four"
260    menu$(5)="At last!!"
270 ENDPROC
280
290
1000 DEF FNselect(lo%, hi%)
1010    REM  Displays a menu of items using menu$(lo%)
1020    REM  to menu$(hi%) and returns the item selected
1030    LOCAL i%, selected%, item%
```

```
1040    REM  Print the menu
1050    CLS
1060    PRINT TAB(0,3);"Press a key when the correct item"'
1070    PRINT "is lit-up."
1080    FOR i%=lo% TO hi%
1090       PROCprint(i%,"normal")
1100    NEXT i%
1110    selected%=FALSE
1120    REM   Now cycle through the items
1130    item%=-1
1140    REPEAT
1150       item%=(item%+1) MOD (hi%-lo%+1)
1160       PROCprint(item%+lo%, "inverse")
1170       IF INKEY(200)<>-1 THEN selected%=TRUE
1180       IF NOT selected% THEN PROCprint(item%+lo%, "normal")
1190    UNTIL selected%
1200    VDU 20: PRINT
1210 =item%+lo%
1220
1230
1500 DEF PROCprint(i%, mode$)
1510    REM   Prints menu$(i%) at the correct position
1520    REM   in normal or inverse text
1530    IF mode$="inverse" THEN COLOUR 0: COLOUR 129
1540    IF mode$="normal"  THEN COLOUR 1: COLOUR 128
1550    PRINT TAB(5,(i%-lo%)*2+9);menu$(i%);
1560 ENDPROC
```

The program assumes the current display mode is a "soft" one (0 to 6), as the inverse text commands won't work in MODE 7 (see Chapter 3). After the array of strings has been set-up, the program calls FNselect. This starts by printing the menu with a small message above it. The routine PROCprint is used to do the actual printing. It takes two parameters, a subscript into the array menu$() and a string representing the way in which the string will be printed. This is restricted to "inverse" and "normal" in the present program. FNselect then cycles through the menu inverting each option for two seconds to give the user a chance to hit a key. If he does, the current item is returned, otherwise the next string is inverted. This cycle continues until a key has been pressed.

There are (hi%–lo%+1) items on the menu. Using MOD, item% is made to count in the range 0 to (hi%–lo%), after which it "wraps-round" to zero again. To get the particular string selected, lo% must be added to item%.

From the definition of MOD (a% MOD b% = a%–b%*(a% DIV b%)), it can be seen that if (a% MOD b%)=0 then b% divides exactly into a%. We can therefore write a program which prints all the factors of an input number:

```
10 REPEAT
20    INPUT ''"Give us a number ",num%
30    FOR i%=2 TO num%
40       IF num% MOD i%=0 THEN PRINT i%;" is a factor of ";num%
50    NEXT i%
60 UNTIL num%=-1
70 END
```

The program is very simple and hardly needs explaining. A similar routine is embedded in the prime number program of the next chapter (a prime number is one with no factors apart from itself and 1). Another use of MOD is given below in a function which returns the GCD (greatest common divisor) of two numbers:

```
1000 DEF FNgcd(a%,b%)
1010    IF a%>b% THEN =FNgcd(b%,a%)
1020    IF b% MOD a%=0 THEN =a%
1030 =FNgcd(b% MOD a%, a%)
```

This is another recursive definition and may make more sense after you have read Chapter two. It is based on what is known as the Euclidean algorithm for finding two numbers' GCD.

Another property about the expression "a% MOD b%" is that if a% is a counter which is changed in steps of one then the expression will yield a zero result every b% steps. For example, suppose you wanted to label the lines going down the screen, every five lines, the top line being line one. In MODE 4 this could be done with:

```
100 FOR line%=0 TO 31
110    IF line% MOD 5=0 THEN P. TAB(0,line%);line%+1
120 NEXT line%
```

Another example is to update a time display every so often. The program below waits in a loop until the built-in timer is exactly on a second (which happens every 100 "ticks") and then prints the time. Of course, if the program were a game or something, there would be much more going on in the loop, so the computer wouldn't really be idle for the whole second between screen updates.

```
100 REPEAT
110    REPEAT t%=TIME: UNTIL t% MOD 100 = 0
120    PRINTTAB(10,2);FNhrs(t%);":";FNmins(t%);":";FNsecs(t%)
130 UNTIL FALSE
140
150
1000 DEF FNhrs(t%)=RIGHT$("00"+STR$(t% DIV 360000 MOD 24),2)
1010 DEF FNmins(t%)=RIGHT$("00"+STR$(t% DIV 6000 MOD 60),2)
1020 DEF FNsecs(t%)=RIGHT$("00"+STR$(t% DIV 100 MOD 60),2)
```

There are four more operators which deal specifically with integers. These are the logical operators OR, AND, EOR and NOT. The first three are similar to +, *, / etc. in that they operate on two values (e.g. a% AND 255). NOT is a unary operator; it operates on the number which follows it. Like unary minus it has high binding power (precedence) thus NOT a% OR b% is interpreted as (NOT a%) OR b% rather than NOT(a% OR b%). The logical operators can be used in two distinct ways — as bit-wise operators on integers, or as combinators of relational expressions working on boolean values TRUE and FALSE. I will discuss these in turn, the latter first.

The relational operators are =, <, >, <>, <= and >=. They are used in comparing strings or numbers. Most ancient BASICs treat them as special operators which can only be used in IF statements, as in:

```
100 IF A>B THEN 130
```

The majority of micro BASICs, however, treat the relationals as normal arithmetic operators. From the table on pp. 144–5 of the User Guide you can see that all the relationals have lower precedence than the normal +, * DIV etc. Thus a typical relational expression would be:

```
a%+b% <= c%/d%*SIN(RAD(45))
```

Because of the relative binding powers of the operators there is no need for brackets, and the computer will compare the two arithmetic expressions (a%+b%) and (c%/d%*SIN(RAD(45))). The <= operator, like the other relationals will return one of two values. These are given the names TRUE and FALSE. There are two functions of the same names which return these two values whenever they are called. Another name for these truth values is "boolean" quantities, as they obey the rules of the so-called boolean algebra which deals with variables that can take on one of two values.

The logical operators mentioned above work on two (or one in the case of NOT) truth values and give another truth value as their result. As truth values can only be either TRUE or FALSE the actions of the logical operators are very simple. In the following, t1 and t2 represent any boolean expressions, e.g. a%>=b%, TRUE, a$<>b$ and so on. Note that as boolean results can be stored in integers, t1 or t2 could also be simply integers. In the menu program above, for example, the variable selected% was assigned the values FALSE and TRUE at various times. This use of a variable is called a flag; it flags whether a certain condition has been met.

The operator OR works as follows:

```
t1 OR t2     is TRUE if t1 and/or t2 are TRUE
```

IN the statement:

```
120 IF a%>100 OR finished% THEN END
```

the program will end if the variable a% is greater than 100 or the flag finished% is TRUE, or both. There is a way of defining the actions of the logical operators with things called truth tables. The truth table for the OR operator is:

t1	t2	Result
FALSE	FALSE	FALSE
FALSE	TRUE	TRUE
TRUE	FALSE	TRUE
TRUE	TRUE	TRUE

The English explanation of OR should be apparent from this. The truth table for the AND operator is:

t1	t2	Result
FALSE	FALSE	FALSE
FALSE	TRUE	FALSE
TRUE	FALSE	FALSE
TRUE	TRUE	TRUE

In English, then, the result of t1 AND t2 is TRUE only if both t1 and t2 are TRUE, otherwise it is FALSE. The truth table for NOT is even simpler, as it only has one operand:

t1	NOT t1
FALSE	TRUE
TRUE	FALSE

NOT therefore gives the opposite to its operand. Two BASIC statements using AND and NOT respectively are:

```
130 IF trace_on% AND line%<max_line% THEN PRINT "[";line%;"]";
140 IF NOT ok% THEN PROCerror
```

The first example is a BASIC equivalent of the action of the TRACE command (see page 367 of the User Guide). In the second example the flag ok% is presumed to have been set elsewhere in the program.

The EOR operator is probably not as useful as the other three for joining relational expressions. It has the truth table:

t1	t2	Result
FALSE	FALSE	FALSE
FALSE	TRUE	TRUE
TRUE	FALSE	TRUE
TRUE	TRUE	FALSE

It is sometimes called the NOT equivalent operator as it gives a TRUE result only when t1 isn't equivalent (i.e. not equal) to t2. EOR has more uses as a bit-wise operator (see below). Notice though that FALSE EOR TRUE=TRUE and TRUE EOR TRUE=FALSE, thus t1 EOR TRUE=NOT t1, where t1 is any truth value.

Expressions such as those given above can be used anywhere a truth value is required, e.g. in an IF or UNTIL statement, and they can also be stored in integers. Thus it is perfectly OK to define as function which returns a truth value. The one below returns TRUE if its second parameter is a factor of the first, otherwise FALSE is returned:

```
1000 DEF FNis_a_factor(a%,b%)=   a% MOD b% = 0
```

Notice that the two "=" have very different uses. the first one belongs to the function definition and the second is a relational operator between the two expressions (a% MOD b%) and 0. The function could be used in lines such as:

```
100 IF FNis_a_factor(x%,10) THEN PRINT x%;" ends in a 0"
```

The fact that truth values can be stored as integers means that they must have numerical values. This is indeed the case, and the statement "PRINT FALSE, TRUE" will yield the two numbers 0 and −1. Most computers use 0 for FALSE, but some BASICs use +1 for TRUE. The BBC version is more sensible, as −1 is the four-byte number with all 32 bits set to 1. This is a useful feature when the logical operators are used in bit-wise mode. Actually, the IF and UNTIL statements are a little less pedantic about what TRUE is. Any number which isn't zero is counted as TRUE. The result of

```
100 a%=1234
110 IF a% THEN PRINT "TRUE" ELSE PRINT "FALSE"
```

will cause "TRUE" to be printed, as 1234 is non-zero. However, although single variables may be used as truth values, be wary of combining them with the logical operators. For example, a% is TRUE as it isn't zero. We would therefore expect NOT a% to be FALSE. This is not the case; NOT 1234 is actually −1235, non-zero. Similarly, although both 5 and 10 would count as TRUE in an IF, 5 AND 10 is FALSE as that expression evaluates to zero.

The problems just described are simply accounted for when the actions of the logical operators are examined a little more closely. As I said, TRUE and FALSE are really just particular integers, whose bits are all ones and all zeroes respectively. The operators AND, OR etc. work on all integers, whether they have "pure" boolean values or not. That is, they are bit-wise operators: the logical function is applied to all the bits of each number at the same time. To keep things simple (i.e. to save my having to type thousands of digits) I will use examples of eight-bit numbers, but the same principles hold for all four bytes of BBC BASIC integers.

It is necessary to treat each separate bit in the integer as a truth value; a one bit is TRUE and a zero bit represents FALSE. When two eight-bit numbers are ORed, for example, the corresponding bits of both numbers are ORed to get the result. This is illustrated by:

```
11001100 OR 10101010 = 11101110
```

This comes from exactly the same rules for OR that were given earlier. Starting from the left-most (most significant) digits of both the operands: 1 OR 1 = 1, 1

OR 0 = 1, 0 OR 1 = 1 and so on, down to 0 OR 0 = 0 for the right-most (least significant) bits. Similar rules apply for the other logical operators:

```
11001100 AND 10101010 = 10001000
11001100 EOR 10101010 = 01100110
         NOT 10101010 = 01010101
```

When we write TRUE as 11111111 (strictly there should be 32 ones for a BBC BASIC integer) and FALSE as 00000000, it can be seen that the rules such as TRUE OR FALSE = TRUE still hold.

What use are these facts? In a word, masking. It is usual to express numbers in hexadecimal when the logical operators are used, as the underlying bit-patterns are a little easier to make out than with decimal. Remember that each hex digit (0 to F) stands for four binary digits (0000 to 1111). The term "masking" refers to the operation of including some bits of a number in a calculation and excluding others. For example, suppose we know there is an address at locations &20E and &20F which might be useful to know. The four bytes at &20E to &211 can be obtained by the term !&20E. To access the lower two bytes only, the upper two must be "masked-off". This is done with the AND operator:

```
100 addr%=!&20E AND &FFFF
```

Hex &FFFF is 16 ones so the 32-bit number accessed by ! is effectively ANDed with (deep breath) 00000000000000001111111111111111, which sets the unrequired high-order bytes to zero, leaving the wanted address. A similar situation arises when using the USR function. This returns a 32-bit number which represents the registers of the 6502 upon return from a user machine code routine (see Chapter 5). The format of this number is &PYXA, where the bytes are the contents of the accumulator, X register, Y register and status register. These could be separated using the following lines:

```
100 usr%=USR(addr%): REM Get four-byte number
110 A%=usr% AND &FF: REM Least sig. byte
120 X%=(usr% AND &FF00) DIV &100: REM Second byte
130 Y%=(usr% AND &FF0000) DIV &10000: REM Third byte
140 P%=(usr% AND &FF000000) DIV &1000000: REM Most sig. byte
```

The DIVs shift the byte the correct number of places to the right to give a value in the proper range of 0–255. The brackets are important as AND has a lower priority than DIV. They force the masking of the relevant byte before the divison takes place. It is more usual to access a particular *bit* of the status register. For example, the carry bit could be retrieved with:

```
150 C%=(usr% AND &01000000) DIV &1000000
```

as this bit is the least significant one in the status register. C% will of course have either a 0 or 1 value after the assignment.

It is sometimes wasteful to use all four bytes of an integer variable if only a small range of numbers is to be stored. This is especially true when arrays are used. You could, for example, save four numbers in the range 0 to 255 in a single integer. This is called data-packing, and can be very useful if storage space is limited. Let us take an extreme example. Suppose lots of dates need to be stored. There are several ways of saving dates: a string of the form "ddmmyy" (or "mmddyy" if you happen to be American), which takes six bytes, plus the overhead associated with a string variable (another four bytes). We can do much better than that by considering the ranges of numbers involved. Days go from 1 to 31. This range fits nicely into five bits, as these can hold the numbers 0 to 31. Months are 1 to 12, which will need four bits (0 to 15). Finally a year in this century will be 0 to 99, which is another seven bits (0 to 127). In binary then a date will be the 16 bits:

    yyyyyyymmmmddddd

The day bits' appearance at the right-hand side is natural as the day part of a date is the least significant. As an example, a very important date (my birthday, cards c/o John Wiley, please) would appear as:

    0111110 0011 00111 = 62 3 7 or 07.03.62

The spaces are inserted to make the parts easier to distinguish. All we need now are some easy-to-use procedures to convert numbers to and from the format. Since the dates are stored as 16 bits, we shouldn't overlook the possibility of storing two dates in each BBC BASIC integer. First, though, two simple functions to convert single dates. FNcompact takes a string of the form "ddmmyy" and returns the equivalent 16-bit number. FNexpand does the opposite: you give it a number and it returns the string.

```
1000 DEF FNcompact(date$)
1010    LOCAL dd%, mm%, yy%
1020    dd%=VAL(LEFT$(date$,2))
1030    mm%=VAL(MID$(date$,3,2))
1040    yy%=VAL(MID$(date$,5))
1050 =dd% OR mm%*&20 OR yy%*&200
1060
1070
1100 DEF FNexpand(date%)
1110    LOCAL dd$, mm$, yy$
1120    dd$=STR$(date% AND &1F)
1130    mm$=STR$((date% AND &1E0) DIV &20)
1140    yy$=STR$((date% AND &FE00) DIV &200)
1150 =RIGHT$("0"+dd$,2)+RIGHT$("0"+mm$,2)+RIGHT$("0"+yy$,2)
```

Both functions assume that they have been given sensible data, and will give silly results if fed silly values. The ORs in line 1050 could equally well have been +'s for this application. ORs just seemed a little more natural. Once FNexpand and

FNcompact are available, it is a simple matter to write 32-bit versions. I have called these FNcompact2 and FNexpand2, as I am a very imaginative programmer.

```
2000 DEF FNcompact2(date$)
2010    !&70=FNcompact(MID$(date$,7))
2020    !&72=FNcompact(LEFT$(date$,6))
2030 =!&70
2040
2050
2100 DEF FNexpand2(date%)
2110 =FNexpand((date% AND &FFFF0000) DIV &10000)+FNexpand(date% AND
     &FFFF)
```

FNcompact2 is more complex than it should have been. Originally it was:

```
2000 DEF FNcompact2(date$)
2010 =&10000*FNcompact(LEFT$(date$,6)) OR FNcompact(MID$(date$))
```

The problem was that if the first date in the string (which is now of the form "ddmmyyddmmyy") had a year greater than '63, the resultant compacted form was large enough to cause a "Too big" error when multiplied by &10000. The answer is to insert the two 16-bit numbers into the four locations at &70 to &73, then make a single number with the assignment in line 2030. The result in the case where the first year >= '64 is negative, but that doesn't matter.

Using the method just described, two dates can be saved in each integer variable, a saving of 300% over the "string" method. This could be handy when trying to cram information onto a disc. Similar techniques can be used for other types of information, especially when it is in the form of a range of integers. Remember though that there is a certain amount of extra processing needed to convert between formats.

1.1.2   Reals

We have seen that integer variables have several uses. The advantages of their use are speed (a comparative term; microprocessors of the 6502's ilk weren't really designed for heavy "number crunching". However, adding two integers is rather more straightforward than the equivalent real operation, as we shall see) and accuracy (within the obvious limits that the operands have to be whole, integer operations are always totally accurate). However, although it is useful to represent abstract items such as colours by integers, they are just not sufficient to deal with real quantities.

By "real" I mean things which occur in nature and are of a continuous nature. Voltages and masses don't change in convenient steps of one volt or gramme. There are an infinite number of speeds between one and two kilometres per hour.

To represent such items on a computer, a different method is required from the simple 32-bit integers. The method normally used is to store numbers in a so-called floating-point format. In this there are two parts to the number: the mantissa, which gives significant digits, and the exponent, which acts as a kind of scaling factor. You are probably familiar with the "E" notation of writing floating-point numbers. The value:

    1.2345E3

is typical. The mantissa in this case is 1.2345. Then comes the "E", which can be read as "times ten to the". This is followed by the exponent. Thus 1.2345E3 is "1.2345 times ten to the 3". Ten to the 3 is a thousand, so 12345E3 is the same as 1234.5. The value of using the exponent comes when dealing with very large or small numbers. Two examples:

    1.2345E24
    1.2345E-10

Notice that whenever numbers are written in "E" notation it is usual to write one digit, then a decimal point then the rest of the digits. This is just a convention; others use the form "0.12345E25", always having the part before the decimal point as zero. The first example above could be written:

    1234500000000000000000000

This gives another advantage of reals over integers. Using the mantissa+ exponent method very much larger numbers may be represented. In BBC BASIC reals can have values up to about +/−1E38, compared to +/−1E9 for integers. Of course, the number of significant digits is much smaller than 38 − about 9.5, as with integers. The second example above has a negative exponent. This means that the mantissa is divided by 1E10 instead of being multiplied by it. Notice that the number itself is still positive, i.e. greater than zero. 1.2345E−10 is the same as:

    0.00000000012345

Reals, then, can hold numbers with a much greater range than integers, and can have fractional parts too. So what are the drawbacks? One is that they are processed slower than integers. Whereas 32-bit integers are just elongated versions of the microprocessor's eight-bit word (the unit of information which it is most at home with when doing calculations), reals are something totally different. It might be advantageous to have a look at how reals are stored. If you don't feel too comfortable with binary you could skip this bit. Come back to it when you've had a go at assembly language programming. BBC BASIC reals are stored in five bytes. These are divided into two parts. One byte is used as the exponent, the other four are the mantissa (which explains why reals have the same number of significant digits as integers). As the base used is binary, the exponent gives the power of two by which the mantissa must be multiplied, not the power of ten.

Below is the representation in binary and decimal of the number 1.5:

```
                Exponent        Mantissa
   Binary       10000001        01000000 00000000 00000000 00000000
   Decimal        129             64       0        0        0
```

How does this relate to the number 1.5? First consider the mantissa. The first byte is slightly different from the other three. The most significant bit in this byte is used as a sign bit for the whole number. If the bit is zero, the number is positive; a one in this position indicates a negative number. We have a zero in this example. So far so good. Next, imagine that there is a binary point immediately before the first proper digit. This acts just like the decimal point in decimal numbers. Having the point in this position is called making the numbers normalised. For example, the decimal numbers:

```
    0.1234E12,  0.4321E-2,  0.7648E23
```

are all normalised as there are no significant digits before the point. On the other hand:

```
    123,         1.234E12,   -.001
```

are not normalised.

Applying this principle to our mantissa, we get:

```
    .1000000 00000000 00000000 00000000
```

However (this is where it gets hairy) normalised binary numbers must have the first digit as a 1, otherwise they wouldn't be normalised. So, we assume that there is a 1 just after the binary point. The 1 in the byte above is therefore the second 1 in the mantissa. Thus the mantissa is actually:

```
    .11000000 00000000 00000000 00000000
```

Now to bring the exponent in. Remember that this represents the power of two by which the mantissa must be multiplied to get the number we're after. As exponents can be negative, there has to be a way of giving the exponent a sign. The method used in this case is called excess-128. The exponent is worked-out, then 128 is added to this. Thus if the exponent was found to be −32, it would be stored as −32+128=96. As the values 0 to 255 can be stored in a byte, exponents range from −128 to 127.

In the present example the exponent byte is 129. This gives an actual value of 129−128=1. Thus our mantissa of .11000 ... must be multiplied by two the power of one, which is simply two. Multiplying a binary number by two is the same as shifting it one place to the left. Thus the number becomes 1.100 ... Now, with binary fractions, numbers to the right of the point are sub-powers of two. The first digit after the point gives the $2(-1)$ part (the halves), the next one the $2^(-2)$ (the quarters), then $2^(-3)$ (the eighths), and so on. Thus 1.1 is 1+0.5=1.5, the number we first thought of.

The foregoing is not supposed to be easy. In fact, it's probably confusing, even if you understand how binary integers work. Try to work out where the following come from:

Number	Exponent	Mantissa
10	132	32 0 0 0
0.125	126	0 0 0 0
0.1	125	76 204 204 205
0	0	0 0 0 0 (you can't work this out as normal;
		0 is stored as all zero bytes.)

Remember: the exponent should be decreased by 128; an exponent of n means shift the mantissa n places to the left; a negative exponent implies a right shift. The most significant bit of the first mantissa byte is the sign bit, not part of the mantissa proper. Then comes the assumed ".1", after which the rest of the mantissa bits are placed.

What has this sortie into the unknown taught us about real numbers? Firstly, they are stored in a complex form. Before any operations can be performed, a real number must be unpacked into a more easily-manipulated format. The reverse operation has to be performed when a result is to be stored in a real variable. Furthermore, even simple operations such as add require a fair amount of preparation; the numbers must have their mantissas shifted (whilst adjusting the exponents) so that the exponents are equal. All this takes time, so the claim that dealing with reals is slower than integers is clearly justified.

More importantly, look at the representation of 0.1 given above. The last three mantissa bytes are very similar. In fact, 0.1 is a recurring binary fraction; it is impossible to represent it exactly in a finite number of bits. This is much the same as trying to represent a third in decimal: 0.3333333 . . .; you could go on for days and still not have represented a third exactly. This means that of all the infinite number of numbers between $-10E38$ and $+10E38$, only a very small proportion of them (about $1E12$) can be stored exactly; all the rest are mere approximations. The outcome is that whenever reals are used in calculations, small errors will creep in. Of course, these will generally only occur in the eighth or ninth decimal place in any single calculation. Errors can, however, accumulate and can become quite noticeable, especially when the quantities involved have large magnitudes. For example, an error in the least significant bit of a result of $1E20$ corresponds to a discrepancy of $2.3E10$, a sizeable number.

The next two examples show how cumulative real errors can lead to erroneous program operation. First, the infamous FOR ... NEXT loop. BASIC is one of the only languages which permits the use of real variables to control such a loop. In fact, some BASICs actually FORBID the use of integer looping variables! Consider the "program" below:

```
100 FOR i=0 TO 10 STEP 0.1
110    IF i=10 THEN PRINT "FINISHED!"
120 NEXT i
```

The idea is that on the last iteration of the loop the text "FINISHED!" is printed.

If you run the program, you will find that this does not happen. In fact, i never reaches the value of 10 in the loop at all. The reason is, of course, the presence of rounding errors. As 0.1 can't be stored exactly in binary, every time it is added to i there is a small discrepancy. When the final NEXT is reached, i is equal to something like 9.9000000001. When 0.1 is added, the result is 10.00000001. The action of NEXT is to branch back to the FOR if i is less than or equal to 10. As it is slightly above this (even though by a very small amount) the condition fails and the last iteration never takes place. If you PRINT i after the loop has finished, "10" will appear. Now after a loop has terminated, the looping variable should be equal to the final value plus the step (prove this to yourself with some integer loops, but don't expect it to necessarily be the case for other BASICs). Thus i should be 10.1. The fact that it is only 10 implies that the last iteration never took place.

In fact, even if the last iteration had occurred, the IF still would have failed. This brings us to another danger point with reals: testing for equality. Real numbers are very rarely equal, and should never be tested as such. The situation gets even more confusing when the computer prints two decimal numbers identically, but then refuses to say they have the same value. This is demonstrated by the following:

```
100 A=0.1
110 B=0.01*10
120 PRINT A,B
130 IF A=B THEN PRINT"THEY'RE EQUAL"
140 END
```

The PRINT at line 120 produces the expected "0.1   0.1". However, the PRINT at line 130 is less forthcoming. The fact is that although the two numbers are "more or less" equal, there is a very small difference which leads to the test for equality failing. In fact, the error is exactly one bit: the last byte of B's mantissa is 204 instead of 205. Although this is not detected by PRINT (which only looks at enough bits to get at most nine decimal digits), the "=" operator tests every bit of every byte of the number.

The problems just described are unique to neither BASIC nor the BBC Computer. Rather, they are a consequence of all computers' finite store and speed. The problems can be reduced by increasing the number of bits given to variable's mantissa, but they can never be removed altogether. This calls for a certain degree of care from the programmer; two precautions which can be taken have already been implied by the foregoing: don't use real looping variables, and never test reals for equality. Integers can be used as scaled-up reals in most cases. There may be small errors which creep in when they are scaled-down again for calculations within the loop, but the important point is that they don't accumulate in the looping variable if it is an integer. As for IF tests on reals (and the same applies to UNTIL conditions, too), it usually suffices to test for the expressions lying within a small distance, e.g. :

```
100 IF ABS(th-COS(PI/4)) < epsilon THEN ....
```

where epsilon has previously been set to some small value. Notice the use of ABS. This is because we don't know if errors will make th be slightly smaller or greater than COS(PI/4). ABS forces the error to be positive so the test always works.

The error tested above is an absolute one: it is simply the magnitude of the difference between two expressions. However, if the expressions are themselves very small, their difference may be smaller than epsilon, even the error is still a tiny fraction of each expression. What we need is a way of measuring the relative error, which takes the size of the numbers being compared into account. This is similar to expressing the error as a percentage. For example, if we wanted to test a variable quantity for being equal to "limit" +/− 0.1%, we would use:

```
100 IF ABS(i-limit)/limit <= 0.001 THEN ...
```

The division scales the absolute error so it can be measured relative to limit, then the $<=$ compares it with 0.001, which is the same as 0.1%. Different, but equivalent, versions of this are:

```
100 IF ABS(i-limit) <= 0.001*limit THEN ...
100 IF ABS(i-limit) <= limit/1000 THEN ...
```

The first alternative is probably the faster in operation, as multiplication is slightly quicker than division in microprocessors.

Now we know some of the pros and cons of real numbers, it's possible to give some examples of their use. An application which springs to mind immediately is financial – most currencies are based on the 100 doohs to a dah principle, e.g. 100 pence to a pound, 100 bututs to a dalasi (in The Gambia). Some have a 1000:1 ratio instead, e.g. 1000 dirhams to a dinar (Libya). It would seem sensible, therefore, to express prices as reals. If you are considering entrusting the records of your earthly wealth to the BBC Computer, it would be wise to consider the effects of cumulative errors that have been discussed. If the TOTAL amounts being handled are below, say, £1M then all should be well. Of course it depends on the calculations being performed. Pure addition would create errors rather smaller than 0.1 of a penny for the sum of about 1000 numbers. However, if the amounts had previously been adjusted by some multiplicative function, there may be odd bits lurking around which would accumulate to create significant errors. Such a calculation may be a mark-up, for instance. It is a wise precaution to round to the nearest penny:

```
1000 DEF FNround(£x)=INT(£x*100+0.5)/100
```

If, on the other hand, you aren't too keen on staking the whole financial future of your small-but-expanding business on the vagaries of real arithmetic, it is possible to use scaled integers. In this, everything is done in pence instead of pounds. Then, using only integer variables, calculations should stay accurate to totals of £9999999.99 (this is also the maximum number of digits which PRINT will produce). Notice that when converting pounds and pence to pence it is not sufficient to say:

```
pence%=£pounds*100
```

The truncation implicit in the conversion to integer means that if the product pounds*100 yields something like 123411.9999 (which would be printed as 123412), pence% will in fact become 123411, a penny out. To be on the safe side, the conversion:

```
pence%=£pounds*100+0.5
```

should be used.

When the numbers are to be printed, they must naturally be divided by 100 if scaled integers are used. BBC BASIC conveniently provides a degree of print-formatting, by way of @%. This is discussed more fully in Chapter three, but a particular case in point is "F2" mode. This is set-up by assigning @% with &2020A (or 131594 in decimal). This prints numbers with exactly 2 decimal places and a leading zero if necessary (see the examples on page 327 of the User Guide). F2 also rounds to the nearest penny on printing.

I mentioned the use of real numbers to represent measurements taken in nature. Being a general purpose language, BASIC provides a number of functions to perform scientific functions. These aren't as exhaustive as many scientific calculators, but rather form a subset from which most others may be derived. BBC BASIC has a few additions to the "standard". For completeness these are listed below:

```
ACS - Returns the arccosine of its argument in radians

ASN - Returns the arcsine of its argument in radians

ATN - Returns the arctangent of its argument in radians

COS - Returns the cosine of its radian argument

DEG - Returns the degrees of its radian argument

EXP - Returns "e" raised to the power of its argument

 LN - Returns the natural (base "e") of its argument

LOG - Returns the common (base 10) of its argument

 PI - Returns the value of PI=3.14159265

RAD - Returns the radians of its degree argument

RND - Returns a random number

SIN - Returns the sine of its radian argument

SQR - Returns the square root of its positive argument

TAN - Returns the tangent of its radian argument
```

I have omitted some of the common functions which work on integers too, e.g. SGN. Some of the functions may need explaining. The "arc" functions are the inverse trig. functions. Normally only ATN is provided. Notice that all the trig. functions use radians. Since everyone thinks in degrees (at least I do, in spite of the valiant attempts by my applied maths teacher to convert me), the two functions DEG and RAD are provided. DEG take its argument and converts this to degrees by multiplying it by the consant conversion factor 180/PI. The RAD function is the opposite of this, returning the number of radians of its argument in degrees. The radian is a slightly more sensible unit of angular measurement than the degree, at least in mathematical terms. The problem is that there are only 6 or so of them in a circle, so angles expressed in radians invariably have lots of hard-to-remember decimal places. As one degree is fairly small, there is rarely a need to express angles in degrees to better than say 0.01 degs. However, computers like radians, so in this book you will see several examples such as:

```
100 x=Len%*COS(RAD(th%))
```

where th% is some angle in degreees. The DEG function is less used as the inverse trig. functions don't seem to crop up very often. The kind of thing is:

```
110 th%=DEG(ATN(y/x))
```

The choice of names for the log. functions is a little unfortunate. The majority of BASICs (and indeed languages) only provide the natural log. function, whose base is "e", 2.71828... This function is called LOG. However, the BBC machine also has common or base 10 logs, so they called this function LOG and renamed base "e" log. LN. If your programs seem to give results which are out by a factor of about 2.3, this curious design decision may have something to do with it. It is very easy to convert between log. bases, which is why only one type is usually given. Another common base is two, especially in communications calculations:

```
100 DEF FNlog2(x)=LN(x)/LN(2)
```

If the function is much used it would be wiser defining 1/LN(2) as a constant and multiplying LN(x) by that in order to save one log. calculation per call. (The trig. and log. functions are by far the least efficient part of BBC BASIC's maths package. If you compare the benchmarks with other computers, the relative superiority of BM8 is far less than all the others. {See PCW Nov. 1982, page 110}.)

The inverse log. function is EXP, "e" raised to a power. There is no "ten to the power of" function. This requires the use of the ˆ operator, viz.

```
100 DEF FNpower_of_ten(x)=10ˆx
```

Speaking of ˆ, it is quite intelligent. Most BASICs complain quite bitterly if you try to raise a negative number to a power. However, if the exponent (the thing after the ˆ) is an integer then this operation is legal. BBC BASIC's ˆ spots this, and uses repeated multiplication to work out, e.g. -2.3^4. (Note this is worked out as $(-2.3)^4$, as − has a higher priority than ˆ.) In fact, ˆ will use repeated multiplication whenever it can, as this is generally faster than the usual method (aˆb = EXP(b*LN(a))).

I've included RND in the list of functions, as it returns a real number sometimes. There are five ways in which RND may be used. (See page 342 in the User Guide.) The one we are interested in here is RND(1). This generates a number in the range 0–0.999999, and as such is compatible with most BASICs' random number generators. Here is a program to find PI. (There is a better way, I believe):

```
100 REM  How to find PI
110 total%=0
```

```
120 in_total%=0
130 CLS
140 REPEAT
150     x=RND(1)
160     y=RND(1)
170     rad=SQR(x*x+y*y)
180     IF rad<=1 THEN in_total%=in_total%+1
190     total%=total%+1
200     pi=in_total%/total%*4
210     PRINT TAB(10,10);"PI=";pi;"  ";
220 UNTIL pi=PI
230 END
```

Don't expect the program to terminate. I won't say exactly how it works, but if you imagine a square one unit on a side, with a quadrant of radius one with its centre at the origin, then consider the two areas involved. . .

The program also uses the SQR function. Not much can be said about this. It gives the square-root of its argument. Pascal programmers who have moved up to BBC BASIC (joke) should realise that this is different from Pascal's sqr, and the same as sqrt. The use of SQR above is to find the distance of the point (x,y) from the origin. It is a special case of the formula for the distance between two points (x1,y1) and (x2,y2), which is:

```
100 DEF FNdistance_between_two_points(x1,y1,  x2,y2)
110 =SQR((x2-x1)^2 + (y2-y1)^2)
```

If everyone used names like that all our problems would be over.

The problem to which the PI program is a solution comes from [Goodman]. Another exercise in that book is to simulate the movement of some beetles. (If you don't like creepy-crawlies you can skip this bit.) There are five of the insects; four of them start from each corner of a square and the fifth is placed at a random position in the square. The rule governing their movement is that each beetle always moves towards (sorry, toward; they're American beetles) its nearest neighbour. The program to perform this simulation is given below. It uses the MODE 4 graphics screen to plot the paths of the insect.

```
100 REM      Beetle Simulation
110 MODE 4
120 PROCinit
130 REPEAT
140     REM For each beetle, move to its nearest neighbour
150     FOR btl%=0 TO max_btl%
160         nrst%=FNnear(btl%)
170         REM  Work out distance to that one
180         dx=x(nrst%)-x(btl%)
190         dy=y(nrst%)-y(btl%)
```

```
 200       dist=SQR(dx*dx+dy*dy)
 210       REM  Update the beetle's pos.
 220       x(btl%)=x(btl%)+dx*speed*dt/dist
 230       y(btl%)=y(btl%)+dy*speed*dt/dist
 240       REM   And plot him
 250       PLOT 69,x(btl%), y(btl%)
 260     NEXT btl%
 270 UNTIL FALSE
 280
1000 DEF PROCinit
1010     REM  Set up the co-ordinates of max_btl%+1 beetles
1020     REM  and define the speed and time interval
1030     max_btl%=4
1040     DIM x(max_btl%), y(max_btl%)
1050     x(0)=RND(511)-256:   y(0)=RND(511)-256
1060     x(1)=-256:           y(1)=-256
1070     x(2)=255:            y(2)=-256
1080     x(3)=255:            y(3)=255
1090     x(4)=-256:           y(4)=255
1100     dt=8: REM    Time interval
1110     speed=1: REM Speed of beetles
1120     REM  Put graphics origin in the middle of the screen
1130     VDU 29,640;512;
1140 ENDPROC
1150
1160
2000 DEF FNnear(btl%)
2010     REM   Finds the btl%'s nearest neighbour
2020     LOCAL dx, dy, dist, min_dist, bt%, min_bt%
2030     min_dist=1E6
2080     FOR bt%=0 TO max_btl%
2090        IF bt%=btl% THEN 2140
2100        dx=x(btl%)-x(bt%)
2110        dy=y(btl%)-y(bt%)
2120        dist=dx*dx+dy*dy
2130        IF dist<min_dist THEN min_bt%=bt%: min_dist=dist
2140     NEXT bt%
2150 =min_bt%
```

After the beetles' co-ordinates have been initialised, the speed and time increment (speed and dt respectively) are set-up. The product of these two determines how far apart the dots on the screen are. The body of the program is an infinite REPEAT loop. Within this loop is a FOR loop which processes each beetle in turn. First, the beetle's nearest neighbour is located by FNnear. The distance between the creature and its neighbour is then calculated using the method given earlier. The next calculation updates the beetle's x and y co-ordinates. FNnear is quite simple. The reason no SQR is used at line 2120 is that as the distances are only being compared, rather than calculated, the expression dx*dx+dy*dy suffices.

Some questions to test your understanding: why, when two beetles' paths meet, do they carry on moving? What would happen in this case if all the co-ordinates and distances used integers? The beetles indiscriminately chase after whoever happens to be nearest. What does this tell you about the sex life of a beetle?

If the fifth beetle is removed, and the rule for movement changed, the beetles trace a somewhat more interesting path. If we change the rule (for the beetles on the square's corners) to "each beetle moves towards the neighbour on its right", the paths traced out are Archimedean spirals. The changes to the program to make this happen are:

```
DELETE 2000,2150
2000 DEF FNnear(btl%)
2010 IF btl%=4 THEN =1 ELSE =btl%+1
 150    FOR btl%=1 TO max_btl%
```

FNnear is so short due to the way the co-ordinates were initialised, in an anti-clockwise direction starting from the bottom left corner.

Computers are often used to solve complex equations or sets of equations which would take too long to work out using conventional techniques. A large amount has been written about this subject of numerical methods. By way of illustration the program below uses a common technique known as the Newton-Raphson method to solve an equation of the form

```
f(x)=0
```

The work is done by a function FNnewton which takes three parameters. These are the function in the form of a string, e.g. "SIN(x)—COS(x)", a guess to start from, and "epsilon", the maximum absolute error permitted. Since it is necessary to give the function an initial guess, the user should have a fair idea about the locations of the root(s) (i.e. the places on the curve which cross the x-axis). As shown, the program finds the roots of the equation "x*x+x-2=0".

```
100 f$="x*x+x-2"
110 PRINT "One root is ";FNnewton(f$, -10, .000001)
120 PRINT "The other is ";FNnewton(f$, 10, .000001)
130 END
140
150
1000 DEF FNnewton(f$, guess, epsilon)
1010    LOCAL x1, x2, y, dx, dy
1020    dx=1E-5
```

```
1030      x2=guess
1040      REPEAT
1045         x1=x2
1050         y=FNy(x1)
1060         dy=FNy(x1+dx)-y
1070         x2=x1-y/(dy/dx)
1080      UNTIL ABS(x2-x1) <= epsilon
1090 =x1
1100
1110
2000 DEF FNy(x)=EVAL(f$)
```

The operation of the Newton-Raphson method is explained in [Beech]. An improvement to the current program could be made by asking for two functions, the equation to be solved and its derivative. At the moment, the slope (dy/dx) is calculated numerically, which could lead to errors. The second method would require that the user have a knowledge of calculus, so that he could, for example, give f1$="2*x+1" for the function used in the listing above.

Another common numerical method is finding the area under a curve, known as numerical integration. This has many uses in practice. For example, if a graph is plotted of speed versus time, the area enclosed between the y-axis, the x-axis, the curve itself and the ordinate through some positive value of x gives the distance travelled in time x. It is sometimes possible to integrate the function symbolically using the various rules. For example, suppose we have an equation for the speed:

```
speed=1+SIN(time)
```

where speed and time would be plotted as y and x respectively. If we assume that at time=0 we are at distance zero, it can be found that:

```
distance=1-COS(time)+time
```

Thus for any value of time, it can be calculated how far we have gone. (If you were in a car travelling with this kind of motion, you would probably need to resort to travel sickness pills quite quickly.)

For some functions it is not possible to perform this manipulation of the function to integrate it, so a numerical technique must be devised. This is especially true if the function is in the form of readings taken in an experiment. You may have a set of readings of, say, heart rate versus time, as the voltage applied to the brain was steadily increased. Integrating this would give some information about the total number of heart beats during the experiment. One way of finding this integral is by Simpson's formula. The program below implements this.

```
100 MODE 4
110 REPEAT
120    INPUT TAB(0,3),"How many readings ", readings%
```

```
130    IF readings% MOD 2 = O THEN PRINT"Must be odd"
140 UNTIL readings% MOD 2
150 INPUT TAB(O,5),"What x-interval ",h
160 INPUT TAB(O,7),"Reading #1 ",yO
170 FOR i%=2 TO readings%-1
180    PRINT TAB(O,7),"Reading #";i%;" ";
190    INPUT y
200    IF i% MOD 2 THEN y=y*2 ELSE y=y*4
210    yO=yO+y
220 NEXT i%
230 PRINT TAB(O,7);"Reading #";readings%;" ";
240 INPUT y
250 yO=yO+y
260 area=h*yO/3
270 PRINT ''"Area is ";area
280 END
```

To work, Simpson's formula needs an odd number of y-readings (e.g. the heartbeat rate of above) and an increment along the x-axis (the time between readings in our example). The actual formula used is:

```
area = h/3*(y(1) + 4*y(2) + 2*y(3)....+4*y(n-1) + y(n))
```

where h is the x-increment between successive readings, $y(1)$, $y(2)$ etc. are the readings (which must be given to the program in order of increasing x) and n is the number of readings. The program above is simply a mechanisation of the formula, so should be easy to follow. To test it, let us use the function "$y=x^3-x+1$". We will take three "readings" at $x=1$, 2 and 3. In response to the first two questions posed by the program we should therefore answer "3" and "1" respectively. The three y-values will be:

```
x=1, y=1^3-1+1 = 1
x=2, y=2^3-2+1 = 7
x=3, y=3^3-3+1 = 25
```

When these numbers are entered into the program, the answer "18" results. When the answer is found algebraically, it comes to 18 too. Thus Simpson's rule is a good one. (This is obviously a fiddle, but in general the formula provides exact results for quadratics and cubics, and reasonable results for higher orders if "h" is chosen sensibly.)

1.1.3 Strings

Although numerical work is an important facet of computing, there are a great many other applications which can benefit from the computer's speed and accuracy. One of these is text processing, dealing with character information instead of numbers. As BASIC is meant to be a general purpose language (jack of all trades, master of none, a cynic may say) it has facilities for dealing with text as well as numbers.

Since I am assuming a certain familiarity with BASIC on the reader's part, I will not dwell on the fundamentals of BASIC strings. The implementation is rather similar to Microsoft BASICs; string variables end in a $, and can contain from zero to 255 characters. String constants, or literals, are delimited by the double quotation mark ("). In order to insert that character into a string, the "escape" sequence "" may be used.

There are fewer string operators than numeric ones, but some of the string functions are quite interesting. The operator + can be used to concatenate two or more strings, e.g.

```
100 a$="Hello, "
110 b$="World"
120 c$=a$+b$
130 PRINT c$'"Hello, World"
140 END
```

would cause "Hello, World" to be printed on two lines. Whenever the + operator is used, the maximum length of string obtained must never exceed 255, even if the result is only going to be printed and not assigned to a variable. If it does, a "String too long" error will result.

The comparison operators $<$, $<=$, $=$, $>=$, $=$, and $<>$ work with strings too. Two strings are compared left to right, using the ASCII codes of the characters. (I use "ASCII code" here to mean the number in the range -1 to 255 as returned by ASC, even though strictly speaking ASCII characters only have the codes 0 to 127.) If two strings are the same length and all their corresponding characters are equal, then they are obviously equal. If either of these conditions is not met, then clearly the $<>$ operator would yield a TRUE result. The other comparisons take a little more explaining. To illustrate, the function below emulates the $>$ operator on two strings.

```
1000 DEF FNgreater(a$, b$)
1010    IF ASC(a$) < ASC(b$) THEN =FALSE
1020    IF ASC(a$) > ASC(b$) THEN =TRUE
1030    IF a$="" AND b$="" THEN =FALSE
1040 =FNgreater(MID$(a$,2), MID$(a$,2))
```

The function ASC returns the ASCII code of the first character of its string argument. Thus ASC("A")=ASC("ABC")=65. The first IF tests for a$ being less than b$. For example, the string "ABC" is less than "BCD" as the code for "A" is less than that for "B". Line 1020 tests the opposite: "234" is greater than "1234" on the strength of their first characters. Clearly string comparisons don't work in the same way as numerical ones. The third test, in line 1030, will only succeed in those cases where a$ and b$ are exactly equal. If none of the foregoing tests yield a result, the first characters of the strings must be equal, so it is necessary to examine the subsequent characters. This is achieved by calling FNgreater to test the second and subsequent characters of a$ and b$.

It is clearly important to consider the layout of the ASCII code table when words are being compared. For example, upper case (capital) letters appear lower in the table than the lower case ones. This results in "BIG" being "less than" "big", one of the paradoxes of computer science. The digits appear lower than either of the letter groups. There are some convenient relationships between the characters. For example, the codes for corresponding upper and lower case letters differ only in one bit; this fact is used in a routine given in Chapter two. Also, the digits have their codes from 48 up. In hex this is ASC("0")=&30, ASC("1")=&31 ... Thus an easy way to convert a number between zero and nine to the equivalent ASCII character is by ORing it with &30:

```
1000 DEF FNchr(x%)=CHR$(x% OR &30)
```

If the upper case letters followed immediately on from the digits then this could be extended for hexadecimal digits too. Unfortunately they don't, so it can't, and we need an IF:

```
1000 DEF FNhex(x%) IF x%<10 THEN =CHR$(x% OR &30) ELSE =CHR$(x%+55)
```

The functions which operate on strings can be divided into two sets, those which return a string, and those which return a number. One function can return either type, so this is dealt with separately: EVAL is one of the most powerful devices available in BBC BASIC. It has the form:

```
     var=EVAL(string_expression$)
or   var$=EVAL(string_expression$)
```

The idea is that string_expression$ represents a valid BBC BASIC numeric or string expression, which is then worked out just as if that expression had been on the right-hand side of an assignment statement. The usefulness of this is that users can alter the action of a program by typing an actual expression, rather than just numbers. Obvious applications are those where an equation must be given to the program, for example graph plotting programs, where the user may be required to give a function in a particular variable. Another candidate would be the Newton-Raphson root finder given earlier. Instead of assigning the function from within the program, the user could be prompted by an INPUT:

```
100 INPUT TAB(0,3),"What function to solve (in x) ",f$
110 INPUT TAB(0,5),"Give a guess for the root ",guess
120 ....
```

Taking such input from the user requires a certain familiarity with the syntax of BBC BASIC expressions. The program must provide extra checking in case an illegal expression is entered. This problem is addressed in the next chapter.

Although EVAL is usually made to return numeric results, strings can result if the expression forms a valid string expression. If the argument of EVAL is obtained from the user, he must usually type an extra pair of quotes to make EVAL return a string. For example, in response to:

```
100 INPUT '"What character do you want to define ", in$
110 chr$=EVAL(in$)
```

the user would need to type """"A"""" rather than just A if he wanted to define that letter. It may be argued that the input could be made more straightforward by not using EVAL at all, and making the input:

```
100 INPUT '"What character do you want to define ", chr$
```

This would not permit the use of characters whose codes are inaccessible from the keyboard. Using the former method, the user could type CHRS(224), without quotes, to define that character.

The usefulness of EVAL is marred by a limitation on what it will actually evaluate. For some reason, it will not accept the presence of any of the pseudo-variables TIME, PAGE, LOMEM, HIMEM in the expression. For example,

```
PRINT EVAL("PAGE")
```

meets with a "No such variable" error. This is no great hardship in the line above as PRINT PAGE would have done the trick. However, in the case of a program accepting strings from the user, this limitation could prove awkward. For example, in a disassembler program, the following might be used:

```
1000 INPUT "What start address ",s$
1010 s%=EVAL(s$)
1020 ....
```

If the user knew that EVAL was being used, he might type "PAGE-256", to disassemble a machine program he has loaded just below BASIC. This wouldn't work. What makes this behaviour even stranger is that I use the same technique in a program in Chapter five ("draw"), which accepts PAGE and the other pseudo variables quite happily.

The other string functions which return numerical results are ASC, VAL and INSTR. ASC has already been mentioned. It returns the ASCII code of the first character of its argument string, e.g. ASC("0") is 48 or &30. The ASC of the null string is −1. This is sensible as it makes null strings "less" than non-empty ones, which corresponds to the action of the relational operators ("A">"" etc.). VAL is like a limited version of EVAL. It treats its argument as a number, and calculates the number as it would if it had been typed in response to an INPUT statement. Using VAL can be regarded as "stripping-off" the quotes around a string. Thus:

```
1000 A=VAL("1.234E12")
```

is equivalent to:

```
1000 A=1.234E12
```

The evaluation of the number stops when a character which couldn't be part of the number is encountered:

```
VAL("12Q") = 12
VAL("1.2EA") = 1.2
VAL("") = 0
```

Notice how VAL differs from EVAL in its treatment of the null string. The latter function would give "No such variable" when asked to evaluate "", as this is equivalent to having the line:

```
100 A=
```

BASIC looks for an expression to evaluate, fails and produces the (somewhat misleading) error message.

The INSTR function is a little less commonly found than the aforementioned ones, though no less useful. It has two possible syntaxes:

```
INSTR(long$, short$)
INSTR(long$, short$, start)
```

The first form returns the position of short$ in long$, or zero if no such relationship between the strings holds. For example:

```
INSTR("A long string", "long") = 3
INSTR("ABBCDE", "B") = 2
INSTR("ABBCDE", "b") = 0
INSTR("String", "") = 1
```

In the first example, "long" appears at character number three of "A long string". Similarly, "B" is the second character of "ABBCDE" (note that the FIRST occurrence of the short string is given. Subsequent appearances may be detected using the second form of INSTR). The third example of INSTR would return zero as "b" is nowhere to be found in "ABBCDE". The last example may seem strange. However, careful thought should make clear that the null string can appear anywhere in another string, as it has zero length. Thus there is effectively a null string between the opening quote of "String" and the "S", hence the value returned by INSTR.

In its second form, INSTR starts the search for the second string at a given place in the longer one, rather than the first character. For example:

```
INSTR("Hee Hee", "He", 2) = 5
```

as the search for "He" starts from the second character of "Hee Hee". Hence it is not until character 5 is reached that a match is found.

INSTR has several applications. A common one is to avoid multiple IFs after an input statement. Consider the following:

```
10 REM    Use of INSTR
20 MODE 4
100 col$="BLACK   RED    GREEN   YELLOW  BLUE   MAGENTA CYAN    WHITE"
```

```
110 REPEAT
120    INPUT TAB(0,5),"Which colour ",c$
130    CLS
140    pos%=INSTR(col$,c$)-1
150    ok%=pos%<>-1 AND pos% MOD 8=0
155    IF NOT ok% THEN PRINT TAB(0,28);"Colours are"'col$
160 UNTIL ok%
170 col%=pos% DIV 8
180 PRINT col%
190 END
```

Col$ contains the possible (legal) responses to the INPUT statement, viz. the names of all the BBC Computer's colours. This is searched by INSTR for an occurrence of the user's response, which is in c$. Notice that the colour names are "padded-out" with spaces so that the total number of characters is eight. This mechanism enables the colour to be translated into its numeric form. For example "RED" is at position nine in col$. Thus pos% is assigned the value 8. When this is divided by eight, the actual colour number for red, 1, is obtained. Note that col$ is also used as the "error message" if the user types in an illegal colour or just presses RETURN. Using this method, an abbreviation form can be used, similar to the "." form used when entering BASIC programs. For example, red can be obtained by typing "R", "RE" or "RED". There are some ambiguities, though. For example, "BL" starts both "BLACK" and "BLUE". The former would be selected as it appears before "BLUE" in col$.

The look-up method described above can be used in other applications. If BBC BASIC didn't happen to have a built-in assembler, it could be used to help write one. The 6502 mnemonics could be put in a string, and looked-up using INSTR. In fact, I used this method when generating the DATA statements for the dissassembler in Chapter five. Adventure games are another possible use. In such games, the user has a "conversation" with the computer (anyone who has played "Philospher's Quest" will understand the presence of the quotation marks). A central part of the program is to look-up special keywords which the computer is meant to understand. The skeleton of a program below shows how INSTR may be used in such an application.

```
10 REM    Adventure (not really)
100 PROCinit
110 REPEAT
120    INPUT'"Yeah",in$
130    words%=FNlex(in$)
135    IF words%=0 THEN 190
140    FOR i%=1 TO words%
150       PROCnoun(word$(i%))
160       PROCverb(word$(i%))
170       PROCabuse(word$(i%))
```

```
180    NEXT i%
190 UNTIL ended%
200 PRINT"Bye!"
210 END
220
230
1000 DEF PROCinit
1010    REM Sets-up the vocab. strings and resets ended%
1020    nouns%=2
1030    DIM nouns$(nouns%)
1035    REM    Note: 7 words of exactly 8 characters (cf line 3070)
1040    nouns$(1)="HAMMER  TORCH   AXE     BOTTLE  SPOON   NIPPLE  EARWIG"
1050    nouns$(2)="DUCK    BOG     PAPER   NOUGAT  HERRING WHALE   LIP"
1060    verbs%=1
1070    DIM verbs$(verbs%)
1080    verbs$(1)="END     SHOUT   LISTEN  SPANK   WHIP    SCRAPE  SUCK"
1090    abuses%=1
1100    DIM abuses$(abuses%)
1110    abuses$(1)="!*?@@#  {}{}{}  <OO>"
1120    ended%=FALSE
1130    REM Array for in$ words
1140    DIM word$(10)
1150 ENDPROC
1170
2000 DEF FNlex(in$)
2010    REM  Splits-up in$ into words in word$()
2015    IF in$="" THEN =0
2020    LOCAL pos%, p%, words%
2030    pos%=1: words%=0
2040    REPEAT
2050       p%=INSTR(in$," ",pos%)
2060       IF p%=0 THEN 2100
2070          words%=words%+1
2080          word$(words%)=MID$(in$,pos%,p%-pos%)
2090          pos%=p%+1
2100    UNTIL p%=0
2110    words%=words%+1
2120    word$(words%)=MID$(in$,pos%)
2130 =words%
2140
2150
3000 DEF PROCnoun(n$)
```

```
3010    REM  Look for a noun and process it
3020    LOCAL i%, p%
3030    FOR i%=1 TO nouns%
3040      p%=INSTR(nouns$(i%), n$)
3050     IF p%=0 THEN 3090
3060        REM work out which word it is
3070        p%=(p%-1) DIV 8 + (i%-1)*7 + 1
3080        ON p% GOSUB
3200,3300,3400,3500,3600,3700,3800,3900,4000,4100,4200,4300,4400,4500
3090     NEXT i%
3100 ENDPROC
3110
3200 REM HAMMER
3210    IF RND>0 THEN PRINT"There's no hammer here!" ELSE PRINT"OK!"
3220 RETURN
3230
3300 REM TORCH
3310    IF TIME<50000 THEN PRINT"It's too dark to see the torch" ELSE
PRINT"OK!"
3320 RETURN
3400 REM  and so on and so on....
3420 RETURN
3430
3440
5000 DEF PROCverb(v$) REM  Similar to PROCnoun
5010 ENDPROC
5020
5030
6000 DEF PROCabuse(a$) REM  Similar to PROCnoun & PROCverb
6010 ENDPROC
6020
6030
```

Like the previous example, the INSTR function is used to convert a string given by the user into a number which can then be processed in some way. There are three sets of words: nouns, verbs and abuse. The main loop takes a string from the keyboard, splits this into words (where a word is assumed to be a group of non-space characters separated by spaces) and then calls the three procedures PROCnoun, PROCverb and PROCabuse for each of these words. PROCinit sets-up the arrays of search strings. I have not included any actual "abuse" examples, as I'm not familiar with the publisher's censorial policies, nor do I wish to find out. Notice that the length of the words in the search strings must be constant to enable the conversion from position to "word number" to be made. Also, the number of words in a given string array (nouns$() etc.) must be constant, as this is also used in the calculation for the ON . . . GOSUB expression.

The program, as presented, is far from complete, and probably very inefficient in terms of memory space used (the strings take up space in both the program text and the variable space). One way to get round this would be to read the strings from a data file on disc or cassette. The program's vocabulary would need to be greatly enhanced, of course. Only one of the word-processing procedures is given; the others follow a very similar pattern of looking-up the word and performing some action if it is valid. To make the program act intelligently, there would need to be many more variables than the present one implies, to keep track of where the adventurer is/has been, what he is holding and so on.

The string functions which actually return a string are recognisable by the $ which appears after their names (except EVAL, of course, whose type varies). Three of these functions are used to access a substring of their argument. These are LEFT$, RIGHT$ and MID$. The syntax of the trio is exactly the same as Microsoft's versions:

```
LEFT$:          A$=LEFT$(str$, num)
RIGHT$:         A$=RIGHT$(str$, num)
MID$:           A$=MID$(str$, start [,num])
```

The LEFT$ function returns the num left-most characters of its first (string) argument. As with all functions in BASIC, the arguments may be arbitrarily complex expressions of the appropriate type. Some examples of LEFT$ are:

```
LEFT$("abcd", 2)="ab"
LEFT$("abcd", 0)=""
LEFT$("abcd", 10)="abcd"
```

The first case is the norm, where num is between 1 and LEN(str$). The second example provides the expected result: the zero left-most characters of any string the the null string. The last example shows that the most characters that LEFT$ (or indeed RIGHT$) will return is LEN(str$). If num is greater than this, the argument string str$ is returned in its entirety. The len parameter is treated as a one-byte quantity. One way of looking at it is that num is ANDed with &000000FF before LEFT$ is applied. This means that giving LEFT$ or RIGHT$ negative values for num will not cause errors directly, but will probably cause erroneous results to be generated. For example, LEFT$(a$,−1) is the same as LEFT$(a$,255); LEFT$(a$,−2) is the same as LEFT$(a$,254), and so on, until LEFT$(a$,−256) which is the same LEFT$(a$,0).

The RIGHT$ function complements LEFT$ by returning the right-most num characters of str$. Thus, to extract the day and year from a string which has the form "dd/mm/yy", the two assignments:

```
dd%=VAL(LEFT$(date$,2))
yy%=VAL(RIGHT$(date$,2))
```

would be used. Extraction of the month field takes a little more effort using LEFT$ and RIGHT$:

```
date$=RIGHT$(date$,5)
mm%=VAL(LEFT$(date$,2))
```

Not only does this require two assignments, but it also changes the value of date$. A superior method is to use the more usual form of MID$. This is:

```
a$=MID$(str$,start,num)
```

str$ is the usual argument string, start is the first character we want to extract and num is the number of characters desired. The mm% assignment using MID$ would be:

```
mm%=VAL(MID$(date$,4,2))
```

MID$ can be considered to be equivalent to a LEFT$, but starting at character start. As the first description given above implies, the third argument is optional. If it is omitted, all the characters of str$ from start to the end of str$ are returned. If start > LEN(str$) the null string is returned. In the present example, MID$(date$,4) would return a string of the form "mm/yy". People familiar with ZX80 BASIC may realise that the function TL$ (tail string) is equivalent to MID$(a$,2). This can be used to write a simple, though impractical function to emulate LEN:

```
1000 DEF FNLen(a$)
1010    IF a$="" THEN =0 ELSE =FNLen(MID$(a$,2))+1
```

This states that if a$ is null, then its length is zero, otherwise its length is 1 plus the length of its tail (a$ minus the first character). The three substring functions LEFT$, RIGHT$ and MID$ have many applications in data validation and field extraction. The date example exemplifies data validation. The procedure below validates a date given in its argument string. The string can be: "d/m/yy", "dd/m/yy", "d/mm/yy" or "dd/mm/yy", so that the leading zeroes do not have to be included in the day and month numbers. The procedure assumes the existence of an array, days%(), which holds the number days in the months 1 (January) to 12 (December). The results are returned in four global variables, dd%, mm%, yy% and err%. The latter is an error code: zero means the values of the other three variables is valid; non-zero codes imply some sort of error:

```
1000 DEF PROCdate(date$)
1010    REM   Validates and converts date$ into numeric
1020    REM   form, with an error code in err%
1030    LOCAL p1%, p2%
1040    err%=0: REM   No error yet
1060    IF LEN(date$)<6 OR LEN(date$)>8 THEN err%=1: ENDPROC
1070    p1%=INSTR(date$,"/")
```

```
1080    IF p1%=0 OR p1%>3 THEN            err%=2: ENDPROC
1090    dd%=VAL(LEFT$(date$,p1%-1))
1100    p2%=INSTR(date$,"/",p1%+1)
1110    IF p2%=0 OR p2%>6 THEN            err%=3: ENDPROC
1120    mm%=VAL(MID$(date$,p1%+1,p2%-p1%-1))
1130    IF mm%<1 OR mm%>12 THEN           err%=4: ENDPROC
1140    IF dd%<1 OR dd%>days%(mm%) THEN   err%=5: ENDPROC
1150    yy%=VAL(MID$(date$,p2%+1))
1160    IF yy%<0 OR yy%>99 THEN           err%=6: ENDPROC
1170 ENDPROC
```

As an exercise you may like to alter the procedure so that it takes leap years into account, or produces explicit error messages rather than codes.

It is sometimes desirable to ensure that a string has a particular length. This is known as "padding" or "justifying" the string. The LEFT$ and RIGHT$ functions are used to perform this task, the particular one used depending on whether the string is to be left- or right-justified. A common example is to right-justify monetary values with zeroes, so that £12.34, £1.23 and £123.4 would be printed as £0012.34, £0001.23 and £0123.40. This practice discourages shady characters from adding a few non-zero figures to the left of the decimal point where such an action might be beneficial to them. Notice also that the last example has a zero after the 4 to ensure there are two characters after the decimal point. Apart from anything else, this makes it look neater. The function below takes three arguments. The first is the number to be justified, and the second and third are the number digits required before and after the decimal point respectively:

```
1000 DEF FNjust(num, left%, right%)
1010    REM   returns a justified version of num
1020    LOCAL num$, dp%, len%, left$, right$
1030    num$=STR$(num)
1040    len%=LEN(num$)
1050    dp%=INSTR(num$, ".")
1060    IF dp%=0 THEN len%=len%+1: dp%=len%: num$=num$+"."
1063    REM   Make sure no figures are chopped off!
1065    IF left% < dp%-1    THEN left%=dp%-1
1067    IF right% < len%-dp% THEN right%=len%-dp%
1070    left$=LEFT$(num$,dp%-1):    REM Get figures left of d.p.
1080    right$=MID$(num$,dp%+1):    REM Get figures right of d.p.
1085    REM     Pad on appropriate side with 0's
1090    left$=RIGHT$(STRING$(left%,"0")+left$,left%)
1100    right$=LEFT$(right$+STRING$(right%,"0"),right%)
1110 =left$+"."+right$
```

The function conveniently introduces two more string functions: STR$ and STRING$. These similar sounding functions have not a lot in common. The first one is the opposite of VAL: it takes a numeric argument and converts this into a string representation. Normally the format of the string returned is exactly as the number would be PRINTed. This can be changed by altering @%, which variable is discussed in Chapter three. If the number is an integer, no decimal point would be produced, so this has to be introduced explicitly in FNjust. A not-very-widely-known-fact about STR$ is that it has a special form, viz. STR$~. This produces a hex representation of its argument. (The argument is made into an integer first if necessary.) This feature is useful when printing addresses in hex:

```
1000 DEF FNhex(h%)=RIGHT$("0000"+STR$~(h%),4)
```

The other function, STRING$, is used for making a number of copies of a given string. It has the form:

```
a$=STRING$(num, str$)
```

and returns num concatenated versions of str$. For example,

```
STRING$(2,"0") = "00"
STRING$(4,"}{") = "}{}{}{}{"
STRING$(10," ") = "          "
```

The number is treated MOD 256, as usual. There is an important difference between BBC STRING$ and the Microsoft "standard". The second example above would produce "}}}}" in Microsoft, as only the first character of the string argument is duplicated (cf. ASC). Also, Microsoft STRING$ allows a numeric second argument, in which case it is treated as an ASCII code. Thus:

```
Microsoft BASIC     BBC BASIC
STRING$(num,asc)    STRING$(num,CHR$(asc))
```

CHR$ is the last string function I will discuss here (GET$ and INKEY$ are covered in Chapter three). It complements the ASC function. Whereas that converts a string (or, more accurately, a character) to its ASCII code, CHR$ takes a byte-sized number and makes it into a character. Thus, for the most part:

```
a$=CHR$(ASC(a$))   and   a%=ASC(CHR$(a%))
```

The symmetry of this relationship is spoiled by that string which is not a string, "". When given a null string for an argument, ASC returns the (illegal) ASCII code −1. This is a useful feature, as it ties in with the INKEY and INKEY$ functions (which return −1 and "" respectively when no character is available). However, CHR$(−1) is treated as CHR$(−1 AND 255), which is the same as CHR$(255). Thus, CHR$(ASC(""))<>"" and ASC(CHR$(−1))<>−1. Notice also that although ASCII code 0 is called NUL, it is not the same as "". The former has a proper ASCII code and a length of 1; the latter has neither of these properties.

On the BBC Micro, one of CHR$'s main uses has been supplanted by the VDU statement. It is common to see the statement:

```
PRINT CHR$(expr);
```

in BASIC programs. This is often used to obtain special characters which are unavailable from the keyboard, or to output a control character from a program (e.g. to clear the screen). The VDU statement is covered later on, but for now it is suffice to say that the above statement can be replaced with:

```
VDU expr
```

This doesn't exactly make the advantage of the latter form abundantly clear, but it involves less typing if nothing else.

On the BBC Machine, the characters printed on the screen can be redefined by the user to give any required pattern. The most convenient ones to redefine tend to have ASCII codes which aren't readily accessible from the keyboard (especially under MOS 0.1). Thus CHR$ finds use in defining composite strings made up from redefined characters. It is also possible to include text formatting and colour changing codes in these strings. This application of CHR$ is discussed in Chapter three. For another use, see the date compaction/expansion routines given above.

1.2 Arrays

The numbers and strings dealt with in the last section were all single quantities, one integer, one real, one string. These are sometimes called simple types. Arrays, on the other hand, are known as structured types. Arrays are very important in many branches of computing, as the idea of a list, or sequence, of identical items crops up often in real life. In BASIC, there can be arrays of numbers and strings, and these can have several dimensions. Because of these variations, there are three subsections to this section. 1.2.1 deals with numeric one-dimensional arrays, or vectors as they are sometimes called. 1.2.2 briefly discusses two-dimensional arrays, also known as matrices. These have importance in various branches of mathematics, physics and computer graphics. 1.2.3 deals with string arrays, with special regard to the searching thereof.

The method for introducing arrays in BASIC is with the DIM statement. A typical DIM statement is:

```
100 DIM a(100), a%(4,4), a$(50)
```

This statement would reserve the space for the following: 101 real variables called a(0) to a(100), 25 integers known as a%(0,0) to a%(4,4), and 51 strings, a$(0) to a$(50). Some BASICs have the OPTION BASE statement which lets the subscripts start from 0 or 1 as desired. All BBC BASIC arrays start from element zero. When using arrays, it is wise to remember the space they can take up, especially strings. For example, DIM a$(20,20) would reserve space for 441 string variables. Each of these takes at least 4 bytes (for its string information block). If each element is then given a 20 character value, 10584 bytes of memory would be needed!

1.2.1 Numeric Vectors

It is very common to have a DIM statement of the form:

```
100 DIM a%(100)
```

This is a numeric vector as each of its elements is numeric and it only has one dimension. A common use for vectors is as a function. In the familar sense of the word, a function returns a value which is determined by its argument. Consider the two statements:

```
100 a=SIN(45)
110 b=TWO(10)
```

syntactically (i.e. the way they look), there is no difference between the two. The first one uses the built-in function SIN to return the sine of 45 radians, and the second example accesses an array (assuming one of that name has previously been declared by a DIM) called TWO. This array could be set-up such that the TWO(i) happens to contain 2^i. This makes TWO effectively become a function with an integer argument which returns an integer. It could be set-up as below:

```
100 DIM TWO(31)
110 TWO(0)=1
120 FOR i%=1 TO
130    TWO(i%)=2*TWO(i%-1)
140 NEXT i%
```

What is the advantage of using the array TWO() over a function defined as below?

```
1000 DEF FNtwo(i%)=2^i%
```

Mainly it is one of speed. Once the array has been initialised, finding the value of 2^0 to 2^{31} becomes a very rapid business. It would be even faster if TWO() were made TWO%() instead. If a program used a lot of arithmetic involving powers of two (e.g. the character pattern display procedure of Chapter three), this pseudo function could speed things significantly. Notice, though, that this improved efficiency costs 128 or 160 bytes of storage for the array. It is very common in computing that there is a trade-off between speed and program storage size. Another example of this is in sorting. There is a very efficient way of sorting arrays known as the two-way merge sort. To work so quickly, this requires an auxiliary array the same size as the one being sorted. This is bad news if the original array only just fits in the computer's memory. On the other hand, the bubble sort is about as inefficient as a sort can be, but it only needs the use of one variable of the same type as the array elements being processed.

The pseudo-function use of arrays is restricted (in BASIC, at least) to arguments of an integer type lying in the range 0 to n, where n is not too large. Other examples are tables of trig. functions (see Chapter four) and factorials. All of the so-called transcendental functions are very slow on microcomputers. Storing scaled versions of them in integer arrays in the range 0 to 359 degrees (for trig. functions) can greatly enhance the speed of a program. Factorials are often calculated, when needed, by a FOR. . .NEXT loop. However, since there are only 13 numbers whose factorials can be stored exactly in BBC BASIC integers, it may be advantageous to calculate them once and for all at the start of the program:

```
100 DIM fac%(12)
110 fac%(0)=1
120 FOR i%=1 TO 12
130     fac%(i%)=fac%(i%-1)*i%
140 NEXT i%
```

Another storage/speed type problem is that of finding primes. Later, a slow but low space-requirement method of calculating primes is given. A much faster method, known as the Sieve of Eratosthenes, uses an array p%(n%), where n% is the highest number to be tested. The program works as follows. Initially, all the elements of p%() are set to TRUE, indicating that as far as we know they are all primes. The program then enters a loop in which each element is examined in turn. If the value of the current element is TRUE, its value is printed and all its multiples (up to n%) are made FALSE (indicating that they are no longer considered as primes). Naturally the process starts at 2. If 1 was the first number examined, all the elements would be eliminated immediately.

```
100 REM     Sieve of Eratosthenes
110 MODE 7
120 n%=1000: REM    max. prime
130 DIM p%(n%)
140 FOR i%=1 TO n%
150     p%(i%)=TRUE
160 NEXT i%
170 PRINT 1;
180 FOR i%=2 TO n%
190     IF NOT p%(i%) THEN 240
193        REM   Don't cross any out if i%>n%/2
195        IF i%+i%>n% THEN 230
200        FOR j%=i%+i% TO n% STEP i%
210            p%(j%)=FALSE
220        NEXT j%
230        PRINT i%;
240 NEXT i%
250 PRINT
260 END
```

You will probably have noticed that there is a gross ineffiency present in the program, in that 32-bit integers are being used to store quantities of a boolean nature, where one bit would suffice. One way to make a saving would be to use a byte array instead of an integer array. Byte arrays use the alternative form of DIM which is covered in the next section. Quite a challenging task is to optimise the Sieve algorithm to make it as efficient as possible.

Vectors of integers can be used to store a sequence of accumulated numbers. For example, it is possible to have a look at the distribution of BBC BASIC's random number generator:

```
100 REM    Random Distribution
110 MODE 4
120 DIM y%(159)
130 REPEAT
140    x%=RND(160)-1
150    y%(x%)=y%(x%)+4
160    PLOT 69,x%*16,y%(x%)
170 UNTIL y%(x%)>1020
180 END
```

The graphical evidence from the program suggests that the random number generator works OK. The distribution pattern of a random variable is, by definition, boring. Slightly more interesting is this. Imagine the integers in the range 0–999. If the digits of these numbers are added, they have the range 0 to 27 (9+9+9). It would be interesting to see how these sums are distributed for the range 0–999. The program below shows this distribution:

```
100 REM  Not so random distribution
110 MODE 5
120 DIM tot%(27)
130 FOR i%=0 TO 999
140    i$=STR$(i%)
150    t%=0
160    FOR j%=1 TO LEN(i$)
170       t%=t%+VAL(MID$(i$,j%,1))
180    NEXT j%
190    tot%(t%)=tot%(t%)+8
200    PLOT 69,t%/27*1279,tot%(t%)
210 NEXT i%
220 END
```

The distribution thus obtained is a normal one: the high and low totals are comparatively rare, most of them being in the middle around 13 and 14. It is interesting to note that if the summing process is repeated until only one digit remains (e.g. 456; 4+5+6=15; 1+5=6), then the distribution of the sums is a flat one. The digits 1 to 9 have 111 numbers each whose ultimate digit-sum is that digit. There is, of course, one number whose sum is zero, namely 000.

A variation on the theme discussed above is to examine the way the bytes in a cassette or disc file are distributed. It is very easy to see by looking at this what sort of file it is. For example, if the bytes 0–255 are distributed across the screen, then for a BASIC program the right half of the page should be much higher than the left-hand side. If the program is well laid-out, there should be a peak at CHR$(32), for the spaces. Similarly, text files should have most of their bytes in the range 32 to 126, with the odd control character. Machine code programs should be relatively random. A program to plot such a distribution is given below.

```
100 REM    File examiner
110 MODE 4
120 DIM count%(255)
130 chan%=OPENIN("")
140 REPEAT
150    b%=BGET#chan%
160    count%(b%)=count%(b%)+4
170    PLOT 69,b%*4,count%(b%)
180 UNTIL EOF#chan%
190 END
```

If the program is run on a cassette-based system, the cassette will have to have motor control, otherwise BASIC can't keep up with the tape and "Block?" errors result. The range of characters examined could be reduced to, say, just the printable ones for text files. This will give a less cramped display.

There is a classic chess problem in which eight queens must be placed on a board in such a way that no piece may be in check with another. (A queen can check if its "opponent" is on the same vertical, horizontal or diagonal line as itself.) When solving this problem by computer, there are at least two ways of proceeding, an exhaustive test of all possible arrangements of eight queens on a board, or by using a technique known as backtracking. The second method will only find one arrangement of the queens for each of the eight possible starting positions, whereas the exhaustive search, as its name suggests, will find all possibilities. The two methods provide an interesting comparison of different problem solving techniques, so I give programs to implement both.

A proper exhaustive search would take far too long on any computer, let alone a micro, so certain observations have to be made which drastically reduce the number of arrangements tested for legality. The first is an obvious one: two queens cannot occupy the same column of the board, and each column must have at least one queen in it. Thus, the board can be envisioned as eight adjacent columns, each with exactly one queen. This gives a clue to how the board can be represented. We dimension a vector, board%() whose elements give the row number of the queen in that column. A typical solution, and the associated values of board%(1) to board%(8) is shown in Figure 1.1.

The way the algorithm proceeds is as follows. The main program calls the procedure PROCqueens(1). This procedure finds all the valid arrangements of queens from column col%, its parameter, to column eight, assuming that all the preceding queens are placed legally. If it is called with a value of 9, then eight

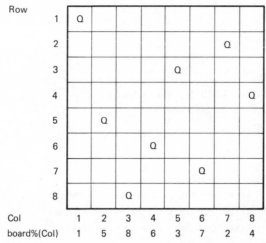

Figure 1.1   Solution to the Eight Queens Problem

queens must have been correctly placed, and the board may be printed out (by PROCprint). If col% is less than eight, it calls PROCmore, with the same parameter, col%. PROCmore tries to place a queen in each of the eight rows of column col%. FNsafe tells it if the current placement is OK. If it is, it uses PROCqueens(col%+1) to find the legal placements for the next column.

The circular way in which PROCqueens calls PROCmore, which then calls PROCqueens again may seem a bit dodgy. It is, however, a perfectly sound technique, and goes by the name of mutual recursion: PROCqueens and PROCmore are mutually recursive. The two remaining procedures are FNsafe and PROCprint. The latter simply displays the current state of board%() in MODE 4. FNsafe takes a column and a row and decides if placing a queen there is safe. It returns TRUE or FALSE dependent upon this fact. First part of the IF test sees if there is a queen on the same row; the second part looks at the diagonals. The ABS enable both diagonals to be examined at once.

Computers have the advantage of allowing generalisations to be made. In this case, the queens program has been generalised to allow for n queens to be placed on an n*n board, where n=1 to 9. The upper limit is determined solely by the FOR ... NEXT loop nesting limit of BBC BASIC. This is very low; only ten loops may be "active" at once. The program is listed below:

```
100 REM    N Queens - 1
110 MODE 4
115 DIM board%(9):    REM  Largest possible board
120 REPEAT
130    PROCinit
140    PROCqueens(1)
160 UNTIL n%=0
170 END
```

```
 180
 190
1000 DEF PROCinit
1020    CLS
1030    REPEAT
1040       INPUT TAB(0,5),"What size board ",n%
1050    UNTIL n%>=0 AND n%<=9
1070 ENDPROC
1080
1090
2000 DEF PROCqueens(col%)
2010    REM  Generates the possibilites for column col%
2020    REM  If col%>n%, a solution has been found & is printed
2030    IF col%>n% THEN PROCprint ELSE PROCmore(col%)
2040 ENDPROC
2050
2060
2070
4000 DEF PROCmore(col%)
4010    REM  Calls PROCqueens to try more possibilites
4040    FOR board%(col%)=1 TO n%
4050       IF FNsafe(col%,board%(col%)) THEN PROCqueens(col%+1)
4060    NEXT board%(col%)
4070 ENDPROC
4080
4090
5000 DEF FNsafe(col%, row%)
5010    REM  Returns TRUE if puting a queen at (col%,row%)
5020    REM  is safe, else returns FALSE
5025    IF col%=1 THEN =TRUE
5030    LOCAL i%, sf%
5040    sf%=TRUE
5050    FOR i%=1 TO col%-1
5060       rowi%=board%(i%)
5070       IF rowi%=row% OR ABS(rowi%-row%)=col%-i% THEN sf%=FALSE
5080    NEXT i%
5090 =sf%
5100
5110
6000 DEF PROCprint
6010    REM   Prints the board after a solution is found
6020    LOCAL i%, row%, col%
```

```
6030     CLS
6035     MOVE 31,992: DRAW 31,988-n%*32
6037     DRAW (n%+1)*32,988-n%*32: DRAW (n%+1)*32,992
6039     DRAW 31,992
6040     IF n%=0 THEN ENDPROC
6050     FOR i%=0 TO n%*n%-1
6060        row%=i% DIV n% + 1
6070        col%=i% MOD n% + 1
6080        IF (row%+col%) AND 1 THEN COLOUR0:COLOUR129 ELSE COLOUR1:COLOUR128
6090        PRINT TAB(col%,row%);
6100        IF row%=board%(col%) THEN PRINT"*"; ELSE PRINT " ";
6110     NEXT i%
6120     VDU 20: REM Back to normal colours
6130     INPUT''"<RETURN>"in$
6140 ENDPROC
```

The other method is of solving the Eight Queens again uses mutually recursive routines, but in a different way. PROCqueens and PROCmore are replaced by three procedures, PROCqueens, PROCback and PROCfind. Once again, the initial call is PROCqueens(1). This procedure calls PROCprint if its parameter is greater than n%; then it returns, which is why only one solution is printed. If col% is <=n%, the procedure PROCfind is called. This looks for a position to place the queen in the current row. If it can't find one, PROCback is called to move the process back by one column (resetting the current column's row to 0 beforehand), and then call PROCfind to look for a suitable position in the new row. This mutual recursion continues until either a queen can be placed, or PROCback tries to backtrack beyond the first column, in which the program halts with the message "No more solutions". When PROCfind eventually returns to PROCqueens, a queen will have been placed, and the next column can be allocated with the recursive call PROCqueens(col%+1).

An extra routine in the second version is PROCtrace, which will show the backtracking motion if the static variable T% has a non-zero value. The program is given below.

```
100 REM    N Queens - 2
110 MODE 4
115 DIM board%(9):    REM  Largest possible board
120 REPEAT
130     PROCinit
140     PROCqueens(1)
150 UNTIL n%=0
220 END
230
240
```

```
1000 DEF PROCinit
1010 LOCAL i%
1020   CLS
1030   REPEAT
1040     INPUT TAB(0,5),"What size board ",n%
1050   UNTIL n%>=0 AND n%<=9
1070   FOR i%=1 TO n%
1080     board%(i%)=0
1090   NEXT i%
1100 ENDPROC
1110
1120
2000 DEF PROCqueens(col%)
2010   REM   If col%>n% then prints the board, else finds a
2020   REM   new queen position (PROCfind), backtracking if nec.
2060   IF col%>n% THEN PROCprint ELSE PROCfind: PROCqueens(col%+1)
2070 ENDPROC
2080
2090
3000 DEF PROCback
3010   REM  Decrements col% and finds a new queen position
3030   board%(col%)=0
3040   col%=col%-1: IF col%<1 THEN PRINT''"No more solutions": END
3050   PROCfind
3070 ENDPROC
3080
3090
4000 DEF PROCfind
4010   REM  Looks for a place to put the queen
4020   LOCAL r%
4030   REPEAT
4040     r%=board%(col%)+1
4050     board%(col%)=r%
4055     IF T% THEN PROCtrace
4060   UNTIL r% > n% OR FNsafe(col%,r%)
4070   IF r% > n% THEN PROCback
4080 ENDPROC
4090
4100
4500 DEF PROCtrace
4510   REM  Traces the progress of the pieces
4520   LOCAL i%
```

```
4530    CLS
4540    FOR i%=1 TO n%
4550        IF board%(i%)<>0 THEN PRINT TAB(i%,board%(i%));"*";
4560    NEXT i%
4570    INPUT TAB(0,n%+2)"<RETURN>"in$
4580 ENDPROC
4590
4600
5000 DEF FNsafe(col%, row%)
5010    REM  Returns TRUE if puting a queen at (col%,row%)
5020    REM  is safe, else returns FALSE
5025    IF col%=1 THEN =TRUE
5030    LOCAL i%, sf%
5040    sf%=TRUE
5050    FOR i%=1 TO col%-1
5060        rowi%=board%(i%)
5070        IF rowi%=row% OR ABS(rowi%-row%)=col%-i% THEN sf%=FALSE
5080    NEXT i%
5090 =sf%
5100
5110
6000 DEF PROCprint
6010    REM   Prints the board after a solution is found
6020    LOCAL i%, row%, col%
6030    CLS
6035    MOVE 31,992: DRAW 31,988-n%*32
6037    DRAW (n%+1)*32,988-n%*32: DRAW (n%+1)*32,992
6039    DRAW 31,992
6040    IF n%=0 THEN ENDPROC
6050    FOR i%=0 TO n%*n%-1
6060        row%=i% DIV n% + 1
6070        col%=i% MOD n% + 1
6080        IF (row%+col%) AND 1 THEN COLOUR0:COLOUR129 ELSE COLOUR1:COLOUR128
6090        PRINT TAB(col%,row%);
6100        IF row%=board%(col%) THEN PRINT"*"; ELSE PRINT " ";
6110    NEXT i%
6120    VDU 20: REM Back to normal colours
6130    INPUT''"<RETURN>"in$
6140 ENDPROC
```

Actually, there are only a couple of minor changes required to make this version print out all the solutions. The modification is to PROCqueens and you may like to try to discover them yourself before reading the next few lines. If these changes are made:

```
2060    IF col%>n% THEN PROCprint: PROCback ELSE PROCfind
2065    PROCqueens(col%+1)
```

then once a solution has been found, PROCback takes the process back to look for subsequent solutions. This terminates in the same way as before, with the "No more solutions" message.

1.2.2   Matrices

Arrays of numbers with two dimensions are known as matrices, or tables. There is a branch of mathematics which is concerned with the manipulation of matrices and their properties. Some versions of BASIC provide special statements which, for example, add two matrices and zero matrices. The BASIC used in [Rogers] is one of these, and if you want to use any of the programs given therein, they will have to be converted to BBC BASIC. This subsection gives a set of procedures which emulate most of the BASIC MAT commands.

In the following procedures and functions, I will assume that the following declarations have been made:

```
100 DIM A(maxi,maxj), B(maxk,maxl), C(maxm,maxn)
```

As BBC BASIC procedures cannot have array parameters, each routine will act on a particular array or arrays. There are two simple statements:

```
MAT A=ZER    and    MAT A=IDN
```

The first causes each of the elements of A() to become zero, the second makes A() into the identity matrix. This has all elements as zero except for A(1,1), A(2,2) ... A(maxi,maxj). Notice that for IDN to work, A() must be a square matrix, i.e. maxi=maxj. Also, it is usual to start matrix subscripts from 1 instead of zero. The two procedures are:

```
1000 DEF PROCzerA(maxi%,maxj%)
1010    LOCAL i%, j%
1020    FOR i%=1 TO maxi%
1030       FOR j%=1 TO maxj%
1040          A(i%,j%)=0
1050       NEXT j%
1060    NEXT i%
1070 ENDPROC
1080
1090
2000 DEF PROCidnA(maxi%,maxj%)
2010    LOCAL i%, j%
2020    FOR i%=1 TO maxi%
```

```
2030        FOR j%=1 TO maxj%
2040            IF i%=j% THEN A(i%,j%)=1 ELSE A(i%,j%)=0
2050        NEXT j%
2060    NEXT i%
2070 ENDPROC
```

It is clear that the differences between the two procedures are few. Using the fact that the relational operators return the truth values 0 and −1, line 2040 can be shortened to:

```
2040            A(i%,j%)=-(i%=j%)
```

An important property of a square matrix is its determinant. The function below will return the determinant of A(). Maxi and maxj must be two or three. The BASIC:

```
100 LET D=DET(A)
```

becomes

```
100 D=FNdetA(maxi)
```

in BBC BASIC.

```
1000 DEF FNdetA(size%)
1010    REM    Give the determinant of A()
1020    LOCAL d
1030    IF size%=2 THEN =FNdet2A(1,1)
1040    d= A(1,1)*FNdet2A(2,2)
1050    d=d+A(2,1)*FNdet2A(3,2)
1060      =d+A(3,1)*FNdet2A(1,2)
1070
1080
1500 DEF FNdet2A(i%,j%)
1510    REM    Gives the determinant of the 2*2
1520    REM    matrix at (i%,j%)
1530    LOCAL i1%,j1%
1540    i1%=i% MOD maxi + 1
1550    j1%=j% MOD maxj + 1
1560 =A(i%,j%)*A(i1%,j1%) - A(i1%,j%)*A(i%,j1%)
```

A procedure which uses the determinant of a matrix is one which finds its inverse. The inverse of a matrix is equivalent to the reciprocal (one over) of a normal number. It is of use in solving simultaneous equations, amongst other things. In BASIC, the inverse is normally used as in:

```
100 MAT A=INV(B)
```

It is not usually possible to assign the inverse of a matrix to itself, i.e. MAT

A=INV(A) is illegal. PROCBinvA(size%) below performs the BASIC assignment
MAT B=INV(A).

```
2000 DEF PROCBinvA(size%)
2010    LOCAL d
2020    d=FNdetA(size%)
2030    IF d=0 THEN PRINT"Singular Matrix":END
2031    IF size%=3 THEN 2040
2032      B(1,1)=A(2,2)/d: B(1,2)=-A(1,2)/d
2033      B(2,1)=-A(2,1)/d: B(2,2)=A(1,1)/d
2034    ENDPROC
2040    FOR i%=1 TO size%
2050      FOR j%=1 TO size%
2060        B(j%,i%)=FNdet2A(i% MOD maxi + 1,j% MOD maxi + 1)/d
2080      NEXT j%
2090    NEXT i%
2100 ENDPROC
```

The error message at line 2030 is the equivalent to "Divide by zero" with
numbers. A matrix which has a zero determinant is called singular and has no
inverse. Other than this exception, all matrices yield the identity matrix when multiplied by their inverse. If you are lost at the moment, and wish you weren't, then a
good book to read is [Jennings].

Matrices can be multiplied and added just like normal numbers. To add two
matrices, they must be of the same size. The sum matrix is the matrix whose elements are the sums of the corresponding ones in the operand matrices. The procedure below, which assumes that maxi=maxk=maxm and maxj=maxl=maxn, and
which is equivalent to the BASIC statement:

```
100 MAT C=A+B
```

should make this clearer

```
3000 DEF PROCC_AplusB(maxi%,maxj%)
3010    REM  Add A() and B(), sum in C()
3020    LOCAL i%,j%
3030    FOR i%=1 TO maxi%
3040      FOR j%=1 TO maxj%
3050        C(i%,j%)=A(i%,j%)+B(i%,j%)
3060      NEXT j%
3070    NEXT i%
3080 ENDPROC
```

Matrix multiplication is a little more involved, and the above reference should
be consulted for an explanation. The next procedure emulates the statement:

```
100 MAT C=A*B
```

with the conditions that maxj=maxk and that maxm>=maxi and maxn>=maxl:

```
4000 DEF PROCC_AtimesB(maxi%,maxj%,maxl%)
4010    REM Multiply A() by B(), product in C()
4020    LOCAL i%,j%,l%,sum
4030    FOR i%=1 TO maxi%
4040       FOR l%=1 TO maxl%
4050          sum=0
4060          FOR j%=1 TO maxj%
4070             sum=sum+A(i%,j%)*B(j%,l%)
4080          NEXT j%
4090          C(i%,l%)=sum
4100       NEXT l%
4110    NEXT i%
4120 ENDPROC
```

Just to prove that all these procedures can be used for something, the program below solves a pair of simultaneous equations with their help. There are six numbers required by the program, the X and Y co-efficients and the two constants. For example, suppose it was required to find the solution to the pair:

```
x+2y=3
3x+2y=1
```

then the required numbers are 1,2,3 and 3,2,1. After a short pause, the solution x=−1,y−2 will be displayed. One more procedure is required which hasn't been given yet. It is simply the equivalent to the statement:

```
100 MAT A=B
```

and goes by the name PROCA_B. Its parameters are the ranges of columns and rows to be copied. The program is listed below, followed by PROCA_B.

```
100 REM Simultaneous equations
110 DIM A(2,2),B(2,2),C(2,2)
115 maxi=2: maxj=2
120 CLS
130 PRINT''"Ax+By=C"'"Dx+Ey=F"
140 INPUT''"What values for A, B and C ",A,B,C
150 INPUT'"What values for D, E and F ",D,E,F
160 A(1,1)=A: A(1,2)=B
170 A(2,1)=D: A(2,2)=E
180 PROCBinvA(2)
190 PROCA_B(2,2)
195 B(1,1)=C: B(2,1)=F
200 PROCC_AtimesB(2,2,1)
210 PRINT''"Solution is x=";C(1,1);",    y=";C(2,1)
```

```
220 END
230
240
5000 DEF PROCA_B(maxi%,maxj%)
5010    REM Performs the assignment A()=B()
5020    LOCAL i%,j%
5030    FOR i%=1 TO maxi%
5040       FOR j%=1 TO maxj%
5050          A(i%,j%)=B(i%,j%)
5060       NEXT j%
5070    NEXT i%
5080 ENDPROC
```

All the foregoing was probably of interest only to readers already familiar with matrices and matrix algebra. If it is the case that you aren't, don't panic. There are several books which explain the use of arrays in much more detail than I have space for here. They are, unfortunately, mostly of an academic nature, and assume that the reader is engaged in some associated course. [Beech] is a very useful exception to this rule, especially if you can cope with TRS-80 BASIC. More technical, but more thorough, are [Horowitz], [Goodman] and [Page]. For those interested in the graphics applications, [Rogers] and [Newman] both have short sections on the use of matrices.

1.2.3   String Arrays

Numbers aren't the only things we like to keep lists of. Since humans have a predilection for giving objects names, it is desirable to be able to store lists of these as well. Strings are, of course, the natural way of representing names, as these usually comprise sequences of letters, digits and other symbols, e.g. "Pete the Great", "ELO" and "Walkman 2". In this section, I discuss the various ways in which string arrays can be arranged to provide easy retrieval of particular values. For example, if you stored a list of your lovers' names and marks out of ten, it might be necessary to one day list all the lovers called Toni (the most asexual name I could think of). Or if you've just won a World Cruise for two, it would be helpful to list all those who got more than eight out of ten before choosing your partner.

Being able to store and retrieve strings in arrays is particularly useful on cassette-based machines when trying to implement any kind of data base. The sequential nature of cassette files precludes the use of "random" search techniques which all data base applications require. The usual technique is to read the whole file into an array (or arrays), perform any processing which is necessary, then re-write the complete file. This obviously places a limit on the size of the file used, so the information must be stored in as compact a form as possible. A complete program to implement a simple cassette-based filing system is given at the end of this section. It should be noted that most of what is said below about processing arrays of strings also applies to direct-access disc files, which can be regarded as arrays of records which happen to reside on a discette instead of in the machine itself. Unfortunately, the lack of access to a disc-based system on my part means that the subject of disc-files must remain "beyond the scope of this book".

When processing data in arrays, there are several operations which can be provided, regardless of the actual way in which the data is organised. These are: Initialise the array; Insert an item; Delete an item and Search for an item. There are other operations which depend on the representation of the data. For example, it may be very easy to give an alphabetical listing of a range of items under some organisations but not others.

The first method can simply be described as "sequential". Strings are stored in the data array in the order in which they occur, i.e. a new item is appended to the "end" of the array. The variable last% holds the subscript of the latest item. This is incremented and decremented as necessary. Size%, whose value is constant throughout the program, holds the largest legal element of data$(), the array of data strings. The initialisation procedure, PROCinit, is quite simple:

```
1000 DEF PROCinit
1010    LOCAL i%
1020    size%=100: len%=20
1030    DIM data$(size%): REM  Plus other fields
1040    FOR i%=0 TO size%
1050       data$(i%)=STRING$(len%, " ")
1060       data$(i%)=""
1070    NEXT i%
1090    last%=0
1100 ENDPROC
```

The (constant) variable len% holds the maximum length to which any element of data$() will grow. This enables data$() to be set-up in the most space-efficient way by the FOR loop at lines 1040 to 1070. The necessity to do this is due to a foible of BBC BASIC and may not exist in other BASICs.

To insert a new item, it is first necessary to check that the data is not already present. Multiple identical strings tend to cause problems when retrieving data later on, so we will assume it is illegal. It would be possible to hold a count of the number of occurrences of an item if this were important. This involves dimensioning a parallel array to data$(). Parallel arrays are dimensioned with the same limits and arranged such that all corresponding elements refer to the same item. For example, referring back to the lovers example, data$() could hold the name and there could be two parallel arrays, phone%(), which holds the phone number, and, of course, score%(), the marks out of ten. (Since integers can hold a larger range than 0–10, you could make the marking even finer, say a percentage.) The three items of data are called the fields of the file. The field by which data is retrieved is known as the key field. There can be more than one key field, but this usually causes undue complexity. It is an advantage of the current scheme that all fields could be used with equal ease to retrieve a particular item (or set of items). This is not always the case, as we shall see below.

The procedure to search for a particular item is a function. It returns the subscript of element whose value is its parameter. If the item cannot be found, the unused subscript 0 is returned.

```
2000 DEF FNsearch(data$)
2010    LOCAL i%
2020    REM   Set-up sentinel
2030    data$(0)=data$
2040    i%=last%+1
2050    REPEAT
2060        i%=i%-1
2070    UNTIL data$(i%)=data$
2080 =i%
```

Notice the way that data$(0) is assigned with data$. This ensures that even if data$ is not in the array per se, it will still be found. Furthermore, i% will hold the correct value (0) when upon return. This technique simplifies the UNTIL condition (by avoiding "OR i%=0"), thus speeding things up.

The insert procedure can now be written. Again, it takes the value of the item to be inserted as a parameter. If there were parallel fields in the file, these could be passed to an assigned by PROCinsert as well, e.g.:

```
100 PROCinsert("Debbie", 559207, 101)
```

The procedure for inserting is very easy. Last% is incremented and the new data placed at that position. It is first necessary to check that there is room, though.

```
3000 DEF PROCinsert(data$): REM  Plus other fields
3005    IF FNsearch(data$)<>0 THEN PROCerror(data$+" already exists"):ENDPROC
3010    IF last%=size% THEN PROCerror("No room"): ENDPROC
3020    last%=last%+1
3030    data$(last%)=data$:  REM  Plus other fields
3040 ENDPROC
```

The procedure PROCerror is defined according to taste. It might simply print the error message and stop the program (bad), or it could set a global variable to tell the caller that an error has occurred and place the error string (or error number) in another variable.

The deletion routine is quite short too. First FNsearch is used to look for the item given as a parameter. If the item is present, it is removed by shifting all the items above down by one. Last% is decremented to reflect this change. If data$ cannot be found, an error is given.

```
4000 DEF PROCdelete(data$)
4010    LOCAL pos%, i%
```

```
4020      pos%=FNsearch(data$)
4030      IF pos%=0 THEN PROCerror("No such item"): ENDPROC
4040      last%=last%-1
4050      IF last%+1=pos% THEN ENDPROC
4060      FOR i%=pos% TO last%
4070         data$(i%)=data$(i%+1): REM Plus other fields
4080      NEXT i%
4090 ENDPROC
```

If there are parallel arrays, their elements should also be shifted down in the body of the FOR loop. The IF at line 4050 would not be necessary if FOR loops could execute zero times.

Only the tape save and load procedures remain to be defined. These are just FOR loops which print and input from tape files respectively.

```
5000 DEF PROCload_file(name$)
5010      LOCAL chan%, i%
5020      chan%=OPENIN(name$)
5030      INPUT#chan%,last%
5040      FOR i%=1 TO last%
5050         INPUT#chan%,data$(i%): REM  Plus other fields
5060      NEXT i%
5070      CLOSE#chan%
5080 ENDPROC
5090
5100
6000 DEF PROCsave_file(name$)
6010      LOCAL chan%, i%
6020      chan%=OPENOUT(name$)
6030      PRINT#chan%,last%
6040      FOR i%=1 TO last%
6050         PRINT#chan%,data$(i%): REM  Plus other fields
6060      NEXT i%
6070      CLOSE#chan%
6080 ENDPROC
```

As usual, other arrays being used in parallel with data$() would have to be PRINTed or INPUT in the loops. It is possible to do this in the same PRINT# and INPUT# statements, i.e.:

```
6050         PRINT#chan%,data$(i%),phone%(i%),score%(i%)
```

is legal.

Below is a "main program" listing which implements the whole lovers filing system, along with a couple of miscellaneous procedures. Your mission reader, should you decide to accept it, is to convert the previous procedures to deal with the three arrays data$(size%), phone%(size%) and score%(size%). This will involve the modification of PROCinit, PROCinsert, PROCdelete, PROCload_file and PRCsave_file.

```
100 REM    Lovers Filing System
110 PROCinit
120 REPEAT
130     c%=FNmenu
140     IF c%<>0 THEN ON c% GOSUB 300,400,500,600,700,800
150 UNTIL c%=0
160 END
300 REM    Add a lover
310     CLS:INPUT TAB(0,2),"What name ",name$
320     INPUT TAB(0,4),"What phone number ",num%
330     INPUT TAB(0,6),"What score ",score%
340     PROCinsert(name$,num%,score%)
350 RETURN
360
400 REM    Chuck a lover
410     CLS:INPUT TAB(0,2),"Whom do you wish to blow-out ",name$
420     PROCdelete(name$)
430 RETURN
440
500 REM    Look-up a lover
510     CLS:INPUT TAB(0,2),"Whom do you wish to look-up ",name$
520     i%=FNsearch(name$)
530     IF i%=0 THEN PROCerror("You haven't met him/her yet!"):RETURN
540     PRINT''"Name: ";name$''"Phone: ";phone%(i%)''"Score: ";score%(i%)'
550     in%=GET
560 RETURN
570
600 REM    List by score
610     CLS:INPUT TAB(0,2),"What minimum score ",min%
615     PRINT
620     FOR i%=1 TO last%
630         IF score%(i%)>=min% THEN PRINTdata$(i%),phone%(i%),score%(i%)
640     NEXT i%
650     in%=GET
660 RETURN
670
700 REM    Load a file
710     CLS:INPUT TAB(0,2),"What file name ",name$
720     PROCload_file(name$)
```

```
 730 RETURN
 740
 800 REM    Save a file
 810    CLS:INPUT TAB(0,2),"What file name ",name$
 820    PROCsave_file(name$)
 830 RETURN
 840
7000 DEF PROCerror(er$)
7010    PRINT ''"ERROR: ";CHR$(7);
7020    PRINT er$
7030    in%=INKEY(500)
7050 ENDPROC
7060
7070
8000 DEF FNmenu
8010    LOCAL choice$
8020    CLS
8030    PRINT'''"0. End program"'
8040    PRINT"1. Add a lover"'
8050    PRINT"2. Blow-out a lover"'
8060    PRINT"3. Look-up a lover"'
8070    PRINT"4. List lovers by score"'
8080    PRINT"5. Load a file"'
8090    PRINT"6. Save a file"
8100    REPEAT
8110       INPUT TAB(0,18),"Which one (0-6) ",choice$
8120    UNTIL VAL(choice$)>=0 AND VAL(choice$)<=6 AND choice$<>""
8130 =VAL(choice$)
8140
```

The sequential organisation described above has the advantage of being easy to implement. All the procedures are short and easy to understand. There is, however, a price to be paid for this straightforwardness. The key field (data$()) is the one which is used by FNsearch to locate a particular item. This search involves stepping through each element until a match to data$ is found. It can be shown that on average this will take last%/2 comparisons, or iterations. As last% gets bigger, then, the time taken to insert, delete and locate items grows steadily. What's more, if an alphabetical list of data$() were required, the array would need to be sorted. (See Chapter two. Any of the procedures given there will work by changing A%() to data$(). Remember that whenever a pair of elements is swapped, the corresponding secondary fields [e.g. phone%(), score%()] must also be swapped.) The next method described solves both these problems; data$() is held in ASCII order at all times, which in turn leads to the ability to retrieve a given data$ very quickly.

The initialisation procedure is similar to the previous one. To describe the procedures, an "inventory" example will be used. This means that the fields will be data$() (the key field), which is the name of the item, price(), the price of an item, and quan%(), the quantity. PROCinit is given below.

```
1000 DEF PROCinit
1010    LOCAL i%
1020    size%=100: len%=10
1030    DIM data$(size%), price(size%), quan%(size%)
1040    FOR i%=0 TO size%
1050       data$(i%)=STRING$(len%," ")
1060       data$(i%)=""
1070    NEXT i%
1080    last%=1
1090    data$(last%)=STRING$(len%,"~")
1100 ENDPROC
```

The immediately noticeable difference is that last% is initialised to 1, and that this first element of data$() is set to lots of "~". This is the character with the highest (printable) ASCII code, and serves to mark the upper limit of the array. Data$(0) was assigned "" by line 1060, so that serves well as the lower limit. The utility of these assignments will become clear from the listing of FNsearch below.

```
2000 DEF FNsearch(data$)
2010    LOCAL lo%, hi%, mid%, found%
2020    lo%=0:  hi%=last%:  found%=FALSE
2030    REPEAT
2040       mid%=(lo%+hi%) DIV 2
2050       IF data$(mid%)=data$ THEN found%=TRUE: GOTO 2070
2060       IF data$(mid%)<data$ THEN lo%=mid%+1 ELSE hi%=mid%-1
2070    UNTIL lo%>hi% OR found%
2090 IF found% THEN =mid% ELSE =-lo%
```

The function is probably easier to understand than at first it looks. The value returned must tell the caller whether the item was found, and where it is if it was. FNsearch also tells the calling program where to put the new item if it is not already in the array. If data$ is located, the number returned is positive and is the subscript of the element containing that value. If FNsearch cannot locate its parameter, it gives a negative result. The absolute value of this is the position where data$ should be placed to insert it into the array. As the idea is keep data$() in order, the position returned is not necessarily at the end.

The method for locating data$ is called a binary search. First, two array indices, lo% and hi%, and set to the lower and upper limits of data$(). The flag found% is also reset. Although this is done for you by LOCAL, it is good practice for when you graduate to more fussy languages. The REPEAT loop starts by setting the mid-point index, mid%, to halfway between lo% and hi%. If the value at this position is equal to data$, i.e. is the one we're looking for, the loop is exited, and FNsearch returns with mid%. If data$(mid%) is not the required item, there are two courses of action. If data$(mid%) is less than (in ASCII order) data$, then the element required must be in the half of data$() above data$(mid%), bearing in mind that the array is in ASCII order. Similarly, if data$(mid%) is greater than data$, the required item can't possibly lie in the range data$(mid%) to data$(hi%), so hi% is decreased to just below mid%.

Notice that the action of the REPEAT loop halves the size of the section which is being searched on each iteration. This means that for an array of size n, the most number of tries required is log to the base two of n. Typical values are four searches when n=16, six searches when n=64, and only ten searches when n has grown to 1024. This compares to an average of over 500 comparisons for the sequential search.

The insert routine is given next. Like the last time, it calls search to make sure the item to be inserted is not already present. The body of the procedure is concerned with shifting up all the items whose key values are "greater" than the one being inserted. This leaves a "hole" in which the item can be placed.

```
3000 DEF PROCinsert(data$,price,quan%)
3010    LOCAL pos%, i%
3020    pos%=FNsearch(data$)
3030    IF pos%>0 THEN PROCerror("Already present"): ENDPROC
3040    pos%=ABS(pos%)
3045    IF last%=size% THEN PROCerror("No room"): ENDPROC
3050    last%=last%+1
3060    FOR i%=last% TO pos%+1 STEP -1
3070       data$(i%)=data$(i%-1)
3080       price(i%)=price(i%-1)
3090       quan%(i%)=quan%(i%-1)
3100    NEXT i%
3110    data$(pos%)=data$
3120    price(pos%)=price
3130    quan%(pos%)=quan%
3140 ENDPROC
```

Deleting an item is almost the exact opposite. The error occurs this time if the item does exist, and the FOR loop moves elements down one instead of up.

```
4000 DEF PROCdelete(data$)
4010    LOCAL pos%, i%
4020    pos%=FNsearch(data$)
4030    IF pos%<0 THEN PROCerror("Can't find "+data$): ENDPROC
4040    last%=last%-1
4050    FOR i%=pos% TO last%
4060       data$(i%)=data$(i%+1)
```

```
4070       price(i%)=price(i%+1)
4080       quan%(i%)=quan%(i%+1)
4090    NEXT i%
4100 ENDPROC
```

Once these fundamental procedures have been written, they can be used to provide particular listings. For example, list all items in a given range:

```
5000 DEF PROCList_range(data1$, data2$)
5010    LOCAL pos%, temp$
5020    IF data1$>data2$ THEN temp$=data1$:data1$=data2$:data2$=temp$
5030    pos%=ABS(FNsearch(data1$))
5040    IF pos%=last% THEN ENDPROC
5050    REM    Enable printer here if required
5060    PRINT"Part No.";TAB(15);"Price";TAB(25);"Quantity"
5070    PRINT STRING$(33,"~")'
5080    REPEAT
5090       PRINT data$(pos%);TAB(15);price(pos%);TAB(25);quan%(pos%)
5100       pos%=pos%+1
5120    UNTIL pos%=last% OR data$(pos%)>data2$
5130    PRINT 'STRING$(33,"_")'
5140    REM    Disable printer here if necessary
5150 ENDPROC
```

The procedure is very friendly; it will never produce an error. At worst it will return without doing anything. As there are many different ways of preparing a printer, the exact code is left to you to devise. See pp. 404–408 of the User Guide for details. The fact that the key field is held in ASCII order is a great boon for listings, as it makes it much easier to find a particular item. The procedure below prints all items whose quantity is below a given level. The one which follows that does a count of all the items in a given range, and also totals the value of the items.

```
6000 DEF PROClevels(quan%)
6010    LOCAL i%
6020    IF last%=1 THEN ENDPROC
6030    REM    Enable printer
6040    PRINT"Part No.";TAB(15);"Quantity"
6050    PRINT STRING$(23,"~")'
6060    FOR i%=1 TO last%-1
6070       IF quan%(i%)<quan% THEN PRINTdata$(i%);TAB(15);quan%(i%)
6080    NEXT i%
6090    PRINT 'STRING$(23,"_")
6100    REM    Disable printer
6110 ENDPROC
```

```
6120
6130
7000 DEF PROCtotals(data1$,data2$)
7010    REM   Puts total units and values between data1$
7020    REM   and data2$ in "units%" and "val" resp.
7030    LOCAL pos%, temp$
7040    units%=0: val=0
7050    IF data1$>data2$ THEN temp$=data1$:data1$=data2$:data2$=temp$
7060    pos%=ABS(FNsearch(data1$))
7070    IF pos%=last% THEN ENDPROC
7080    REM    Enable printer
7090    REPEAT
7100       units%=units%+quan%(pos%)
7110       val=val+price(pos%)*quan%(pos%)
7120       pos%=pos%+1
7130    UNTIL pos%=last% OR data$(pos%)>data2$
7140    REM    Disable printer
7150 ENDPROC
```

As they stand, the procedures listed so far can be called in immediate mode to provide a casual enquiry-type system. Obviously the tape save and load procedures must be written, and PROCerror provided. When this has been done, the function keys can be programmed as:

```
*key0 PROCinit
*key1 PROCinsert(
*key2 PROCdelete(
*key3 PROClist_range(
*key4 PROCload_file(
*key5 PROCsave_file(
```

and so on. This would just about give a useable, interactive system. It is, of course, far better to tie all the procedures together with a proper program which provides error/range checking, as well as some other functions you might care to think of. If you didn't have anything to do, you have now. Pretend that you are being paid £5000 for writing a user-friendly, idiot-proof system for an influential company who could put a lot more business your way. Write a driving program to provide such a system, paying particular attention to error messages (what the hell does "No room" mean??) This will undoubtedly involve changing some of the procedures given above. Can you make them safer, or more efficient? As a reward, when you've got a perfect program, you can change all the variable names, pretend you wrote it all and sell it to someone. (Don't blame me if Wiley's sue you, though.)

The sorted array/binary search method has several advantages over the simple sequential method, but also has some drawbacks of its own. In order to keep the array sorted, the deletion and insertion of items requires that a proportion of the elements be shifted, a time-consuming exercise. This was offset by the rapidity with which items could be located. The last technique for storing information I discuss here has the advantage of rapid retrieval combined with comparatively fast insertion and deletion. This could be especially vital in disc systems, where shifting hundreds of records about could prove disastrously slow.

The technique discussed is known variously as key-address transformation and hashing. The latter name is shorter, so will be used here. Imagine a filing system where the key field happened to be a number in the range 0 to 999. Assuming that the computer had enough storage space to hold one thousand complete records, each possible key value could be given its own slot in the array/file. Thus, to store a record with key value 345, the 345th element would be used, similarly for retrieving. In this ideal situation, each operation would require only one access, and would therefore be very efficient.

Unfortunately it is very rarely possible to get away with such a simple scheme. Firstly, the key field would probably be alphanumeric, for example a part number, "M68B45", or a name, "Kewney G.". Also, even if an entirely numeric field were used (in the early days of micro software, many companies persuaded clients that this was a good thing, to their eternal grief) the chances are that it would be "sparse". For example, a six digit part number would have 1 million different possible values, but only a thousand of these might occur in practice. Reserving an element for each possible value on the off chance that it might be used would obviously be impractical.

The solution to these problems is found in hashing. The idea is allow for a certain maximum number of records in the file, which remains fixed throughout the file's life, then convert the key field values to a number in the range 0 to N−1, where N is the size of the file. The method of performing this "key to address" conversion is called the hashing algorithm. A simple example will demonstrate the principles. Suppose we allow for 1000 records in the file (the size chosen is very important for reasons which will become apparent). Suppose the key field is a four digit number in the range 1000 to 9999. We will define the hashing algorithm thus: to get the location in which the item is to be located, just take the last three digits of the key field. Thus if we want to locate item "1234", we will look in record number (or array subscript) 234. Likewise, to delete the item called "5439", record 439 would be used. This provides the same ideal one-access performance as described above. Consider this, though. Suppose two items "1234" and "6234" were to be inserted. The first would go in with no trouble, at location 234. However, the second item, under our simple hashing algorithm, should also go in record 234. What is aptly termed a collision has occurred. It is an inevitable fact that if there are more possible key values than available locations (9000 and 1000 respectively in this example), then collisions will occur. The question of what to do about this has many answers. Again, the simplest approach will be adopted here. Suppose a record has a hash address of H, and this location is already occupied. Our "re-hashing" function is to try H+1, H+2 ... until a free space is found. Thus in the example above, "6234" would be placed in the first free slot after 234. Note that if we reach the end of the file, it is usual to "wrap-round" to the beginning. In this example the sequence would go 998, 999, 0, 1 . . . and so on.

It is clear that as the hash table (as these structures are called) becomes more full, the number of collisions will increase rapidly. This will in turn increase the number of comparisons required before a given item can be found in the table. It can be shown that this number is determined not to be the size of the file, as might be expected, but by its loading factor. This is the ratio of occupied records to the total. For example, a file which is three quarters full has a loading factor of 0.75. If the loading factor is a, then for the simple method described above $(2-a)/(2-2a)$ searches are needed to find an item, on average. To show how this varies with a, the table below gives the theoretical number of searches required for various loading factors.

Per cent full (a*100)	Number of searches
0	1.0
10	1.1
20	1.1
30	1.2
40	1.3
50	1.5
60	1.8
70	2.2
80	3.0
90	5.5
95	10.5
100	infinity

Since the results obtained in real life are invariably much worse than the theoretical ones, it is clear that the file should not become much more than half full if long sequences of re-hashing are to be avoided.

The second criterion used for determining the file size again comes from theory. It can be shown that the simple "add one" re-hashing technique causes a clumping effect, where many items are concentrated around a relatively small area, and other parts of the file remain empty. There is another re-hashing method known as quadratic probing which avoids this problem. In order for this to work, the file must have size equal to a prime number. What is more, the prime must be of the form $4j+3$, where j is some positive integer. (See [Horowitz].) In the procedures given below this re-hashing method will be adopted, with a file size of 127, which is a prime of the appropriate form $(127=4*31+3)$. All that is required now is an initial hashing algorithm. The one given above cannot be used in the general case, as alphanumeric keys must be allowed. The one I give is quite simple, but seems to work in practice. The method is to start with a variable, say h%, set to 1. Then for each character in the string to be hashed, h% is multiplied by the character's ASCII code. h% is then set back to range 0–126 by MODing it with 127.

The foregoing is a very diluted account of hashing techniques. There are many hashing/re-hashing algorithms, and the subject is still the area of much research. [Horowitz], [Page] and many other data structures and algorithms books cover hashing in more mathematical detail. Interested readers are referred to them for more detail (and many more equations). The procedures given below should serve as a suitable introduction to the subject. As I mentioned earlier, hashing is particularly well suited to disc files as there are relatively few data transfers involved.

The initialisation procedure is much the same as the previous two. The procedures given below don't keep track of the number of items in the file, as there is no need to keep a length count. Such a facility could be added so that a warning is given when the file becomes more than, say, 70 percent full. The count would be incremented after a successful insertion and decremented after a deletion.

```
1000 DEF PROCinit
1010    LOCAL i%
1020    size%=127: len%=10
1030    DIM data$(size%)
1040    FOR i%=1 TO size%:   REM Don't use element 0
1050       data$(i%)=STRING$(len%, " ")
1060       data$(i%)=""
1070    NEXT i%
1080 ENDPROC
```

Notice that element zero isn't used at all. This enables FNsearch to return a positive or negative number depending on whether its argument was found or not. If zero was used, it would be impossible to distinguish between the item being found at location zero, and the item not found, with the next empty location at position zero. The search function and its two auxiliary functions are given below.

```
2000 DEF FNsearch(data$)
2010    LOCAL h%, try%, found%
2020    h%=FNhash(data$)
2030    try%=1: free%=0: found%=FALSE
2040    REPEAT
2050       IF data$(h%)=data$ THEN found%=TRUE: GOTO 2080
2060       IF data$(h%)="[DELETED]" THEN free%=h%
2070       IF data$(h%)<>"" THEN h%=FNrehash(h%,try%): try%=try%+1
2080    UNTIL found% OR data$(h%)=""
2090    IF free% AND NOT found% THEN =-free%
2100 IF found% THEN =h% ELSE =-h%
2110
2200 DEF FNhash(data$)
```

```
2210    LOCAL h%, i%, c%
2220    h%=1
2230    FOR i%=1 TO LEN(data$)
2240        c%=ASC(MID$(data$, i%, 1))
2250        h%=(h%*c%*c%) MOD size% + 1
2260    NEXT i%
2270 =h%
2280
2300 DEF FNrehash(h%, try%)=(h%+try%*try%) MOD size% + 1
```

The search process is complicated by the need to make provision for deleted records. When an item is deleted, it is not enough to simply make that string null, to mark it as empty. If this were the case, all the items which come after it (in the re-hashing sequence) would effectively be cut-off, as the search terminates once the empty marker is found. Instead, a "deleted record" marker is used. This has the value "[DELETED]", but could be set to any string which is unlikely to occur in practice.

When the function is entered, the initial hash address is found by calling FNhash. This uses the character codes of the string in the way described earlier to calculate a number between 1 and size%. (MOD size% gives a value between 0 and size%−1, hence the +1.) The flag found%, the free location pointer, free%, and the tries count, try% are also initialised. The REPEAT loop makes three tests. The first is to see if the item data$(h%) is the one being sought. If so, found% is set to TRUE, and a branch made to the UNTIL to exit the loop. Next, the current record is checked for being a deleted one. If so, free% is set to the current record number. This may be used after the loop as the result of the function. The final IF within the REPEAT ... UNTIL performs the rehash and increments try% if an empty record hasn't been encountered yet.

The value returned after the loop depends on (a) whether data$ was found and (b) if it wasn't, whether a deleted record was found. The first check returns −free% if (a) is false and (b) is true. This is what is desired as a negative result will be produced and the magnitude of the result will be a free record number.

If the previous test fails, there are two more possibilities. If data$ was found, the (positive) record number associated with it is returned. Otherwise, the negated value of h% is returned, as this will contain the address of the blank record just found. The code to achieve all of this is slightly convoluted because REPEAT always executes at least once (hence the need for the GOTO which would be unnecessary in a WHILE loop) and the restrictions of the IF ... THEN ... ELSE statement make two lines necessary.

Although FNsearch is fairly complicated, it makes PROCinsert and PROCdelete quite short. They are given below.

```
3000 DEF PROCinsert(data$)
3010    LOCAL p%
3020    p%=FNsearch(data$)
```

```
3030    IF p%>0 THEN PROCerror(data$+" already exists"): ENDPROC
3040    data$(ABS(p%))=data$
3050 ENDPROC
3060
3070
4000 DEF PROCdelete(data$)
4010    LOCAL p%
4020    p%=FNsearch(data$)
4030    IF p%<0 THEN PROCerror("Can't find "+data$): ENDPROC
4040    data$(p%)="[DELETED]"
4050 ENDPROC
```

The way these two procedures are used should be quite clear. The anti-symmetric relationship between insertion and deletion is very apparent from lines 3020–3040 and the corresponding ones in PROCdelete. Once again, PROCerror should be suitably defined somewhere in the program.

The performance of hash tables does tend to improve, to a certain extent, with size, even if the theory doesn't say so. Small tables tend to have a worse performance than ones say ten times bigger, even of the loading factors are the same. This rule obeys the law of diminishing returns so that above a certain size increasing the size of a table will not better its performance for a given loading factor. One reason for the procedures above not giving the theoretical best performance (in addition to the rather small "file" size) is the presence of the deletion routine. Hash tables of the sort described tend to be happiest with static or slowly increasing amounts of data. For example, if a manufacturer produces 500 types of component, and is certain that this won't change by more than about 10 percent in either direction, then a suitable file of size 1000–1500 records (to provide a suitably low loading factor) could be set-up and would provide very rapid access. However, when a hash file holds more dynamically changing data things slow down. The total number of records may not vary by much, but the presence of lots of [DELETED] records creates longer sequences of re-hashing. There are several ways in which the performance can be improved. Firstly, more than one search routine can be written: one to find a record, one to look for an empty space and so on. Another method is to "chain" records with the same initial hash address together in a linked list (see later). This avoids the need for re-hashing altogether. For more details see the references already given.

1.3   Using the Indirection Operators

The Acorn BASICs are unique in their provision of indirection operators. (Unique amongst other BASICs, that is. Like many of BBC BASIC's novel features, the indirection operators were inspired by the existence of a similar idea in the language BCPL.) There are three of the operators, ?, ! and $. These operate on bytes, four-byte integers and strings respectively. The action of the operators is probably best illustrated with the so-called word operator, !. In the assignment:

```
100 A%=1234
```

the variable A% is given the value 1234. However, placing a ! before the number, thus:

```
100 A%=!1234
```

changes the meaning to "make A% the value the integer AT ADDRESS 1234". Those familiar with assembler language should understand the derivation of the term "indirection" from this. When an object is accessed indirectly, the object itself is not specified, but an address related to it is. So in this example, 1234 is the address and !1234 is the object being referred to. Suppose the four addresses 1234 to 1237 held the values 0, 2, 0 and 0 respectively. Then the value of !1234 would be $(1*0+2*256+0*65536+0*16777216)$, or just 512. This is a consequence of the way integers are stored in BBC BASIC, with the least significant byte first.

The other two operators can be interpreted in the same way.

```
100 A%=?1234
```

assigns to A% the value of the one-byte value (in the range 0-255) which is at address 1234. This is directly equivalent to:

```
100 A%=PEEK(1234)
```

in many other BASICs, but we shall see that the ? method is far more powerful than this. The string indirection operator, $, returns the value of the string (which is terminated by a carriage-return character) at the address specified. Thus:

```
100 A$=$1234
```

sets A$ to the string at starting at 1234, so long as there is a sequence of 255 or less characters followed by a C-R at that address. If not, A$ is set to the null string.

The numeric indirection operators ? and ! have a variation on their use. The assignment:

```
100 A%=tab%!12
```

set A% to the value of the integer which starts 12 bytes after address tab%. This is exactly equivalent to:

```
100 A%=!(tab%+12)
```

The brackets are necessary as, like −, ! has a high binding power and tries to operate on the smallest possible item (technically speaking, the item following ! is a factor, where a factor is a variable, a function or unary operator [−, +, NOT] followed by its argument, or an expression in brackets. See page 144 of the User Guide). When ! or ? is used with two values, the first one has to be a variable name, e.g. var% above. In BCPL, the binary (i.e. two-operand) use of ! is called subscripting. Consider:

```
100 A%=tab%?23
```

In this case, the item accessed could be thought of as the 24th item in an array of bytes, hence the term subscripting. The $ operator can only be used in the unary mode, with one expression coming after the operator. The reason for this is probably that, for example, start$12 would be indistinguishable from the string start$ immediately followed by the number 12. Such a combination would be perfectly OK in a PRINT statement. No such ambiguity arises with ? and ! as these symbols don't have any other uses.

Since indirection can be interpreted as accessing an array, it would be expected that the indirection operator-equivalent to:

```
100 A%(12)=1234
```

is possible. Indeed it is, and all the operators can be used on the left hand of an assignment statement. Thus:

```
100 tab%?5=128
110 tab%!6=65535
120 $str%="Indirect"
```

are all permissible. Line 100 set the byte at address (tab%+5) to 128; line 110 sets the four bytes (tab%+6) to (tab%+9) to 255, 255, 0 and 0 repectively, and line 120 has the following effect:

Location	Value
str%	ASC("I") = 73
str%+1	ASC("n") = 110
str%+2	ASC("d") = 100
str%+3	ASC("i") = 105
str%+4	ASC("r") = 114
str%+5	ASC("e") = 101
str%+6	ASC("c") = 99
str%+7	ASC("t") = 116
str%+8	ASC(C-R) = 13

Notice that in this usage, ? acts as POKE, i.e.:

```
100 POKE A,B        and        100 ?A=B
```

are equivalent.

One reason why indirection is so useful in BBC BASIC is that the idea of the variable has been extended to "addressable object", where variables and indirection expressions are addressable objects. This means that anywhere a variable is allowed in BASIC, an indirection expression of the same type can be used instead. This includes FOR loops, procedure declarations and calls to machine code. So:

```
100 FOR !&70=1 TO 100 .... NEXT !&70
110 DEF PROC(!a%, $b%)
120 CALL code, !&70, !&74
130 READ !&4000
150 INPUT $buff
```

are all perfectly valid. In most cases, there is no advantage in using these types of variables over the more usual ones. One occasion when they might be useful is when memory space is limited. It would be possible to use some of the space before the program to store values, rather than creating "visible" variables which appear after it. For example, the spare page at &D00 could be used as a string buffer with $&D00. This would also provide room for 64 integer variables. Such techniques are last resort ones, as they drastically reduce the readability of the statements which use them.

Note that although an analogy was made earlier between ? and PEEK and POKE, the uses are very different. PEEK and POKE are very good names, as they are designed to let you do just that, peek around the inner workings of the interpreter/operating system. Almost all micro owners have a memorised list of "useful pokes". These range from setting the text windows in Applesoft and disabling the STOP key on the PET to inserting machine code programs (on almost all BASIC oriented machines). Between them, the BBC BASIC interpreter and the Machine operating System try to provide all the possible values you would otherwise have to PEEK or POKE. This is all part of the philosophy of ensuring that programs will run on the second processors. It is therefore very rarely that you should want to use ? or ! to access BASIC or MOS values. On the other hand, if Tube compatability doesn't concern you, there is nothing to stop you peeking and poking around to see what you come up with. Just as a token example:

```
100 FOR i%=HIMEM TO &8000 STEP 4
110    !i%=NOT !i%
120 NEXT i%
130 END
```

Assuming that the indirection operators are not used to manipulate "system" information, their use must be restricted to data belonging explicitly to the program. The two categories of use I will discuss are (1) more efficient representation of arrays of small ranges, e.g. arrays of 0–255, or arrays of boolean; and (2) the constructions of composite data types (i.e. records) and dynamic data structures which use them.

1.3.1 Efficient Arrays

In an earlier program, the Sieve of Eratosthenes, an array of integers was used to store truth values. As was stated then, this is a bit of an overkill, as one bit suffices to hold TRUE/FALSE, whereas each element of an integer array requires 32 bits. Using the indirection operator ? it is possible to create arrays of bytes, each element of which needs only eight bits.

Declaring a byte array uses a special form of the DIM statement. The statement:

```
100 DIM tab% 100
```

would reserve 101 bytes of memory space. It is useful to know where this space resides, and the address of the first element of the byte array is put into tab%. Notice that the important difference between the above form and the usual DIM is the presence of at least one space after the variable name, not the absence of brackets. For example:

```
100 DIM tab% (100)
```

would have the same effect as the previous example, not as:

```
100 DIM tab%(100)
```

which would declare an array of 101 four-byte integers whose first and last elements are tab%(0) and tab%(100). In this case, the simple variable tab% would not be created.

When a byte array is declared, its elements are not initialised, so it is usual to follow the DIM by some kind of loop to set-up the array:

```
100 DIM tab% n%
100 FOR i%=0 TO n%
110    tab%?i%=0
120 NEXT i%
```

The similarity between array subscripting and the binary use of ? should be clear from this example. The ? and ! operators are commutative, which means that they don't mind the order in which their operands are placed (like + and *, but not − and /). Thus:

```
        tab%?i%    is the same as    i%?tab%
and     tab%!i%    is the same as    i%!tab%
```

This is useful to remember as sometimes when accessing an array of bytes, the "base address" of the array is not held in a simple variable. An example would be when looking at the first few bytes of a program:

```
100 FOR i%=0 TO 15
110    c%=PAGE?i%
120    PRINT ~PAGE+i%,~c%;"    ";
```

```
130    IF c%>31 THEN PRINT CHR$(c%) ELSE PRINT
140 NEXT i%
150 END
```

Unfortunately, the program above will fail at line 110. This is because, although the indirection expression seems natural under the circumstances, it is illegal to precede ? (or !) by anything but a numeric variable name. There are a couple of alternatives to line 110 which will work. It could be written as either of:

```
110    c%=?(PAGE+i%)
110    c%=i%?PAGE
```

The second example executes slightly faster, and conveys the array idea better. For another example of this form, see any of the Acornsoft programs. When the first program is run, it transfers the Acornsoft logo from just above the program onto the screen using a FOR loop with the ! operator. In effect the loop transfers a thousand bytes from the "word" array starting at TOP to the word array commencing at HIMEM (which happens to be the first screen address).

One of the uses of numeric arrays given earlier was as functions or look-up tables. The same applies to byte arrays too. One such application is in adding a parity bit to the seven bit ASCII codes which the BBC Computer produces. For example, it was recently necessary to find a quick way of interfacing one of the University's BBC Computers to the main-frame so that files could be transferred between them, and so that the BBC could be used as an intelligent graphics terminal. The interface used was the RS-423 serial one. The format required by the main-frame was seven bits of data, and one parity bit. This is an extra bit added to the data to provide some sort of error checking. The method is to count the number of ones in the binary representation of the data byte. If this is odd, then a parity bit is added (at the most significant position of the data byte) to ensure that all bytes have an even number of 1 bits. Thus if a byte with an odd number of one bits is ever received, an error has occurred during transmission and some action can be taken. The parity calculations for the characters "A" and "C" are shown below.

Character	Hex	Binary	Binary with Parity
"A"	41	1000001	01000001
"C"	43	1000011	11000011

Although the 6850 chip used in the BBC Computer's serial interface is capable of producing the desired format of seven data bits, an even parity bit and one stop bit (to mark the end of the data byte), the RS-423 routines in the Machine Operating System use a different format of eight data bits and no parity. The need arises, therefore, to add the parity bit explicitly. Since BASIC was being used, efficiency was important, so instead of working out the parity bit each time a character was to be transmitted, a table was made containing the "paritirised" code for each character from CHR$(0) to CHR$(127). The program to do this is reproduced below, with thanks to Steve Binns:

```
100 REM    BASIC Terminal Program
110 REM    or part thereof, anyway
120 DIM c% 127
130 REM    Set-up c%?i% with i%+parity bit
140 FOR i%=0 TO 127
150    c%?i%=i%+FNparity(i%)
160 NEXT i%
170 REM    Stuff to set-up the RS-423
180 ...
190 REM    Main Loop
200 REPEAT
210    ch%=INKEY(0)
220    IF ch%<>-1 THEN VDU 1,c%?ch%: REM Send ch% down RS-423
230    REM   Stuff to receive from RS-423
240    ...
250 UNTIL FALSE
260
1000 DEF FNparity(c%)
1010    REM   Returns 128 or 0 as required to
1020    REM   make c% even parity
1030    LOCAL count%
1040    REPEAT
1050       count%=count% + c% MOD 2
1060       c%=c% DIV 2
1070    UNTIL c%=0
1080 IF count% MOD 2=0 THEN =0 ELSE =128
1090
```

It does not matter if FNparity is inefficient (which it is) as the calculations are only performed once, when c%? is initialised. After that, the mapping from ch% to ch%+parity is made as quickly as a byte can be accessed with the indirection operator. Note that only the parts of the program relevant to the current topic are given. There are other things to do, such as echo characters received from the RS-423 port (which is tedious under MOS 0.1 as no receive routine is available), and deal with errors generated by the user pressing ESCAPE.

Other functions can be provided in a similar manner using byte arrays. One example would be converting between character sets. Although the ASCII code is very widely accepted in the computer industry, there are several alternatives which are sometimes used. For example, IBM and ICL computers use the EBDIC code. If the BBC Computer is to be connected to a device which uses EBDIC, the incoming and outgoing characters would need to be changed as appropriate. [Saville] contains a 6502 assembly language version of such a conversion which could be the used as the basis for a BASIC program similar to that given above.

The programs given in section 1.2.1 could all be converted to use byte arrays instead of integer ones. As already mentioned, the Sieve program will be 4 times as efficient if bytes are used instead of whole integers. In fact, it is possible to write a couple of routines to simulate arrays of bits using ?. The procedure listed below takes three parameters. These are the address of a bit array, the element of the array to be changed, and the new state of the bit (TRUE or FALSE). The DIM statement for an array of bits has the form:

```
100 DIM b% (n%-1) DIV 8
```

where n% is the number of bits in the array. Thus to define a boolean array of 30 elements, the statement:

```
100 DIM b% 3
```

would be used. b% is then the address of the first eight bits of the array. PROCset is given below:

```
1000 DEF PROCset(addr%, ele%, state%)
1010    REM   Set bit ele% (from 0) of the boolean array
1020    REM   starting at addr% to state%
1030    LOCAL bit%, byte%, data%
1040    byte%=ele% DIV 8
1050    bit% =ele% MOD 8
1060    data%=addr%?byte%
1070    IF state% THEN addr%?byte%=data% OR 2^bit%: ENDPROC
1080    addr%?byte%=data% AND NOT (2^bit%)
1090 ENDPROC
```

As with normal arrays, the bits in a boolean array would be numbered from zero to n%−1. Note that state% has to be simply non-zero to be interpreted as true, so that PROCset(a%, 1, 1) and PROSset(a%, 1, TRUE) would both set the second bit of the array at a% to 1.

It should be possible to complement the procedure above to find out the current state of a bit. This is FNstate and, as presented below, it returns FALSE if bit ele% of the boolean array at addr% is a zero, otherwise it gives TRUE.

```
2000 DEF FNstate(addr%,ele%)
2010    REM  Returns the state of addr%(ele%)
2020    LOCAL bit%, byte%
2030    byte%=ele% DIV 8
2040    bit% =ele% MOD 8
2050 =(addr%?byte% AND 2^bit%)<>FALSE
```

The <>FALSE part is not strictly necessary. It just ensures that if the bit is a 1, the proper version of TRUE, i.e. −1 is returned. Another way of putting it is:

```
2050 =-(addr%?byte% AND 2^bit%)
```

By using PROCset and FNstate it is possible to convert the Sieve program to find much higher primes than before. As only one bit per number is used, primes up to 32 times bigger than before can be tested. Don't try to go in for any records, though; the highest known prime has more digits than can be stored in the BBC Computer's memory, and the proof that it is prime takes a couple of days' execution time on a huge mainframe!

The bit-manipulation routines are a typical example of speed versus storage trade-off. Although the elements of the boolean array are stored as efficiently as possible, the routines to access them are not very efficient. This is mainly due to the presence of the exponentiation operator, ˆ. As was mentioned earlier, the power of two function is a good candidate for a look-up table. The present application could have an eight-element array of bytes whose values are the powers of two, from 1 to 128. Then occurrences of the expression "2ˆbit%" could be replaced by "two%?bit%", where two% is the address of the power table. The desirability for bit manipulation is reflected in some computers' instruction sets, which in turn shows up in high-level languages on these machines. Unfortunately the 6502 microprocessor in the BBC Computer has no bit operators, so accessing boolean arrays (which are freely available in languages like Pascal) is none too efficient.

1.3.2   Dynamic Arrays and Pointers

When an array is declared with a statement of the form:

```
100 DIM tot%(expr%)
```

its size, i.e. the number of elements, is fixed for the rest of the program's life. This implies that expr% had better be big enough for the use to which tot% will be put, or we're in trouble. In many applications this isn't a problem, as expr% is very predictable: the program given earlier which counted the occurrences of the various ASCII codes in a file was like this as there will always be 256 eight-bit codes (unless someone somewhere has made a rather fundamental error in the design of the universe).

Sometimes, though, predicting the size of an array is not so easy, and the DIM expression has to be a sensible guess. The string arrays of the last section were like this. A maximum number of items had to be allowed for. This means that, if expr% is too small, the program fails for lack of space or, if expr% proved far too large, space has been wasted which could have been used elsewhere, e.g. making the program better. A nice thing to have would be arrays which "grow" as elements are added, and "shrink" again when some elements are no longer needed. Using the byte array form of DIM, the first of these can be implemented in BBC BASIC.

The scheme for dynamic arrays described below relies on the fact that the areas of memory allocated by successive DIMs are contiguous provided that no other variables are created (i.e. referenced for the first time) in between. Thus:

```
100 REM Create variables first
110 a%=0: b%=0
120 DIM a% 9, b% 9
```

would allocate 20 bytes of storage. The variable a% would hold the address of the first ten; b% would be set to the address of the next ten bytes, and its value would be exactly ten greater than a%. Strictly speaking, only b% had to be created before the DIM. If it wasn't, the entry for b% itself would have appeared between the two ten-byte areas, upsetting the continuity which lets us use the two areas as one array. The procedure below adds an element of size n% bytes to the array whose base address is at first%

```
1000 DEF PROCnew(n%)
1010     last%=last%+1
1020     IF last%=0 THEN DIM first% n%-1 ELSE DIM x% n%-1
1030 ENDPROC
```

It works as follows. Initially, last% is set to −1. This means that the array hasn't been created yet, as last% holds the highest subscript which may be used, starting from zero. After last% has been incremented at line 1010, its value will be zero if this is the first call to PROCnew. In this case, the n% bytes are allocated and the address of the element (the first of the array) placed in first%, which should then remain unchanged for the rest of the program. If last% was greater than zero, the bytes are allocated again, but this time their address is placed in the dummy variable x% (which should have been created before the very first call to PROCnew). In either case, last% now holds the subscript of the highest available element of the array.

It must be stressed that the above will only work if all the variables which the program will use have already been created by the time the first call to PROCnew is made. If the array is to be one of integers, using the ! operator to store and retrieve elements, n% should be 4. For strings, n% should be (1 + the longest string to be used). Also, n% should remain the same, so only one array can be handled like this. The address of the element i% is:

```
first% + i%*n%
```

with i% between zero and last% inclusive. Thus to get the i%th element when the array is of 4-byte integers,

```
val%=first%!(i%*4)
```

would be used. For 20-byte strings (remember to count the CR character on the end), the equivalent assignment would be:

```
str$=$(first% + i%*20)
```

Actually, it is just possible to "shrink" the array by changing one of BASIC's pointers. I'm really loath to explain this, as it reminds me of those "<your favourite computer> REVEALED" books, which just seem to encourage devious (i.e. incomprehensible) programming. BASIC has a pointer (i.e. a couple of bytes which hold an important address) to the next free location in memory for putting variables. When using PROCnew as described above, this will point to the first byte after the last element declared. Thus it is possible, by changing this pointer's value, to make BASIC forget about the last few bytes of the array. The procedure to do this is given below:

```
2000 DEF PROCdelete(n%, num%)
2010    IF num%>last%+1 THEN num%=last%+1
2020    vt%=!2 AND &FFFF
2030    vt%=vt%-n%*num%
2040    !2=!2 AND &FFFF0000 OR vt%
2050    last%=last%-num%
2060 ENDPROC
```

n% is the number of bytes in each element and num% holds the number of elements to be deleted from the end of the array. The test at line 2010 checks that we're not trying to delete more elements than actually exist. If this is the case, num% is reduced so that only the array elements will be removed, not all the variables (and possibly program) which lie below it. The pointer (coined VARTOP by PCW) is at locations 2 and 3. Its current value is put in vt% at line 2020. The AND part ensures that only the two bytes of interest are used. Line 2030 reduces vt% by the appropriate number of bytes, and line 2040 puts this new value of VARTOP where BASIC can find it. Line 2050 changes last% to reflect the deletion of the elements.

Although the above procedures will work, they place a restriction on the way in which variables are declared, and use some pretty disgusting tricks to achieve their aims. These two weaknesses can be avoided by altering the view we have of the data. If we say, OK, the elements don't have to be contiguous (thus can't be used as an array), so long as they are all accessible, then it is possible to use a structure known as a linked list to save the values. This technique uses an extra few bytes tagged on to the end of the data which hold the address of the next element in the array. The address of the first element of the list is held in a separate variable, and the end of the list is denoted by the address field being set to zero. The advantage of referencing the list by pointers is that it doesn't matter if variables are declared in between elements of the list, as they don't need to be contiguous. The set of procedures below implements a simple scheme for creating a linked list of strings, with the ability to insert and delete elements as required. A couple of procedures also print the list in alphabetical and reverse alphabetical order.

```
1000 DEF PROCinit
1010    REM  Initiaise the list heads and constants
1020    NIL=0
```

```
1030     free_hd%=NIL
1040     size%=20: REM 21 bytes: 16+1 for data, 4 for link
1050     REM    Set-up a dummy end record
1060     data_hd%=FNget
1070     PROCset_data(data_hd%,STRING$(16,"~"))
1080     PROCset_link(data_hd%,NIL)
1090 ENDPROC
1100
1120
2000 DEF PROCinsert(data$)
2010     REM    Inserts the item with value data$ into
2020     REM    list, maintaining alphabetical order
2030     LOCAL ptr%, new%, last%
2040     REM    Get pointer to a new item & save old head
2050     new%=FNget: ptr%=data_hd%
2060     REM    Check for special case that data$
2070     REM    is the first item in the list
2080     IF data$>FNdata(data_hd%) THEN 2180
2090         REM    Insert data$ just after data_hd%
2120         REM    Point the head to the new one
2130         data_hd%=new%
2140         REM    and set-up the new one
2150         PROCset_data(new%, data$)
2160         PROCset_link(new%, ptr%)
2170     ENDPROC
2180     REM    Look for the place to insert new%
2190     REPEAT
2200         last%=ptr%
2210         ptr%=FNlink(ptr%)
2220     UNTIL FNdata(ptr%)>=data$
2225     REM    Could have an "Already Exists" error here
2230     REM    Insert new% between last% and ptr%
2240     PROCset_link(last%, new%)
2250     PROCset_data(new%, data$)
2260     PROCset_link(new%, ptr%)
2270 ENDPROC
2280
2290
3000 DEF PROCdelete(data$)
3010     REM    Delete the item data$ and put it in the free list
3020     LOCAL ptr%, last%
3030     IF FNlink(data_hd%)=NIL THEN PROCerror("Doesn't Exist"):ENDPROC
```

```
3040    ptr%=data_hd%
3045    REM   Is data$ the first item?
3050    IF FNdata(ptr%)=data$ THEN data_hd%=FNlink(ptr%): GOTO 3130
3060    REPEAT
3070       last%=ptr%
3080       ptr%=FNlink(ptr%)
3090    UNTIL FNdata(ptr%)>=data$
3100    IF FNdata(ptr%)<>data$ THEN PROCerror("Doesn't Exist"):ENDPROC
3110    REM   Change last%'s link to ptr%'s link
3120    PROCset_link(last%, FNlink(ptr%))
3130    REM   Then insert ptr% into free list
3140    PROCset_link(ptr%, free_hd%)
3150    free_hd%=ptr%
3160 ENDPROC
3170
3180
4000 DEF PROCforward_print(head%)
4010    REM   Print the list starting at head% in forward order
4020    IF head%<>NIL THEN PRINT FNdata(head%):PROCforward_print(FNlink(head%))
4040 ENDPROC
4050
4060
4100 DEF PROCreverse_print(head%)
4110    REM   Print the list starting at head% in reverse order
4120    IF head%<>NIL THEN PROCreverse_print(FNlink(head%)):PRINT FNdata(head%)
4140 ENDPROC
4150
4160
5000 DEF FNget
5010    REM   Returns a pointer to a free item
5020    LOCAL ptr%
5030    REM   Any in the free list?
5040    IF free_hd%=NIL THEN 5090
5050       REM   Get a free one then
5060       ptr%=free_hd%
5070       free_hd%=FNlink(free_hd%)
5080    =ptr%
5090    REM   Create a new one
5100    DIM ptr% size%
5110 =ptr%
5120
5130
```

```
6000 DEF PROCset_data(ptr%, str$)
6010    REM   Set the data field of ptr% to str$
6020    $ptr%=LEFT$(str$,16)
6030 ENDPROC
6040
6050
6100 DEF PROCset_link(ptr%, link%)
6110    REM   Set the link field of ptr% to link%
6120    ptr%!17=link%
6130 ENDPROC
6140
6150
7000 DEF FNdata(ptr%)
7010    REM   Returns the data field of ptr%
7020 =$(ptr%)
7030
7040
7100 DEF FNlink(ptr%)
7110    REM   Returns the link field of ptr%
7120 =ptr%!17
7130
7140
8000 DEF PROCerror(err$)
8010    PRINT''"Oh dear: ";err$''
8020 ENDPROC
8030
8040
```

Actually, there are two linked lists. Both have the same types of element, i.e. 21 bytes long, 17 of which are for the data and the last four for the link information. The main list is the list of elements which have been inserted by PROCinsert and is arranged in ASCII order. The variable data_hd% points to the first element of the list. To make insertion and deletion easier, there is a dummy element at the end whose value is the very high ASCII string "~~~~~~...." This is used in the same way as the similar element in the sorted array procedures given earlier. The insert and delete procedures are much longer than they really need to be because of the REMs. I hope these make them a little more comprehensible.

The second list is the free list. This is structured in exactly the same manner as the data list, except that it is possible for it to be empty (i.e. there is no dummy element) as the order in which its elements are stored is unimportant. The free list holds all the elements which have been used but were subsequently deleted. When PROCinsert is then called to create a new element, it asks FNget for the address of a suitable area of store to use. FNget first checks the free list to see if it has anything to offer. If it has (i.e. free_hd% is not NIL), an element is deleted from the free list and its address given to PROCinsert. If the free list is empty, a new area is created using DIM. Using this technique, the bare minimum of memory is used so that items can be deleted and inserted often without fear of running out of store.

The print routines show the beauty of using recursive procedures with recursive data structures (see the next Chapter). PROCforward_print says "if this isn't the last element, print it and go onto the next one" and PROCreverse_print says "if this isn't the last element, print the rest, then print this one". Notice that the parameter to both procedures is a pointer, so you can start printing a list from any element whose address happens to be available. Usually, though, calls would be of the form:

```
PROCforward_print(data_hd%)
PROCreverse_print(data_hd%)
```

It is equally possible to print the free list by changing the head pointer given to PROCforward_print, but don't expect the data to come out in order. (In fact, as items inserted into the free list are put in at the head, the statement:

```
PROCreverse_print(free_hd%)
```

will print items in the order in which they were deleted.)

The other procedures are concerned with setting and interrogating the elements whose addresses are supplied to them.

The linked list is a very useful structure. Most books on BASIC which cover them use arrays to simulate lists, which goes against the grain really as they are inherently dynamic. See [Grogono] for a good introduction to Pascal linked lists. These use pointer types, which are just addresses, and records, which are just composite data types like our 21-byte record used above.

Many types of data structure can be built using pointers. Examples are queues, deques, trees and stacks. [Page] and [Horowitz] are the books to read on this subject, and I give another example in the next chapter of the use of lists. To conclude this chapter (and the book as far as I'm concerned, due to the strange reverse_print algorithm I used to write it) I give an example of a tree structure using pointers.

The particular trees to be discussed are binary ones. This means that connected to each data item (or node) there are two pointers. Each pointer can be NIL, which means the node has no children in that direction, or it can point to another node, which in turn can point to more children. Nodes with no children are called leaves, and the very first node is called the root node. Tree structures have many applications, for example arithmetic expressions (or whole programs) can be held in tree form when they are being analysed by a compiler. Another application is sorting. Since there are two possible sub-trees sprouting from each node, the nodes can be assigned in such a way that all nodes which are reached through one pointer have a greater ASCII value than the current one, and the other pointer points to a sub-tree whose nodes are all less than the current one. The two pointers are usually called the left and right pointer. We shall use the convention that the left pointer gives the sub-tree whose nodes are less than the current one and the right pointer points to the greater nodes.

Once the data has been put into a tree, it can be displayed using very simple recursive procedures. There are three principal ways of visiting the nodes of a tree (i.e. traversing the tree). These are called prefix, suffix and symmetric traversals. The prefix walk is defined as:

```
Print the current node
If there is a left child, do a prefix walk of it
If there is a right child, do a prefix walk of it
```

The suffix walk is:

```
If there is a left child, do a suffix walk of it
If there is a right child, do a suffix walk of it
Print the current node
```

The recursive definition of the symmetric walk is:

```
If there is a left child, do a symmetric walk of it
Print the current node
If there is a right child, do a symmetric walk of it
```

The last one is the most interesting, as if the nodes have been entered properly, the list produced will be in ASCII order. If the first and third statements are reversed, the list will be in reverse order. The suffix walk is interesting when the tree represents an arithmetic expression. In this case, the nodes which aren't leaves are the operators of the expression and their children are the operands. The leaf nodes are the "terminal" symbols, such as variables names and numbers. The suffix walk of such a tree produces the reverse-Polish string representing the expression. This is the notation where the operands follow the operator. For example:

```
       a+b          becomes      a b + in RPN
      a+b*c          becomes      a b c * + in RPN
   (a+b)/(c-d)       becomes      a b + c d - / in RPN
```

The advantage of reverse-Polish is that expressions are easier to evaluate by machine than the normal infix ones (i.e. where the operator is fixed in between the operands). Also, as the last example illustrates, RPN avoids the necessity for brackets. I know I'm supposed to be talking about trees, but infix to RPN conversion provides such a good example of recursive procedures that trees will have to wait a minute. The set of procedures below converts a string which represents an expression with operands which are letters and with operators which are $+, -, *, /,$ $\hat{\ }$, (and) into its postfix or RPN equivalent. This would be a trivial task but for the fact that the precedence of operators has to be taken into account. For example, a+b*c has to be converted to a b c * + so that the *, which has a higher precedence than + is done first.

```
100 REM    Infix to Postfix Conversion
110 REPEAT
120    INPUT'"Give me an expression (e.g. a+b*c) ",expr$
130    ptr%=1
```

```
140    ch$=FNgetch
150    PRINT expr$;" in RPN is ";
160    PROCadd
170    IF ptr%<LEN(expr$)+2 THEN PROCerror("Syntax Error")
180 UNTIL FALSE
190
200
1000 DEF PROCadd
1005    LOCAL add_op$
1010    PROCmult
1020    IF ch$<>"+" AND ch$<>"-" THEN ENDPROC
1030    REPEAT
1040       add_op$=ch$
1050       ch$=FNgetch
1060       PROCmult
1070       PRINT add_op$;
1080    UNTIL ch$<>"+" AND ch$<>"-"
1090 ENDPROC
1100
2000 DEF PROCmult
2005    LOCAL mult_op$
2010    PROCexp
2020    IF ch$<>"*" AND ch$<>"/" THEN ENDPROC
2030    REPEAT
2040       mult_op$=ch$
2050       ch$=FNgetch
2060       PROCexp
2070       PRINT mult_op$;
2080    UNTIL ch$<>"*" AND ch$<>"/"
2090 ENDPROC
2100
3000 DEF PROCexp
3010    PROCfactor
3020    IF ch$<>"^" THEN ENDPROC
3030    REPEAT
3050       ch$=FNgetch
3060       PROCfactor
3070       PRINT "^";
3080    UNTIL ch$<>"^"
3090 ENDPROC
3100
3120
```

```
4000 DEF PROCfactor
4010    IF FNletter(ch$) THEN PRINTch$;: ch$=FNgetch:ENDPROC
4020    IF ch$="(" THEN PROCbrackets :ENDPROC
4030    IF ch$="" THEN PROCerror("Missing variable"):ENDPROC
4040    IF INSTR("+-*/^",ch$) THEN PROCerror("No unary operators"):ENDPROC
4050    PROCerror("Syntax error")
4060 ENDPROC
4070
5000 DEF PROCbrackets
5010    ch$=FNgetch
5020    PROCadd
5030    IF ch$<>")" THEN PROCerror("Missing )") ELSE ch$=FNgetch
5040 ENDPROC
5050
5060
6000 DEF FNgetch
6010    LOCAL ch$
6020    ch$=MID$(expr$,ptr%,1)
6030    ptr%=ptr%+1
6040 IF ch$<>" " THEN =ch$ ELSE =FNgetch
6050
6060
6100 DEF FNletter(ch$)=("A" <= ch$ AND ch$ <= "Z") OR ("a" <= ch$ AND ch$ <=
"z")
7000 DEF PROCerror(err$)
7010    PRINT'"ERROR: ";expr$
7020    PRINT TAB(ptr%+5);"^  ";err$
7030 RUN
```

The method used to convert the expression is called recursive descent (see any book on compilers) and is similar to that used by BBC BASIC when evaluating expressions. Of course, the procedures above only deal with four levels of precedence, whereas BBC BASIC has seven levels altogether, and also has to deal with factors (the highest precedence items) which are numbers as well as variables. Add the fact that there are strings and array subscripts to contend with, and built-in and user-defined functions, and it becomes clear why the expression evaluator often forms a substantial part of a BASIC interpreter on micros.

The meanings of the error messages should be obvious. They are similar to those emitted by BASIC in similar circumstances, except that with such a simple expression to work with it is possible to pin-point the error quite accurately so this is done with an up arrow (^).

We return now to the original topic of binary trees. The procedures below implement a very simple system which will accept strings and insert them into a binary tree. The tree can be printed in reverse or forward ASCII order. There is

no provision for deleting items as this is considerably more tedious than deleting
an item from a list, hence there is no free list.

```
100 PROCinit
110 FOR i%=1 TO 40
120    PROCinsert(RIGHT$("00000"+STR$RND(99999),5))
130 NEXT i%
140 PROCforward_print(root%)
150 PROCreverse_print(root%)
160 END
170
180
1000 DEF PROCinit
1010    size%=21
1020    NIL=0
1030    root%=FNget
1040    PROCset_data(root%,"MIDDLE")
1050    PROCset_left(root%, NIL)
1060    PROCset_right(root%, NIL)
1070 ENDPROC
1080
1090
2000 DEF PROCinsert(data$)
2010    LOCAL ptr%, last%, new%
2015    ptr%=root%
2020    REPEAT
2030       last%=ptr%
2040       IF FNdata(ptr%)>data$ THEN ptr%=FNleft(ptr%) ELSE
ptr%=FNright(ptr%)
2050    UNTIL ptr%=NIL OR FNdata(last%)=data$
2060    IF FNdata(last%)=data$ THEN PROCerror(data$+" Already
exists"):ENDPROC
2070    new%=FNget
2080    PROCset_data(new%,data$)
2090    PROCset_left(new%,NIL)
2100    PROCset_right(new%,NIL)
2110    IF data$<FNdata(last%) THEN PROCset_left(last%,new%) ELSE
PROCset_right(last%,new%)
2120 ENDPROC
2130
2140
3000 DEF PROCforward_print(ptr%)
3010    IF ptr%=NIL THEN ENDPROC
```

```
3020    PROCforward_print(FNleft(ptr%))
3030    IF FNdata(ptr%)<>"MIDDLE" THEN PRINT FNdata(ptr%)
3040    PROCforward_print(FNright(ptr%))
3050 ENDPROC
3060
3070
3100 DEF PROCreverse_print(ptr%)
3110    IF ptr%=NIL THEN ENDPROC
3120    PROCreverse_print(FNright(ptr%))
3130    IF FNdata(ptr%)<>"MIDDLE" THEN PRINT FNdata(ptr%)
3140    PROCreverse_print(FNleft(ptr%))
3150 ENDPROC
3160
3170
4000 DEF FNget
4010    LOCAL x%
4020    DIM x% size%-1
4030 =x%
4040
4050
5000 DEF PROCset_data(ptr%,data$)
5010    $(ptr%)=LEFT$(data$,16)
5020 ENDPROC
5030
5100 DEF PROCset_left(ptr%,new%)
5110    ptr%!17=ptr%!17 AND &FFFF0000 OR new%
5120 ENDPROC
5130
5140
5200 DEF PROCset_right(ptr%,new%)
5210    ptr%!17=ptr%!17 AND &FFFF OR new%*2^16
5220 ENDPROC
5230
5240
6000 DEF FNdata(ptr%)=$ptr%
6010
6100 DEF FNleft(ptr%)=ptr%!17 AND &FFFF
6110
6200 DEF FNright(ptr%)=(ptr%!17 AND &FFFF0000) DIV 2^16
6210
6220
7000 DEF PROCerror(err$)
```

```
7010    PRINT'"Error: ";err$
7020 ENDPROC
7030
7040
```

The program before the procedures inserts 40 five-digit strings into the tree, and then prints them out in forward and reverse order. When you consider that the input and output statements can be changed quite easily to use files, it can be seen that the program could be changed to a file sorter very quickly. The dummy record which is inserted at the beginning of the tree ensures, assuming the strings are alphabetic and the first letter is in upper case, that there is an equal spread of letters on both halves of the tree. This makes it more efficient when inserting and searching for a particular item.

The exercise for this section is to get a book on data structures and relate what it tells you about binary trees to the program above. Then do some of the exercises in that book. This is called indirection (or redirection) in computing circles.

Chapter Two

The Structured Bits

2.1 Structured Programming

One of BBC BASIC's most heralded features is the provision of statements which help the programmer to write well structured programs. To see why this is a good thing, it is first necessary to know what structured programming is. About fifteen years ago, some of the Great Men of computing began to express their concern about the way in which many large programs used in the commercial, military and even academic environments did not work very well, due to the prevalence of mistakes (bugs, as they are called) in said programs. In all probability, it wasn't only the Great Men who were concerned, but Great Men have a greater ability to get their views heard by others.

This unreliability was caused by the lack of suitable "programming rules". At that time, there was no real formal definition of how one should go about writing a program to solve a particular problem. It was all down to intuition and experience. Also, a great lack of foresight was often exhibited by the authors of large systems – programs were written with no regard to future expansion, and when they came to be amended or upgraded, the task often proved harder than rewriting the whole thing from scratch.

Because of the difficulty in improving or correcting programs which had been written in an ad hoc fashion, a "software crisis" was predicted (and many say has arrived), where programmers would spend more time trying to get old programs to work than writing new ones. This makes software very expensive to produce. Clearly, what was needed was a formal methodology which one could use to construct programs that work first time and that can be easily understood and therefore changed by programmers other than the author. It was in 1972 that three of the aforementioned Great Men produced a book entitled simply "Structured Programming". This has since become a standard reference work, and the more mathematically inclined reader might do well to obtain a copy if he wishes to delve into the finer points of designing well structured programs. See [Dijkstra].

In this chapter, I will restrict the discussion to the points which I feel are especially relevant to using the BBC BASIC structured constructs well. I will write only in very general terms about structuring programs. As well as the reference given above, any book about the Pascal language worth its salt should provide good advice on structured programming. I mention a couple of these in the Bibliography, though the reader should realise that Pascal is much more sophisticated than any form of BASIC, even the BBC version, so many of the concepts introduced in Pascal programming books would be very hard, if not impossible to transfer to the BBC Computer.

The first part of this chapter is concerned with two of the important concepts of structured programming – controlling the flow of a program, and program decomposition. It also discusses where standard BASIC goes wrong in relation to these two topics. The second part describes the BBC BASIC programming structures in detail. The last two sections deal with more minor but still very important subjects – error detection and handling in programs, and the way programs can be laid out to make them more readable. The latter point is very important when you come to change the program later on. It is entirely for the benefit of the human reader – the computer doesn't mind how the program is arranged, so long as the statements are syntactically correct. Because of this, programmers often compromise the clarity of a program by putting dozens of statements on one line and using short, uninformative variable names. Learning to avoid this tendency can be half the skill of writing good programs.

2.1.1 Two Important Concepts

For a program to stand any chance of working properly, it must be perfectly clear just by looking at the listing which statements are executed in given conditions and which are not. This may seem an obvious quality possessed by all programs, but if you have access to some largish (say more than 100 lines) BASIC listings try to follow exactly where the program "goes" for various sets of input data. If you are lucky, the path to follow is perfectly straight forward, and it is clear at all times why certain lines are executed instead of others. Tracing the program in this way is called tracing the "control of flow" of the program.

In the book "Structured Programming", Dijkstra notes three types of control of flow which are needed to write well structured programs in a transparent way. The "transparent" part is important – it must be obvious from the listing what the structure is. These three flow control devices are as follows:

1. Sequences. This is the "default" way in which programs are executed. Statements are executed in the order in which they appear (which is in order of increasing line number in BASIC). The sequence of statements represents the steps involved in solving the problem – if an individual step is too complex to be performed by an easily understood sequence, it must be broken down into a set of smaller steps which can. This is "decomposition", which is discussed below.

2. Selection. Obviously, it must be possible to execute some statements only if a certain condition holds. The ability to "make decisions" is one of the computer's most useful facilities. This is implemented in high level languages (i.e. computer languages which contain many English-like words and other features which make the programming of a computer a comparatively easy

task) with statements such as IF ... THEN. The generality of a language's IF ... THEN is an important factor when trying to write "transparent" code.

3. Repetition. This is the computer's other strength – the ability to execute statements over and over again very rapidly until a certain condition is met, or until the statements have been performed a predetermined number of times. Again, the way in which repetition is implemented in a language contributes significantly to the usefulness of the language.

These three flow control mechanisms are present in all programs written in traditional computer languages. Some languages make this obvious by the various statements they provide (such as "if ... then ... else" and "while ... do ..." in Pascal). Others (like BASIC) "hide" the structures with lots of GOTO statements. In the three descriptions above, note that nowhere does the ability to "jump to a certain part of the program" appear explicitly. This action is implicit in the operation of the selection and repetition devices, but is only used in a very controlled way – giving the programmer the power to jump to any part of the program willy-nilly is generally considered undesirable. The reasons behind this thinking are discussed in section 2.1.2.

The way in which flow control devices (2) and (3) above are implemented varies between languages. At one end of the spectrum is Pascal, which has a comprehensive set of statements to aid the programmer in making selections and performing loops. At the other end is BASIC, which is in some respects only a comparatively small step up from assembly language (the computer's "native" language). BBC BASIC falls somewhere between these two stalls, so it can be praised for being better than standard BASIC, and criticised for not going the whole way. Section 2.2 deals with the constructs available in BBC BASIC in some detail.

Important concept number two is program decomposition. This does not mean that after a while a program goes rotten and starts to decompose (though this fate is surely met by many an unstructured program), but describes the way in which complex problems are broken up into smaller, more easily solved ones. When combined, the sub-problems' solutions (called subroutines or procedures in programming terms) form a solution to the whole problem – if they have been well designed. This technique is by no means confined to programming; any form of construction project must be broken down into smaller sub-assemblies which can be dealt with individually and then combined when completed. The BBC Computer is a fine example of this; the sub-units on the main printed circuit board are clearly visible, and they combine to make a reliable whole. What is surprising is that the decomposition methodology took so long to be adopted by programmers.

Any useful program can be broken down into three main steps – input, processing and output. If anything worthwhile is being done on the input data, it is likely that the processing step can itself be decomposed into some smaller processes. How this is done determines how well structured a program will be. It is no good just thinking of random ways of splitting up the main process and then hoping the end product will be nice and modular. It is at this point where the "science" of programming starts to veer towards being an art. It is only very simple problems which enable the programmer to say "Oh yes, that's how it's done." without any planning or forethought. Non-trivial programs demand some thinking to be done first. Because the thought process cannot be described mathematically, it will always be impossible to totally formalise the method of program writing. This is probably just as well, as this is where the enjoyment of writing a good program is derived from – it is the intellectual achievement of solving a problem which is rewarding, not typing the program into the computer (though obviously seeing the object of your labours in action is a pleasing sight).

Once the germ of a solution has been born, the best thing to do is write it down IN ENGLISH. The strongest urge in humans must be to start writing out a program before they have even thought about the problem. Well, second strongest anyway. To quote one of the Great Men, "Think before you code!". After the thinking, the way the program develops depends on the programmer's experience and ability to think logically. The major sub-problems should be identifiable from the English solution. Examination of these should determine whether they are simple enough to solve immediately, or if they themselves need to be broken down. All this is very abstract, and at the end of this chapter there are a couple of "case studies" which bring together all the topics covered in this and subsequent sections.

You have probably realised that sub-problems and their solutions discussed above are connected with subroutines in BASIC. Unfortunately, most people who learn programming via BASIC are taught that the GOSUB statement is used only to group "commonly used" statements together, where they can be accessed from different parts of the program. Although this is partly true, it gives the impression that a group of statements has to appear several times in a program before it earns the status of a "subroutine". This is definitely not the case – a subroutine should represent the solution of a sub-problem which is part of the main program. It does not matter if the subroutine is called only once from the main program: the body of a program could simply be a list of GOSUBs with a couple of loops. The idea is that by looking at the main body of a program, the method of solution is clearly visible, without the reader knowing how each sub-program actually works. In view of this, the main part of even a relatively complex program should rarely be more than two pages long. If it is, the initial solution may have been given in too fine detail, and this might compromise the clarity of the program when someone comes to try to understand it later.

The decomposition of the problem into sub-problems (and sub-sub-problems if necessary) obviously gives a hierarchy of solutions. This can be represented in various ways. Unfortunately, the linear program listing is not one of the best, as a hierarchy is fundamentally two dimensional, like a family tree, which progresses down and outwards at the same time. Actually, a "tree" is a common way of expressing the relationships between sub-programs. (See [Bowles].) However, it is not very easy to show repetition or selection in a tree, so a more flexible method is required. One of the best is Warnier-Orr diagrams. This is a pictorial way of representing a well structured solution in an abstract way (i.e. independently of the language in which it will finally be implemented). Anyone who is at all keen to write programs which work first time, regardless of the complexity of the problem and the programming language to be used would do well to read the section by Higgins in [Liffick].

Now that the fundamentals of structured programming have been covered, albeit in a very superficial way, I will discuss why standard BASIC fails in may people's eyes to provide a tool (which is, after all, what a language should be – a tool with which to craft a solution) that supports the ideas of structured programming. This is not to say that it is impossible to write well structured solutions in BASIC, only that whereas Pascal, as noted above, provides many language constructs to support structuring of not only programs, but data as well, BASIC provides very few of these in its "raw" form. BBC BASIC goes some way to correct this deficiency, as described in section 2.2.

2.1.2   Why BASIC is BAD

Now that two of the most important structuring concepts have been covered, it is possible to examine BASIC and see why so many computing intellectuals verbally crucify it. I will discuss the two main points of control of flow and program decomposition in that order.

I mentioned in the last section that Pascal has a generous number of language constructs that implement the two concepts of selection and repetition in a way that makes it very easy to keep track of what the program is doing. Programmers can use these facilities to greater or lesser advantage, but it would be a very poor programmer indeed who produced a totally illegible Pascal program. This is certainly not the case in BASIC, and it takes at least a careful programmer to write a readable BASIC program. To illustrate this, let us consider the way BASIC implements selection. I said in section 2.1.1 that this is the IF . . . THEN . . . ELSE of programming languages. Suppose in the English version of a solution to a problem there was the sentence:

```
If the total is more than £100, give a 10%
discount, otherwise add £2.50 for postage.
```

How would this be implemented in BASIC? It depends on what version of BASIC you are using. In ANSI Minimal BASIC (which only allows IF statements of the form "IF condition THEN line num.", and limited variable names) it would look like:

```
100 IF TO > 100 THEN 130
110 LET TO=TO+2.50
120 GOTO 140
130 LET TO=TO*.90
140 .....
```

Notice that there was no mention of jumping from one line to another in the English version – these were introduced in the translation to BASIC. Even in

Microsoft BASIC the situation isn't that much better:

```
100 IF TO > 100 THEN TO=TO*.9:GOTO 120
110 TO=TO+2.50
120 .....
```

Even here, the GOTO hasn't been totally eliminated. You may wonder why we should want to eliminate the GOTO; what harm does it do? Well, for a start it does not belong to the problem, and therefore shouldn't appear in its solution. A programming language is a means to an end. It is a means for humans to express problems which can then be converted into a form suitable for the computer to solve. Humans don't think in GOTOs. The way BASIC forces the programmer to think down to that level is contrary to the whole idea of using high level languages in the first place. By imposing such restrictions on the way humans communicate their ideas to the computer, the bandwidth of the communication channel is similarly reduced – the result is a loss of productivity.

Enough of the deep stuff, suffice to say the GOTO IS BAD. Below are the Pascal and BBC BASIC versions of the IF example given above:

```
(Pascal)  if total > 100.0 then
              total:=total*0.90 { 10% discount }
          else
              total:=total+2.50; { post and packing }


(BASIC)   100 IF total>100 THEN total=total*0.9 ELSE total=total+2.50
```

Even if you've never seen a piece of Pascal before, it should be clear what the segment above does. Note that Pascal is a free-format language; statements can be placed anywhere on the line, and comments (included between braces {}) can be placed anywhere. BASIC (including BBC BASIC) is a line-oriented language; each statement can occupy at most one line (see line 100 above).

The example that has been discussed so far is a relatively simple one. Both parts of the IF ... THEN ... ELSE ... were single statements. Even so, the clarity was severely reduced between the English version and the BASIC transla-tion, due to the combination of the sudden appearance of GOTOs and the limited variable names. This situation worsens as the THEN and ELSE parts grow more complex. Repetition suffers in a similar way when translated to BASIC.

Consider the English version of an input loop and its interpretation in minimal BASIC given below:

```
Keep on getting the quantity and cost, updating

the total amount, until the quantity is a negative

number, or ten pairs of numbers have been given.


100 REM    INITIALISE COUNT
```

```
110 LET C=0
120 PRINT "Quantity, Cost ";
130 INPUT Q,C1
140 IF Q<0 THEN 190
150 REM     UPDATE TOTAL
160 LET T=T+Q*C1
170 LET C=C+1
180 IF C<10 THEN 120
190 .....
```

Again, the BASIC version totally disguises the problem. There are two GOTOs (albeit conditional ones), both of which are used in controlling the operation of a loop. The Pascal and BBC BASIC versions of the segment are shown below:

```
count := 0;
repeat
   write('Quantity, Cost ');
   readln(qty, cost);
   if qty>=0 then
      begin
         total := total + qty*cost;
         count := count + 1
      end
until (count=10) or (qty<0);
```

```
100 count=0
110 REPEAT
120    PRINT"Quantity, Count ";
130    INPUT qty, cost
140    IF qty>=0 THEN total=total+qty*cost: count=count+1
150 UNTIL count=10 OR qty<0
```

The Pascal and BBC BASIC versions differ in very few respects. All the statements controlled by a THEN have to be on the same line in BASIC, whereas in Pascal they are "bracketed" together by "begin" and "end". Both versions reflect the nature of the English expression of the problem; they are uncluttered by confusing GOTOs. The words REPEAT and UNTIL express the nature loop much more clearly than backward branches using IF . . . THEN.

In summary, after expressing a solution in English (or a similar very high level language), try to do the conversion into BASIC using the structures provided, instead of automatically GOTOing all over the place. The conditional branches of BASIC (i.e. IF . . . THEN line) have all the shortcomings of assembly language (easily confused code due to erroneous jumps, weak powers of expression), with none of the advantages (speed mainly). It is not usually possible to eliminate the GOTO completely in BBC BASIC due to the compromises which have been made in implementing the structured bits, but there should be far fewer than in most BASIC programs.

The other disadvantage with normal BASIC is the poor subroutine calling mechanism. To someone who has never used a "grown up" language, this deficiency may not be readily apparent. I will go through a fairly simple example, and derive the BBC BASIC "DEF PROC" facility from the primitive GOSUB statement. The example is a routine which draws a circle using high-resolution graphics. At the moment, there is no need to know how the routine works – all we are interested in is how it is called from the main BASIC program. This is the whole point of a program being structured; it is possible to look at the upper levels of the hierarchy and understand what is going on without getting down to the nitty-gritty.

To specify the circle we require, there are certain values which have to be given to the subroutine. For example, the circle drawing routine will need to know the position of circle (i.e. its X and Y co-ordinates), its radius, and perhaps other quantities such as the colour in which it is to be drawn. These values are called parameters. Below is the section of BASIC which would be needed to set-up the parameters and call a subroutine at line 2000 which draws a circle:

```
100 LET X=200
110 LET Y=100
120 LET R=150
130 LET C=3: REM COLOUR
150 GOSUB 2000
```

It takes five statements just to call the subroutine. That, however, is the least of our problems. Firstly, there's the question of these four variables "X", "Y", "R" and "C". They are obviously the ones used by the subroutine in drawing the circle. However, this precludes their use anywhere else in the program, as whenever the subroutine at line 2000 is used, the values will have to be changed when setting up the parameters. Also, why should the main program have to know what variables the subroutine uses? Surely that is of concern only to the subroutine itself. Let's change the GOSUB statement so that the parameters are placed after the destination line number. That way no special variables have to be remembered; you only need to know the meaning of each value in the parameter list. The call to line 2000 now becomes:

```
100 GOSUB 2000, 200, 100, 150, 3
```

where the "200" is passed to the subroutine as the X value, the "100" as the Y co-ordinate and so on. This is better than previously as it eliminates the need for a knowledge of the internal variables of the subroutine. (We assume that the values given after the "2000" above are somehow transferred to the subroutine.)

Line 100 above is still not exactly "transparent". What does the routine at line 2000 do exactly? (Put yourself in the position of a stranger to the program, or even its author a few weeks after he wrote it.) The only way to find out is look down a few pages of listing till the relevant section is found. This is hardly conducive to understanding the program by browsing through the higher levels of the listing. What the subroutine needs is a name. It would be possible to use "GOSUB CIRCLE....", but the syntax of GOSUB is well established already, so it wouldn't be very wise to start changing it now. Instead, we will adapt the syntax of BASIC's user-defined functions. These use "DEF FNname" to define a function which can then be called using "FNname" in an expression. Since subroutines are related to the procedures found in adult languages (Pascal, Algol), we will invent the "DEF PROCname" statement to define a procedure which can subsquently be executed using "PROCname". Actually, it was the designers of BBC BASIC who invented this notation. The circle call would be expressed:

```
100 PROCcircle(200, 100, 150, 3)
```

This completes the transformation of the subroutine calling procedure from GOSUB (which BBC BASIC implements for the sake of completeness) to the BBC BASIC procedure calling mechanism. Even as it stands, the latter method renders GOSUBs superfluous, and they should never really appear in a new BBC BASIC program (i.e. one which hasn't been directly translated from another machine).

The lack of parameters and meaningful names are not the only deficiencies in the standard BASIC GOSUB system. Remember I mentioned that when the passing of parameters relied on setting up special variables whose names are known to the main program, it means that these names cannot be used elsewhere in case their values are corrupted by calling the subroutine. A similar effect occurs when the subroutine uses variables to store temporary results. For example, consider the section of code below, which could have been taken from a circle drawing routine:

```
2030 LET S=1/R
2040 FOR I=0 TO 2*3.142 STEP S
2050 .....
```

The two variables S (standing for "step") and I are used by the subroutine to draw the circle; they have no use outside this routine. However, say the author of the program which contains the routine at line 2000 decides to extend it in some fashion. In this extension, he calls the circle routine from inside a FOR ... NEXT loop thus:

```
560 FOR I=0 TO 200
570     LET X=I*2
580     LET Y=I*4
590     GOSUB 2000
600 NEXT I
610 ....
```

The programmer has forgotten about the FOR I loop used inside the subroutine and has used the same looping variable in the loop at line 560. This results in two nested FOR ... NEXT loops using the same variable, which is of course erroneous as the inner loop will corrupt the value of the outer loop's "I". (Section 2.2.3.) This phenomenom is known as a side-effect; the subroutine has a side effect on the main program caused by the fact that it changes a variable currently being used by the "outside". It could be argued that the programmer should keep track of his variables better, but this is a lot to ask in a 2000 line program, with loops and subroutines which may be nested five or six levels deep.

The solution to the "side-effect" problem is the use of local variables. As already noted, I and S above are "local" to the circle routine. Ideally they should exist only for the duration of the routine being active, i.e. when it is being executed. This is impossible to achieve in standard BASIC; all variables are global, which means any variable can be accessed with equal ease by any part of the program, so the same name always refers to the same value. In BBC BASIC there is a statements called LOCAL. It has the syntax shown below:

```
1000 LOCAL A$,B,C%
```

i.e. the word LOCAL followed by a list of string, real or integer variables. When it is executed (which can only be from within a user-defined procedure or function), the variables named are "created" for use within the procedure (or function). The local variables are stored in a different area of memory to the global variables. This area is searched first when any variable is accessed. As a result, if there are two variables called "I", one global and one local to the current procedure, only the local version of "I" will be affected by statements inside the procedure. Once the procedure has finished (via an ENDPROC statement – section 2.2.5), the local "I" is forgotten, and references to that name now refer to the global "I".

The LOCAL statement is the last feature of BBC BASIC DEF FN/PROCs which improves the subroutine calling mechanism (apart from recursion, which is a more subtle change – see sections 2.2.5 and 2.2.6). It still doesn't achieve the power available by Pascal procedures for reasons explained later. It does, however, go a long way in enabling structured solutions to problems to be expressed much more elegantly than in standard BASIC, and as such should be used to the full. Most of the programs in this book (apart from trivial explanatory examples) use a procedure or two to make them more understandable. If you adopt the same habit (but at the same time avoid the temptation to split-up a program into random "chunks" just for the sake of using procedures), your programs should become more reliable and easier to understand later on. They will also stand more chance of being published in a computer magazine.

In this section I have looked at BASIC's principal weaknesses in the area of structured programming, and touched upon the improvements made by the BBC version of the language. The next sections describe these improvements in some detail. The only way to get to know them well (and therefore use them well) is by writing a lot of programs. It takes a conscious effort to write well structured programs – using a decent language can only make the task easier. Practice using the facilities provided (perhaps by re-writing some old programs, or other people's) and you should soon be thinking automatically in terms of REPEATS and IF ... THEN ... ELSE instead of GOTOs. With this half of the battle won, practice recognising how large problems can be simplified into smaller ones. Always remember the "Think before you code!" rule (after all, it *is* a quotation from a Great Man). Even if you suddenly have a brainwave while sitting at the computer, take a while to clarify in your mind exactly what you want to achieve. Writing things down always helps. This is different from typing it in – the BBC Computer doesn't understand English (I'm working on it though). If all this seems obvious, good. If not, get one of the Structured Programming books mentioned in the Bibliography. But don't just read it – practice it!

2.2   BBC BASIC's Structured Constructs

The last part discussed in general terms the features that are desirable in a language in order to write structured programs. It also revealed that standard BASIC has a dearth of useful facilities to aid the programmer in the writing of such programs. BBC BASIC goes some way to remove this deficiency. Unfortunately, it seems like a half-hearted attempt; enough features are implemented to give the language a certain amount of respectability in the eyes of BASIC's critics, but this has not been taken far enough. The limitations are pointed out as they are encountered in the following sections. Obviously, there is only a certain amount by which you can change a language and still say it is that language. BASIC has suffered particularly badly from this – nearly every machine's version differs from all the others. Given this, combined with the criticism that BASIC attracts anyway, it's a shame that the designers of BBC BASIC didn't scrap the "Structured BASIC" notion altogether, and implement something like Comal, which combines the advantages of Pascal with those of BASIC, omitting many of the disadvantages of both.

The comments above notwithstanding, the BBC version of BASIC is a very powerful one, and is certainly an improvement on nearly every other version available on microcomputers. The main advantages are the virtual elimination of the GOTO statement, with all the confusion that it causes, and the greater ease with which programs can be modularised into simple, understandable procedures and functions. The first four sections in this part deal with the flow control statements – IF ... THEN ... ELSE, ON ... GOTO/GOSUB, FOR ... NEXT and REPEAT ... UNTIL. The last two parts cover the program decomposition statements – DEF FN and DEF PROC.

When describing the form of computer language statements (i.e. the statements' syntax), it is usual to use a special notation. This makes it much easier to express parts which are optional or repeats. I use a simple scheme to explain the syntax of BBC BASIC statements. This is summarised below:

```
statement      means any legal BBC BASIC statement

{word}         means that the presence of word is optional

word*          means word may occur any number of times,
               including zero. Multiple statements are of
               course separated by colons (:)

[w1 w2]        means that w1 and w2 must occur together
```

2.2.1 The IF ... THEN ... ELSE Statement

An example of this statement's use has already been given in section 2.1.2. It has two forms:

```
100 IF expression {THEN} statement* {ELSE statement*}
200 IF expression THEN line number {ELSE line number}
```

It can be seen that most parts are optional, which leads to all sorts of weird-looking statements which are perfectly legal. "expression" is any valid expression which yields a number as a result. If the number is non-zero, the result is taken as TRUE, and the THEN statement(s) (if present) will be executed. If the number is zero, it is taken as FALSE and the ELSE statement(s) (if present) are executed. Most often, "expression" is a comparison between two numbers or strings. Groups of comparisons can be combined by using the AND, OR, EOR and NOT operators (see Chapter one). The statements can be any legal statements, including another IF. Some examples of typical and not so typical IF statements are shown below with their "English" translations:

```
      100 REM     print the larger of A and B
      110 IF A>B THEN PRINT A ELSE PRINT B
      120 REM     if A% divides exactly into B% then
      130 REM     print their quotient
      140 IF B% MOD A% = 0 THEN PRINT B% DIV A%
or    140 IF B% MOD A% ELSE PRINT B% DIV A%
      150 REM     if A$ is "greater" in ASCII order
      160 REM     than B$ then concatenate A$ to B$,
      170 REM     otherwise concatenate B$ to A$
      180 IF A$>B$ THEN B$=B$+A$ ELSE A$=A$+B$
      190 REM     limit A to a maximum of 100
      200 IF A>100 THEN A=100
      210 REM     if 0<=a<=100 then half a
      220 IF a>=0 AND a<=100 THEN a=a/2
      230 REM     if a>b, or b>c, but not both or neither, print b
      240 IF a>b EOR b>c THEN PRINT b
```

Occasionally, the "statement" part will be a GOTO. This may be omitted, giving the familiar "IF expression THEN line number" form. This statement should only be used to jump over a large number of statements which could not fit comfortably on one line. For example, it may be necessary to jump over a REPEAT ... UNTIL section to emulate a WHILE facility (section 2.2.4). Another example is given below. It could be part of a sort routine:

```
      100 REM     Swap unordered elements - unwieldy version
      110 IF A%(I%) > A%(I%+1) THEN T%=A%(I%):A%(I%)=A%(I%+1):A%(I%+1)=
          T%:F%=FALSE
```

```
120 REM     Swap unordered elements - better version
130 IF A%(I%) <= A%(I%+1) THEN 180
140    T%=A%(I%)
150    A%(I%)=A%(I%+1)
160    A%(I%+1)=T%
170    F%=FALSE
180 ....
```

This is one of the few opportunties to use the GOTO which arises. It is a consequence of BASIC's insistence that all the statements controlled by an IF should
appear on one line. There is no real need for this; the statements controlled by
FOR ... NEXT can be spread over many lines. The two versions of the swap
given above compromise elegance and the "no GOTO" rule respectively.
Personally I think more than two or three statements on one line is highly unreadable, especially when they wrap around the screen. This is obviously a matter of
taste – I'm sure the people who wrote the Welcome tape programs would beg to
differ; most of those programs have about ten statements per line. Notice that
lines 140–170 above are indented slightly. This helps to show the lines that are
skipped by the GOTO implicit in the IF ... THEN.

As the "statement" part of a THEN or ELSE can be another IF statement, it is
not always clear which statements will be executed. Consider the following
English conditional statement:

> If the cost is less than £100 then no discount, otherwise if the cost is less than
> £200 then give a 10% discount, otherwise give a 15% discount.

The obvious way to express this in BBC BASIC is:

```
100 IF cost>=100 THEN IF cost>=200 THEN cost=cost*0.85 ELSE cost=cost*0.9
```

Unfortunately, this statement will give a 15% discount if the cost is less than
£100. The reason is the way BASIC deals with the ELSE part of IF statements.
First, the condition after the IF is evaluated. If this is non-zero (TRUE), the
THEN statement is executed. Otherwise, the line is scanned for an ELSE. If one is
present, the statements following it are executed. Thus, in line 100 above, when
cost<100 the ELSE statement "cost=cost*0.9" is executed, even though this is
supposed to belong to the second IF. To make the statement behave correctly,
there are a couple of possible changes:

```
100 IF cost<=100 ELSE IF cost>=200 THEN cost=cost*0.85 ELSE cost=cost*0.9
100 IF cost>=200 THEN cost=cost*0.85 ELSE IF cost>=100 THEN cost=cost*0.9
```

As a general rule, the combination "THEN IF" should be avoided, though "ELSE
IF" is OK. Note that:

```
100 IF c1 THEN IF c2 THEN s1
```

can be replaced by:

```
100 IF c1 AND c2 THEN s1
```

and that:

```
100 IF c1 ELSE IF c2 THEN s1
```

is equivalent to:

```
100 IF NOT (c1) AND c2 THEN s1
```

2.2.2 The ON ... GOTO/GOSUB Statement

This is (almost) a logical extension to the IF ... THEN ... ELSE statement of the previous section. Whereas that statememt allowed the choice between two actions (either or both of which could be null actions) selected by a boolean value, the ON ... statement allows the selection of an arbitrary number of actions, chosen by the value of an expression. The form of the statement is:

```
100 ON expression GOTO line [,line]* {ELSE statement*}
110 ON expression GOSUB line [,line]* {ELSE statement*}
```

Once again, the parts between braces are optional. The * means that that part can be repeated as many times as desired. Actually, the "line"s can be expressions; this is a general case with destination line numbers in BBC BASIC. For example "GOTO A+B" is perfectly legal. It is not a good idea to take advantage of this facility for reasons given later.

The actions of ON ... GOTO and ON ... GOSUB are very similar; only the first form will be described in detail. All comments apply equally to the latter version; the difference is that when a RETURN is encountered after an ON ... GOSUB has been executed, control returns to the line following the ON ..., much the same as a normal GOSUB.

When an ON ... GOTO is encountered, the expression after the ON is evaluated. It should preferably be an integer. If not, it is truncated as if the INT function had been applied. When evaluated, the expression should lie in the range from one to N, where N is the number of line numbers which appear after the GOTO (or GOSUB). For example, in the statement:

```
230 ON A% GOTO 1000, 2000, 3000, 4000
```

A% must be in the range 1 to 4, otherwise an error "ON range" error would occur. If A% is 1, then a GOTO 1000 is performed. If it equals 2, a GOTO 2000 is executed and so on. A common use for the ON ... statement is in selecting one of several actions from a "menu" of items presented to the user. The section of program below illustrates this.

```
100 REM       print menu
110 CLS
120 PRINT'''"1. Add some stock"
130 PRINT'"2. Remove some stock"
140 PRINT'"3. Insert a new item"
```

```
150 PRINT'"4. Delete an item"
160 REPEAT
170    INPUT TAB(0,11),"Which one (1-4) ",choice%
180 UNTIL choice%>=1 AND choice%<=4
190 ON choice% GOTO 1000, 2000, 3000, 4000
200 .....
1000 REM    Add stock
1010 .....
1020 .....
1230 GOTO 100
2000 REM    Remove stock
2010 .....
2020 .....
2400 GOTO 100
3000 REM    Insert an item
3010 .....
3020 .....
3500 GOTO 100
4000 REM    Delete an item
4010 .....
4020 .....
4230 GOTO 100
```

The action of the "program" should be clear, despite its skeletal nature. The menu of four items is printed. The user is asked to make a choice, and has to type in a number between 1 and 4 before the ON ... at line 190 is executed. Once a number in the correct range has been entered, the ON statement selects the appropriate line. If the user chose number 3, for example, the section of program starting at line 3000 would be jumped to.

The example above illustrates some deficiencies of the ON ... GOTO which can be rectified by the use of ON ... GOSUB and the ELSE part. First, notice that after each of the routines at 1000, 2000 etc., there is a GOTO which branches back to the beginning of the section. There will almost always be a need for a branch such as this after the relevant piece of program has been executed, otherwise all the sections would run into each other. This clearly opens the door for plenty of mistakes, especially if the sections selected by the ON ... are large and the GOTO has to be made to a distant destination. The ON ... GOSUB version alleviates this problem. If each section is terminated by a RETURN, it can be guaranteed that control will be returned to the statement following the ON ... GOSUB, so it is much easier to keep track of the flow of control. There is some loss of flexibility, because all the sections have to return to the same place in the program. Using the GOTO method, control could be transferred to any place in the program. However, this very flexibility detracts from the program's robustness, so there is no real advantage to be gained by using ON . . . GOTO instead of ON . . . GOSUB.

The second problem is the need to check the range of the ON expression before the ON . . . statement could actually be executed. This adds a significant amount to the complexity of the menu routine, and can be avoided if the optional "ELSE statement" part is included. When this is added to the ON . . . statement, the part after the ELSE is executed if the expression evaluates to a number less than 1 or greater than the number of line numbers given. The statement can be any general set of instructions (separated by colons as usual), but will usually be an error message of some sort followed by a jump to a "default" routine in the program. The section given above is re-presented below, incorporating the two improvements over the ON . . . GOTO just discussed.

```
100 REM      print menu
110 CLS
120 PRINT'''"1. Add some stock"
130 PRINT'"2. Remove some stock"
140 PRINT'"3. Insert a new item"
150 PRINT'"4. Delete an item"
160 INPUT TAB(0,11),"Which one (1-4) ",choice%
170 ON choice% GOSUB 1000, 2000, 3000, 4000 ELSE 100
180 .....
1000 REM      Add stock
1010 .....
1020 .....
1230 RETURN
2000 REM    Remove stock
2010 .....
2020 .....
2400 RETURN
3000 REM    Insert an item
3010 .....
3020 .....
3500 RETURN
4000 REM    Delete an item
4010 .....
4020 .....
4230 RETURN
```

It is obviously a good idea to place the subroutines as close to the ON statement as possible. They could be separated by a few blank lines and indented to make the individual routines stand out. Remember that the null line is valid in BBC BASIC. A line number number followed by one or more spaces is inserted into the program just as any other statement, and is treated much the same as a REM, i.e. is ignored. There has to be at least one space, otherwise BASIC will think you just want to delete the line with the line number given.

Although the ELSE part above was simply another line number, it could have been any of:

```
170 ON choice% GOSUB 1000, 2000, 3000, 4000 ELSE PROCerror(170)
170 ON choice% GOSUB 1000, 2000, 3000, 4000 ELSE PRLNT "Wrong!":GOTO 20
170 ON choice% GOSUB 1000, 2000, 3000, 4000 ELSE STOP
```

The only "extra" BBC BASIC provides over the standard ON ... facility is the ELSE clause. This is quite useful as it obviates the need to check the range of the ON expression before the statement is executed Given the way in which the GOSUB idea has been enhanced to provide the DEF PROC statement, it is a shame a parallel development of the ON ... statement wasn't made. For example, there could be an "ON expression PROC" statement, where one of a list of procedures is executed dependent upon the value of the expression. More generally, a statement such as:

```
100 ON expression DO statement {,statement}* [ELSE statement*]
```

could have been provided. This nearly provides the generality of the Pascal "case" statement. If enough people write to Acorn, maybe they can be persuaded to enhance BBC BASIC even further. (It worked for the Star Trek fans who wanted Paramount to make a Trek film – they got two!) On the other hand, you may as well wait for Pascal to arrive on the BBC Computer if you want to write large, structured programs.

The Computed GOTO

The ON ... statement is often called the computed GOTO, clearly because the destination of the GOTO/GOSUB is computed from the expression after the ON. However, all GOTOs in BBC BASIC (and many other micro BASICs) can be called "computed", as the actual form of the statement is "GOTO expression" (or "GOSUB expression"). The expression is usually a line number constant (e.g. 900, 1234), but could be more complex, such as A%, 100*L%+100 and so on. This section is dedicated to deterring the user from taking advantage of this form of statement.

The first two reasons are readability and robustness. The ON ... GOTO used in the example above could be replaced by the much shorter line:

```
140 GOTO choice%*1000
```

It uses a simple expression. However, its presence does mean that anyone trying to follow the program has to do some multiplications just to find out where the program is going. This becomes worse when the expression becomes more complex, and if many such computed GOTOs are used in the program. Also, there is no equivalent of an ELSE part in the "GOTO expression" form. The range of "expression" has to be checked before each GOTO is executed. This checking can be omitted if the programmer is "sure" that the expression will in all cases yield a proper line number. This decreases the robustness of the program, and if the wrong line number is generated by the expression, the fault can be very hard to detect and correct.

The other reason for not using GOTO expression manifests itself when the program comes to be renumbered. The renumber command in BBC BASIC changes all the line numbers in the program so that they start at 10 (or whatever number is specified by the first optional parameter of RENUMBER), and increase in steps of 10 (or the step given by the second optional parameter). RENUMBER also changes all GOTO, GOSUB etc. statements so that the destination lines correspond to the renumbered lines. However, the GOTOs can only be changed correctly if the statements are of the form "GOTO line", where "line" is a constant (100, 23452), NOT a general expression. The consequence of this is that if your program uses statements such as GOTO X%, or even GOTO 100*10, it will not work properly after it has been renumbered.

Given the arguments presented above, there should be very few cases that justify the "GOTO expression" form of the statement. It's not as if there is no alternative (i.e. the ON ... GOTO/GOSUB ... ELSE). I recently saw a ZX BASIC program that included the line:

```
136 GOTO VAL(MIDS("0100030012001400", A*4+1,4))
```

(I translated it into BBC BASIC to make it more understandable.) I will leave it as an exercise for the reader to calculate the probability that any program incorporating such a line will work.

2.2.3   The FOR ... NEXT Loop

The last two sections dealt with the "selection" statements of BBC BASIC. The next two describe the "repetition" or looping constructs. Every version of BASIC worthy of that name implements the FOR ... NEXT loop. The general form of the construct is shown below.

```
100 FOR var=expr TO expr {STEP expr}
110 statement*
120 ..... (ditto)
130 NEXT {var}
```

Stated another way, the FOR statement is followed by a number (possibly zero) of statements, which are followed by a NEXT statement. The statements enclosed between the FOR and NEXT parts are executed a number of times, the number being determined by the two (or three) expressions in the FOR part. An actual example will make things clearer.

```
100 FOR I%=32 TO 126
110    PRINT CHR$(I%);
120 NEXT I%
130 END
```

The variable I% is called the looping variable. (This is the "var" part in the general form given above.) The looping variable can be any type of numeric variable, e.g. a%, ABC, L%(12,2), !&70. The last example is not a variable per se, but the four memory locations &70 ... &73 are used as if they are one, and can be treated just as a normal integer, e.g. A%. This applies to other statements, e.g. READ !&70, INPUT !&70 are perfectly acceptable.

The FOR statement in line 100 above sets the variable I% to 32. This is called the start value of the loop. The statements between the FOR and the NEXT are now executed. This is just the PRINT at line 110. When the NEXT is encountered, the looping variable is incremented by one. If there had been a STEP part in line 100, I% would have been incremented by the value of the expression after the word STEP. Since it was omitted, the step is taken as being one. The value of I% is compared with 126 – the end value. Since it is less than this, the statement in the body of the loop (line 110) is re-executed. This continues until I% has been incremented to a value greater than the end value, i.e. 127 in this example.

The numeric expressions for the start, end and step value can of course be arbitrarily complex; they are evaluated just once when the FOR is first encountered. After that, the end and step values are stored for use by the NEXT statement. The step can be negative, in which case the condition for the loop terminating (instead of jumping back to the statement after the NEXT) is that the looping variable is less than the limit. For example, to print the character set of the computer backwards, the following would be used

```
100 FOR I%=126 TO 32 STEP -1
110    PRINT CHR$(I%);
120 NEXT I%
130 END
```

In this case, I% would be initialised to 126, and would be "incremented" by −1 each time through the loop, until I% was less than 32. Note that since I% is not tested until the NEXT is reached, the statements in the loop are always executed at least once. This is not the way FOR ... NEXT loops should operate. For example, the loop with an initial line:

```
100 FOR I%=10 TO 5
```

should never have its statements executed, as the start value is greater than the end value and the step is positive. The test should be made at the FOR instead of the NEXT, but this way of implementing FOR ... NEXTs is rarely used on micro computer BASICs (an exception being ZX BASIC). Bearing this behaviour in mind (something you should do whenever using FOR ... NEXT loops), it is possible to obtain a formula for the number of times, N%, that a loop will be executed, viz.

```
IF (end-start)*step < 0 THEN N%=1 ELSE N%=(end-start)/step + 1
```

For example, the loop with initial line:

```
100 FOR I=3.5 TO 12 STEP .25
```

will execute $(12-3.5)/0.25+1 = 35$ times. Beware though! When using loops with non-integer looping variables and non-integer steps, the behaviour of the loop is not always so predictable. The example above is all right, as all the expressions used can be represented as exact quantities in binary (see Chapter 1). However, the loop below has a step of 0.1, which is a recurring binary fraction. That means it cannot be represented exactly in binary notation, and when it is repeatedly added to I, the small but significant error involved accumulates. Eventually the error becomes so great that I is printed with a fractional part of 3.59999999 instead 3.6. Errors such as this mean that FOR ... NEXT loops with real numbers for steps may execute for one iteration more or less than intended.

```
100 FOR I=0 TO 5 STEP .1
110     PRINT I
120 NEXT I
130 END
```

The cure for this ailment is to use integer looping variables wherever possible. This has the added advantage of executing much more quickly than the equivalent real loop. Obviously integer loops cannot be used as a substitute for fractional valued real loops without some scaling. For example, the loop above could become

```
100 FOR I%=0 TO 50
110     PRINT I%/10
120 NEXT I%
130 END
```

It is possible to have nested FOR ... NEXT loops. This means that some of the statements between a FOR and NEXT themselves form a FOR ... NEXT loop. The example below shows a rather slow way of finding prime numbers.

```
100 REM     THE PRIMES BETWEEN 2 AND 997
110 PRINT 2,3;
120 FOR I%=5 TO 997 STEP 2
130     FOR J%=3 TO SQR(I%) STEP 2
140         IF I% MOD J% = 0 THEN 170
150     NEXT J%
160     PRINT I%;
170 NEXT I%
180 END
```

Recall from the general form of the FOR ... NEXT statement that including the name of the looping variable after the NEXT is optional. The program above illustrates why it is a good idea always to include it. Line 140 jumps out of the inner loop under certain conditions. (The condition is that J% divides exactly into I% and is therefore a factor. This means that I% cannot be a prime number, so a jump to the NEXT I% is made to start testing the next number.) Imagine that the J% and I% were omitted from the NEXTs at lines 150 and 170 respectively. When the jump is made at line 140, the next statement to be executed is the NEXT at line 170. If the I% were not present after the NEXT, BASIC would execute by default the NEXT of the innermost FOR ... loop. (There is no way that BASIC can detect a jump out of a loop, so it assumes the first NEXT to be encountered belongs to the most recent FOR.) A NEXT J% would therefore be executed, and a jump would be made to line 140 (the line after the FOR J%=..). This is of course erroneous. What was intended was a NEXT I%. When the looping variable is included after a NEXT, BASIC automatically discards all loops until the one matching the looping variable given is found. In this example, the FOR J%... loop is "forgotten" when the NEXT I% is encountered, and the program executes correctly.

You may argue that jumping out of FOR ... NEXT loop is not exactly the height of elegance and should not even be contemplated. You might even argue that instead, J% should be assigned a value greater than the end value. In most people's eyes, this is even worse – the value of a looping variable is sacrosanct and should never be altered inside the loop apart from by the NEXT statement. Branching out of a loop is sometimes unavoidable and should cause no problems as long as all the NEXTs have their appropriate looping variable names included. What you should never do is branch back into a loop after exiting it. (Except of course when returning from a subroutine or user-defined procedure. This is different as the branching is under the control of BASIC, and is therefore much safer than GOTOs programmed by the user.) A similarly abysmal practice is having multiple NEXTs belonging to one FOR. I have actually seen this in a com-mercially sold stock control program. Presumably the programmer knew what he was doing. I certainly didn't, and it was I who had to try to modify the program to accept more items of stock. In the end I re-wrote the whole thing. Avoid such tricks, they may make the program run slightly quicker (which I believe was the "benefit" claimed by the author of the stock control program in its only REM statement), but when it comes to changing the program later, the misery caused quickly nullifies any such advantage. When one of my lecturers suspects a student of trying to make his program "too clever by half", he only gives the work half marks. It's a shame a similar practice can't be adopted with the wages of some programmers claiming to write "commercial quality" software on micros.

It is possible to close more than one FOR loop with a single NEXT:

```
100 FOR i%=0 TO 100
110    FOR j%=1 TO 51 STEP 2
120       REM blah blah
130 NEXT j%,i%
```

This is convenient, but it mucks up the indentation of LIST under LISTO2. LIST only decreases the indentation when a NEXT is encountered. In the example above, there are two FORs and one NEXT, so the second loop isn't closed as far as LIST is concerned.

A common use for FOR ... NEXT loops is to cause a delay in the execution of the program, i.e. it "does nothing" for a certain amount of time. The line below is typical:

```
100 FOR I%=0 TO 10000:NEXT I%
```

The body of the loop is a null statement. Since even updating the value of the looping variable takes a finite amount of time, the loop above will "halt" the program for a significant period. I mention this use of the FOR . . . NEXT simply to advise against using it on the BBC Micro. The reason is two fold. Firstly, the time delay obtained will vary depending on what type of operating system you have in your machine, and what external devices (e.g. Teletext adaptor, disc drives) are connected to it. Early BBC Computers came fitted with MOS 0.1 in EPROM. This is a bug-infested version which is housed in four chips placed in the ROM sockets on the main board. When these are fitted, the machine works at slower than normal speed, "normal" being when the MOS 0.1 or 1.0 ROMs are fitted. Line 100 above takes 2.27 seconds on my (MOS 0.1 EPROM) machine. The chances are that it will take less on your machine. This unpredictability makes it pointless using (in BBC BASIC) FOR . . . NEXT loops for delays, especially when (the second reason) there is a very accurate built-in timer on the BBC machine. This is accessed in BASIC using the TIME pseudo-variable. By using TIME in a null-bodied REPEAT . . . UNTIL loop (see next section), you can program delays from 10 milliseconds to a year and four months, which should be long enough for most purposes.

2.2.4   The REPEAT . . . UNTIL Loop

The subject of this section is loosely related to the FOR . . . NEXT loop. In fact, the REPEAT . . . UNTIL construct is just a more general way of performing repetition. The statement's syntax is:

```
100 REPEAT statement*
110 statement*
120 ..... (ditto)
130 UNTIL expression
```

The similarities to the construct described in the previous section are apparent from the skeleton above: a number (possibly zero) of statements are enclosed between two special statements. In this case REPEAT marks the start of the loop, UNTIL its end. The expression after UNTIL can be any expression that yields a numerical value, as with the IF . . . statement. It is usually a comparison between two or more numerical or string expressions (i.e. a relational expression), possibly using the logical operators such as AND and OR.

When the REPEAT is encountered during execution of a program, nothing happens overtly; however, BASIC remembers the point in the program that comes immediately after the REPEAT. This information is used later. The statements which precede the UNTIL are then executed. When then UNTIL is reached, the expression that follows is evaluated. If the result is non-zero (TRUE), the program carries on as if nothing had happened. IF the expression yields a FALSE result though, the program branches back to the point in the program immediately following the REPEAT. The process of executing statements and branching back is REPEATed UNTIL the expression yields a TRUE value, hence the construct's name.

The statements below cause a delay of one second in the execution of the program.

```
100 T%=TIME
110 REPEAT
120 UNTIL TIME-T%=100
```

The variable T% is used to store the value of the built-in timer "now". Lines 110 and 120 then do nothing (there are no statements in the body of the loop) until 100 units have elapsed on the timer. Since the timer counts in hundredths of seconds, this represents a delay of one second. The pseudo-variable TIME is treated as a normal integer variable (except that it must not be assigned using LET; TIME=123 suffices). It is therefore possible to program delays from 10 milliseconds to $2^{32}/100$ seconds, which is about a year and four months. The program below uses the BBC Computer as a £300 alarm clock. The alarm sounds eight hours from when the program is run.

```
100 T%=TIME:REPEAT UNTIL TIME-T%=2880000
110 F%=0
120 REPEAT
130    SOUND 1,F%,-15,0
140    F%=(F%+1) MOD 50
150 UNTIL FALSE
```

Short as it is, the program contains a couple of noteworthy details. The whole of the time delay part is on one line. This is such a common use of the REPEAT ... UNTIL construct that it is hardly worth putting each statement on a line of its own. Notice that there is no colon (:) between the REPEAT and UNTIL. This is the general case with REPEAT − it does not have to be separated from the next statement, unlike the FOR in a FOR ... NEXT loop. The "2880000" in line 100 could be replaced by the expression

```
100*(3600*hrs + 60*mins + secs)
```

where the meanings of the three variables are obvious. The second thing to notice is that the second loop never terminates. The expression after the UNTIL is simply the function FALSE, which always returns zero. Therefore, the opportunity to leave the loop never arises, and the alarm sounds until ESCAPE is pressed or the power is removed.

The program below illustrates a more typical use of the REPEAT loop. It sorts an array of numbers into ascending order using the bubble sort. This method is noted for its simplicity and inefficiency. The sort works by interchanging adjacent pairs of numbers in the array which are out of order until all the numbers are sorted. I won't go into further detail about how the sort works, partly because it is not important to the current topic, and also because a couple of far better sort routines are presented in section 2.2.5.

```
100 REM     Sort Program
120 REM     Fill A%() with random numbers
130 n%=50
140 DIM a%(n%)
150 FOR i%=0 TO n%
160     a%(i%)=RND(100)
170 NEXT i%
180
190 REM    Now sort a%()
200 j%=n%-1
210 REPEAT
220    end%=TRUE
230    FOR i%=0 TO j%
240       IF a%(i%) <= a%(i%+1) THEN 300
250          REM     Exchange elements and reset end%
260          temp%=a%(i%)
270          a%(i%)=a%(i%+1)
280          a%(i%+1)=temp%
290          end%=FALSE
300    NEXT i%
310    j%=j%-1
320 UNTIL end% OR j%=0
330
340 REM    Now print the sorted array
350 FOR i%=0 TO n%
360    PRINT a%(i%);
370 NEXT i%
380 PRINT
390 END
```

There are a couple of points of interest. The IF at line 240 actually causes a branch over the five lines between it and line 300, just the kind of thing I was criticising BASIC for earlier. My excuse is that if the condition were reversed, i.e "a%(i%) > a%(i%+1)", there would be four statements on the IF line. It is far easier to read a program with only a couple of statements on each line, so I opted for the method shown above instead of the more "structured" but less tidy approach. I will add IFs used in this way to the list of "acceptable GOTOs" presented at the end of the chapter.

The other thing to realise is that the use of the integer array "a%()" is by no means mandatory; the program will sort arrays of reals and strings equally well by replacing all occurrences of a%() with a() or a$() repectively (or of course any other valid name).

Although not very good practice, jumping out of FOR ... NEXT loops is acceptable in certain situations. This is not true of REPEAT loops. Unlike FORs, there is no way to distinguish which REPEAT a particular UNTIL belongs to. Because of this, jumping out of a REPEAT loop which is embedded in another loop will cause an error. It is wise not to jump out of any REPEAT loop, even if it is at the outermost level – cultivating good habits from the start will pay dividends later. The need to exit a REPEAT loop from a place other than the corresponding UNTIL can usually be avoided by making the UNTIL expression test all possible exit conditions. I was surprised to see the segment below (which I have translated into BBC BASIC) given in a fairly "heavy" computer science book.

```
100 REPEAT
110    IF i<j THEN GOSUB 1000 ELSE GOTO 130
120 UNTIL FALSE
130 .....
```

This can easily be changed to obviate the need for a GOTO out of the loop.

```
100 REPEAT
110    IF i<j THEN GOSUB 1000
120 UNTIL i>=j
130 .....
```

Jumping out of an infinite loop is particularly stupid – why make it impossible to exit normally (via the UNTIL) and then make an explicit branch out?

The next example program plays a number guessing game. The user thinks of a number between 0 and 100. The computer tries to guess what the number is by asking the user if it is above or below successive guesses. The statements which generate the guess and accept the user's response are embedded in a REPEAT loop. The loop has two exit conditions. The first is that the guess is correct. The second is that the computer has generated enough guesses to ensure a correct guess, no matter what number the user originally thought of. It is possible to predict the maximum number of guesses required to locate a number within a certain range because of the method used to generate each try. This is a version of the binary search given in the last chapter.

```
100 REM      Number Guesser
110
120 PRINT"You think of a number between 0 and 100"
130 PRINT"and I'll try to guess what it is."
140 hi%=100
150 lo%=0
160 count%=0
170 REPEAT
```

```
180    guess%=(lo% + hi%) DIV 2
190    PRINT'"I reckon it's ";guess%
210    PRINT"high, low or correct (h, l or c) ";
210    REPEAT
220        rep$=CHR$(GET OR 32)
230    UNTIL INSTR("hlc", rep$)
240    PRINT rep$
250    IF rep$ = "h" THEN hi%=guess% - 1
260    IF rep$ = "l" THEN lo%=guess% + 1
280    count%=count% + 1
290    IF rep$ = "c" THEN PRINT'"In a mere ";count%;" guesses!!"
300 UNTIL count% > 6 OR rep$ = "c"
310 IF count% > 7 THEN PRINT'"CHEAT - I must have got it by now!!"
320 END
```

The embedded loop between line 210 and 230 is used to ignore anything the user types apart from the legal responses "h", "l" and "c", and the upper case equivalents. Such input loops are very useful, and are discussed in detail in the next chapter.

I said at the start of this section that the REPEAT loop is more general than the FOR loop because the number of times it iterates is determined by a relation rather than a formula. However, there are some situations where even the REPEAT loop is not sufficiently general. The reason is that, like the FOR ... NEXT, the statements in the body of the loop are always excuted at least once. The situation sometimes arises where it is desirable for the statements not to be executed at all. The "null-situation" arises frequently in computer science, and programs are not robust if they cannot deal with empty input data as easily as the more normal cases. This problem can be illustrated in terms of the FOR ... NEXT loop. (Remember that strictly speaking, it should be possible to avoid the statements in the body of a FOR ... NEXT, though this is not possible in the BBC BASIC version.) The short piece of program below converts each character in a string to its lower case equivalent if it is an upper case letter; other characters remain unchanged.

```
100 INPUT"Type in a string ",a$
110 b$=""
120 FOR i%=1 TO LEN(a$)
130     b$=b$+CHR$(ASC(MID$(a$, i%, 1)) OR 32)
140 NEXT i%
150 PRINT a$;" is ";b$;" in lower case"
160 END
```

This program works in all cases except one – when the user just presses RETURN in response to the INPUT at line 100. This makes a$ as the null string whose length is zero. In an ideal world, the FOR ... NEXT loop scanning lines

120 to 140 would not be executed in this case, as the end value (0) is less than the start value and the step is positive. The world of BBC BASIC is not quite ideal, and line 130 is executed. The ASC function returns −1 when given a null argument. −1 OR 32 is −1, so b$ becomes CHR$(−1). BBC BASIC only uses the eight least significant bits, so b$ actually becomes CHR$(255). This is of course wrong; b$ should be the null string if a$ is. The discrepancy caused by the FOR ... NEXT executing once when it wasn't supposed to may not seem too drastic, but any error is serious, especially when it is due to a weakness of the programming language. The example below shows a similar problem caused by the REPEAT loop's inability to iterate zero times.

```
100 INPUT"Type in two numbers ",a%,b%
110 REPEAT
120    IF a% > b% THEN a%=a%-b% ELSE b%=b%-a%
130 UNTIL a% = b%
140 PRINT"Their HCF is ";a%
150 END
```

The program finds the highest common factor (HCF) of two numbers. This is the highest number which will divide exactly into both numbers. The method used in the program is called the euclidean method, and can be stated in English as "repeatedly subtract the smaller number from the larger until they are equal". The program works fine with pairs of numbers that are different. For example, given 32 and 24, the program returns 8. A little thought will reveal that eight is the largest number that will divide exactly into 24 and 32. When the two numbers are the same, however, the program fails. The problem occurs because of the subtraction at line 120. The ELSE part makes b% equal to the difference of the two numbers, this being zero if they are the same. From then on, the THEN part repeatedly subtracts b% (zero) from a% in a vain attempt to reduce the value of the latter to the former. This results in an infinite loop, the UNTIL condition never being satisfied.

Both the examples given have been simple, and their failures easy to understand when examined in isolation. However, when the incorrect handling of null or special cases causes a whole program to fail, the fault can be very hard to track down. In the case of the FOR ... NEXT loop, the fault is one of implementation – the structure does not operate exactly as it should. The REPEAT ... UNTIL is slightly different; it works exactly as it should, but could be replaced by the more versatile WHILE loop, whose operation deals properly with null cases. The ways the two loops have been implemented suggests a certain degree of "opting out". The correct FOR loop and the WHILE loop are both harder to implement than BBC BASIC's equivalents. In the example above, correct operation can be achieved inserting the line

```
105 IF a% = b% THEN 140
```

The moral is: if you suspect the program may be given null or "border line" data, perform checks before loops which will not work correctly in such situations.

It useful to see how REPEAT loops are implemented using GOTOs. The inspection of most BASIC programs reveals loops that arise from backwards branches. The examples below show some skeleton programs in standard BASIC, along with the BBC BASIC translations.

Standard BASIC

```
260 F=1
270 IF ABS(H)>0 THEN 290
280 GOTO 320
290 GOSUB 2000
300 F=F*M
310 GOTO 270
320 .....
```

BBC BASIC

```
260 f=1
270 IF ABS(h) <= 0 THEN 320
280 REPEAT
290    GOSUB 2000
300    f=f*m
310 UNTIL ABS(h) <= 0
320 .....
```

The standard BASIC program actually implements a WHILE loop, as the body (GOSUB 2000 and F=F*M) might never be executed. Because of this the BBC BASIC version still needs an IF ... to jump over the REPEAT loop. The Pascal version of this segment is the clearest:

```
while abs(h) > 0 do
   begin
      sub2000;
      f := f*m
   end;
```

The while works like the REPEAT loop, but the condition is the opposite to the UNTIL condition; the statements are executed while abs(h)>0 instead of UNTIL ABS(h)<=0. The difference is that in the former case there is the chance that the statements are executed while abs(h)>0 instead of UNTIL ABS(h)<=0. This difference means that in the former case there is the chance that the body of the loops will never be executed (if the while condition is initially false).

The next example is a common type of processing, taking some input from a file and manipulating it in some way until the file is exhausted. More generally, the processed data would be written onto another file, but that would cloud the issue. The program below (written in standard BASIC but using BBC BASIC's file commands) read numbers from a file and makes a count of the number of positive and negative numbers.

Standard BASIC

```
100 C=OPENIN("DATA")
110 REM     ZERO COUNTS
120 C1=0
130 C2=0
140 INPUT#C,N
150 IF N<0 THEN 180
160 C1=C1+1
170 GOTO 190
180 C2=C2+1
190 IF NOT EOF#C THEN 140
200 .....
```

The BBC BASIC version is as follows:

```
100 chan=OPENIN("DATA")
110 pos_count=0
120 neg_count=0
130 REPEAT
140    INPUT#chan, num
150    IF num < 0 THEN neg_count=neg_count+1 ELSE pos_count=pos_count+1
160 UNTIL EOF#chan
170 ....
```

Few people would deny that the second version is much clearer. Line 150 can be changed to two simple assignments by realising that the relational operators return numbers, 0 for FALSE and −1 for TRUE.

```
150 pos_count=pos_count - (num >= 0)
155 neg_count=neg_count - (num < 0)
```

The brackets are necessary because all the arithmetic operators have higher precedences than the relational ones. Without the brackets, the expression in line 150 would be "(pos_count−num) >=0", which is of course totally different. Whether such "tricks" should be used is very debatable. They make the program less readable, especially if the reader doesn't know about the 0/−1 truth values. This example isn't a very good one, because there are always two assignments in the second form, whereas in the first version the assignments were mutually exclusive (i.e. appeared in different clauses of an IF ... THEN ... ELSE), so only one was executed on each iteration of the loop.

Another form of trickery related to the one above is shortening IF ... THEN ... ELSEs of the form

```
100 IF condition THEN a=expression ELSE a=0
```

to

```
100 a=expression AND condition
```

An example might be

```
      100 IF z1>=z2 THEN x=z1+z2 ELSE x=0
to    100 x=z1+z2 AND z1>=z2
```

There is a restriction in that "expression" must yield an integer value. Again, statements such as this detract from the legibility of programs. However, it is as well to know about such devices; some BASICs require their use to achieve a limited IF . . . THEN . . . ELSE capability. One such BASIC is the ZX variety. Since at least some of the half million ZX81 owners will move up to the BBC Micro, statements such as line 100 above will no doubt be used in BBC BASIC programs. Understanding tricks used by other people is good preparation for debugging their programs; the hard thing is to resist the temptation of using such contrivances in your own programs.

2.2.5 User-defined Procedures

The last four sections have dealt with the flow control statements, selection and repetition. I now move on to the two major subprogram features of BBC BASIC. These are user-defined procedures and functions. The former is the subject of this section; user-defined functions are covered in section 2.2.6. The standard GOSUB . . . RETURN combination is not described because it is so much less useful than the BBC BASIC DEF PROC statement. I do assume, however, that you have a fair idea of how the GOSUB statement works. A procedure is a group of statements which forms a particular section of the solution to a Problem. The statements which forms a particular section of the solution to a problem. The statements example, a filing program might need a routine to sort an array of numbers into ascending order. This routine could be written as a procedure and tested in a small program, and when it works incorporated into the filing program. By writing and testing useful procedures in this way, a "library" of routines can be built up, and whenever a particular problem needs to be solved, the library can be consulted to see if any procedures which are required in the solution have already been written. This saves much re-writing of programs, and is a standard feature of almost all large computer systems. The term "software tools" has been coined to describe programs which are used over and over again, and there is no reason why the same techniques cannot be applied to microcomputer software.

Apart from assisting in the creation of software tool libraries, the use of procedures in programs is a great aid to readability and reliability. One of the limitations of the human programmer (which description applies to most of the current users of computers) is his inability to thoroughly understand more than about a page of program at a time. Dijkstra calls this "our inability to do much". It means that when we are faced with a listing a thousand lines long, the task of reading it and understanding the purpose of each statement in detail is hopelessly beyond the capabilities of any human (even a Great Man). Unless, that is, the program has been written in such a way that the whole solution is stated in a relatively small space, say one page, and this page contains numerous calls to subprograms (which have been descriptively named) which perform the low-level work. Of course, a subprogram may itself be too complex to write in a manageable number of lines, so is in turn written using calls to even lower-level routines.

The foregoing is all very abstract, and cannot be properly explained without the use of examples. The programs developed at the end of this chapter go some way in satisying this requirement; however, there is nothing like experience to improve one's programming skills. I urge you to try to adopt the techniques touched upon in this chapter when writing programs of any length, and to read the books dedicated to spreading the use of structured programming. It is a little hard to think of sources of "good BASIC programs"; that phrase has almost become a contradiction in terms. However, the book by [Beech] given in the Bibliography is one of the best for BASIC, and most Pascal text books are worth reading just for the example programs.

The syntax of user-defined procedures looks quite formidable when given in the notation I have adopted for expressing such things, but it is really very simple. Formally, it is

```
1000 DEF PROCname{(var [,var]*)} statement*
1010 statement*
1020 ..... (ditto)
1030 ENDPROC
```

The very first statement is the complex one. The DEF PROC statement has two purposes. Firstly, it marks the beginning of the statements that make up the procedure. Secondly, it gives the procedure a name, and also gives the parameters the procedure uses and their types. The "name" has the same rules as other variables. It is best to use lower case so that the name is clearly separated from the PROC part (there can be no space between PROC and "name"). The ENDPROC marks the end of the procedure's statements, and is akin to the RETURN from a GOSUB. Notice that it is only possible to enter a procedure from one place – via the DEF PROC line – whereas the first line of GOSUB routine can vary depending on the calling line. The latter method is not very satisfactory as if a subroutine is entered from many places, it is not very clear exactly what it does. The first examples of procedure definitions ignore the possibility of using parameters; these are described in detail below. The definition below shows a common use of procedures, to set up the values of various variables used in the program. Most programs require some form of initialisation, and it is a good idea to keep that part separate from the rest to make it easier to change without accidentally changing other unrelated lines.

```
10000 DEF PROCinit
10010    REM Set up-the look-up table
10020    n%=99
10030    DIM a%(n%)
10040    FOR i%=0 to n%
10050       READ a%(i%)
10060    NEXT i%
```

```
10070    DATA 12, -13, 42, 12, .......
10080 ENDPROC
11000 DEF PROCins
11010    REM Print instructions
11020    CLS
11030    PRINT''"    The object of this game is ....."
11040    PRINT"blah blah blah ......"
11050    PRINT"yak yak yak ......"
11090 ENDPROC
```

The second procedure prints out the instructions to some hypothetical game. Notice that the line numbers of the procedure definitions are quite high. This is because procedures (and functions) are defined in a part of the program that is not actually executed in normal circumstances. At the end is as good a place as any. Some people claim that placing definitions at the end slows the program down, as when the procedures come to be called (see below), BASIC has to search through the whole of the preceding code to find the definition. This is rubbish – after the very first time a user-defined procedure or function is used, BASIC remembers exactly where the DEF statement is stored, and using a procedure is then as fast as accessing a normal variable, irrespective of its position in the program. A procedure is called by stating its name preceded with PROC. This is equivalent of saying "GOSUB line", though you only need to remember the name of the procedure instead of its first line number. A program using the two procedures above might contain the following lines.

```
100 REM   Spac Invaders
110 PROCinit
120 PRINT"Do you need instructions ";
130 INPUT yn$
140 IF LEFT$(yn$,1)="Y" THEN PROCins
150 ......
160 ......
300 END
500 REM    procedure and function definitions
```

The PROCname statement may be used wherever a statement is required, including from within the definition of another procedure or function. The statements inside a definition can be anything except MODE (the reason for this will become clear later).

The procedure definitions given above are really nothing more than glorified versions of the GOSUB statement. The advantage of giving a routine a name instead of a line number is significant but not really dramatic. The addition of parameters to the routine is rather more useful. The majority of subroutines written in standard BASIC use parameters, though in a way obscured by the necessity to set them up with lots of assignments and the use of global variables. I will use the circle example given in section 2.1.1 to illustrate a procedure definition with parameters.

```
10000 DEF PROCcircle(x%, y%, r%, col%)
10010    REM    draws a circle at (x%,y%) of
10020    REM    radius r% in colour col%.
10030    REM    (see chapter four)
10040    step=4 / r%
10050    GCOL 0, col%
10060    MOVE x%+r%, y%
10070    FOR th=step TO 2*PI STEP step
10080       DRAW x%+r%*COS(th), y%+r%*SIN(th)
10090    NEXT th
10100 ENDPROC
```

The mechanics of the procedure are unimportant at the moment; the point of interest in this chapter is the parameter passing mechanism. The parameters of the procedure are listed in brackets after the DEF part. In the present example, there are four parameters, all integers. It is possible to have real and string parameters as well. The variables x%, y%, r% and col% above are called the formal parameters of the procedure. They are used inside the procedure definition to represent the values passed to the procedure when it is called. The listing below is an example of how PROCcircle might be used.

```
100 FOR r%=10 TO 320 STEP 16
110    PROCcircle(r%*4, 512, r%, 1)
120 NEXT r%
130 END
```

It is assumed that the computer is in a graphics mode and that PROCcircle has been defined somewhere in the program. When the procedure is called at line 110, the expressions given in brackets after the PROCcircle (i.e. "r%*4", "512", "r%"and "1") are evaluated. These values are then assigned to the variables x%, y%, r% and col% respectively. These variables are special; they exist only when PROCcircle is "active", i.e. between the statements PROCcircle and ENDPROC being executed. After the ENDPROC, they are forgotten. These formal parameter variables are special in other ways too. Notice that r% is used as a parameter inside the procedure, and also as a looping variable outside it. These two versions of r% are distinct from each other. It so happens in this example that they have the same value because the value given to the parameter r% is just the looping variable r%. However, if PROCcircle performed some assignment which changed r%, it would only be r% the parameter that is altered, not the other (global) r%. To show this more clearly, and to explain why you can't use MODE in a procedure (or function), I will use a skeletal program containing a parameterised procedure and some clashing names.

```
100 REM   Trivial example program
```

```
110 a%=1: b%=2: c%=3
120 PRINT a%, b%, c%
130 PROCdemo(a%, b%, c%)
140 PRINT a%, b%, c%
150 END
160
170
10000 DEF PROCdemo(a%, b%, x%)
10010    REM   Trivial example procedure
10020    a%=a%*2: b%=b%*2
10030    c%=c%*2: x%=x%*2
10040    PRINT a%, b%, c%, x%
10050 ENDPROC
```

When run, the program will print out the following:

```
1        2        3
2        4        6        6
1        2        6
```

The three lines of output can be explained as follows: the first one is straight-forward; line 120 simply prints the values of a%, b%, c% that have just been assigned to them in line 110. The next PRINT to be executed is that at line 10040. Lines 10020 and 10030 multiply all the variables accessible from PROCdemo by two. These variables a% (local), b% (local), c% (global; as there is no parameter c% the external version is still accessible from inside the procedure) and x% (local). The multiplication of a% and b% by two has no effect on the global variables a% and b% as these are effectively "hidden" by the existence of the parameters with the same names. When the last PRINT is executed at line 140, the global variables a% and b% are used, as the parameters a% and b% are local to PROCdemo and are lost when the ENDPROC is encountered. Thus, the first two values are the same as in the very first PRINT statement; a% and b% being unaffected by the assignments to the parameters a% and b%. The value of c%, however, was changed inside the procedure because there was no local variable of that name to use.

The way in which global variables suddenly disappear when the program enters a procedure with parameters of the same name, and reappear after the ENDPROC is executed is not as magical as it seems. When a PROC is executed, BASIC looks for all the variable names in the parameter list, if one is present. If a parameter variable doesn't exist already, one of that name is created, as if by a LET statement. Once all the parameters have been created (if necessary), BASIC stores their current values in an area of memory called the stack. This is located at HIMEM, and "grows" down as more values are added to it. Then the parameter variables are set-up with the corresponding values in the calling PROC for use inside the procedure. When the ENDPROC is executed, the values that were saved on the stack are re-assigned to the parameter variables.

The way in which the value of the global variable c% is changed by PROCdemo is called a side-effect. The procedure has altered the value of a global variable, an action which may sometimes be desirable (for reasons explained below), but often we want to guard against the use of a procedure producing unwanted changes in global variables. The obvious way to achieve this is to give all the variables used in a procedure definition special names. This is tedious, as it limits the way in which variables can be given meaningful names. For example, consider the circle routine, PROCcircle, given earlier. There are two variables, "step" and "th", which are used only within the procedure itself. If the program that contained PROCcircle also had variables of the same names, these would have their values unwantedly altered by the procedure. By inserting the line

```
10035 LOCAL step, th
```

into the procedure declaration, two new temporary variables are created for use in PROCcircle. The assignments to step and th would have no effect on global variables of the same names, and after the procedure had finished executing, any variable called step or th would be retrieved as normal. LOCAL variables can be viewed as parameters which aren't initialised when the procedure is called. Actually, the LOCAL statement initialises its numeric variables to zero and strings to the null string "". The way LOCAL is used is a little like DIM, viz.

```
10010 LOCAL A%, str$, x, y
```
cf.
```
10010 DIM A%(100), str$(10), x(10), y(10)
```

Like LOCAL, DIM initialises its variables to zero or null as appropriate.

With the exception of recursion, all of the facilities of BBC BASIC procedures have been discussed. I now present a few examples of procedure definitions to consolidate the points covered above. The first example of a procedure is one that draws a bar-chart or histogram. The data for the histogram is held in an array a%(), and the parameters of the procedure determine which of the elements in the array are used, and what character is used to draw the bars.

```
10000 DEF PROChistogram(first%, last%, ch$)
10010    REM    draws a histogram of the values
10020    REM    in a%(first%) to a%(last%). Uses
10030    REM    the character ch$ to draw bars.
10040    REM    Check that ch$ is valid
10050    IF LEN(ch$) <> 1 OR ASC(ch$) < 32 THEN PRINT
             "Illegal Character":ENDPROC
10060    LOCAL max%, len%, i%, pc%, l%
10070    REM    Find the highest value for scaling
10080    max%=a%(first%)
10090    FOR i%=first%+1 TO last%
10100       IF a%(i%) > max% THEN max%=a%(i%)
10110    NEXT i%
10120    REM    Draw horizontal axis
```

```
10130    len%=60 : REM    maximum length of line
10140    CLS
10150    PRINT TAB(0,4);"Element";TAB(40);"per cent of ";max%
10160    PRINT TAB(13,6);STRING$(len%, ".")
10170    FOR i%=0 TO len%
10180       pc%=100*i% DIV len%
10190       IF pc% MOD 10 = 0 THEN PRINT TAB(13+i%,6);pc%;TAB(13+i%,7);"|"
10200    NEXT i%
10210    REM    Now the bars themselves
10220    FOR i%=first% TO last%
10230       l%=a%(i%)*len% DIV max%
10240       PRINT i%;" - ";STRING$(l%, ch$)
10250    NEXT i%
10260 ENDPROC
```

The procedure first finds the value of the highest element in the array (which must be greater then zero) which is used for scaling the bars. Most of the work is the drawing of the axes; the actual bar-drawing routine is only four lines long. The ENDPROC in line 10050 means that the procedure does not adhere to the "one entrance, one exit" principle. The only way to avoid this is to change the ENDPROC to a GOTO 10260, which is really not much better. At least with the ENDPROC statement you can be sure that control will return to the calling program; a GOTO always leaves scope for error in the destination line number. The histogram program is quite rudimentary, and needs an 80 column screen to work well (you could reduce len% to 25 for a 40 column mode, but this has even more limited resolution). In Chapter four, I give a better version using graphics instead of text characters.

The array a%() which holds the values to be plotted by PROChistogram is not passed to the procedure as a parameter, but is used globally. The reason is that it is only possible to have parameters which are single items such as abc, abc% and abc$. If array parameters were allowed, the whole array would have to copied to the local variable storage area. This is obviously very wasteful of space when large arrays are being used. When using arrays then, the procedure and main program must both know the name of the array to be used.

The next procedure is a more efficient sort routine than the bubble sort given earlier. The reason for the bubble sort's slowness is that it has to examine (and possibly swap) N elements on the first pass, N−1 elements on the second pass, then N−2 and so on until finally it examines just the first two elements. This is the mathematical series $1+2+3+...N$ where N is the number of elements being sorted. Mathematically inclined readers will find that the series can be expressed as $N*(N+1)/2$. This expression has an N squared term in, so the number of operations needed to sort N elements of an array using the bubble sort is proportional to the square of N. This means the time taken is also proportional to N squared. If

N is 10, and the time is 2 seconds, it would take 8 seconds to sort 20 elements, and 200 seconds to sort 100 elements. Obviously as N grows, the time taken to sort the array increases rather rapidly. It is this that makes the bubble sort inefficient.

There are several different sorting methods (algorithms) that have much better performance. It can be shown that the fastest sorts of the "compare and exchange" type we are interested in are O(N*LOG(N)). This means that the time taken to sort N elements is proportional to N*LOG(N). The bubble sort is O(N*N). The expression N*LOG(N) increases much slower with N than N*N, so obviously these O(N*LOG(N)) sorts are much better than the bubble sort. One such sort is the Shell sort. The procedure below uses this method to sort a%() into ascending order between the elements first% and last%.

```
20000 DEF PROCshell(first%, last%)
20010    REM    Sorts the array a%() into ascending
20020    REM    order between a%(first%) and a%(last%)
20030    LOCAL i%, j%, dist%, i1%, t%
20040    dist%=(last%-first%+1) DIV 2
20050    REPEAT
20060       FOR j%=first%+dist% TO last%
20070          FOR i%=j%-dist% TO first% STEP -dist%
20080             i1%=i%+dist%
20090             IF a%(i%) <= a%(i1%) THEN 20140
20100                t%=a%(i%)
20110                a%(i%)=a%(i1%)
20120                a%(i1%)=t%
20130          NEXT i%
20140       NEXT j%
20150       dist%=dist% DIV 2
20160    UNTIL dist%=0
20170 ENDPROC
```

An explanation of how the sort routine works will not be given, as not knowing how the numbers are actually sorted does not prevent you from using the procedure (not knowing how the internal combustion engine works doesn't stop people from driving to work). A couple of the books given in the Bibliography discuss sorting techniques in some detail, and the interested user is referred to them. As I mentioned above, the Shell sort is much more efficient than the bubble sort: the PROCshell sorts an array of 1000 integers in 110 seconds on my MOS 0.1 EPROM machine. The bubble sort would take about half an hour (I calculated that from the N*N rule combined with the fact that it takes 20.1 seconds to sort 100 numbers.) An even more efficient sort is given later to illustrate the use of recursion. The short program below can be used to illustrate graphically the effect of sorting an array. The histogram procedure is used to illustrate the state of an array of random numbers before and after sorting. The best mode to use is MODE 0, if you have sufficient memory, otherwise the histogram procedure will need to be altered.

```
100 REM     Demo for PROChistogram & PROCshell
110 n%=20
120 DIM a%(n%)
130 FOR i%=0 TO n%
140     a%(i%)=RND(50)+20
150 NEXT i%
160 PROChistogram(0, n%, "*")
170 PROCshell(0, n%)
180 INPUT"RETURN "in$
190 PROChistogram(0, n%, "*")
200 END
```

The next example is used to reveal a weakness in the way procedures are implemented in BBC BASIC. Specifically, there is a weakness in the way parameters are used. It is sometimes desirable to have a procedure perform some calculations on its parameters and then return the results of these calculations back to the main program. For example, it might be necessary to perform lots of polar to cartesian co-ordinate conversions in a program. (If you don't know what these terms mean, let alone why anyone should want to convert them, Chapter four might prove enlightening.) A procedure to perform this conversion might be written as follows:

```
10000 DEF PROCpol_cart(r, theta, x, y)
10010    REM    Converts from polar to rectangular
10020    REM    co-ordinates: (r, theta) -> (x, y)
10030    x=r*COS(theta)
10040    y=r*SIN(theta)
10050 ENDPROC
```

A typical call to the procedure would be "PROCpol_cart(12*r1,th1,x,y)". The idea is that the values of "r" and "theta" given in the call (12*r1 and th1 respectively) are used to find the corresponding x and y, which are then passed back to the main program in the global variables x and y. This will not work, as the two assignments in lines 10030 and 10040 only affect the parameters x and y, which are local to PROCpol_cart. When the ENDPROC is executed, the global x and y have their values restored from the stack as usual.

What we need to make this example work is the provision of what is known as "variable" or "reference" parameters. These work differently to the parameters already discussed in that any assignments to the formal parameters in the procedure's body also change the values of the actual parameters. In the example above, if x and y were variable parameters, the two assignments would also assign the global variables used in the calling PROC statement. Pascal and other languages use variable parameters to pass values back from a procedure to the main program. Their absence in BBC BASIC means that information can only be passed from the main program to a procedure, not the other way round. It is possible to use global variables whose names are known both to the main program and the procedure, but this is just the kind of thing we wanted to avoid by using parameters.

Recursive Procedures

The concept of recursion is usually introduced with recursive functions, and indeed the next section does contain examples of such functions. But since procedures are the subject of this section, recursive procedures will be explained first. Recursion is a mathematical device, and is akin to induction. If an object is defined recursively, the definition contains a reference to the object itself. I propose to illustrate this by giving a version of the Quicksort devised by C. A. R. Hoare (one of the co-authors of "Structured Programming", which puts him into the demigod league.) Imagine an array of numbers, say a%(), which is unsorted between elements 0 and 100. Choose the first element, a%(0). Use some method to move the value of a%(0) to the position in which it would appear in the sorted version of a%(). Call this element a%(n). Furthermore, say that a%(n) is swapped with a%(0), and that after they have been swapped, all elements a%(0) ... a%(n−1) are less than or equal to a%(n), and all elements a%(n+1)..a%(100) are greater or equal to a%(n). The array has now been split into two parts, with a%(n) in its correct final place. If the two parts of a%() below and above a%(n) are sorted (using the same technique), the whole array will be sorted. The procedure to do this is given in a rough form below.

```
10000 DEF PROCquick(first%, last%)
10010    REM    Sorts a%(first%) to a%(last%)
10020    REM    Find the correct place for a%(first%) in
10030    REM    a%(). Call this a%(n%). All elements below
10040    REM    n% <= a%(n%), all above n% >= a%(n%).
10050    REM    Swap a%(first%) and a%(n%)
10060    PROCquick(first%, n%-1)
10070    PROCquick(n%+1, last%)
10080 ENDPROC
```

The PROCquick in lines 10060 and 10070 may seem strange, but they are perfectly valid. Apart from the fact that the first part of the procedure is missing, there is something wrong with the definition above. Whenever a procedure calls itself, or recurses, there has to be the possibility that it will return eventually. This means that it has to be possible to call the procedure under certain conditions when the procedure will not recurse. The example above is "inifinitely recursive", as each call to PROCquick generates two more calls. What we need is a termination condition. In this case it is simply when first%>=last%; if there is only one or

124

less elements, they must already be sorted. All recursive definitions must eventually reach a point where it is unnecessary to make a recursive call. It occurs when the solution to that particular invocation of the procedure or function is trivial. The complete PROCquick is given below.

```
10000 DEF PROCquick(first%, last%)
10010    REM     Sorts a%(first%)..a%(last%)
10020    REM     Check for trivial case
10030    IF first% >= last% THEN ENDPROC
10040    REM     If not, we need some locals
10050    LOCAL i%, j%, temp%, test%
10060    i%=first%
10070    j%=last%+1
10080    test%=a%(first%)
10090    REM     Find correct position of test%
10100    REPEAT
10110       REPEAT i%=i%+1
10120       UNTIL a%(i%) >= test% OR i% = last%
10130       REPEAT j%=j%-1
10140       UNTIL a%(j%)= test%
10150       IF i%<j% THEN temp%=a%(i%):a%(i%)=a%(j%):a%(j%)=temp%
10160    UNTIL i% >= j%
10170    REM     Put test% into position
10180    a%(first%)=a%(j%)
10190    a%(j%)=test%
10200    REM     Now sort the other two parts
10210    PROCquick(first%, j%-1)
10220    PROCquick(j%+1, last%)
10230 ENDPROC
```

The Quicksort is nearly twice as fast as the Shell sort. The procedure above takes 58 seconds on average to sort 1000 integers. Note that although the Quicksort has a O(N*LOG(N)) behaviour, this is only for arrays that are unsorted. If the array is already almost sorted (in the same order or opposite order to which the routine is sorting), the performance degenerates to O(N*N) i.e. as bad as the bubble sort. Steps can be taken to avoid this behaviour by choosing the value of test% (which is called the pivot element) in a different manner. This is outside the scope of this book, but [Bowles] discusses it. See also [Horowitz] and/or [Goodman] for pictorial explanations of this and other sorting methods.

The iterative constructs such as FOR ... NEXT and REPEAT ... UNTIL can be expressed recursively. In fact, some languages only use recursion to perform repetition (for example, Logo and LISP, which are two languages oriented towards the manipulation of lists, themselves recursively defined objects). It is interesting to see how well-known constructs can be implemented recursively. First, consider the procedure below, which just counts.

```
1000 DEF PROCcount(n%)
1010    PRINT n%
1020    IF n%>0 THEN PROCcount(n%-1)
1030 ENDPROC
```

The statement "PROCcount(10)" will cause a "countdown" of the numbers 10 to 0. Note that each time the procedure recurses, the current value of n% is saved on the stack. These successive saves ensure that the value of n% is preserved at each level of recursion, so that it may be used again on the return from the next level. Figure 2.1 shows how the stack grows and shrinks after the call "PROCcount(3)".

To test your understanding of the saving and retrieval of parameters, try to predict the effect of adding the line:

```
1025    PRINT n%
```

to PROCcount. If you got it wrong, think hard!

PROCcount is a little like a FOR ... NEXT loop. The full recursive version of a FOR ... NEXT is given below.

```
1000 DEF PROCfor(i,last,step)
1010    REM Test for termination
1020    IF (last-i)*step < 0 THEN ENDPROC
1030    REM Do the "body" statements
1040    PROCbody
1050    REM Next iteration
1060    PROCfor(i+step,last,step)
1070 ENDPROC
2000 DEF PROCbody
2010    PRINT i
2020 ENDPROC
```

The line "FOR i=0 TO 20 STEP 5" would be performed by the call "PROCfor(0,20,5)". The statements which would occupy the body of the loop must be defined in PROCbody. Notice that the call "PROCfor(1,0,1)" would result in the initial call returning immediately, with no action. Thus the version of FOR ... NEXT implemented by PROCfor is the proper one, rather than the normal micro BASIC method. Also, it is quite general, and will work with negative steps, as in "PROCfor(10,0,-1)". The BBC BASIC FOR ... NEXT loop would be:

```
1000 DEF PROCfor(i,last,step)
1010    PROCbody
```

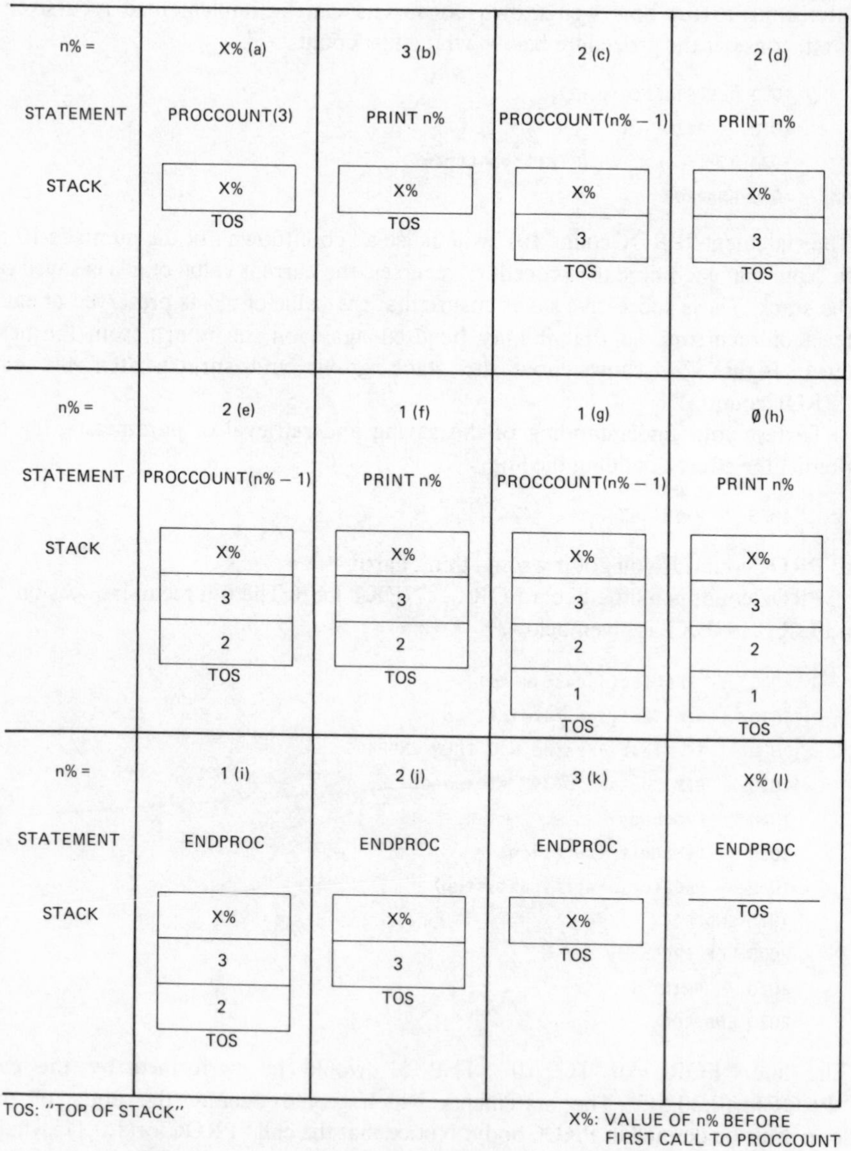

n% =	X% (a)	3 (b)	2 (c)	2 (d)
STATEMENT	PROCCOUNT(3)	PRINT n%	PROCCOUNT(n% − 1)	PRINT n%
STACK	X% TOS	X% TOS	X% 3 TOS	X% 3 TOS

n% =	2 (e)	1 (f)	1 (g)	Ø (h)
STATEMENT	PROCCOUNT(n% − 1)	PRINT n%	PROCCOUNT(n% − 1)	PRINT n%
STACK	X% 3 2 TOS	X% 3 2 TOS	X% 3 2 1 TOS	X% 3 2 1 TOS

n% =	1 (i)	2 (j)	3 (k)	X% (l)
STATEMENT	ENDPROC	ENDPROC	ENDPROC	ENDPROC
STACK	X% 3 2 TOS	X% 3 TOS	X% TOS	TOS

TOS: "TOP OF STACK"

X%: VALUE OF n% BEFORE
FIRST CALL TO PROCCOUNT

Figure 2.1   Action of the BASIC Stack during Recursion

```
1020     IF (last-i)*step > 0 THEN PROCfor(i+step,last,step)
1030 ENDPROC
```

Notice how there is a call to PROCbody before any termination test has been performed. This corresponds to the "at least once" rule of BBC FOR ... NEXT loops.

REPEAT and WHILE loops are a little harder to implement, as the termination/continuation condition has to be passed to the routine. The best way of doing this is as a string, which can then be EVALuated. Below is a recursive WHILE loop:

```
100 count=0
110 i=125
120 PROCwhile("i>=1")
130 PRINT count
140 END
150
1000 DEF PROCwhile(a$)
1010     IF NOT EVAL(a$) THEN ENDPROC
1020     PROCbody
1030     PROCwhile(a$)
1040 ENDPROC
1050
2000 DEF PROCbody
2010     count=count+1
2020     i=i / 2
2030 ENDPROC
```

PROCwhile itself is very straightforward. As long as the condition given in a$ is TRUE, the statements in PROCbody will be executed. How would you write a recursive REPEAT?

The above examples are really just for illustration, as it is much quicker to implement a WHILE (for example) with a REPEAT preceded by a conditional GOTO. However, it seems recursive and functional languages have a role to play in the future, so there's certainly no harm in playing around with recursive procedures to see what can be done.

2.2.6 User-defined Functions

In the last section I criticised BBC BASIC for not implementing any "safe" method of transferring data from a procedure to the calling program. However, using the user-defined function facility, it is possible to return a single value. This works in much the same way as the built-in functions such as INT and RND. A user-defined function may have zero or more parameters, and may return a number or a string (or either). A function is defined in a very similar way to a procedure:

```
10000 DEF FNname{(var [,var]*)}statement*
10010 statment*
10020 ..... (ditto)
10030 =expression
```

The =expression part is similar to the ENDPROC in a user-defined procedure. Because all the "statements" can occur zero or more times, the simplest legal definition is of the form:

```
10000 DEF FNname=expression
```

This is similar to the limited version of the DEF FN statement found in many BASICs. A couple of functions with no parameters are defined below:

```
10000 DEF FNsize=TOP - PAGE
10010 DEF FNfree=HIMEM - TOP
```

These two functions return the size of the program and the amount of free space remaining. They might be used as follows:

```
100 PRINT"The program is ";FNsize;" bytes long."
110 PRINT"There are ";FNfree;" bytes free."
120 END
```

As with user-defined procedures, the definition of a function should be placed somewhere in the program where it will not be executed, except when intentionally invoked using FNname. Obviously the usefulness of a function with no parameters is quite limited. The examples below gives some function definitions with parameters:

```
10000 DEF FNchar(low$, high$)
10010    REM      Returns a character in the range
10020    REM      low$..high$ from keyboard
10030    LOCAL c$
10040    REPEAT
10050       c$=GET$
10060    UNTIL low$ = c$ AND c$ = high$
10070 =c$
10080
10090
11000 DEF FNmax(a, b) IF a >= b THEN =a ELSE =b
11010
11020
12000 DEF FNlog(a, b) REM    Returns log of b to the base a
12010 =LN(b) / LN(a)
12020
12030
13000 DEF FNfact(n%) REM    Factorial n%
13010    IF n% = 0 THEN =1
13020    LOCAL i%, f%
13030    f%=1
```

```
13040    FOR i%=1 TO n%
13050       f%=f%*i%
13060    NEXT i%
13070 =f%
13080
13090
14000 DEF FNrev(a$) REM     Returns a$ backwards
14010    LOCAL i%, c$
14020    c$="":  REM  not strictly necessary
14030    FOR i%=1 to LEN(a$)
14040       c$=MID$(a$, i%, 1) + c$
14050    NEXT i%
14060 =c$
```

It can be seen that function and procedure definitions have a lot in common: local variables and parameters are treated in exactly the same way. Also, both support recursion. Whenever the =expression statement in encountered in a function definition (it is illegal to use =expression outside of a function), the expression is evaluated and the value returned in place of the FNname which invoked the function. There can be more than one =expression, just as there can be more than one ENDPROC in a procedure definition. All the statements which come after that =expression are not used by the function definition. This is different from Pascal functions, which don't return to the main program until the "end" is encountered. You should remember this if you convert Pascal to BBC BASIC, or vice versa.

One of the most common uses of user-defined functions is to provide the scientific functions that appear on many calculators nowadays, but which aren't standard in BASIC. Factorial is given above, and there is a more complete list of useful function definitions at the end of this chapter. It is usually a simple matter to convert a formula into BASIC notation. A couple of useful functions using INT are:

```
10000 DEF FNround(x)=INT(x+0.5)
10100 DEF FNtrunc(x)=SGN(x)*INT(ABS(x))
```

The first one rounds x up to the nearest integer, the second returns x without its decimal part, which for negative numbers is different from simply INT(x).

I said in section 2.2.5 that recursion is usually presented in terms of functions rather than procedures. This is because procedures are an invention of computer science, and recursion (like functions) is a purely mathematical concept. It is customary to use Factorials to illustrate recursion in functions. Not wishing to be accused of being a sheep, I will use a totally different example. I don't pretend it is any better, but at least it's original. Suppose a function is required to return a string which is the lower case equivalent of its parameter. Call this function FNlower, so that FNlower ("PETE WAS 'ERE.") would be "pete was 'ere.". Notice that only the letters are affected; punctuation symbols stay the same. The recursive function to perform this feat is given below:

```
10000 DEF FNlower(a$) REM      Returns a$ in lower case
10010     IF a$="" THEN =""
10020     LOCAL first%
10030     first%=ASC(LEFT$(a$,1))
10040 =CHR$(first% OR 32) + FNlower(MID$(a$,2))
```

The function really has two solutions, one for the trivial case when a$ is the null string "", and one for when a$ actually contains some characters. The first case is the "end condition" mentioned in conjunction with recursive procedures in the last section. The lower case of the null string is just the null string, so the function can return its result, "", immediately.

When a$ is not empty, things become more interesting. Stated in English the result is "the lower case version of the first character, followed by the lower case version of the rest of the string". It so happens that converting a single letter to lower case is easy. Examination of the ASCII codes of "A" to "Z" and "a" to "z" reveals that they only differ in a single bit, bit five. In particular, this bit is zero for upper case and one for lower case. To convert the former to the latter, all you have to do is OR the ASCII code with 00100000 in binary, which is 32 in decimal. So, line 10050 returns the lower case version of the first character, and then calls FNlower recursively to convert the rest of the string.

The action of the function is traced for the string "PETE" below.

```
FNlower("PETE")  = "p" + FNlower("ETE")
= "p" + "e" + FNlower("TE")
= "p" + "e" + "t" + FNlower("E")
= "p" + "e" + "t" + "e" + FNlower("")
= "p" + "e" + "t" + "e" + ""
= "pete"
```

To convert a string of N characters, the function recurses to a depth of N. At each level, the current version of a$ must be remembered, and these strings are kept on the stack as with any other parameters. In the example above, the string "PETE", "ETE", "TE", and "E" are all held on the stack when the FNlower("") is finally reached. The lengths of the strings form another one of those $1+2+3...+N$ series. This means that the amount of storage required to convert an N character string is roughly proportional to N*N. This limits the size of string you can convert, the actual limit depending on the size of the program in the machine and the display mode etc. In contrast, a non-recursive (iterative) function to perform the same job would have a much lower storage overhead. This is a common failing of recursive solutions; they are mathematically beautiful but practically unattractive because of speed or storage inefficiency.

There is a programming language called LISP which is used in list processing applications (hence its name). In computing terms, a list can be described recursively: a list is either empty or is an object followed by a list. In LISP, the "object" can be a number, a character string or a list. Because of the recursive definition of a list, the functions in LISP are frequently themselves recursive. The character strings of BASIC can be defined in a similar way to the LISP lists: a string is a null, "", or a character followed by a string. It is this property that makes it possible to define recursive functions on strings in a fairly natural way. The recursive procedures/functions in Chapter one which operate on trees and lists might be a little easier to understand now. Below are some more function definitions which use the recursive nature of strings.

```
10000 DEF FNlen(a$)
10010 IF a$="" THEN =0 ELSE =1 + FNlen(MID$(a$,2))
10020
11000 DEF FNreverse(a$)
11010 IF a$="" THEN ="" ELSE =FNreverse(MID$(a$,2)) + LEFT$(a$,1)
11020
12000 DEF FNval(a$)
12010 IF a$="" THEN =0
12020 IF LEN(a$)=1 THEN =ASC(a$)-ASC("0")
12030 =FNval(RIGHT$(a$,1)) + 10*FNval(LEFT$(a$,LEN(a$)-1))
```

Obviously the functions defined above are already available in BASIC (FNlen and FNval) or can be programmed just as easily using a FOR ... NEXT loops (FNreverse). However, if you understand how recursion is used in their definitions then they have served their purpose. The next example is also more illustrative than useful. Examine the text below:

```
 Line 1 is:
'Line 1 is:'
 Line 2 is:
''Line 1 is:''
 Line 3 is:
'Line 2 is:'
 Line 4 is:
'''Line 1 is'''
(and so on)
```

The problem is to write a program which produces the output above for as many lines as required. There will need to be a function that returns the string to be printed at a given line. After a little thought, the rule governing what is printed becomes clear. The odd numbered lines are always unquoted and introduce the next line. If the text of line N (where N is odd) is "Line M is:", then M is always (N+1) DIV 2. So, the first line is "Line 1 is:", the third "Line 2 is:" and so on. The even lines are a little more complex. The text at line N (N is even) is the text at line N DIV 2, but in quotes. So, line two is "'Line 1 is:'", line four is line two in quotes, i.e. "''Line 2 is:''" and so on. The program to produce the desired output is given (1+SQR(5))/2. Readers interested in the recreational manipulation of numbers

```
100 REM     Lines program
110 n%=20
120 FOR i%=1 TO n%
130     p$=FNprint(i%)
140     PRINT TAB(20-LEN(p$) DIV 2);p$
150 NEXT i%
160 END
170
180
1000 DEF FNprint(n%)
1010     IF n% MOD 2 THEN ="Line "+STR$((n%+1) DIV 2)+" is:"
1020 ="'"+FNprint(n% DIV 2)+"'"
```

The most quotes occur when n% is a large power of two, as the function must recurse many times before n% becomes odd. For example, try

```
PRINT FNprint(2^30)
```

There are LOG(n%)/LOG(2) (i.e. the log to base two of n%) pairs of quotes, which is 30 pairs in the example above. Although the program is almost trivial in its recursive form, a far greater amount of work is required in the non-recursive version. I will therefore leave that as an exercise for the reader.

Although the examples of recursive functions presented so far have all used strings, there are several purely numeric functions that can be defined recursively. Unfortunately, most of them can be implemented much more efficiently using iterative methods. A case in point is the Fibonacci series. This is the series of numbers that begins 1, 1, 2, 3..., and so on, each number being the sum of its two predecessors and the first two numbers being one. The series is of use in various branches of computing, for example generating random numbers. The function F(n) gives the nth number in the series, and can be defined recursively:

```
F(1) = 1,
F(2) = 1,
F(n) = F(n-1) + F(n-2), n > 2
```

This definition can be converted almost directly into a BBC BASIC function:

```
10000 DEF FNF(n%)   REM     Returns the n%th Fibonacci number
10010 IF n% > 2 THEN =FNF(n%-1)+FNF(n%-2) ELSE =1
```

The problem with this definition is the amount of recursion involved. In general, FNF(n%) requires a total of 2*FNF(n%)-1 calls (itself a recursive definition). FNF(17) for example needs 3193 calls to FNF. Even given the speed of BBC BASIC, this is a lot of calculation. A much better way to implement the function is using a FOR ... NEXT loop to add the last two terms the appropriate number of times. This version is given below.

```
10100 DEF FNF(n%)
```

```
10110     LOCAL i%, last%, fib%
10120     last%=1
10130     fib%=1
10140     IF n% <= 2 THEN =fib%
10150     FOR i%=1 TO n%
10160        fib%=last%+fib%
10170        last%=fib%-last%
10180     NEXT i%
10190 =fib%
```

The difference in the time taken by the two versions of FNF is vast. When finding F(20), the recursive version takes 41.35 seconds, the iterative version 0.11 seconds! There are many interesting properties of the Fibonacci series, such as the ratio between consecutive terms. This tends to the so-called golden ratio phi, $(1+SQR(5))/2$. Readers interested in the recreational manipulation of numbers are referred to [Gardner], which contains several fascinating examples of the occurrence of Fibonacci series and phi.

In summary, it can be said that recursion is a technique whose use leads to mathematically beautiful but practically inferior solutions. There are circumstances, however, where a recursive solution is attractive from both points of view, and a good programmer should be prepared to investigate such a solution when it presents itself. The examples in this book should give you at least some idea of when recursive techniques can be applied, for example when using recursively defined data structures.

2.3   Error Handling

The handling of errors in a program is not exactly central to the concept of structured programming; it is, however, a very important part of programs that are going to be used by inexperienced users. The word "error" in this context covers a multitude of sins. It is well known that if a computer operator can make a program go wrong, he will. One particular function in BBC BASIC, EVAL, opens the door to all sorts of errors. Consider the section of program below. It is part of a hypothetical graph plotting program. The user types in a function which is evaluated for various values of x.

```
100 PRINT"Type in the function in 'x' ";
110 INPUT fx$
120 FOR x=x1 TO x2 STEP dx
130     y=EVAL(fx$)
140     REM    and so on
```

Suppose the user types in "4*X+3" in response to the INPUT at line 110. This is a perfectly valid function in X. Unfortunately, the variable used in the program is the lower case x. These two variables are of course separate objects in BBC BASIC. When the EVAL at line 130 tries to evaluate fx$, it will not be able to find

X. This will cause a "No such variable at line 140" error. With luck, the user of the program may have some knowledge of programming, and will be able to work out what he did wrong. On the other hand, the user may be totally inexperienced with computers. The apparition of the strange "No such. . .." message, combined with the lack of useful replies to commands such as "help!" would cause a great deal of confusion for the poor user.

Another kind of fault is the filing error. These occur when data is being transferred to or from some storage device (tape or disc). When such an error occurs, the operating system usually comes out with a helpful "Block?"-type message. If the error actually occurs on a read operation, the program will stop. Again, the computer-generated error messages are only meaningful to experienced users. They are useless to naive operators, and as such should never be allowed to escape from the computer.

Having recognised the need for some kind of error trapping, i.e. the ability to stop an error from causing the termination of the program, how do we go about it? BBC BASIC comes equipped with a very useful statement. It is called ON ERROR. The form of the statement is:

```
     100 ON ERROR statement*
or   100 ON ERROR OFF
```

I will deal with the former case first, after which the meaning of the second form should become apparent. The piece of code below shows how rudimentary error trapping could be added to the "graph-plotter" example given above.

```
100 ON ERROR PROCerror
110 PRINT "Type in function in 'x' ";
120 INPUT fx$
130 FOR x=x1 TO x2 STEP dx
140     y=EVAL(fx$)
150     REM and so on
........
........
1000 DEF PROCerror
1010    IF ERL<>140 THEN REPORT:PRINT" at line ";ERL:END
1020    PRINT TAB(0,28);"Sorry, I can't work that one out."
1030    PRINT "Try another function (remember it's 'x', not 'X')"
1040 ENDPROC
```

The action of the program is as follows: when the ON ERROR statement in line 100 is encountered, nothing overt happens. However, BASIC does make a note of the current location in the program that is being executed. More precisely, it notes the location of the first byte in the program after the word "ERROR". Execution then continues as normal until an error occurs in the program. When this happens, instead of printing the normal "such an error at line such a line"-type message, the program jumps to the location that was remembered by the ON

ERROR statement. It's very similar to a "GOTO the last ON ERROR statement". Execution then carries on. Before control passes to the ON ERROR line, however, BASIC saves some useful information, namely the line number at which the error occurred, the code for that error (as given in the User Guide pp. 474–482) and also the text that would have been printed if no ON ERROR had been encountered.

Once control is passed to the ON ERROR line, the statements that follow it can be executed. In the present example, the only statement is PROCerror. This just calls the procedure named, as you would expect. If the action you wanted to take was very simple, such as re-running the program, this could be done on the ON ERROR line rather than by calling a procedure. For example "ON ERROR RUN" would cause the program to start afresh if an error were encountered. Of course, no error message would be given, so such an action would hardly merit the term "user-friendly". PROCerror simply deals with the case of an error in the EVAL function of line 140. All other errors are treated as normal, i.e. cause the termination of the program. Line 1010 determines where the error happened. As I mentioned, the computer stores the erroneous line number. This is accessed via the ERL function. (ERL returns 0 if the error is an immediate one.) If the error line is not 140, i.e. the error was caused by something other than EVAL statement, the statements:

```
REPORT:PRINT" at Line ";ERL:END
```

are executed. The action of REPORT is to print the error message corresponding to the latest error. First it prints a new line, then the text of the error message, without a new-line at the end. The PRINT statement then gives the line number of the error, and finally the program finishes with the END statement. This is, of course, the exact effect obtained when errors are reported as normal by BASIC.

If the error did occur in line 140, then the procedure assumes that the EVAL statement was the cause (there's not much else that can go wrong in that line). A relatively helpful message is printed, and the procedure ends. This returns control back to the ON ERROR statement. Because there are no more statements to execute on that line, control continues on the next line down. This is convenient in the present example because this causes the INPUT to be executed again, a desirable action in view of the error concerned. Sometimes, though, it is more sensible to restart the program somewhere other than the line after the ON ERROR. In this case, a GOTO could follow the error handling statements.

The other error function, ERR, can be used to isolate particular errors. A different message could be printed depending on the exact cause of the error. In all situations, though, the report should be phrased in a fashion that makes it meaningful to the user of the program, rather than a computer expert. When composing error messages, try to test them on your mum/girlfriend/wife (or for the feminists who are already looking for the sex discrimination board's phone number, dad/boyfriend/husband). If an error message is comprehensible to a complete novice, it has done its job. Otherwise, it should be simplified. One case where ERR is very useful is in error logging. Suppose you have written a filing program for a disc-based system. Assume, also, that the program is being used by a naive operator. The chances are that eventually an error will occur. The program's user will telephone you the next day and say "your program's gone wrong!". If you then ask what the error message was, the chances are the user will not remember. Trying to de-bug a program with an unknown error is not easy, especially as such errors are never reproducible. The solution is to get the computer to remember the error for you. This is done by saving all the information you can on the disc. For example:

```
2000 DEF PROCerror
2010    LOCAL chan%
2020    chan%=OPENOUT("Error file")
2030    PTR#chan%=EXT#chan%
2040    PRINT#chan%,ERL,ERR,date$,id$
2050    CLOSE#chan%
2060    REM    Rest of error routine
2070    .......
2080    .......
```

The statement "PTR#chan%=EXT#chan%" means "add what comes next to the end of the file". In addition to the important ERR and ERL, two other quantities are written onto the file. These are the date, which the program thoughtfully remembered to ask at the beginning, and some kind of identification, so that when the error file is inspected, it is clear which program actually caused the error. It is the use of the EXT# & PTR# functions that limits the use of this type of procedure to disc systems; they don't work for cassette files.

When a program is still being debugged, it is useful to only have error trapping in the parts that you "know" work, and let the computer generate error messages as normal for the other bits. Disabling error trapping after an ON ERROR has been encountered is achieved by the use of the "ON ERROR OFF" form of the statement. This returns BASIC to the default error reporting state. Interestingly enough, even the default error handling routine is written in BASIC. The interpreter ROM has the text:

```
REPORT:IF ERL<>0 THEN PRINT "at line ";ERL;:PRINT:END
```

Before an ON ERROR statement is encountered, or after an ON ERROR OFF is executed, the computer jumps to the small program above. You can prove that this is executed in a couple of ways. Firstly, if you enter a line such as "0 PRUNT" and then run the program, the error message "Mistake" is given. There is no " at line 0" because the BASIC thinks the error is an immediate mode one. In view of this, it is strange that line 0 is legal in BBC BASIC. Another way is to change the print formatting (see section 3.2.1). If you execute the statement "@%=&2020A", the line numbers in error messages will be printed as 100.00 etc., because the normal PRINT routine is being used.

In the example I have been using, the error occurs inside a FOR ... NEXT loop. The loop is re-entered after the error routine has done its thing. You may think this is bad practice, as the same loop is being exited and re-entered, possibly many times. In normal circumstances this could lead to a "Too many FORs" error. Not in this case, though. As soon as BASIC detects an error, it clears all the stacks (the main stack which has all the return addresses and local variables for procedures and functions, and the separate stack used to store information on REPEAT/FOR/GOSUBs). This means that if the program is in the middle of any sort of control structure when an error arises, all knowledge of this is forgotten by the time the error handling routine is executed. This is quite desirable if the error routine causes execution to terminate. However, if the program is to continue after the error has been processed, it can only jump to the outer-most level. Many BASICs with error trapping provide a statement called RESUME. This is equivalent to BBC BASIC's "GOTO ERL", i.e. the program restarts where it left-off (the source of error presumably having been corrected). This will not work if the error occurred in a REPEAT or FOR loop, or a subroutine, procedure or function. Actually, this raises the interesting question of "what happens if the error routine itself causes an error?". In the example above, if ON ERROR line made a jump back into the FOR x loop, as soon as the NEXT x was encountered, a "No FOR" error would be generated. This would lead to PROCerror being called once more. Because the error line would no longer be 140, PROCerror would report the error as normal and stop the program.

2.4 Program Layout

The more astute readers will no doubt have already noticed a certain method in the way the programs in this book have been laid out. Program formatting is a very neglected subject in BASIC programming books. There are a variety of reasons for this. Firstly, BASIC is an interactive interpreted language. This means that each program line is processed in some way as soon as it is typed in. At the very least, the keywords of the language (PRINT, IF, SIN etc) are tokenised – converted to a single one byte code. Most BASICs go somewhat further than this; they delete any spaces that appear between the line number and the first non-space character. Some actually remove all the spaces in a line. When the program is listed, the interpreter inserts spaces where its author sees fit, for example before and after each keyword. This behaviour differs from compiled languages (Pascal, Forth, Algol etc.). In these, the text of a program is created using a text editor. The programmer can insert spaces, blank lines and comments wherever he wants; they are all ignored by the compiler.

The difference between the way that BASIC treats its text (the "source") and the way compiled languages do means that offering advice on formatting BASIC programs is usually in vain. Some BASICs, though, credit their users with a little more common sense. They take the view that any spaces in the program are there for a reason, and as such should be left untouched. Fortunately, BBC BASIC is one of those dialects where any processing performed on the source (and there is quite a lot) is kept hidden from the user, and a program always LISTs in exactly the same way as it was typed in. Readers who take this facility for granted should try typing in a short program into an Applesoft machine, then listing it. The changes made by the interpreter often makes the listing unreadable compared to the original.

Although the default action of BBC BASIC's LIST command in to reproduce the program unaltered, there exists the option of having REPEAT and FOR loops indented, and having a space inserted after the line number. This is achieved by using the LISTO command. The command is followed by an integer which is treated as a three-bit number. The first bit is for a space after the line number, the second for indenting FOR loops and the third for indenting REPEAT loops. If a bit is a one, indenting occurs. The table below summarises the eight possible combinations.

LISTO option	REPEATs	FURs	Line number
0	NO	NO	NO
1	NO	NO	YES
2	NO	YES	NO
3	NO	YES	YES
4	YES	NO	NO
5	YES	NO	YES
6	YES	YES	NO
7	YES	YES	YES

As the User Guide states, the most common options are 0 and 7, no indenting and full indenting respectively. Unfortunately, only the first option of having a space after the line number is at all useful in my (humble) opinion. The reason is the way UNTILs and NEXTs are handled. Consider the skeletal program segment below, as listed with LISTO 0 and 7 respectively.

```
LISTO 0    100 FOR I.....
           110 REPEAT
           120 FOR J.....
           130 REM .....
           140 NEXT J
           150 UNTIL .....
           160 NEXT I
           170 END

LISTO 7    100 FOR I.....
           110   REPEAT
           120     FOR J.....
           130       REM .....
           140     NEXT J
           150   UNTIL .....
           160 NEXT I
           170 END
```

At first sight, the LISTO 7 version looks nicely indented. However, notice that the UNTIL appears underneath the FOR j, and the NEXT I appears under the REPEAT. I was always brought up to believe that a statement that closes a loop should always appear directly beneath its corresponding start-loop statement. When one is used to a certain way of formatting programs, being confronted with a different way can be very confusing. This is of course exactly the opposite effect to that required; formatting should be used to clarify the meaning of the program for the human reader. The reasons for the strange behaviour of BBC BASIC's LISTO is easy to explain. Stated in English, LIST does the following: "If I just listed a REPEAT or FOR, increase the indentation factor by two spaces. If I just listed an UNTIL or a NEXT, decrease it by two." Of course, decreasing the indentation after the NEXT or UNTIL has been printed is too late. What the LIST program should do is look to see if the first statement on the line is a loop termination statement. If it is, it should decrease the indentation count before it lists the statement. If you find the way LIST works acceptable (which means you've never used a free-format language before), fine. I dislike it so intensely that I wrote my own version, which is given in Chapter six. I now present my views on how BBC BASIC programs should be laid out. This is of course a very subjective thing. However, any form of (consistent) formatting is useful. Useful, that is, for the human reader trying to grasp the meaning of your program. The BBC Computer is totally indifferent to the spaces, blank lines, REMs and variable names you choose to use. As long as the text forms a syntactically correct program, BASIC will be happy. All the redundant characters used to make a program look "pretty" may even slow it down a bit. This is rarely a major concern, though. Just as a program's error messages should be designed to benefit the user, the text itself should be arranged to help anyone trying to decipher it.

Indentation is one of the most useful devices. I always indent blocks (groups of statements between a pair of delimiters) by three spaces. This includes REPEAT loops, FOR loops, subroutines (whose first delimiting statement should be a REM) and user-defined functions and procedures. Nested blocks should of course have a cumulative effect on the indentation. And, most importantly, the delimiting statements should be made to align, as in:

```
100   FOR i.....
110      REPEAT
130         FOR i.....
140            REM.....
150         NEXT j
160      UNTIL .....
170   NEXT i
180   END
10000 DEF PROCstart
10010    REM.....
10020    LOCAL i%
10030    FOR i%.....
10040       REM .....
```

```
10050    NEXT i%
10060 ENDPROC
```

Another case for indentation is when a group of statements is avoided by using a conditional GOTO, e.g.

```
100 IF vat = 0 THEN 140
110     PRINT"There's ";vat*100"% VAT on that"
120     PRINT"The total price is `";`cost*(1+vat)
130     total_vat=total_vat + `cost*vat:GOTO 150
140 total_cost=total_cost + `cost
150 .....
```

Putting the three conditional statements (lines 110–130) on one line would prove cumbersome. It is better in situations like this to reverse the condition, and skip over those lines. In order to make the intention clear, the lines that are skipped have been indented.

As I mentioned before, the necessity that all an IF statement's THEN and ELSE parts are on one line is a major shortcoming of BBC BASIC. Some programs may have the vast majority of their statements conditional on a single IF. An example is the procedure PROCquick given earlier. The most logical way of expressing the first line is:

```
1000 DEF PROCquick(m%, n%)
1010    LOCAL ......
1020    IF m% < n% THEN REM do the procedure
1030 END PROC
```

This form is impossible in BBC BASIC because the "do the procedure" part would all have to be on line 1020. A quick look back at the procedure would show that this would be impractical, to say the least. Instead, the programmer has the choice of two "unstructured" alternatives. The first (the one I used) is to reverse the condition and perform an ENDPROC in the THEN part. This breaks the "one entrance, one exit" rule of structured blocks of program. The second alternative is to perform a GOTO to the last statement if m%>=n%. This invites errors in the destination line number. Given that this "one statement, one line" policy exists, it's a shame that the LIST routine hasn't got an option to make IF ... THEN .. ELSEs a little more readable. For example, the line:

```
1000 IF a>=b OR a=c AND c=d THEN q=q+1:r=r-1 ELSE PROCerror:count=count+1
```

is a little cumbersome. Two more readable alternatives are:

```
1000 IF a>=b OR a=c AND c=d THEN q=q+1:r=r-1
                            ELSE PROCerror:count=count+1

1000 IF a>=b OR a=c AND c=d
        THEN q=q+1:r=r-1
        ELSE PROCerror:count=count+1
```

Such enhancements are not very expensive to provide, as my list program in

Chapter five shows. The main thing is that the two parts of the IF do not appear on the same line. After all, there is no way that both parts will be executed on the same time through the IF, so they should be clearly separated. Unfortunately, it is not possible to format an IF statement like this without recourse to a special program. Unless enough people complain to Acorn Computers about their idea of a clever LIST command. . . .

Apart from indentation, the spaces that occur within individual statements can add a great deal to legibility. There are very few places where BBC BASIC actually requires a space. The most common is when a real variable precedes a reserved word as in "I MOD J" and "FOR i=a TO b". The spaces between the I and MOD and between the a and TO are absolutely necessary; none of the others are though. If they were absent, BASIC would think references were being made to the two variables IMODJ and aTOb respectively. The reason is that once BASIC recognises the start of a variable (a letter or "_" or "£"), any letters, digits, "_" or "£" that follow are taken as part of that variable. In the two examples above, the MOD and TO are just counted as letters in the variables being read. A space or any punctuation marks the end of a variable, which is why names such as a% to demo$ don't need a space after them.

Now that we know exactly when a space necessary from the computer's point of view, I will say that humans deserve a little more verbosity. At the very least all reserved words should be sandwiched between spaces. (The one exception I sometimes make is with PRINT "stuff". This doesn't exactly detract from the clarity of the statement, though.) Looking through programs published for the PET, you might be forgiven for thinking that the computer didn't possess a space bar. Here's a line from a program given in a recent (as I write this in August 1982) edition of "Britain's Largest Selling Micro Magazine":

```
57 FORZ=1TOI:IFPEEK(Y+2*Z)<60THENW=Z:Z=I:NEXT:GOTO62
```

The only reason there is a space after the line number is that the PET puts it in automatically.

As I said before, some BASICs insert spaces where the program is listed. This has the advantage that it relieves the programmer of the responsibility. Conversely, if you don't like the way the spacing is done, you're stuck. BBC BASIC's non-interference policy is probably the best. It means that the onus to make the program legible is with the programmer, but he is given greater flexibility in return. Apart from the obvious separation of keywords from the other symbols, spacing can be added to clarify the meaning of individual expressions. For example, different operators have different precedences or binding powers. This can be reflected in the spacing:

```
a + b*c
a * b^c
-a ^ b
a+b >= c-d
b*b > 4*a*c
```

```
a>b AND q<>10
flag   OR   b+c>2 AND NOT finished
```

There is no rule that says that operators of a certain precedence should be surrounded by so many spaces; rather that the high precedence operators have their operands closer to them than the lower precedence ones. This becomes a little difficult when there are more than a couple of different precedence operators in an expression, such as the last example above. In those cases, brackets can be used to show the order in which the expression will be evaluated:

```
flag OR ( (b+c > 2) AND NOT finished)
```

This is especially useful when you're not actually sure about the various binding powers in a complex expression: you can force the evaluation in the order you want by using brackets. Speaking of brackets, all the functions in BBC BASIC with only one argument are perfectly happy without them. They act more like very high precedence unary operators (like the minus sign in "−a^b"), so that brackets are only required when the function is to act on more than a simple term. Some examples:

```
SQR1          is    SQR(1)
SINRADth+45   is    SIN(RAD(th))+45   NOT   SIN(RAD(th+45))
SQRLNa+b      is    SQR(LN(a))+b      NOT   SQR(LN(a+b))
COS2*a        is    COS(2)*a          NOT   COS(2*a)
```

As a matter of style, and to avoid confusion, I have used brackets at all times in this book. I recommend you do the same, as people used to other languages which require brackets around function arguments (which includes almost every language known to man) will be able to read your programs with greater ease. A place where spaces would be useful, but aren't allowed is between a PROC or FN and its name. "FN status" is illegal, unfortunately. As an alternative, FN_status is nearly as good, but does mean you have to remember the "_". If spaces were allowed, they would not actually be part of the name, so you could forget to put them in with no ill effects. Apart from that, there is nowhere in BBC BASIC statements that you can't put a space if you need to. Obviously spaces aren't allowed in the middle of numbers or reserved words, but that is not a restriction in making the program legible.

Another type of spacing is between the individual lines of the program. In BBC BASIC, as in any other BASIC, typing a line number followed by RETURN deletes that line, if it exists. However, if there is at least one space after the line number, the line is entered into the program. Such blank lines act like REM statements when the program is executed, but are less obtrusive in the listing. Blank lines are used to section off the important blocks of a program. At the very least, individual procedure, functions and subroutines (if you can find an excuse for using the latter) should be separated with a number of blank lines; three seems as good a number as any. Important parts within the main blocks could also be partitioned. For example, the input/processing/output sections I mentioned at the start of this chapter could be separated. There is no advantage to be gained from typing more than one space after the line number. They are all stored, so the extra ones just take up room that could be used elsewhere. A line followed by one space takes up five bytes in the program, which is not too great a price pay for the increased readability it can bring.

Because most of the programs so far have been of the "here is an example" type, there has been no need to use long, descriptive variable names. However, this facility does exist and should be used. The only restriction on the length of a name is the number of characters that can be typed on one input line: about 240. Even so, it is best not to go mad with names. The reasons are of space (each occurrence of the name "total_cost" takes ten bytes of the program space), and, ironically enough, readability. On a model A, with only 40 columns of screen, statements involving lengthy variable names quickly grow larger than a single line. This is particularly true of IF ... THEN ... ELSE statements. If a single page is the unit of information that the brain can cope with at once, then the line is the eye's useful limit. As soon as a line grows longer than one display line, its legibility decreases rapidly. This is especially true when individual words are split between lines. Considering that "total_cost" takes up a quarter of a MODE 4 line, it is obvious that long variable names can get in the way. The moral is obviously to upgrade to a model B so that you can take advantage of the 80 columns modes.

The above notwithstanding, names should always bear some relation to what they are being used for. This is very important with procedures and functions. PROCsort, PROCinit, PROCexplode etc. give a good impression of what is going on without the reader of the program having to actually travel down the page to find the procedure definitions. As I said earlier, the main body of a program might just be a list of procedure calls with a few flow control constructs. Other names can be as long or short as is deemed necessary. It is not particularly useful to give looping variables long names. "i", "j" and "k" are good for three levels of nesting, and most people associate these names with FOR loops. Sometimes "x" is used, particularly in algebraic programs such as graph plotters or equation solvers. Variables which are used as flags (logical values) can be named in such a way as to make some statements read like English:

```
REPEAT ..... UNTIL finished OR error
IF OK THEN PROCinit ELSE PROCerror
```

The "_" and "£" symbols can be used to good effect. Obviously "£" implies some sort of monetary value, and "_" can separate words in variable names: amount_due. These two symbols are treated as letters, in that they can be the first character of a name. Whether the letters are upper or lower case is a matter of taste. Upper case names look more uniform in a listing, as all the reserved words are upper case. However, there is the problem of clashes between variables and keywords: COST would not be acceptable as it would be parsed as COS(T). If you're lucky, the variable T will not exist and an error will be generated. On the other hand, the program may just produce erroneous results for no apparent reason. Some programming language books recommend the use of upper case for "manifest constants". These are values that don't change in the program, so would appear as numbers (or string literals) such as 2.71828, "Z". The use of such quantities may not be obvious at first sight, so they are given names; E, LEFT$. Also, such values could change from time to time. For example, when you buy a memory upgrade the number of array elements you can sort more than doubles. If your sort program has lots of lines such as:

```
100 IF N>1500 THEN.....
```

then you'll have to go through the program looking for all the places where "1500" is present and change them to "3500". A better method would be to have a manifest constant defined at the beginning of the program as "MAX=1500". All the statements that depend on the value of MAX can then be changed in one fell swoop. The reason upper case is recommended for such "variables" is that it makes them stand out in languages where the reserved words are in lower case, as well as the variables. (The language "C" is a notable example.) This is not so in BBC BASIC, but the principle still holds. Values used many times (in the same way) in a program, and which might be changed occasionally to alter the characteristics of the program should be named.

Not directly related to program layout, but of equal or greater import is the use of REMs. The first rule of BASIC programming seems to be "avoid REM statements at all costs". This is not strictly true; ZX81 owners use REMs all the time, to reserve space for machine code routines. It is ironic that the language that is second only to assembly language in its impenetrability attracts the least documentation-conscious users. BBC BASIC is very good because it lets the programmer express actions whose meaning would be totally hidden in standard BASIC (see the examples at the start of this chapter). This reduces the need for certain types of REM statement. However, there is no programming language in existence that can get by with the total exclusion of English comments. You should let common sense and experience guide you in the use of REMs. Most books warn the reader of such silliness as:

```
100 REM    add 1 to a%
110 a%=a%+1
```

but I credit my readers with more intelligence, so I won't mention it.

The main use of REMs is to introduce blocks of code whose action may not be obvious just by looking at the individual lines. This applies to segments within the main program, as well as procedure/function/subroutine blocks. A common use in minimal BASIC of the REM statement is to list the variables used and their functions. This is mainly because the names are limited to the "A" and "Z9" variety. In BBC BASIC, the name itself should be enough to provide such information, though there is certainly no harm in making absolutely sure the reader knows what a variable is for. Any "trickery" indulged in should certainly be expounded with comments. Better still, avoid trickery. If you can write the program in such a way that every statement is crystal clear in its meaning, it does you far greater credit than a program half the size and twice the speed which is incapable of being understood by anyone. The best book for advice on document-ing BASIC programs is [Nevison]. It is also very cheap.

2.5   Example Programs

The following programs try to illustrate the principles introduced in this chapter. They are presented with clarity in mind, rather than efficiency. This is especially obvious from the Life program. It is hard to think of problems which are difficult enough to warrant a non-trivial solution but easy enough to present in a book such as this. For example, a compiler for BASIC would be difficult enough to require a well thought-out structured approach, but would make boring reading. On the other hand a quadratic equation solver is really just a couple of equations converted into BASIC. The interesting part in the latter case would be to make the program as robust as possible, so that it deals with imaginary roots, zero x^2 co-efficients etc.

The first program illustrates recursion, and the use of list structures (see Chapter one). I "stole" the problem from a competition which is currently being run by PCW (the original one) and W. H. Smith's. The idea is to guess the number of ways it is possible to get to the Smith's shop from "home". There is a road map of one-way streets which connect these two places. This is reproduced in Figure 2.2. The obvious way to solve the problem is to manually trace the roads, trying to remember the ones that have already been counted. The solution pre-sented here is more reliable. The method is to define a procedure which will trace a path between any two of the junctions, keeping a list of the points which have already been visited. All routes can be examined by calling the procedure recursively and looking out for the end condition which in this case will be that the "destination" junction has been reached.

Before such a procedure can be written, it is necessary to decide how the map will be represented in the computer. As all the roads are one-way, the map is an example of a structure called a directed graph. A graph in this context is a set of

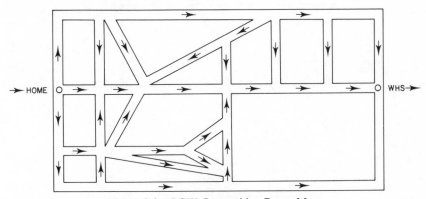

Figure 2.2   PCW Competition Route Map

points (called nodes) which are connected by some lines (called edges). The "directed" part stems from the fact that it is only possible to travel along an edge in one direction. Digraph is a common abbreviation for directed graph. The digraph equivalent to the W. H. Smith's map is shown in Figure 2.3.

The nodes have been numbered for convenience, with "home" as node one and the destination node numbered 17. The way of storing the digraph is as a set of linked lists. There is one list for each node. The pointers to the first elements of the lists are stored in a array called heads%(). Each item in the list has a data part and a pointer to the next item. A zero pointer marks the end of the list. The data parts for the list pointed to by heads%(n) hold the numbers of the nodes connected to and accessible to node n. This is illustrated in Figure 2.4 with a simpler digraph. The order in which the nodes appear in the list is unimportant for the present program. A final list is kept which holds the nodes which have been visited so far by the procedure. This list is pointed to by the zeroth element of heads%(). It is initially empty.

It is now possible to explain PROCpath. It has two parameters, start% and end%. Start% is the number of the node from where the path must start. It is altered as the various paths are explored. End% is the destination node number and remains constant. The initial call to PROCpath from the main program is "PROCpath(1, nodes%)". On entering the procedure, the value of start% is added to the list of nodes visited. There are then two courses of action. If start%=end%, the destination node has been reached. In this case, the current path is printed by the call "PROCprintlist(0)" and a jump is made to end of the procedure, where the last node in the "path" list is deleted. If, on the other hand, start%<>end% it is necessary to continue the search for end%. This is achieved by recursively using PROCpath to visit all the nodes connected to start%. For safety's sake this is done with a WHILE rather than a REPEAT loop, so that the possibility of no nodes connected to first% is dealt with properly. This is not necessary with the Smith's map, as all nodes except the last one have at least one direct neighbour.

The above description of the walk makes it sound much more complex than it

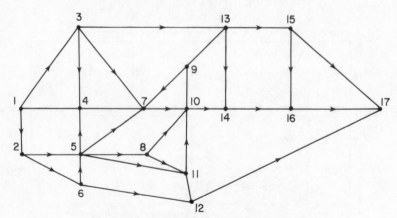

Figure 2.3   Route Map as a Directed Graph

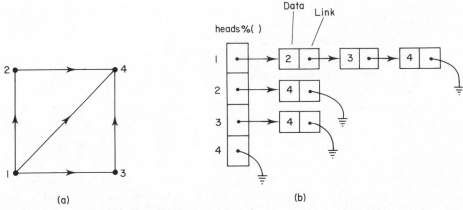

Figure 2.4   Simple Graph and its Array Representation

really is. The best way to understand the action of **PROC**draw is to work through a simple example by hand, e.g. with the square digraph given above. The other recursive procedure is the one which prints the list backwards. This is necessary as when a path has been completed, the most recently added item in the list is the last node. This should appear last in the print-out, hence the list must be printed backwards. You may have noticed that the way the path list grows and shrinks by adding and deleting the same item upon entering and leaving the path procedure makes it a stack. As such, it could have been implemented in an array of its own with an associated variable to act as the stack pointer. The procedure to print this could be non-recursive, by printing the stacked nodes from the bottom of the stack to the top.

The ancillary procedures to manipulate the lists should be easy to understand. The complete program, with the DATA statements for the particular digraph under discussion, is given below.

```
100 REM     Directed Graph Walk Program
110 PROCinit
120 start%=1: end%=nodes%
130 PROCpath(start%,end%)
140 PRINT '"There are ";count%;" ways."
150 END
160
170
1000 DEF PROCinit
1010    REM Set-up the linked list
1020    LOCAL i%, edges%, from%, to%
1030    REM This uses data statements, but it could be
1040    REM input by the user
1050    READ nodes%, edges%
1060    DIM heads%(nodes%):  REM Array containing "head" pointers
```

```
1070    FOR i%=1 TO edges%
1080       READ from%, to%
1090       PROCadd_edge(from%,to%)
1100    NEXT i%
1110    REM    Init count of paths
1120    count%=0
1130 ENDPROC
1140
1150
1200 DATA 17,31
1210 DATA 1,2,    1,3,    1,4,    2,5,    2,6,    4,4,    3,7,    3,13,   4,7
1220 DATA 5,4,    5,7,    5,8,    5,11,   6,5,    6,12,   7,10,   8,10,   8,11
1230 DATA 9,7,    9,10,   10,14,  11,10,  12,11,  12,17,  13,9,   13,14,  13,15
1240 DATA 14,16,  15,16,  15,17,  16,17
1250
1260
2000 DEF PROCadd_edge(from%, to%)
2010    REM  Add the edge to node "to%" to the list
2020    REM  of start node "from%"
2030    LOCAL ptr%
2040    ptr%=FNnew(4):    REM  get four bytes of memory
2050    REM  Set-up node with data part "to%" and pointer to next node
2060    PROCassign(ptr%, to%, heads%(from%))
2070    REM  Make this the new first node
2080    heads%(from%)=ptr%
2090 ENDPROC
2100
2110
2500 DEF FNnew(n%)
2510    REM  Return address of n% bytes of store
2520    LOCAL ptr%
2530    DIM ptr% (n%-1):  REM  The space before the ( is important
2540 =ptr%
2550
2560
2600 DEF PROCassign(ptr%, data%, link%)
2610    REM  Set-up the node pointed to by ptr% with
2630    REM  "data%" and "link%" as data and link fields
2640    !ptr%=data%*&10000 OR link%
2650 ENDPROC
2660
```

```
2670
3000 DEF PROCpath(first%, last%)
3010    REM Do a walk from first% to all the adjacent nodes
3020    REM If first% = last%, print the path it took to get there
3030    LOCAL ptr%, node%
3040    PROCadd_edge(0,first%): REM   Add this edge to the walk
3050    IF first%=last% THEN PROCprint_list(0):  GOTO 3130
3060       REM  We're not at the end, so visit the adjacent nodes
3070       ptr%=heads%(first%)
3075       IF ptr%=0 THEN 3130: REM   Make it a "WHILE" loop
3080       REPEAT
3090          node%=FNdata(ptr%):     REM Get an adjacent node
3100          PROCpath(node%, last%): REM Visit its neighbours
3110          ptr%=FNlink(ptr%):      REM Get pointer to next one
3120       UNTIL ptr%=0
3130    PROCtail(0):  REM  Delete first% from the path
3140 ENDPROC
3150
3160
3500 DEF FNlink(ptr%)
3510    REM  Returns link field of node at ptr%
3520 =!ptr% AND &FFFF
3530
3550
3600 DEF FNdata(ptr%)
3610    REM  Returns data field of node at ptr%
3620 =(!ptr% AND &FFFF0000) DIV &10000
3630
3640
4000 DEF PROCprint_list(node%)
4010    REM   Print the list from node "node%"
4020    REM   and update "count" etc.
4040    count%=count%+1
4050    PRINT"Path number ";count%;":"
4060    PROCprint1(heads%(node%))
4070    PRINT'
4080 ENDPROC
4090
4100
4500 DEF PROCprint1(ptr%)
4510    REM  Recursive procedure to print list from "ptr%"
```

```
4520    REM  in reverse order
4530    LOCAL link%, data%
4540    link%=FNlink(ptr%)
4550    data%=FNdata(ptr%)
4560    IF link%<>0 THEN PROCprint1(link%)
4570    PRINT "-";data%;"-";
4580 ENDPROC
4590
4600
500U DEF PROCtail(node%)
5010    REM  Remove first element of list "node%"
5020    LOCAL first%
5030    first%=heads%(node%)
5050    heads%(node%)=FNlink(first%)
5060 ENDPROC
```

The Game of Life

Life is a game invented by a John Horton Conway of Cambridge. Some might claim it was invented by a certain slightly more powerful being, but the version presented here is certainly of human conception. The game, which is more accurately termed a simulation, is played on a grid of cells. This grid should ideally stretch to infinity in all directions, but for the purposes of computer implementation, it is given a finite size. The version given below allows the user to define a grid of cells (1–38) by (1–19) in the X and Y directions respectively.

Each cell can contain an organism. If so, the cell is said to be alive, otherwise it is dead. Initially, cells are set-up with organisms in a pattern defined by the user. The present program uses an asterisk to denote a live cell and a blank to show the absence of an organism. The initial pattern is altered by applying some simple rules to each cell. Its survival into the next generation depends on its current state (dead or alive) and the number of live neighbours it has. The rules are:

1. A cell will survive into the next generation if it has two or three neighbours.
2. A dead cell will gain life if it has exactly three neighbours.

These can be simplified by saying that a cell will live in the next generation if it has three neighbours, or is currently living and has two neighbours. To count the live neighbours of a particular cell, imagine it to be in the centre of a noughts and crosses board. It has eight immediate neighbours. The cells on the edges of the board can be treated in various ways. In the present version of the game, all cells have eight neighbours, irrespective of their position. The neighbour to the right a cell on the right-most edge of the board is the cell on the same row at the left-most edge, i.e. the board "wraps-around" at the edges.

In order to keep track of the current and next generation, two versions of the grid must be stored. One, the "active" one, holds the state of the cells for the present generation. These are counted in order to find the cells' conditions in the next generation, which states are stored on the "inactive" board. At the end of a generation, the two boards or grids are reversed, so that the previously inactive one becomes active, and vice versa. The program is listed below.

```
100 REM    The Game of Life
110 MODE 7
120 PROCinit
130 REPEAT
140    active%=0
150    PROCset_up(num_x%,num_y%,active%)
155    CLS
160    REPEAT
170       PROCgeneration(num_x%,num_y%,active%)
175       active%=1-active%:  REM  Swap "active" board
180    UNTIL count%=0 OR INKEY(0)<>-1
190    INPUT''"Another go (Y/N) ",yn$
200 UNTIL yn$="N" OR yn$="n"
210 MODE 7
220 *FX4,0
230 END
240
250
1000 DEF PROCinit
1010    REM  Get size of board, set-up function keys etc.
1020    REPEAT
1030       INPUT TAB(0,3),"Horizontal cells (1-38) ",num_x%
1040    UNTIL num_x%>=1 AND num_x<=38
1050    REPEAT
1070       INPUT TAB(0,5),"Vertical cells (1-19) ",num_y%
1080    UNTIL num_y%>=1 AND num_y<=19
1090    DIM board%(num_x%-1, num_y %-1, 1)
1100    *key0 |!|a
1110    *key1 |!|A
1120    REM  Codes for cursor keys
1130    copy=135:  up=139
1140    REM  Make the cursor keys give ASCII codes
1150    *fx4,1
1160 ENDPROC
1170
1180
2000 DEF PROCset_up(num_x%, num_y%, to%)
2010    REM  Initialise the board with dimensions num_x%,num-y%
```

```
2020     REM   on board number "to%"
2030     LOCAL vert$, cx%, cy%, com%
2035     CLS
2040     REM   Print the borders with indicating arrows
2050     PRINT TAB(1,num_y%+1);"^";STRING$(num_x%-1, "|")
2060     vert$=CHR$(8)+CHR$(10)+"-"
2070     PRINT TAB(0,1);"]";STRING$(num_y%-1, vert$)
2110     PRINT'"Cursor keys to move, COPY to finish"
2120     PRINT"f0 to reset a point,"
2130     PRINT"f1 to set a point"
2140     REM   Init cursor position
2150     cx%=0:  cy%=0
2160     REPEAT
2170        com%=FNget_com
2180        PROCobey(com%)
2190     UNTIL com%=copy
2200 ENDPROC
2210
2220
2500 DEF FNget_com
2510     REM   Return the ASCII code of a valid command
2520     LOCAL in%
2530     REPEAT
2540        in%=GET
2550     UNTIL in%=128 OR in%=129 OR (in%>=copy AND in%<=up)
2560 =in%
2570
2580
3000 DEF PROCobey(com%)
3010     REM   Carry out action according to com%
3030     REM   Move cursor codes to start from 130 for ON ... GOSUB
3040     IF com%>=copy THEN com%=com%-copy+130
3050     ON com%-127 GOSUB 3100,3200,3300,3400,3500,3600,3700
3060 ENDPROC
3070
3100 REM   Reset point at cursor. Print a space there
3110 REM   and zero appropriate element of board%()
3120     PRINT TAB(cx%+1,cy%+1);" "
3130     board%(cx%,cy%,to%)=FALSE
3140 RETURN
3150
3200 REM   Set point at cursor. Print a star there
```

```
3210 REM  and set appropriate element of board%()
3220    PRINT TAB(cx%+1,cy%+1);"*"
3230    board%(cx%,cy%,to%)=TRUE
3240 RETURN
3250
3300 REM  Copy. Just return
3310 RETURN
3320
3400 REM  Cursor left
3410    REM   Delete old up-arrow
3420    PRINT TAB(cx%+1,num_y%+1);"|"
3430    REM   Update cx%
3440    cx%=cx%-1
3450    IF cx%<0 THEN cx%=num_x%-1
3460    REM   Print new arrow
3470    PRINT TAB(cx%+1,num_y%+1);"^"
3480 RETURN
3490
3500 REM  Cursor right
3510    REM   Delete old up-arrow
3520    PRINT TAB(cx%+1,num_y%+1);"|"
3530    REM   Update cx%
3540    cx%=(cx%+1) MOD num_x%
3550    REM   Print new arrow
3560    PRINT TAB(cx%+1,num_y%+1);"^"
3570 RETURN
3580
3600 REM  Cursor down
3610    REM   Delete old right-arrow
3620    PRINT TAB(0,cy%+1);"-"
3630    REM   Update cy%
3640    cy%=(cy%+1) MOD num_y%
3650    REM   Print new arrow
3660    PRINT TAB(0,cy%+1);"]";
3670 RETURN
3680
3700 REM  Cursor up
3710    REM   Delete old right-arrow
3720    PRINT TAB(0,cy%+1);"-"
3730    REM   Update cy%
3740    cy%=cy%-1
3750    IF cy%<0 THEN cy%=num_y%-1
```

```
3760    REM    Print new arrow
3770    PRINT TAB(0,cy%+1);"]";
3780 RETURN
3790
3800
6000 DEF PROCgeneration(num_x%, num_y%, active%)
6010    REM  Do one generation from "active%" board
6020    REM  onto the other one
6030    LOCAL  i%,j%
6040    count%=0:  REM   Count of live cells
6050    FOR j%=0 TO num_y%-1
6060      FOR i%=0 TO num_x%-1
6070        PROCcell(i%,j%,active%)
6080      NEXT i%
6100    NEXT j%
6110    VDU 30: REM   Home Cursor
6120    FOR j%=0 TO num_y%-1
6130      FOR i%=0 TO num_x%-1
6140        IF board%(i%,j%,1-active%) THEN PRINT"*"; ELSE PRINT" ";
6150      NEXT i%
6160      PRINT
6170    NEXT j%
6180 ENDPROC
6190
6200
7000 DEF PROCcell(i%,j%,active%)
7010    REM  Process one cell at (i%,j%)
7020    LOCAL  state%
7030    state%=FNalive(i%,j%,active%)
7040    board%(i%,j%,1-active%)=state%
7050    IF state% THEN count%=count%+1
7060 ENDPROC
7070
7080
8000 DEF FNalive(i%,j%,active%)
8010    REM Returns TRUE if the cell at (i%,j%) will live in
8020    REM this generation, else returns FALSE
8030    LOCAL count%, dx%, dy%, x%, y%
8040    count%=0
8050    FOR dy%=-1 TO 1
8060      FOR dx%=-1 TO 1
8070        IF (dx% OR dy%)=0 THEN 8130
```

```
8080            x%=(i%+dx%) MOD num_x%
8090            IF x%<0 THEN x%=num_x%-1
8100            y%=(j%+dy%) MOD num_y%
8110            IF y%<0 THEN y%=num_y%-1
8120            count%=count%-board%(x%,y%,active%)
8130          NEXT dx%
8140        NEXT dy%
8150 =count%=3 OR (board%(i%,j%,active%) AND count%=2)
10000 *FX4,0
10010 REPORT:PRINT" at line ";ERL
10020 END
```

As usual, the body of the program is fairly short, the bulk of the work being done by its subordinate procedures. The program is run in MODE 7 so that it will work on a 16K or 32K machine. This mode also has the arrow characters used to position the cursor in the set-up routine. PROCinit obtains the desired board size from the user and dimensions the array board%() accordingly. This has three dimensions, the third being used to store the two grids, the active one and the inactive one. These can be imagined as two parallel planes, board%(x,y,0) and board%(x,y,1). The set-up routine uses the function keys f0 and f1, and also the cursor control keys. The statements to set these up are in PROCinit. Also, two constants are defined. "Copy" is the ASCII value of the COPY key after an *fx4,1 and is the lowest of the cursor control key codes. "Up" is the ASCII code of the cursor-up key that has the highest value. These are used to check for valid entries in FNget_com.

The set-up routine enables the user to initialise the grid in the first generation. There is an invisible cursor whose position is indicated by the up- and right-arrows on the border of the grid. A cell can be made to be alive by pressing the f1 key, or dead by pressing f0. When the pattern has been set-up as desired, the COPY key is used to exit the set-up part, after which the program calculates and displays subsequent generations. Although a 38 by 19 grid is possible, the speed of the program means that 10 by 10 is a practical upper limit, unless you are very patient. PROCset_up calls PROCobey to perform the various cursor actions. The four cursor movements all have the same form. The present arrow is deleted, then the cursor position updated. The cursor wraps-around in all directions. The COPY key signifies the end of "editing" of the board, and the subroutine for this simply returns immediately. The other two commands set and reset a cell. This involves updating the display with a space or star, and storing TRUE (alive) or FALSE (dead) in the appropriate element of board%().

PROCgeneration works out the state of each cell in the inactive board by examining the active board, and then prints the new board out. This is performed by two sets of nested FOR ... NEXT loops. This could be reduced to one set of loops by printing the state of the cells as they are found, but it is more impressive to update the display quickly. PROCgeneration also resets count%, the number of alive cells. This is incremented by PROCcell, which processes one cell at the given co-ordinates.

PROCcell finds the new state of the cell by calling the function FNalive. This returns TRUE if the cell will live in the next generation, FALSE otherwise. Since these are the values used to represent the presence or absence of life, the inactive board is updated by simply assigning the state returned by FNalive to the appropriate element in board%(). Count% is incremented for each live cell encountered.

FNalive is the lowest level routine. It counts the neighbours for the cell given, and does the logic necessary to determine if that cell will live in the next generation. The nested FOR . . . NEXT loops perform a total of 9 iterations, 8 of which count (one of them is the cell itself). It is the necessity of checking for the (0,0) displacement and for wrap-around which slows the routine down quite considerably. FNalive would be a good candidate for a machine code replacement. In this case, the method for storing the states of the cells could be altered. In the limit, each cell only needs one bit to store its state. A more sensible arrangement would be to have one byte per cell, as bytes can be handled efficiently by BASIC as well as machine code.

The remaining routine is the error one. The only error this should ever encounter is the ESCAPE one. Its sole purpose is to reset the cursor control keys to their normal functions if the user decides to escape from the program prematurely.

2.6 Using GOTOs

Here is the list of GOTO dos and don'ts mentioned earlier. As I've already said, it is possible in some languages to write even very long programs without recourse to the GOTO statement. These languages typically make it awkward for the programmer to set-up unconditional branches (Pascal, for example, requires the declaration of each label at the start of the program. See [Brown] for a good example of the way Pascal labels should NOT be used). Others, notably Forth, simply refuse to let you branch at all, the necessity for which is removed by the provision of suitable looping and conditional constructs. The main thing to remember when you find yourself typing "GOTO" in BBC BASIC is that, with few exceptions, there is a better way of doing it.

Situations where GOTOs acceptable (just)

1. To implement a WHILE loop using a REPEAT, or a proper FOR loop. For example:

```
while a>b do
    begin
    a:=a*0.8;
    count:=count+1
    end;
```

in Pascal becomes:

```
100 IF a<=b THEN 150
110 REPEAT
120    a=a*0.8
130    count=count+1
140 UNTIL a<=b
150 ....
```

in BASIC. Notice the way in which the while condition is reversed for the UNTIL termination condition.

2. To avoid the use of a very long IF ... THEN ... ELSE lines. Statements which span more than one screen line are not very readable. In this case it is sometimes better to have just the THEN part on one line, and skip over the ELSE statements with a GOTO:

```
100 IF a<b AND b<c THEN t=a:a=b:b=t:swap%=TRUE ELSE FOR i%=0
    TO 10:data(i%)=a+b*c:NEXT i%
```

This looks better as:

```
100 IF a<b AND b<c THEN t=a:a=b:b=t:swap%=TRUE: GOTO 140
110    FOR i%=0 TO 10
120        data(i%)=a+b*c
130    NEXT i%
140 ....
```

Notice the indentation to indicate the statements affected by the GOTO. If both the THEN and ELSE parts have many statements, it might be better to enclose them in procedures:

```
  100 IF a<b THEN PROCthen ELSE PROCelse
10000 DEF PROCthen      REM   Then statements
10010 ....
10020 ENDPROC
10030
10100 DEF PROCelse      REM   Else statements
10110 ....
10120 ENDPROC
```

This is a very poor substitute for proper statement blocks (as provided by Pascal's begin...end) and should only be used in desperation. A re-think of the program might be a better idea. Of course, there is no reason why user-defined procedures shouldn't appear in IF statements if their use is a NATURAL consequence of the structuring of the program. The method shown above is more of a contrived technique which tries to overcome the weaknesses of the language.

3. In an error situation. After an error has been trapped, either by an ON ERROR statement or by the checking performed by the program, it may be necessary to restart execution somewhere else. A GOTO could be used to jump to this point. Remember though that after an error has been trapped, all loops and procedures etc. are forgotten, so the new start point should be at the outer level of the program.

   If execution is to restart at the beginning, it is possible to use RUN. This obviates the need to know the first line number, but remember that RUN deletes all but the static variables @%–Z%.

4. Jumping out of a FOR ... NEXT loop is preferable to tampering with its looping variable to stop the loop. Remember that BASIC can only keep track of your FOR ... NEXT loops if the variable name is included after the NEXTs. Otherwise jumping out of a loop can cause much confusion. Also, once a FOR loop has been exited, you must stay out. Jumping into a FOR loop is regarded as very poor taste, unless of course it is a result of returning from a GOSUB or PROC. This is under BASIC's control, so the behaviour of the program is quite predictable.

When not to GOTO:

1. Never jump out of a REPEAT loop unless it's to a (terminating) error routine. If the UNTIL statement is phrased properly, all exit conditions can be covered without resorting to IF ... GOTOs. Remember that BASIC can't tell the difference between nested REPEATs, so they must all be terminated properly by an UNTIL.

2. Never GOTO a previous line in order to make a loop. BASIC may not provide all the desired looping constructs, but it certainly provides enough to avoid backward branches. As I mentioned earlier, if you are already familiar with a "standard" BASIC, you must adapt the way you think about programs. There is no "natural" program language, but the GOTO is about as unnatural as you can get. Explicit looping and decision constructs, on the other hand, at least make it clear what the programmer has in mind.

3. The only time a GOSUB should be used in preference to a PROC is in conjunction with ON. The absence of a "case" statement has already been lamented and not much can be done about it until Pascal or BCPL becomes available. In the meantime, ON ... GOSUB does provide a useful construct in certain situations (see Life above).

2.7 Some Function Definitions

The following are some miscellaneous user-defined function definitions. The list is not meant to be exhaustive, but representative of the kind of use to which the FN statement can be put. Several of the definitions are recursive, and as no attempt is made to explain them you could use them to test your understanding of recursion in functions. A book with a lot of useful mathematical formulae is [Pan].

```
1000 DEF FNav(a,b)
1010    REM  Returns average of a and b
1020 =(a+b)/2
1030
1040
1100 DEF FNmean(a,b,c)
1110    REM  Returns mean of a, b and c
1120 =(a+b+c)/3
1130
1140
1200 DEF FNdec(bin$)
1210    REM  Returns decimal number equivalent to bin$
1220    IF bin$="" THEN =0
1230 =VAL(RIGHT$(bin$,1))+2*FNdec(LEFT$(bin$,LEN(bin$)-1))
1240
1250
1300 DEF FNbin(dec%)
1310    REM  Returns binary string of dec%
1320    IF dec%=0 THEN =""
1330 =FNbin(dec% DIV 2)+STR$(dec% MOD 2)
1340
1350
1400 DEF FNcirc_area(r)
1410    REM   Returns the area of the circle radius r
1420 =PI*r*r
1430
1440
1500 DEF FNtri_area(s1,s2,s3)
1510    REM  Returns area of the triangle with
1520    REM  sides length s1,s2 and s3
1530    LOCAL s
1540    s=(s1+s2+s3)/2
1550 =SQR(s*(s-s1)*(s-s2)*(s-s3))
1560
1570
1600 DEF FNis_prime(n%)
1610    REM  Returns TRUE if n% is a prime, otherwise FALSE
1620    IF n%<=1 THEN =FALSE
1630    IF n%=2 THEN =TRUE
1640    IF n% MOD 2 = 0 THEN =FALSE
1650    LOCAL i%, p%
1655    p%=TRUE
```

```
1660    FOR i%=3 TO SQR(n%) STEP 2
1670       IF n% MOD i%=0 THEN p%=FALSE
1680    NEXT i%
1690 =p%
1700
1710
1800 DEF FNdy_dx(f$, x)
1810    REM  Returns the slope of the function
1820    REM  f$ (in x) at x.
1830    LOCAL dx,y1,y2
1840    dx=0.00001
1850    y1=EVAL(f$)
1860    x=x+dx
1870    y2=EVAL(f$)
1880 =(y2-y1)/dx
1890
1900
2000 DEF FNmerge(a$,b$)
2010    REM Returns a$ and b$ merged into one
2015    REM Assumes a$ and b$ are sorted
2020    IF a$="" THEN =b$
2030    IF b$="" THEN =a$
2040    LOCAL a1$,b1$
2050    a1$=LEFT$(a$,1)
2060    b1$=LEFT$(b$,1)
2070    IF a1$<b$ THEN =a1$+FNmerge(MID$(a$,2), b$)
2080 =b1$+FNmerge(MID$(b$,2), a$)
2090
2100
2200 DEF FNncr(n%,r%)
2210    REM  Returns no. of ways of taking r% objects
2220    REM  from n%
2230    IF r%=0 OR n%=r% THEN =1
2240 =FNncr(n%-1,r%-1)+FNncr(n%-1,r%)
2250
2260
2300 DEF FNLine_Len(x1,y1,  x2,y2)
2310    REM  Returns the length of the line bewteen
2320    REM  the points (x1,y1) and (x2,y2)
2330 =SQR((x2-x1)^2 + (y2-y1)^2)
```

Chapter Three

Input and Output

Now that the "building blocks" of BBC BASIC have been dealt with, we can start looking at the more meaty facilities. This chapter looks at the ways in which data is got into and out of the computer. This is called input/output and is usually abbreviated to i/o. BASIC actually has strong i/o facilities compared to some languages, and BBC BASIC has a particularly rich set of i/o operations. The most general statements are INPUT and PRINT for input and output respectively. These are augmented by some lower-level instructions, which enable the programmer to use the display and keyboard with great versatility. It should be noted that by "output" I mean text output to the screen. Graphics output (e.g. the PLOT and DRAW commands) is covered in its own chapter. Similarly, the input of this chapter relates solely to dealing with the computer's keyboard. The choice of what to cover first, "i" or "o", is really arbitrary as they are equally important. Input is slightly simpler, merely because there are less ways of getting information from the user than displaying it to him. Because of this, the input statements are covered in section 3.1, followed by output.

3.1   BBC BASIC Input Methods

3.1.1   The INPUT Statement

This is a very versatile statement, with a seemingly infinite number of different forms. Instead of giving the syntax using the notation adopted in the last chapter, I will present successively more complex forms of INPUT. The most simple version is that which just waits for the user to type a number or string, followed by RETURN. A string is any sequence of characters, except a comma (,).

```
100 INPUT a
110 INPUT a%
120 INPUT !a
130 INPUT a$
```

When the INPUT statement is executed, a question mark (?) is printed, and the computer waits until a line of input is typed by the user. What happens then depends on the sort of value being INPUT. Superficially, the statement "INPUT var" acts as "LET var=whatever is typed in". However, INPUT is much less fussy about the format of right-hand side of the hypothetical assignment statement and never gives "Type mismatch" errors.

If the subject of the INPUT is a number, all the characters up to the first non-numeric one are counted, except initial spaces which are ignored. Below are some examples of the way various input lines are interpreted.

Statement	Line typed in	Interpreted as
INPUT a	123.34	123.34
INPUT a	10+10	10
INPUT a	12e3	12
INPUT a	123E3	123000
INPUT a%	123	123
INPUT a%	123.34	123

Notice that INPUT does not calculate the value of expressions, as shown by the second example. (ZX BASIC devotees take note!) Also, integer INPUTs presented with real numbers will truncate the number (like INT). You can of course type in exponent notation numbers, as long as the "E" is a capital.

When strings are INPUT, all the characters in the line entered are used, with two exceptions. All spaces before the first non-space are ignored and all characters after and including a comma are ignored.

Statement	Line typed in	Interpreted as
INPUT a$	hello there	hello there
INPUT a$	hello, there	hello
INPUT a$	hello there	hello there
INPUT a$	"hello, there"	hello, there
INPUT a$	hello"there	hello"there
INPUT a$	""""	"

If the first non-space character is a quote ("), the input line is treated exactly as a string on the right hand of an assignment, i.e. it needs a closing quote, and to insert a quote in the middle of the string a double quote must be used (""). Quotes embedded in other text have no special meaning.

The INPUT statement can be used to assign more than one variable at once. Multiple variables are separated by commas, as shown below.

```
INPUT a, b$, c%
INPUT A, B, C
INPUT ?&70, ?&71
```

The different items in the INPUT line can be separated by commas or RETURNS, or a combination of both. Each time RETURN is pressed, a question mark is produced if more input is required. You should note that a RETURN on its own is accepted by both string and numeric input. It produces the null string and 0 respectively. In the third example above, the number typed in is treated MOD 256, i.e. only the least significant byte is counted.

Sometimes it is necessary to accept a whole line of input, including leading spaces, commas and all. This only applies to string input of course, and is achieved using the LINE modifier to INPUT. The INPUT LINE sequence is usually used with just one variable, for example

Statement	Line typed in	Interpreted as
INPUT LINE a$	HELLO, WORLD	HELLO, WORLD
INPUT LINE a$	"	"
INPUT LINE a$	"hi	"hi

This form of input is useful in some text processing applications, where the input line must be copied verbatim into the variable. It is also safer in cases where the user may put quotes in the string, without knowing about the rules for matching pairs. "INPUT LINE a" is exactly the same in meaning as "INPUT a", and "INPUT LINE a$,b$" would accept two lines of input, separated by RETURNs.

It is usual to precede an INPUT statement by a PRINT to give the user some idea of what is expected from him, e.g.

```
100 PRINT "How many eggs (1-20) ";
110 INPUT eggs%
```

This is printed as "How many eggs (1–20) ?", the question mark coming from the INPUT statement. It is possible to combine these two statements into one long INPUT, viz.

```
100 INPUT "How many eggs (1-20) ", eggs%
```

Notice that there is a comma after the string instead of a semicolon. In this example, they have exactly the same effect; the comma used in INPUTs should not to be confused with the one in PRINT statements (see section 3.2.1). The only punctuation marks that appear in INPUT statement are the comma and the apostrophe, whose use is explained later. The program below emulates a broken BBC Computer. It issues the standard ">" prompt and accepts a line of input. It then prints "Mistake", regardless of the input.

```
100 ON ERROR REPORT:PRINT
110 REPEAT
120     INPUT ">" a$
130     IF a$<>"" THEN PRINT'"Mistake"
140 UNTIL FALSE
```

Line 120 is yet another form of the INPUT statement. If the comma after the prompt is omitted, no question mark is printed. Here is an exercise for the reader. Extend the program above so that it will appear to accept lines beginning with numbers without comment, and when the program is first run, emulate the BREAK intro. message. Also, program the BREAK key so that it does an OLD then a RUN. (BREAK is *KEY10.) When enhanced in this way, the action of the program should be indistinguishable from the proper BASIC "get line, process it" loop, except that any command produces an error message. When it is finished, save it on a cassette or disc. Take this to the next exhibition at which Acorn Computers are exhibiting. Load the program into one of the BBC Computers on show and run it. Then corner an Acorn person, and tell him the BBC Computer is broken, but you can fix it if he gives you a large sum of money. As long as he doesn't turn the computer off, he will have no option but to succumb to your demands . . .

There are two more INPUT modifiers that are used to provide more versatility when using prompts. These are TAB and the apostrophe. The TAB option is used to position the prompt string anywhere on the screen, and apostrophes (') are used to print blank lines. For example

```
INPUT TAB(20),"Which one (1-5) ", choice%
INPUT TAB(0,15),"How many goes ", num_goes%
INPUT ''"Press return when ready", a$
```

The first line moves the cursor to the 21st column on the screen on the current line and prints the prompt. If the cursor is already past the 21st column, the prompt is printed at the given column on the next line down. The second INPUT moves the cursor to first column on the sixteenth line down, then prints the prompt and INPUTs a number. When the TAB part has two numbers as in this example, it doesn't matter where the cursor is positioned already, the prompt will always be printed at the co-ordinates specified. If the position given is outside the current text window, the prompt is printed at the beginning of the next line down. (All this is explained in greater detail in section 3.2.1.) The third example above prints two new-lines before the prompt is given. The apostrophes can be placed before or after the prompt string, though it is usual to put the prompt immediately before the INPUT's question mark is printed, so the form given above is more common.

All the "extras" to the bare INPUT statement occur as many times as required in any one line, with the exception of LINE, which must appear only once, immediately after the INPUT. After an INPUT LINE, all the string variables being input require a whole line, i.e. the user must separate lines with RETURNs instead of commas. Below are some more general INPUT lines than those already presented.

```
INPUT "Stock no. ", sn%, TAB(20,VPOS-1),"Model no.", mn%
INPUT "Type in your replies separated"'"by commas",a,b,c
INPUT TAB(0,0),q$,TAB(5,5),r$,TAB(11,11),s$
```

The restriction mentioned earlier, that the reply to a numeric INPUT must be a constant, rather than an expression, can be overcome by accepting a string variable instead of a numeric one, and then using the EVAL function on the string. For example,

```
100 INPUT "Starting address ", sa$
110 sa%=EVAL(sa$)
```

This emulates the statement "INPUT "Starting address", sa" in ZX BASIC. It is obviously wise to incorporate some error trapping, in case the user gives an illegal expression. Another example of using EVAL might be in a situation where the user must type in a number in hexadecimal.

```
100 INPUT "Number of bytes (in hex) ", bytes$
110 IF LEFT$(bytes$,1) <> "&" THEN bytes$="&"+bytes$
120 bytes%=EVAL(bytes$)
```

Although the INPUT is very generous with the way prompts may be formatted, it doesn't give much control over what the user actually is allowed to type in. For example, "jam tart" is a perfectly acceptable reply to "INPUT a". The next section deals with some functions that give the programmer the ability to define exactly what characters will be accepted by an input line.

3.1.2   Character Input

It is much easier to provide fool-proof input routines when the program can look at the input on a character by character basis. There are four functions in BBC BASIC with which to do this. They are GET and INKEY, and their string equivalents GET$ and INKEY$. GET is more use in applications where the user must simply type something in his own time. The function waits until the user presses a key, then returns the ASCII code of that key. INKEY needs a time limit in brackets. It will wait for this interval (given in the ubiquitous hundredths of a second), and if the user presses a key in time, the ASCII code of the key is returned. Otherwise, the function returns −1, which is the ASCII code of the null string. INKEY is used in games and other such applications where the keyboard must be examined for only a short period of time, without delaying the program unduly.

The string versions of the functions return the actual characters instead of their codes. Only one pair of functions is really necessary, as the other versions can easily be derived, viz.

```
100 a%=GET   is the same as    100 a%=ASC(GET$)
110 a$=GET$  is the same as    100 a$=CHR$(GET)
```

INKEY can be treated in a similar way. Actually, INKEY can be used to emulate the other three functions quite easily. However, they are all best suited to particular situations, so it is certainly useful having them defined individually in BASIC. Most BASICs just provide one function (e.g. INKEY$ in ZX BASIC and GET, which is a statement, not a function in Applesoft). When you convert programs from different dialects of BASIC, you might think about whether one of the BBC character input functions would do the job better than the one used. Unfortunately it is not always apparent that character input is being done (for example, A%=PEEK(−16384) on the Apple][is the same as A%=INKEY(0) on the BBC machine).

When GET and its counterparts are being used, the characters typed are not "echoed" onto the screen. This means the user can't see what he is typing unless the program explicitly prints the input. The program below emulates a typewriter.

```
100 REPEAT
110    a%=GET
120    IF a% >= 32 THEN PRINT CHR$(a%);
130    IF a% = 13 THEN PRINT
140 UNTIL FALSE
```

The IF at line 120 makes sure that only non-control characters are echoed. This means that the return character (whose code is 13) will not be echoed. In order to enable new lines to be generated, the second IF checks if the user has typed RETURN. Even if the PRINT at line 120 had been unconditional, line 130 would still be needed. This is because "PRINT CHR$(13);" only does the carriage-return part of the new line sequence. That is, the cursor is sent to the beginning if the current line. To perform the line-feed part, another character must be sent, CHR$(11). The simple statement PRINT causes both these characters to be printed, so the correct carriage-return/ line-feed action is achieved.

It is not always desirable to echo what the user types in. A common case is that of password entry. If a program enables the user to perform some drastic operation, such as delete a file, or even just access "sensitive" data, it is a good idea to stop undesirables from using the program by requiring the entry of a password before the program will proceed. This is similar to the Personal Identification Number required by a cash-point machine before it will give you money.

```
100 REPEAT
110    pw$=""
120    PRINT TAB(0,2);"Password: ";
130    REPEAT
140       in$=GET$
150       pw$=pw$+in$
160    UNTIL LEN(pw$)=4 OR in$=CHR$(127)
170 UNTIL in$ <> CHR$(127)
180 IF pw$<>"10cc" THEN PRINT "Sorry":END
190 REM    carry on
```

The routine accepts a password (which must be four characters long) without echoing the characters. If the user makes a mistake, he can press the DELETE key (ASCII code 127) to start again.

The program below is an "reaction tester". The computer pauses for a random interval between 3 and 10 seconds. It then displays a "Now" prompt. The user hits a key as fast as he can. The time taken is then displayed.

```
100 t%=TIME+RND(700)+300
110 REPEAT UNTIL TIME=t%
120 PRINT "Now";: *FX15,0
```

```
130 t%=TIME:REPEAT UNTIL INKEY$(0) <>""
140 PRINT (TIME-t%)/100;" seconds"
150 END
```

The *FX15,0 clears the input buffer so that only keys pressed after this statement has been reached are counted.

The functions GET and INKEY and the INPUT statement all use the routines for getting characters provided in the machine operating system (for example "osrdch"). Because of this, the editing keys still work as normal, i.e. they move the cursor and allow characters to be copied from the screen instead of being typed in. This can sometimes be useful, but can also be a nuisance. The four cursor moving keys are very useful when the user has to give some input to determine a movement. An example appeared in the Life program of the last chapter. When the board was being set up, the cursor moving keys were used to specify the cell to be changed. The editing function of the arrow keys is disabled by the command "*FX4,1" and re-enabled by "FX4,0" After a "*FX4,1", the cursor control keys act as normal keys with high ASCII codes. The codes 135 to 139 are given by the COPY, left-arrow, right-arrow, down-arrow and up-arrow. In the Life program, the fact that the codes of the cursor keys are consecutive makes the use of an ON ... GOSUB statement possible. The program below uses the cursor keys to move a "wiper" which leaves a trail that reveals the contents of the array text$. It could form the basis of a word guessing game.

```
100 REM     Cursor "Game"
110
120 MODE 7
130 PROCinit
140 REPEAT
150    key%=FNget_key
160    PROCmove(key%)
170 UNTIL key%=copy%
180 PRINT
190 *FX 4,0
200 END
210
220
1000 DEF PROCinit    REM  Set-up board etc.
1010    LOCAL row%, col%
1020    rows%=25
1030    cols%=39
1035    copy%=135
1037    PRINT"Please hang on"
1040    DIM text$(rows%-1)
1050    FOR row%=0 TO rows%-1
```

```
1060        text$(row%)=""
1070        FOR col%=1 TO cols%
1080            text$(row%)=text$(row%)+FNchar
1090        NEXT col%
1100     NEXT row%
1110     c_row%=rows% DIV 2
1120     c_col%=cols% DIV 2
1130     *FX 4,1
1140     CLS
1150 ENDPROC
1160
1200 DEF FNchar
1210     REM    Returns a space or letter
1220     REM     with equal probability
1230 IF RND > 0 THEN =" " ELSE =CHR$(RND(26)+ASC("A")-1)
1250
1260
1270
2000 DEF FNget_key
2010     REM    Get an editing key
2020     LOCAL key%
2030     REPEAT
2040        key%=GET
2050     UNTIL key% >= 135 AND key% <= 139
2060 =key%
2070
2080
2090
3000 DEF PROCmove(key%)
3010     REM    Moves the cursor in a direction
3020     REM     determined by key%
3040     ON key%-134 GOSUB 3100, 3200, 3300, 3400, 3500
3050 ENDPROC
3060
3070
3100 REM    Copy key. Do nothing
3110 RETURN
3130
3200 REM    Left-arrow
3210     IF c_col% = 1 THEN RETURN
3220     c_col%=c_col%-1
3230     PRINT TAB(c_col%-1, c_row%); MID$(text$(c_row%), c_col%, 1);
3240 RETURN
```

```
3250
3260
3300 REM     Right-arrow
3310    IF c_col% = cols% THEN RETURN
3320    c_col%=c_col%+1
3330    PRINT TAB(c_col%-1, c_row%); MID$(text$(c_row%), c_col%, 1);
3340 RETURN
3350
3360
3400 REM     Down-arrow
3410    IF c_row% = rows%-1 THEN RETURN
3420    c_row%=c_row%+1
3430    PRINT TAB(c_col%-1, c_row%); MID$(text$(c_row%), c_col%, 1);
3440 RETURN
3450
3460
3500 REM     Up-arrow
3510    IF c_row% = 0 THEN RETURN
3520    c_row%=c_row%-1
3530    PRINT TAB(c_col%-1, c_row%); MID$(text$(c_row%), c_col%, 1);
3550 RETURN
```

The array text$ has rows% elements, each of which is a string of cols% characters. Row zero of the array correponds to the first line of the display. Row rows%−1 is the bottom line. In the current program, the array is initialised to random letters or spaces. In a proper game, the array could be initialised with particular words. The player could be given a certain number of moves in which to get as many words as possible. The variables c_row% and c_col% are the position of the cursor. Lines 3230, 3330 etc. print the character corresponding to the current cursor position.

The red function keys are also quite useful in programs. The idea is that each key is programmed to represent a particular task in the program. For example, "f0" could mean "drop atomic bomb". However, with menu driven programs, where the user selects one option from a list, there is no real advantage to be gained by using the function keys rather than the digits 0–9. I feel that the red keys come into their own in the immediate mode, where they can be programmed to represent strings. For example, when I was writing this book, I typed it in as lots of programs consisting of nothing but PRINT statements. These were then saved on tape. When it came to getting hard-copy, I simply ran the programs with the printer enabled. Throughout all this, the keys f0, f1 and f2 were programmed as

```
*KEY0 "P.""""
*KEY1 """"'|M"
*KEY2 """"'|MP.""""
```

These definitions combined with the AUTO command meant that I only needed to press one key (f2) at the end of each line, once the initial line had been started with a press of f0. The key f1 was used somewhat less frequently, but was still useful.

Under MOS 1.0, it is possible to to make the function keys represent any range of ten consecutive ASCII codes. For example, "*FX227,128" would set f0 to be CHR$(128), f1 as CHR$(129) and so on. The "*FX228" command can be used to set the SHIFTed function key codes. This facility is not available in MOS 0.1, so machines with this version of the operating system must have their red keys programmed in a different way. The vertical bar (|) before a character means "control-character". For example,

```
*KEY0 |@
```

would set f0 to CHR$(0). To obtain the vertical bar itself, ‖. The sequence "|!" means "add 128 to the code of the next character". Thus "|!a" would produce CHR$(128+97) = CHR$(225). "|!|A" would give CHR$(128+1) = CHR$(129). These special sequences are of course only valid in the strings used to program the function keys. Once the keys have been set up in this way, GET etc. can be used to read them as any other key, but with higher ASCII codes. If a function key is programmed as a long string, all the characters can be obtained with successive calls to GET or INKEY.

3.1.3 Input Routines

Now we have seen what GET and INKEY do, it is possible to write some useful input routines. In "casual" programs that you knock up in one evening, and then discard almost immediately, it is obviously not vital to have every piece of input stringently checked; if you make a mistake, it is a simple matter to press ESCAPE and start again. However, most people write, or would like to write, programs that are used by others. These users might be fellow computer enthusiasts, who can cope with the errors caused by poor input checking. On the other hand, they might be "dumb users", people who understand very little about computers, and may even hold them in awe. The message "BAD Hex" may be seen as some kind of curse in the eyes of naive users. The programmer should do all within his power to protect inexperienced users from the underlying unfriendliness of the computer. Whenever possible, get your mum/girlfriend/wife (see Chapter 2) to test your latest masterpiece. Even if what the program does is beyond the guinea-pig's comprehension, it will at least be obvious if the prompts etc. are effective.

Clearly an important part of making a program user-friendly is the way in which data is accepted from the keyboard. As mentioned in section 3.1.1, the INPUT statement is too tolerant for its own good. It is impossible to tell if the user actually typed "0", or he mis-hit the "1" key and pressed "Q" instead. Both will be interpreted as zero by INPUT. Ideally the computer will not accept any character which is illegal in the data required. For example, a numeric input should be made to accept only the digits and decimal point (and possibly "E" in scientific programs).

Another problem is using INPUT in repeat loops. Consider the example below, which gets a number in the range 1–9.

```
100 REPEAT
110     INPUT TAB(0,10),"Quantity (1-9) ",q%
120 UNTIL q% >= 1 AND q% <= 9
```

The problem is that if the user types in an illegal value, the prompt is re-printed, but the previous entry is not deleted from the screen. This can be very confusing to the user. It would be much better if the previous input was erased. Also, the user should be warned that an error occurred, even if only by the sounding of the "bell". When an operator is familiar with a program, a sounding of the bell illicits a Pavlov's dogs-type response. This is good as re-typing an erroneous input becomes a reflex reaction, which in turn leads to efficiency. The function below returns an integer in the range lo%..hi%. The prompt, pr$ is printed at the current cursor position.

```
1000 DEF FNinput(pr$, lo%, hi%)
1010     REM     Returns an integer in the
1020     REM     range lo%..hi%.
1030     ON ERROR VDU 7:GOTO 1090
1040     LOCAL cx%, cy%, line_len%, in, ok%
1050     line_len%=40: REM     Change if necessary
1060     cx%=POS: cy%=VPOS
1070     del$=STRING$(line_len% - LEN(pr$) - cx%, " ")
1080     del$=del$ + STRING$(LEN(del$), CHR$(127))
1090     REPEAT
1100         ok%=TRUE
1120         PRINT TAB(cx%, cy%);pr$;del$;
1130         INPUT in
1140         IF in<>INT(in) THEN ok%=FALSE
1160         IF in < lo% OR in > hi% THEN ok%=FALSE
1170         IF NOT ok% THEN VDU 7
1180     UNTIL ok%
1190     ON ERROR OFF
1200 =in
```

The string del$ is used to clear the line after the prompt. First of all enough spaces are printed to delete any characters from the end of the prompt to the end of the line, then the same number of back-spaces are printed to get back to the end of the prompt. The variable line_len% should be equal to the number of columns in the current display mode. As well as being in the correct range, "in" is also checked for integrality. Another error might be the user pressing the ESCAPE key, or typing in a number with more than 31 digits (which will cause an "Out of range" error). Whenever a number is deemed unacceptable for some reason, the bell is sounded by a VDU 7 statement, and the user must try again.

Some programs, such as the disassembler of Chapter five, deal mainly with numbers expressed in hexadecimal notation. The function below accepts a four digit hex number from the keyboard. Only valid hexadecimal digits are allowed, though the routine will take upper or lower case letters. Lower case letters are converted to upper case before they are echoed.

```
1000 DEF FNget_hex
1010   REM    Get a 4-digit hex address
1020   LOCAL hex$, c$
1030   *FX 4,1
1040   PRINT"Address: &----";
1050   PRINT TAB(POS-4, VPOS);
1060   hex$="&"
1070   REPEAT
1080     REPEAT
1090       c$=GET$
1110     UNTIL FNhex(c$) OR c$=CHR$(127)
1120     IF c$ = CHR$(127) THEN PROCback_space ELSE PROCappend(c$)
1130   UNTIL LEN(hex$)=5
1140   *FX4,0
1150 =EVAL(hex$)
1160
1170
1500 DEF FNhex(c$)
1510   LOCAL h%
1520   h%= c$>="0" AND c$<="9"  OR  c$>="a" AND c$<="f"
1530 =h%  OR  c$>="A" AND c$<="F"
1540
1550
1600 DEF PROCback_space
1610   IF hex$="&" THEN ENDPROC
1620   hex$=LEFT$(hex$, LEN(hex$)-1)
1630   PRINT c$;"-";CHR$(8);
1640 ENDPROC
1650
1660
1700 DEF PROCappend(c$)
1710   REM    Make letters upper case
1720   IF c$>="A" THEN c$=CHR$(ASC(c$) AND 223)
1730   hex$=hex$+c$
1740   PRINT c$;
1750 ENDPROC
```

The four dashes printed after the "&" (which is supposed to tell the user that hexadecimal notation is expected) mark the positions of the four digits to be entered. The only characters that are recognised are the digits, the letters "a"–"f" and "A"–"F", and backspace key. The latter is handled by PROCback_space. If hex$ has only the "&", to which it is initialised, nothing happens. This is equivalent to trying to backspace past the ">" of a BASIC input line. If there is something to delete, hex$ is shortened by one character and the character replaced by a "–" on the screen. The sequence c$;"–";CHR$(8) has the effect: delete the last character (c$ contains CHR$(127)), print the "–" marker, backspace back to the last digit. The difference between CHR$(127) and CHR$(8) is that the former replaces the last character with a space and the latter just moves the cursor back one character in a non-destructive way. The other notable thing is that the routine ends as soon as the last digit has been entered. Because of this, RETURN doesn't have to be pressed. More importantly, a mistake in the last digit cannot be corrected. As an exercise, you could change the routine so that a RETURN is required, and maybe add other features such as making the number of digits allowed a parameter, and sounding a warning if an illegal character is typed.

The next example is a very general input routine. There are two parameters, a prompt and a format string. The latter is used to determine exactly what characters are allowed where in the input string. The letter "a" means a letter is allowed in that position, "0" means a digit must occur. Any other character stands for itself, apart from "~" which means "any character". For example, the format string "0000.00" would accept four digits, a decimal point, then another two digits. "aa00a" is a code that should be recognisable to radio amateurs. It is the code used in a special system used by hams to specify locations to about 2km. For example, my home has the code "AL34j". The function as presented certainly has great scope for improvement. The format codes could be made more versatile. For example, it would be very useful for the user to be able type in a variable number of digits in a numeric input. As with most of the examples in this book, the reader should think about how he can improve the program given, making it more versatile, or more specific to his needs.

```
1000 DEF FNinput(pr$, form$)
1010    REM    Inputs a string of format form$.
1020    REM    pr$ is the prompt
1030    LOCAL in$, bs$, i%, text$
1040    PRINT pr$;STRING$(LEN(form$), "-");
1050    PRINT TAB(POS-LEN(form$), VPOS);
1060    text$=""
1070    bs$=CHR$(127)
1080    i%=1
1090    REPEAT
1100       in$=FNget(MID$(form$, i%, 1))
1110       IF in$=bs$ THEN PROCback_space ELSE PROCappend(in$)
```

```
1130     UNTIL LEN(text$) = LEN(form$)
1140 =text$
1150
1160
1500 DEF FNget(match$)
1510     REM    Gets a character of type match$
1520     LOCAL in$
1530     IF match$="0" THEN =FNdigit
1540     IF match$="a" THEN =FNletter
1550     IF match$="~" THEN =GET$
1560     REM   Get match$ then
1570     REPEAT
1580        in$=GET$
1590     UNTIL in$=match$ OR in$=bs$
1600 =in$
1610
1620
1700 DEF FNdigit
1710     LOCAL in$
1720     REPEAT
1730        in$=GET$
1740     UNTIL "0"<=in$ AND in$<="9"   OR   in$=bs$
1750 =in$
1760
1800 DEF FNletter
1810     LOCAL in$
1820     REPEAT
1830        in$=GET$
1840     UNTIL "a"<=in$ AND in$<="z"   OR   "A"<=in$ AND in$<="Z"   OR in$=bs$
1850 =in$
1860
1870
1880
2000 DEF PROCback_space
2005     IF text$="" THEN ENDPROC
2010     i%=i%-1
2020     text$=LEFT$(text$, LEN(text$)-1)
2030     PRINT in$;"-";CHR$(8);
2040 ENDPROC
2050
2060
3000 DEF PROCappend(in$)
```

```
3005    i%=i%+1
3010    text$=text$+in$
3020    PRINT in$;
3030 ENDPROC
```

3.2   Output

The number of ways of getting information onto the BBC Micro's screen is quite phenomonal. In this chapter, I only deal with purely textual output, i.e. printing characters as opposed to drawing shapes. Even so, there are still eight distinct display modes (four on 16K machines), with various sophisticated options such as changing colour and text windows. All of these facilities are described in this chapter; they provide a good background for graphics, which is the subject of the next chapter.

There are two different types of display on the BBC Computer. Mode 7, the teletext mode, is called a "hard display". The others are all "soft displays". The difference is the way in which the information on the screen is stored. The teletext mode uses only one byte of storage for each character on the screen. This, combined with the "crafty" way colour is obtained in mode 7, means that only 1000 bytes are required for a display with full colour, limited graphics and flashing characters. However, this economy of memory means that certain capabilities that are present in the soft modes cannot be obtained in mode 7. This includes user-defined characters and the high resolution graphics of modes 0,1,2,4 and 5. Because of these differences, I will concentrate on the soft modes in this part. The techniques for obtaining colour and other effects in MODE 7 are described in the User Guide (Chapter 28). In addition, numerous articles have been published in the press about teletext.

There are five different display formats in all. These are combinations of 20, 40 and 80 columns across the screen and 25 or 32 rows down. The table below gives the display data for the eight different modes.

MODE	FORMAT	COLOURS	MEMORY
0	80 X 32	2	20K
1	40 X 32	4	20K
2	20 X 32	16	20K
3	80 X 25	2	16K
4	40 X 32	2	10K
5	20 X 32	4	10K
6	40 X 25	2	8K
7	40 X 25	16	1K

It is obvious that the soft displays use far more memory than the teletext display. In modes 0 to 6 there is a relationship between the number of characters that can be displayed on the screen, the number of colours available and the amount of memory used. Also, the COLOURS column gives the number of different colours on the screen at once. The actual colours displayed can be any from a set of eight steady colours and eight flashing ones. This is explained in section 3.2.2.

3.2.1 The PRINT Statement

This is the work-horse of text output. Like INPUT, PRINT has dozens of options and modifiers. Some of these have already been introduced in section 3.1.1, when the INPUT prompting mechanism was described. The most simple form of PRINT statement is just the word on its own. The line

```
100 PRINT
```

would perform a new-line operation, moving the cursor to the start of the next line and scrolling the display if necessary. Obviously this is not the principal use of PRINT. It is normally used to print the values of expressions. These can be string or numeric expressions. For example:

```
100 PRINT a+b
110 PRINT b*b-4*a*c
120 PRINT a%>=x%
130 PRINT A$+" said "+B$
140 PRINT a$=b$+c$
```

More than one expression can be PRINTed by each statement if the expressions are separated by symbols which have special effects in PRINT statements. In order of how drastic an effect they cause, they are: space (or nothing if no confusion can occur), semicolon, comma, and apostrophe. When two items are separated by a space, they are printed as normal, with no extra gaps between them. Now numbers are usually printed so that they are right-justified, with enough preceding spaces to ensure ten characters are printed in all. (The total number of characters printed is controlled by @%, see below.) This is illustrated below.

```
Statement            Effect
PRINT"a" "b"        ab
PRINT"a"123         a.......123
PRINT"abc"1234      abc......1234
PRINT1 2 "a"        .........1.........2a
PRINT1"a"2          .........1a.........2
```

The "."'s represent spaces. Notice that there is no need for a space between "a" and 123, as the two objects are easily distinguishable. On the other hand, the space between 1 and 2 in the fourth example is compulsory if numbers are not to be interpreted as the single number 12. The numbers always take up ten character positions, whereas strings occupy exactly the length of the string.

The semicolon is used to suppress the leading spaces before a number, and also to stop the computer from printing a new line after all the expressions have been printed. When strings are being printed, separating them with a semicolon is exactly the same as separating them with a space.

```
PRINT "a";"b"         ab
PRINT "a";1;2         a12
PRINT 1 2;
PRINT 3 4             .........1.........2.........3.........4
PRINT "The time is";
PRINT " one pm"       The time is one pm
PRINT 1;2             .........12
PRINT ;1;2            12
```

The action of the comma is defined as "printing enough spaces to ensure that the next item is printed in a new print field". Each line of the display is split up into imaginary sections. When the computer is first turned on, they are initialised to be ten characters wide. Thus there are four print fields in a forty column mode, starting at character positions zero, 10, 20 and 30. When printing is done using commas, the output is aligned with the edges of the print fields. Strings are aligned with the left edges of the print fields, numbers with the right edges. The examples below should illustrate the action of commas.

```
Statement             Effect
                      01234567890123456789 0
PRINT 1,2                      1         2
PRINT "a",1           a                  1
PRINT "a","b"         a         b
PRINT 1,"a"                    1a
```

The comma in BBC BASIC is a little lazy compared to most others. The action of most BASICs' comma is to print a "tab". This means enough spaces are printed to move the cursor into the next print field. However, the BBC comma will only go as far as the next unused field, after which it will refuse to do anything more unless something is printed. This point may be important when converting programs to the BBC machine. The statement "PRINT ,,1,,2" in most BASICs would cause the cursor to move to the third print field, where a 2 is printed, then move to the sixth print field, where a 2 is printed. In BBC BASIC, that statement will have exactly the same effect as simply "PRINT 1,2". Notice that because numbers are right-justified, and strings are left-justified, statements of the form "PRINT number, string" are printed similarly to the last example above, i.e. there is nothing between the two items. This can be avoided by preceding the string with a space, or changing the statement to the form "PRINT;number,string", which would cause the number to be left justified as well.

The apostrophe has exactly the same use as in an INPUT statement, that is, it causes a new-line to be generated. As many apostrophes as required can be placed adjacent to one another, as in

```
PRINT "The object of this game is to"''"see what the";
PRINT "maximum"''"number of ....etc."
```

The TAB modifier works in exactly the same way as in the INPUT statement. There are the two forms, one with just the column number, and the other with the column and row number. The procedure below uses TAB to print a three-part heading. The three parameters left$, mid$ and right$ are left-justified, centred and right-justified. The procedure could be called, for example, with the line

```
100 PROCheading("Using BBC BASIC","--32--","P J Cockerell")
```

The "—32—" is meant to be a page number. The procedure is listed below.

```
1000 DEF PROCheading(left$, mid$, right$)
1010    REM    Prints a three part heading
1020    LOCAL line_len%, tab1%, tab2%
1030    line_len%=80
1040    PRINT left$;
1050    tab1%=(line_len% - LEN(mid$)) DIV 2
1060    IF tab1% >= POS+1 THEN PRINT TAB(tab1%);mid$;
1070    tab2%=line_len% - LEN(right$)
1080    IF tab2% >= POS+1 THEN PRINT TAB(tab2%);right$  ELSE PRINT
1090 ENDPROC
```

If any of the parts overlap, the procedure will miss out the right-most one. The tests at lines 1060 and 1080 ensure that there is at least one space between all three parts. The two co-ordinate form of TAB can be used to print headings vertically. This is useful when labelling the axes of graphs and other diagrams (see next chapter).

```
1000 DEF PROCvertical(x%, y%, heading$)
1010    REM    Prints heading$ vertically, starting
1030    REM    at TAB(x%,y%).
1040    LOCAL i%, line%
1050    lines%=32
1060    FOR i%=1 TO LEN(heading$)
1070        IF i%+y% <= lines% THEN PRINT TAB(x%,i%+y%-1);MID$(heading$,i%,1)
1080    NEXT i%
1090 ENDPROC
```

The variable lines% is used to check that the character will actually be on the screen. This is a useful function that should have been provided.

Another print modifier is SPC. This is used to print a given number of spaces in a PRINT statement, e.g.

```
100 PRINT A$;SPC(4);B$
```

It is an alternative to the form " ". In terms of storage used, SPC is worthwhile if more than two spaces are being printed. SPC(3) is four bytes of storage (the SPC part is stored as one byte), and " " is five bytes long. Obviously the savings are even greater for long spaces. The provision of SPC almost makes up for the fact that commas don't work in the usual way in print statements, but it is still not as useful because it does not automatically move the cursor to a print field boundary. Note that SPC is not a function; it does not return a given number of spaces, but produces them in a PRINT (or INPUT) statement. Below is a function definition to emulate the tabulation property of other BASIC's comma. It returns enough spaces to emulate the action of n% commas.

```
1000 DEF FNcomma(n%)
1010    REM     returns spaces for n% tabs
1020    LOCAL width%
1030    width%=a% AND &FF
1040 =STRING$(width%*n% - POS MOD width%, " ")
```

The function would be used in statements such as

```
100 PRINT a$;FNcomma(5);b$;FNcomma(2);c$
```

It makes use of the value of @%. This is a variable which contains four fields of information used in printing. These will be described in detail below.

As its name implies, @% is an integer variable. It is very similar to the static variables A% to Z%, except that it should not be used to store information – it is reserved especially for use by the PRINT statement (and sometimes the STR$ function). Like all integers, @% is four bytes long. Each of these bytes has a special significance. If you print the value of @% in hexadecimal by the statement

```
PRINT ~a%
```

you will normally get "A0A". The PRINT statement suppresses leading zeroes on numbers, so this is actually "00 00 0A 0A" (I inserted the spaces to separate the individual bytes in the number). Starting with the least significant byte (i.e. the right-most one), the fields have the following meanings. The "0A" on the right is the print field width. The default setting is 10, which means that all numbers are printed with at least ten characters. 10 is of course 0A in hexadecimal. It was this byte of @% that FNcomma used above. The print width can be set to any number between one and 255. Ten is a sensible default, as few numbers actually have more than ten digits when printed (at least they shouldn't; there are very few physical quantities that can be measured to that accuracy), and ten is a factor of 20, 40 and 80, the overall display widths of the various modes, This means that there is always a whole number of print fields on a line. Remember that the field width determines the minimum number of characters printed in a number, not the maximum. If the number has more characters (including the decimal point, "E" and signs if present) than the print field width, the number is still printed, but will spill over into the next print field, which might cause subsequent numbers to be mis-aligned.

The second byte of @%, which is also 10 by default, determines the number of digits actually printed. Since the way this is interpreted depends on the value of the third byte, I will describe them together. The third byte determines the format in which a number will be printed. There are three formats, general (0), exponent, or scientific (1) and fixed (2). The default is "general". In this format, numbers will be printed in the pattern "number.number", if the number is in the range 0.1 to 10 raised to the power B2, where B2 is the value of byte two. All trailing zeroes are suppressed, and all leading zeroes, except one immediately before a decimal point are suppressed. The examples below show how various numbers would be printed with @%=00 00 03 0A.

Number	Printed as
12	12
.01	1E-2
1234	1.23E3
500.51	501
12.456	12.5

Notice that at most B2 significant digits are printed. Numbers are always rounded rather than truncated. If the number is less than 0.1 or greater or equal to 10^B2, then exponent format is used.

Exponent format is what manufacturers of pocket calculators like to call "scientific notation". When printed in this format, numbers are of the form "digit.numberEnumber", or just "digitEnumber". In this format, byte two gives the number of significant digits that are printed. Since there is always one digit before the point, there will be B2-1 digits after it. Below are the same numbers as before, as printed with @%=00 01 03 0A.

Number	Printed as
12	1.20E2
.01	1.00E-2
1234	1.23E3
500.01	5.00E2
12.456	1.25E2

Notice that the computer cleverly lines up all the decimal points. There are four spaces "reserved" for the exponent part, so that the worst case of something like 0.0000000001, or 1.00E-10 will fit in. Then come the B2-1 decimal digits, then the decimal point, the mantissa digit, and finally the sign, if present. BBC BASIC never prints a plus sign, only the minus one for negative numbers.

The last format is the fixed point format. This is the one heralded (by Acorn) as every accountant's dream. Numbers are printed in the form "number.number" whenever possible. Moreover, the number of digits after the decimal point is a constant, specified by B2. The usual examples are given below.

Number	Printed as
12	12.000
.01	0.010
1234	1234.000
500.01	500.010
12.456	12.456

This is with @%=00 02 03 0A. Obviously the accountant's format would have B2 as 02, so that all the pounds and pence line up. If the sums are too large to fit in the print field, general format is used instead. As I mentioned in the last chapter, the built-in error handling routine prints the error line, ERL, using a normal PRINT statement. Consequently, if @% is something like &0001030A, you get error messages such as:

```
Mistake at line 1.24E3
```

The last byte of @% is used not by PRINT but STR$. When STR$ is called to convert a number to a string representation, it first examines the fourth byte of @%. If this byte is not zero, then the string returned has exactly the same format as if it had been printed, except for the leading spaces. This means that bytes 2 and 3 of @% are used to determine the format of the string conversion. If byte 4 is zero (the default case), STR$ does not bother with what @% contains, but just uses the general format, i.e. the string returned is what would be printed if @%=&A0A.

When numbers are being printed in hex, only the width field of @% has any meaning. It is only possible to print integers in hexadecimal in BBC BASIC, so 255.5 would be printed as FF. (The number is truncated rather than rounded.) When ˜ is used to print in hex, it only affects the next item to be printed. If the item is a string, it has no effect at all.

```
PRINT ˜255,4095     prints    FF    4095
PRINT ˜255,˜4095    prints    FF    FFF
PRINT ˜"255",255    prints    255   255
```

There are three more functions and another statement that can be used in conjunction with PRINT. Two of the functions, POS and VPOS have been used in several examples already, so there meaning should be obvious. POS returns the current column of the cursor (from zero to N−1, where N is the number of columns in the present MODE), and VPOS returns the cursor's vertical position (from zero to L−1, L being the number of display lines and line zero being the top line). The functions are sometimes used to remember the current cursor position so that it can be restored after some processing. For example, the routine below prints an error message on the bottom line of the display, then re-positions the cursor.

```
1000 DEF PROCerror
1010    LOCAL x%, y%
1020    x%=POS: y%=VPOS
1030    PRINT TAB(0, 30);
1040    REPORT
1050    PRINT TAB(x%, y%);
1060 ENDPROC
```

Notice that the PRINTs are followed by semicolons to prevent a new-line being generated. Even so, REPORT does its own new-line, so the cursor is positioned on the line above the bottom one; REPORT moves it to the very bottom line. Another use of the two functions is to print text in a position relative to the present one. The procedure below prints its parameter string, then places a box of "*" round it.

```
1000 DEF PROCbox(a$)
1010    LOCAL x%, y%, i%, j%
1020    x%=POS: y%=VPOS
1030    PRINT a$
1040    PRINT TAB(x%-2, y%+2);STRING$(LEN(a$)+4, "*")
1050    PRINT TAB(x%-2, y%-2);STRING$(LEN(a$)+4, "*")
1060    NEXT i%
1070    FOR j%=y%-2 TO y%+2
1080       PRINT TAB(i%-2, j%);"*";TAB(i%+LEN(a$)+1, j%);"*"
1090    NEXT j%
1100 ENDPROC
```

In order for the procedure to work, there must be sufficient space to print the asterisks, i.e. the current cursor position must be at least three spaces from any of the screen edges.

The remaining PRINT-related words are not quite as useful as POS and VPOS. The last function is called COUNT. It returns the number of characters that have been printed since the last new-line. It would be identical to POS but for the fact that some characters do not move the cursor, or if they do, they move it backwards or up. Thus, if you don't print any of these control characters, COUNT will equal POS. Even the Provisional User Guide has some difficulty giving a decent example using the function. The one given prints 16 "*" in a row, something that Mr. Coll admits can be achieved much easier, using STRING$ for example. I think that COUNT may be more useful when sending output to a printer, and as such is outside the scope of this book.

A statement associated with COUNT is WIDTH. It has the form

```
WIDTH expression
```

where the expression yields an integer between zero and 255. Whenever characters are PRINTed, the value of COUNT is compared with the latest

WIDTH specified. If the printing of a character would cause COUNT to exceed this width, a newline is generated to reset COUNT. The same action occurs when a program is being listed. By default, the width is zero, which means that no new-lines will be generated at all. The effect of WIDTH can be seen by typing "WIDTH 20" in MODE 4, then listing a program. Only half the screen will be used in the listing.

Whereas the PRINT statement is usually used to display numeric or string expressions, the VDU statement is used to output individual characters. The relationship between PRINT and VDU is similar to that between INPUT and GET, though VDU is a statement rather than a function. VDU has the form:

```
VDU expression [ ,/; expression ]* {;}
```

The "/" is not part of the syntax, but indicates that there could be either a comma or semicolon in that position. In English, the VDU statement is followed by one or more expressions separated by commas or semicolons. The expressions in this case are integers. If the expression is followed by a comma, or is the last expression in the statement, then it is treated as an eight-bit number, i.e. is "reduced" to the range 0–255. If the expression is followed by a semicolon, it is regarded as a sixteen-bit quantity in the range 0–65535. The first case is easier to grasp: "VDU a" is exactly equivalent to "PRINT CHR$(a);". The statement "VDU a,b,c" has the same effect as "PRINT CHR$(a);CHR$(b);CHR$(c);". You can prove this to yourself by typing "VDU 65,66,67". The string "ABC" is printed. This is because the ASCII codes for A, B, and C are 65, 66 and 67 repectively.

Obviously it is much easier to use PRINT"ABC" than the equivalent VDU statement. However, where VDU does come in useful is when control characters are being output. On pp. 378–389 of the final User Guide, there is a description of the so-called VDU drivers. The ASCII codes 0–31 and 127 perform special tasks when printed. There is a routine in the machine operating system called "oswrch". This is the program that controls all the activity of the display of the BBC Micro, such as changing modes, drawing lines and more mundane tasks like printing the letter "A". All programs that require something to be printed have to call this routine. Since BBC BASIC is just other program, albeit a rather large one, whenever anything is to be printed, the oswrch routine is used. The VDU command allows direct access to this routine. As an example, refer to page 380 of the User Guide. The code 7 is the "bell" character. Whenever an ASCII character with code 7 is sent to the oswrch routine, a "beep" is sounded on the computer's speaker. This can be obtained by

```
1. The statement  "VDU 7"
2. The statement PRINT CHR$(7);
3. Pressing "CTRL" and "G"
```

The last method works because control-G has the ASCII code 7. Whenever a key is pressed during input on the BBC Micro, its code is sent to oswrch so that it is "echoed" on the screen. The exception is, as we have seen, when the keyboard is interrogated by INKEY or GET. In this case, the character is not echoed unless the user specifically arranges it.

Another example is the MODE statement. In BASIC, MODE is followed by a number which should be between 0 and 7 (if it isn't, it is treated as MOD 8). All that MODE does is send two characters to oswrch; the first one is the code 22 (control-V), which informs oswrch that we want to change mode. After this, oswrch waits for the next character to be printed. It interprets this character as the mode that is required. For example, to change the mode to 7 (the teletext mode), we could

```
1. Use the statement VDU 22,7
2. Use the statement PRINT CHR$(22);CHR$(7);
3. Type CTRL-V followed by "7"
4. Use the statement MODE 7
```

The third example is quite interesting. Strictly speaking, CTRL-V should be followed by CTRL-G, as this is the required "7" code. However, since the second byte is treated as MOD 8, only the first three bits of the number are actually examined to determine the mode. The ASCII codes for the digits start at &30 for "0". This means that the lower three bits of the digits are simply the binary representation of those digits. The ASCII code of "5", for example, is &35. This is 00110101 in binary. The lower three digits are therefore 101, or 5 in decimal. Because of this arrangement of the digits' ASCII codes, the oswrch routine treats the two sequences CTRL-V, CTRL-G and CTRL-V, "7" as the same thing. There is one important distinction between changing mode with VDU 22 and using BBC BASIC's MODE statement. As well as sending the appropriate codes to oswrch, MODE also changes the value of HIMEM so that it is equal to the highest address before the screen memory starts. Recall that the BASIC stack, as used by PROCs, FNs and whenever expressions are evaluated, starts from HIMEM. Thus if MODE is changed in the middle of a procedure's execution, HIMEM would be altered and the stack information would be forgotten. Because of this, it is only safe to use VDU 22 (or CTRL-V etc.) to change MODE if HIMEM would stay the same, i.e. as long as the old and new modes are in one of the sets (0,1,2) and (4,5), which are the 20K and 10K modes respectively.

Because certain combinations of oswrch codes are so common, they have been incorporated as special statements in BASIC. These are MODE, just discussed, PLOT, MOVE, DRAW, CLS, CLG, COLOUR and GCOL. All of these simply send the appropriate codes to oswrch, followed by any extra codes which may be required. If they hadn't been given special statement, the same effects could still be obtained with the appropriate VDU sequences. There are some useful control codes which have not been given BASIC keywords. You have to use VDU to obtain these effects. For example, some of the examples above had statements of the form "PRINT TAB(x%,y%);" to move the cursor to given co-ordinates. This could also be written

```
VDU 31, x%, y%
```

The code 31 tells oswrch that the next two characters printed will be screen co-ordinates to which the cursor must be moved. The special case of VDU 31,0,0, which "homes" the cursor to the top left corner has its own code – VDU 30. Other codes are used to move the cursor one space in a certain direction. The codes 8, 9, 10 and 11 (CTRL-H, -I, -J and -K) move the cursor left, right, down and up respectively. Note that these are different from typing the four editing keys with the arrows on. Those keys have a special effect on the "edit cursor", which is separate from the normal text cursor.

The four cursor movement codes can be used to print vertical lines of characters. I have used STRING$ already to print horizontal rows of characters. By following a character with the codes 8 and 11, the cursor will move back to the orginal position, then up to the space above it. To print an "A" above a "B" for example, the statement:

```
VDU 66,8,11,65
```

could be used. This can be extended by using STRING$ to produce columns of characters. To print 10 "|"s up from the current position use

```
PRINT STRING$(10, "|"+CHR$(8)+CHR$(11));
```

Similarly, a column going down could be printed by the single statement:

```
PRINT STRING$(10, "|"+CHR$(8)+CHR$(10));
```

The BBC display is different to most microcomputers in the way that it scrolls. Most screens scroll up when the cursor tries to move past the right-most position on the bottom line. The BBC computer's screen also scrolls down when the cursor tries to move past the left-most position on the top line. This can be used to good effect in games. The outline of a program that uses this facility is given in section 3.2.4.

The VDU statement's arguments can also be separated with semicolons. The difference between this and the first form is best described by an example.

```
VDU a;b;    is exactly equivalent to
VDU a MOD 256,a DIV 256, b MOD 256, b DIV 256
```

If an expression is followed by a semicolon, it is treated as a two-byte, or 16-bit, number. The two bytes are sent to the oswrch separately. The less significant byte is sent first, then the more significant one. Suppose "a" above was 260. First, a byte with the value 4 (260 MOD 256) would be sent, then one with the value 1 (260 DIV 256) would be sent. Hence VDU 260; is the same as VDU 4,1. Similarly, VDU 0; is just the same as saying VDU 0,0. Therefore, VDU 22; is equivalent to MODE 0. This is because 22 MOD 256 is 22, so a byte of value 22 is sent to oswrch. This tells it that the next byte sent will be the new MODE. 22 DIV 256 is 0, so oswrch changes the mode to zero. The main use of the semicolon is to send values that oswrch requires to be sixteen bits long. This includes VDU 24, which specifies the graphics window, and VDU 25, the plot command. Both these VDU options are covered in some detail in the next chapter, so I refer you to there for some examples. Another use of the semicolon form is to save some bytes in a program. Some of the VDU options require a few zero bytes to follow the main information bytes. An example is VDU 19, which defines a logical colour. (See the next section.) The form of this particular VDU option is:

```
VDU a,b,0,0,0
```

The last three zeroes are "for future expansion". The statement could be specified with exactly the same meaning as:

```
VDU a,b;0;
```

as long as "b" is less than 256. The first byte, "a" is sent in the same way in both versions. In the second version, "b" is treated as a 16 bit number. First the lower byte is sent, which corresponds to the "b," in the first version, then the upper byte, which is the first zero in the first version. Then the "0;" of the latter form sends the last two zero bytes. The second method saves a grand total of three bytes in a program, so could be useful if space is not plentiful.

You should take care not to confuse the ways commas and semicolons are used in PRINT and VDU. In the former they are formatting symbols used to determine the way numbers are printed. In the latter they are list separators which determine the way expressions are interpreted.

3.2.2   Coloured Text

Like most modern microcomputers, the BBC Computer can display text in colour (providing a colour monitor or TV is used). This section deals with getting colour from the soft displays. The teletext mode requires very different techniques (see the User Guide). Referring to the table in the introduction to this part, it can be seen that modes zero to six can display between two and 16 colours at once. The colours that are displayed are set-up when the mode is entered, but can be changed if necessary. These default settings are given on page 383 of the User Guide.

The statement that enables us to change the colour of text is simply called COLOUR. The command is used to set both the background and foreground colours of the text. By default, these colours are chosen so that the backgound is black and the foreground white. I will assume that the computer is in mode five or one, the four colour modes. The table in the User Guide just mentioned shows that the four colours are set to black, red, yellow and white. The default background colour is 0 (black) and the foreground is set to 3 (white). The foreground refers to the colour in which the "on" dots of a character is shown. The background colour is the "off" parts of a character. Thus the space character has only the background colour.

To change the foreground colour to red the command:

```
COLOUR 1
```

would be used. If you are using a black and white display, red and yellow should appear as two distinct shades of grey. After the foreground colour has been altered, all subsequent printing is performed in that colour. To return the foregound back to white, the statement "COLOUR 3" would obviously be used. Changing the text background colour is just as easy. To change the background to colour N, the statement COLOUR N+128 is used. Thus to change the background colour to white (colour three in the four colour modes), the statement "COLOUR 131" would be executed. Notice that altering either the foreground or background only affects subsequent printing, not what has gone before. This means that you can have various combinations of foreground and background colours on the screen at any time. In particular, the two colour modes allow four combinations, the four colour modes 16 and the 16 colour modes 256 combinations of colour. Unfortunately, if the foreground and background colours are the same, the text becomes invisible. This reduces the useful combinations to 2, 12 and 240 respectively. The program below prints the 12 four-colour colour combinations.

```
100 FOR back%=128 TO 131
110    FOR fore%=0 TO 3
120       IF fore%+128 = back% THEN 160
130       COLOUR fore%
140       COLOUR back%
150       PRINT fore%, back%;
160    NEXT fore%
170 NEXT back%
180 COLOUR 3
190 COLOUR 128
200 END
```

If the mode is 5, omit the semicolon from line 150. The program produces four bands of background colour, each of which have three possible foregrounds. The COLOUR command is simply just another VDU driver. In this case it is VDU 17. One byte follows the 17 – the value described above. For example, line 130 above could be replaced with "VDU 17, fore%". This would have exactly the same effect as the COLOUR command. It is possible to set the foregound colour directly from the keyboard. ASCII 17 is control Q, so the sequence CTRL-Q "3" would set the foregound colour to white. (You don't type the quotes, of course.) The background colours are a little harder. The codes 128 onwards are not easily accessible from the keyboard, at least not under MOS 0.1. It seems that MOS 1.0 produces the codes 128–138 for the ten function keys when they are pressed with the SHIFT key. However, under MOS 0.1, they have to be explicitly programmed using the "|!|@" method described in section 3.1.

Some computers (e.g. the VIC-20 and ZX Spectrum) enable special colour codes to be inserted into strings and the program from the keyboard. This means that to print a string in red on the VIC, you would type

```
PRINT "<RED>HELLO WORLD"
```

where <RED> means press the key marked RED. This is impossible on the BBC machine, as all control codes are interpreted as they are typed in. When you type CTRL-Q "3", BASIC never actually get the two characters; the MOS "swallows" them and changes colour immediately. It's a shame there isn't a "don't interpret the next character" code, so that control codes can be inserted into strings. If you want to change colours a lot, but also want to avoid using hundreds of COLOUR statements, a good idea is to define special "control strings" which contain the appropriate colour changing characters. For example, suppose part of a program has to print some "status information". The headings "Speed", "Fuel" and "Height" have to be in red, yellow and white on a black background, and the figures that follow each heading are to be in the inverse of those colours, i.e. black on red, yellow and white backgrounds. The following strings could be defined in the initialisation part of the program.

```
1000 red_black$=CHR$(17)+CHR$(1)+CHR$(17)+CHR$(128)
1010 yel_black$=CHR$(17)+CHR$(2)+CHR$(17)+CHR$(128)
1020 wht_black$=CHR$(17)+CHR$(3)+CHR$(17)+CHR$(128)
1030 black_red$=CHR$(17)+CHR$(0)+CHR$(17)+CHR$(129)
1040 black_yel$=CHR$(17)+CHR$(0)+CHR$(17)+CHR$(130)
1050 black_wht$=CHR$(17)+CHR$(0)+CHR$(17)+CHR$(131)
1060 sp$=red_black$+"Speed  "+black_red$
1070 fu$=yel_black$+"Fuel   "+black_yel$
1080 he$=wht_black$+"Height "+black_wht$
```

Obviously the names of the strings have been made verbose for readability's sake. They could be abbreviated to "rb$" etc., providing their purpose was well documented in REMs. The strings would be used in the program in the following way:

```
100 PRINT sp$;speed%
110 PRINT fu$;fuel%
120 PRINT he$;height%
```

This method of changing characters' colours is especially useful when the characters are user-defined ones. An example of this is given in section 3.2.4.

The COLOUR or VDU 17 command only alters the colours of text to be printed. That is to say, it selects which colour to use for the background and foreground of text. These colours are referred to by the numbers zero to N–1, where N is the number of available colours for a particular mode. These are called the "logical colours". The actual colours that the logical colours are displayed as can be varied by another VDU command. The BBC Computer can display eight different colours, and also these eight alternating with their inverse – the so-called flashing colours. Staying with the four colour modes, the table below shows the relationship between the logical colours and the actual colours when the mode is first entered.

Logical colour	Actual colour
0	0 (black)
1	1 (red)
2	3 (yellow)
3	7 (white)

This is a sensible choice, as even on a black and white set all four colours are easily distinguishable. It is very easy to change the logical–actual colour relationship. The table below shows the 16 actual effects available.

F B G R	Actual colour	Effect
0 0 0 0	0	Black
0 0 0 1	1	Red
0 0 1 0	2	Green
0 0 1 1	3	Yellow
0 1 0 0	4	Blue
0 1 0 1	5	Magenta
0 1 1 0	6	Cyan
0 1 1 1	7	White
1 0 0 0	8	Black then White
1 0 0 1	9	Red then Cyan
1 0 1 0	10	Green then Magenta
1 0 1 1	11	Yellow then Blue
1 1 0 0	12	Blue then Yellow
1 1 0 1	13	Magenta then Green
1 1 1 0	14	Cyan then Red
1 1 1 1	15	White then Black

The columns labelled R, G, B, F represent Red, Green, Blue and Flash. The actual colour number can be thought of as having four components. The first three bits represent the guns in a colour TV tube. If a bit is one, then the corresponding gun will be activated. Obviously when no guns are on the colour produced is black; when all guns are activated white results. The intermediate values produce the other colours. The fourth bit is the "flash" bit. When it is a one, the colour produced will alternate with its inverse. The inverse is the colour obtained by inverting the three colour bits, so the inverse of red (001) is cyan (110).

The statement used to assign an actual colour to a logical colour is VDU 19. It has the form:

```
     VDU 19, logical, actual, 0, 0, 0
or   VDU 19, logical, actual;0;
```

The three zeroes are for "future expansion". This means that there may one day be a new video chip that will support more than the present 16 colours. The expansion capability provides for eight bits to be assigned to each gun. This gives a total of over 16 million possible colours, though obviously only the current 16 could be shown at one time. Whether such expansion capability will be used is something only time will tell. To make logical colour 1 show up as red alternating with cyan the statement "VDU 19,1,9;0;" would be used. Similarly to change colour 3 to green, "VDU 19,3,2;0;" is used. Unlike COLOUR, changing the actual colour assigned to a logical one can alter text that has already been printed. For example, if a program has been printing in mode 4 in the default foreground colour of white, as soon as the statement "VDU 19,1,1;0;" is executed, all the white text will turn into red. This property can be used to hide text (and graphics), and then make it appear instantaneously. The program below prints three groups of text in colours 1, 2 and three. It then changes the logical–actual colour relationships so that only one of the groups is visible (i.e. different from the background colour of black) at once.

```
100 MODE 5
110 FOR i%=0 TO 30
120    COLOUR 1:PRINT"Left   ";
130    COLOUR 2:PRINT"Middle ";
140    COLOUR 3:PRINT"Right"
150 NEXT i%
160 REM    Blot out all colours
170 VDU 19,1;0;0
180 VDU 19,2;0;0
190 VDU 19,3;0;0
200 REM    Now cycle through, making each
210 REM    colour white in turn
220 i%=0
230 REPEAT
240    VDU 19,i% MOD 3 + 1,7;0;
250    VDU 19,(i%+1) MOD 3 + 1,0;0;
260    VDU 19,(i%+2) MOD 3 + 1,0;0;
270    t%=TIME+50:REPEAT UNTIL TIME=T%
280    i%=i%+1
290 UNTIL INKEY(0)<>-1
300 END
```

The expressions in lines 240, 250 and 260 simply select the logical colours 1, 2 and 3 depending on i%. One colour is set to white, the others to black. To see that the two non-displayed parts are still there even when they are black, a line such as "165 VDU 19,0,1;0;" could be inserted. This makes the background red instead of black.

If, after altering the text colours and the logical–actual relationships you want to change them back to the default values, you can use the command VDU 20. This sets the background and foreground colours to black and white respectively and the logical colours to their proper actual colours, as they are immediately after a MODE statement.

The flashing colours are quite useful in situations where the user is to be given a headache. By default the flashing rate is 1Hz. This means that each colour is on for half a second. It is possible, though, to vary the period for which each colour is on. This is achieved with a couple of *FX commands, *FX9 and *FX10. The former sets the time for which the colour is shown as the first colour, the latter sets the second colour's period. For example, suppose one of the colours being shown is flashing Blue–Yellow (actual colour 12). By default, the anything printed in that colour will be blue for half a second, then yellow for half a second, then blue again and so on. If the two commands

```
*FX9,10
*FX10,5
```

are executed, the flash rate will change instantaneously to 3.33Hz. This stems from the fact that the figures that follows the *FX9/10 is the time in fiftieths of a second for which the appropriate colour is shown. Thus, blue is displayed for 0.2 seconds, then yellow for 0.01 seconds. This gives a period of 0.3 seconds, or a frequency of 3.33Hz. The shortest time for which a colour can be selected is 0.02 seconds. Therefore the fastest rate at which colours can be made to flash is 25Hz. The maximum value for the flash period is 255, or 5.1 seconds. Thus the lowest frequency possible is 0.098 Hertz, or one complete flash every 10.2 seconds. When using a flashing colour to enhance some text, care should be taken to ensure that the combination of foreground and background does not make the text disappear every so often. For example, suppose in a 4 colour mode it is required to print the text "Fuel Low!!" flashing. One way of doing this would be:

```
130 COLOUR 1
140 VDU 19,1,8;0;
150 PRINT "Fuel Low!!"
```

However, if the text backgound colour has not been changed from its default black, the text will disappear every half a second. An alternative would be to change line 140 to "VDU 19,1,9;0;", so that the two flashing colours are always visible. Better still would be to change the text background colour so that it always complements the foreground, viz.

```
130 COLOUR 1: COLOUR 130
140 VDU 19,1,8;0;: VDU 19,2,15;0;
150 PRINT "Fuel Low!!"
160 COLOUR 3:COLOUR 128
```

3.2.3 Text Windows

When a display mode is first entered, you have the whole screen on which to print. That is, in MODE 4, the cursor can be moved to any of the 40 columns on any of the 32 lines. When you try to print something below the bottom line, or above the top line, the display scrolls in the appropriate direction. Sometimes, though, it is useful to only use some of the display for volatile information, i.e. output that changes. There might be some things displayed which are fixed, and should not be affected by the screen's scrolling action. It is very easy to define a fixed area on the BBC Computer's display. More accurately, it is easy to define the area that scrolls, the rest being "frozen" into place.

The command to define a text or scrolling window is yet another variation on the theme of VDU. In this case, it is VDU 28. The 28 code is followed by four more bytes; they specify the boundaries of the window. The syntax of the statement is given below:

```
VDU 28, left_column, bottom_row, right_column, top_row
```

The row and column numbers start from zero for the top and left-hand edges, and go up to rows−1 and columns−1 for the top and right-hand edges respectively. The co-ordinates are therefore similar to those used in the TAB(x, y) modifier. They are always in terms of the default maximum sized window. For example, in MODE 4, the command:

```
VDU 28, 0, 31, 39, 16
```

would redefine the scrolling window so that text is only printed in the lower half. Similarly, in MODE 7,

```
VDU 28, 0, 24, 19, 0
```

would cause only the left-hand side of the screen to be available. When the text window is redefined, a couple of noteworthy things happen. Firstly, the TAB co-ordinates change so that TAB(0,0) is the top left-hand position in the new window, rather than the top left-hand of the whole screen. In the first example above, the TAB(0,0) position would change to the left-most character of the 16th line of the display. This means that TAB(0,15) would be the first character on the last line of the new window. Another important thing is the way the computer performs scrolling before and after a window has been defined. When the text window is the whole screen, the computer uses a method known as "hardware scrolling". This means that to give the appearance of every line on the display shifting up one, all that need be done is change a special location in the computer's video chip that specifies the very first screen location. For example, if the computer is in MODE 4, by adding 40 (the number of characters on one line) to the value in this special location, the top line is effectively removed, and the display moves up by one line. The point of this is that scrolling can be done very quickly. You have probably noticed this by the way listings disappear off the screen before you've had a chance to read them. Unfortunately, hardware scrolling can only be used when the whole screen is defined as the text window. As soon as this is altered by a VDU 28, a different method has to be used. This is called "software scrolling", as a small program is used to shift all the characters up by the right amount. Because this can involve moving over 20,000 bytes (in modes 0, 1 and 2), it is very slow. Here is an example. Load a reasonably long program and put the computer into MODE 4. When it is listed, the listing should whizz by as usual. Now define a text window with:

```
VDU 28,0,31,39,0
```

This actually defines the whole screen as a window, so the computer could still use hardware scrolling. Unfortunately, the MOS (which perform all the operations on the screen) isn't clever enough to spot this, and reverts to software scrolling. If you list the program again, the difference in speed can be seen to be quite dramatic.

The example above is obviously an extreme one, but the effect is still noticeable on smaller windows, especially on the 20K modes (0, 1 and 2). If, when a VDU 28 is executed, the text cursor is outside of the newly defined window, it is automatically "homed" to the new top left-hand corner. If it is already inside the new scrolling area, its position is unaltered. Once a VDU 28 is executed, all the other VDU commands that affect the text display only work on the new window. For example, CLS (which is VDU 12 or CTRL-L) only clears the new text area. Note that the command CLS means not "fill the text window with black", but "fill the text window with the current text background colour". This is demonstrated by the routine below which defines successively smaller windows in MODE 5, and clears them in cycling background colours. The last window is just a 2×2 square in the centre of the screen. The VDU 19 command is then used to change the actual colours of the logical colours 1, 2 and 3 so that a "moving tunnel" effect is obtained.

```
10 MODE 5
20 FOR size%=20 TO 2 STEP -2
30    COLOUR 129+(size% DIV 2 MOD 3):REM Selects 129, 130 or 131
40    VDU 28, 10-size% DIV 2, 15+size% DIV 2, 9+size% DIV 2, 16-size% DIV 2
50    CLS
60 NEXT size%
70 i%=0
80 REPEAT
90    VDU 19, i% MOD 3+1,1,0,0,0
100   VDU 19,(i%+1) MOD 3+1,3,0,0,0
110   VDU 19,(i%+2) MOD 3+1,7,0,0,0
120   t%=TIME+10: REPEAT UNTIL TIME=t%
130   i%=i%+1
140 UNTIL INKEY(0)<>-1
150 END
```

Although of no great practical value, this program does illustrate a point about the way the logical colours are changed. It is easy to see by the way the bands of colour change that the logical–actual colour relationships are updated immediately. However, if you look carefully, you will see a jagged line which runs horizontally across the screen whenever the colours change. The reason for this is that the picture on the TV is updated 50 times a second. It therefore takes 20ms to draw one frame. Because the colours change very quickly, the chances are they will be updated in the middle of the drawing of a frame. This causes the jagged line. Because the current program is trivial, this interaction is not important. In some applications, though, flickering colours can be quite distracting. Luckily, there is a way to get round this problem. It involves changing colours in the period between actual frames being drawn. One of the many *FX (or osbyte) options is called "wait for field sync.". When it is called, the computer stops whatever it is doing, and waits for a special signal form the TV picture circuitry. This signal marks the beginning of a picture, and because there is a certain portion of the picture not shown on the screen, there is time to change the colours before the picture actually becomes visible. This is especially useful in assembly language programs, as there is quite a lot that can be done between the field sync. occurring and the top of the picture becoming visible. The snag is, the appropriate call (*FX19) is only implemented from MOS 1.0. Not having that on my machine, I cannot guarantee that placing a *FX19 before each of the three VDU 19 statements in the current example will remove the jagged line effect. You could certainly try it if you have a MOS 1.0 machine. (STOP PRESS: It does!)

A common use of defining text windows is to protect a part of the screen from the ravages of scrolling. Often, a program will display some "status" information that is constant. Without a window-defining ability, such information would have to be re-written each time the display was cleared. Not so on the BBC Computer. The example belows prints a key to the meanings of the function keys on the bottom four lines of the screen. It then re-defines the window so that the information is protected from scrolling and CLS.

```
1000 DEF PROCinit
1010    REM    define the function keys and print
1020    REM    a key. Then protect the bottom four
1030    REM    lines (this example for MODE 4)
1040    *KEY0 |!|A
1050    *KEY1 |!|B
1060    *KEY2 |!`
1070    *KEY3 |!a
1080    PRINT TAB(0,28);"f0 - Drop a bomb"
1090    PRINT TAB(0,29);"f1 - Launch an ICBM"
1100    PRINT TAB(0,30);"f2 - Assassinate the President"
1110    PRINT TAB(0,31);"f3 - Send for Rex Kramer";
1120    VDU 28, 0, 26, 39, 0
1130    REM    rest of initialisation
1140    .....
1150    .....
1160 ENDPROC
```

Windows could also be used to selectively clear an area of the screen without having to print lots of space characters, which is comparatively slow. For example, there is a facility in the Apple][monitor to clear all the screen below the current line. A procedure to emulate this feature is given below.

```
10000 DEF PROCclear_below
10010    REM  Clears the screen below the
10020    REM  current cursor position
10030    LOCAL cx%, cy%
10040    cx%=POS:  cy%=VPOS
10050    VDU 28, 0, bot%, right%, cx%+1, 12, 26
10060    VDU 31, cx%, cy%           .
10070 ENDPROC
```

The procedure also illustrates how it is possible to have several VDU commands on one line. First, the current position of the cursor is remembered. This is necessary because when the window below the current line is defined, the cursor will automatically be moved to the top left-hand corner. This is side-effect; a procedure should avoid changing things like the cursor position if such a change is not implied in its name, just as it shouldn't change the values of unconnected global variables. The first five VDU expressions redefine the text window. This is yet another occasion that calls for a knowledge of the format of the current mode. The values "bot%" and "right%" have to be defined somewhere in the program, and must of course be altered for different display modes. After the five window-defining bytes, there is the code 12. This is exactly the same as the CLS statement, or pressing CTRL-L. The "26" which follows that is a new one. This VDU command means "restore default windows". It is used to return the text and graphics (see next chapter) windows to their default settings of the whole screen. For the text window, this is different from using a simple "VDU 28,left, bottom, right, top" statement, because it also reinstates hardware scrolling, rather than the software method that VDU 28 implies. Once the window has been restored, a VDU 31 is used to replace the cursor to its old position. This is the same as using a "PRINT TAB(cx%, cy%);" statement.

With careful management, it is possible to use more than one window to display different sets of information. In a disc system, for example, it would be possible to display the contents of two or more files in separate windows, in order to compare them. Such extravagance is not possible on cassette-based systems, as only one file can be read at once. Instead, I will demonstrate the technique using data generated inside the machine. To keep things simple, I will generate two tables in different windows. One is the table of the sines of angles from zero degrees; the other is a table of the Fibonacci numbers.

To keep things as general as possible, the data for each window are kept in arrays. That way, the number of windows can be altered at will. There is only one routine that deals directly with the display – PROCshow. It takes a window number (1–num_windows%), a pair of co-ordinates and a string to be displayed as parameters. If either or both of the co-ordinates are –1, the string is printed in the position of that window's cursor

```
100 MODE 4
110 PROCinit
120 th%=0: i%=1
130 REPEAT
140     text$=STR$(FNfib(i%))+CHR$(13)
150     PROCshow(1, -1, -1, text$)
160     text$=STR$(SIN(RAD(th%)))+CHR$(13)
170     PROCshow(2, -1, -1, text$)
180     th%=th%+1:  i%=i%+1
190 UNTIL INKEY(0)<>-1
200 END
210
220
230
1000 DEF PROCinit
1010    REM    Initialises the window data
1020    num_windows%=2
1030    DIM cx%(num_windows%), cy%(num_windows%)
1040    DIM left%(num_windows%), bot%(num_windows%)
1050    DIM right%(num_windows%), top%(num_windows%)
1060    left%(1)=0:    left%(2)=20
1070    bot%(1)=31:    bot%(2)=31
1080    right%(1)=19: right%(2)=39
1090    top%(1)=0:    top%(2)=0
1100 ENDPROC
1110
1120
1130
2000 DEF PROCshow(win%, cx%, cy%, text$)
2010    REM    Prints text$ at TAB(cx%,cy%) in
2020    REM    window win%, if it exists
2030    IF win% < 1  OR  win% > num_windows% THEN  ENDPROC
2040    IF cx% = -1  OR   cy% = -1 THEN cx%=cx%(win%):  cy%=cy%(win%)
2050    VDU 28, left%(win%), bot%(win%), right%(win%), top%(win%)
2060    PRINT TAB(cx%, cy%); text$;
2065    IF RIGHT$(text$,1)=CHR$(13) THEN PRINT
2070    cx%(win%)=POS
2080    cy%(win%)=VPOS
2090    VDU 26
2100 ENDPROC
```

If win% is out of range, PROCshow does nothing. After setting up the window in line 2050, the text is printed. It is followed by a semicolon so that no new-line is printed automatically. If a line-feed is required, a CHR$(13) should be appended onto text$. This is tested for in line 2065. Note that "PRINT CHR$(13);" only performs a carriage-return, not a line feed as well. This is why the extra statement is necessary. The new cursor position is stored in cx%() and cy%(), and the default window restored by the VDU 26 at 2090. The need to store the cursor position arises from the fact that when a window is first set-up, the default cursor position in the top left-hand corner. If the cx%() and cy%() weren't used, all the text would appear at the top line of the display. Not very useful. The practical limit on the number of windows using this method is about three or four. After that, things get very slow. I assume that PROCfib is present in the program (see section 2.2.6).

I will return to windows in the next chapter, when the graphics or clipping window is covered. The two types of window can be manipulated independently, which has some very useful applications.

3.2.4   User-defined Characters

The ability to create special characters which can be displayed as normal text is available only in the soft modes, zero to six. If you examine the picture closely on a good quality screen (i.e. a monitor), you should be able to see that each character is actually a pattern of dots. This is most obvious in modes 5 and 2. The way the dots are arranged determines which character is shown. Each character position is made up of an array of eight by eight dots. The patterns for the letter "A" and the "£" sign are shown below:

```
  ****            ***
 **  **          ** **
 **  **          **
 ******          *****
 **  **          **
 **  **          **
 **  **          ******
```

Wherever a " " appears in the patterns above, the corresponding dot on the screen is coloured in the current text backgound colour; a "*" means that the dot will appear in the current text foreground colour. Whenever the computer is asked to print a visible (i.e. non-control) character, it looks up the appropriate pattern of dots in a table located at the start of the MOS ROM. The pattern for each character from CHR$(32) (the space) to CHR$(126) ("~", the tilde) is held as eight consecutive bytes. Each of these bytes represents one row of the two examples above. The eight bits in the byte are the eight horizontal dots in each row. The eight bytes for the letter "A" are:

00111100	=	&3C
01100110	=	&66
01100110	=	&66
01111110	=	&7E
01100110	=	&66
01100110	=	&66
01100110	=	&66
00000000	=	&00

If you want to investigate the dot patterns of other characters, you can use the procedure below. The main procedure, PROCshow, takes a string argument. For each printable character in the string, it calls the MOS routine "osword". The functions performed by osword are listed in the U.G. For now, all you need to know is that the statements at lines 1080 to 1110 cause the eight-byte pattern for the character whose code is c% to be transferred into the eight locations &71–&78. The procedure PROCdisp is then used to convert these bytes into sequences of "*" for 1 bits, and spaces for zero bits. The outer loop (the FOR) steps through the eight bytes, putting the current value in byte%. The inner, REPEAT loop then examines the individual bits. By ANDing the byte with &80 (=128 in decimal), the most significant bit can be examined. If this bit is set, byte% AND &80 will yield a true result, hence a "*" is printed. If the MSB is a zero, byte% AND &80 also yield a zero, so a space is printed. Multiplying byte% by two effectively shifts all the bits to the left, so that on the next iteration of the loop, the second most significant bit is examined and so on. The loop repeats until there are no more "1" bits left. When this is so, a new-line is printed, and the next byte examined. PROCshow is called with a statement such as "PROCshow("Deb")", which would print the dot patterns for the letters "D", "e", and "b" down the screen.

```
1000 DEF PROCshow(a$)
1010    REM   Shows the patterns of all the
1020    REM   characters in a$.
1030    LOCAL i%, c%
1040    FOR i%=1 TO LEN(a$)
1050       c%=ASC(MID$(a$,i%,1))
1060       IF c%<32 OR c%=127 THEN  1130
1070       REM   Set up call to "osword"
1080       ?&70=c%:  A%=&0A
1090       X%=&70:   Y%=0
1110       CALL &FFF1
1120       PROCdisp(&71)
1130    NEXT i%
1140 ENDPROC
1150
```

```
1160
2000 DEF PROCdisp(add%)
2010    REM     Displays the pattern held in
2020    REM     addresses add%-add%+7
2030    LOCAL i%, byte%
2040    FOR i%=add% TO add%+7
2050       byte%=?i%
2060       REPEAT
2070          IF byte% AND &80 THEN PRINT"*"; ELSE PRINT " ";
2080          byte%=byte%*2
2090       UNTIL (byte% AND &FF) = 0
2100       PRINT
2110    NEXT i%
2120 ENDPROC
```

So far, I have only discussed the normal, pre-defined ASCII characters. These are held in ROM, and are therefore fixed. However, certain characters have their dot pattern bytes stored in the normal alterable memory (RAM), so that the patterns produced by printing these characters can be changed by the user. When the machine is switched on, the MOS sets aside a page of memory (a "page" is 256 bytes in this context) in which the patterns of the characters with codes 224 to 255 are stored. A VDU command can be used to redefine these characters as required. The command has the form:

```
VDU 23, ascii_code, byte1, byte2, ... , byte8
```

The command is therefore VDU 23, and it is followed by the ascii code of the character to be defined, followed by the eight pattern-defining bytes. You must ensure that "ascii_code" is between 224 and 255, otherwise the VDU 23 command will place the eight bytes you give in some undesirable place, probably in the middle of your program. This will of course cause the program to become corrupt and un-runnable.

Suppose we required a Starship Enterprise symbol. The first thing to do is work out the pattern of dots that will look reasonably like an Enterprise. For a side view, it is probably best to use two adjacent characters. My idea of what these should be is given below.

```
CHR$(224)  CHR$(225)
       **   ********
   ***  *   ********
 *******    **
 *******     *
       *    **
     ***    *****
     ***    ******
     ***    ******
```

When these patterns are converted into binary, then hexadecimal, the following numbers are obtained:

```
CHR$(224)   CHR$(225)
00000011    11111111    =&03    &FF
00111001    11111111    =&39    &FF
11111110    00110000    =&FE    &30
11111110    00100000    =&FE    &20
00000010    01100000    =&02    &60
00000111    11111000    =&07    &F8
00000111    11111100    =&07    &FC
00000111    11111100    =&07    &FC
```

The two characters CHR$(224) and CHR$(225) can be set to the right and left halves of the Enterprise shape with the two statements:

```
VDU 23,224,&03,&39,&FE,&FE,&02,&07,&07,&07
VDU 23,225,&FF,&FF,&30,&20,&60,&F8,&FC,&FC
```

I have used hexadecimal to make things clearer: there is no reason why decimal could not be used. After these statements have been executed, the statement "PRINT CHR$(224);CHR$(225)", or its equivalent "VDU 224,225" can be used to print the Enterprise shape. Because of the length/height ratio of the screen, the shape only looks at all like its subject in the 20 column modes, 2 and 5. If the shape was to be drawn in MODE 5, with colour 1 as the background, and colour 2 as the foreground, a string could be defined to change colours in addition to actually printing the shape.

```
Ent$=CHR$(17)+CHR$(129)+CHR$(17)+CHR$(2)
Ent$=Ent$+CHR$(224)+CHR$(225)
Ent$=Ent$+CHR$(17)+CHR$(128)+CHR$(17)+CHR$(3)
```

The first line changes the colours, the second line adds the actual printed characters and the last line changes the colours back to the defaults.

The process of thinking up the shape, converting it to binary and hex, then performing the VDU 23 statements and finally making up a string to print the shape is quite time consuming, especially if the shape is made up from more than a couple of characters. In fact, the shape defining task is an ideal candidate for a program to make life easier.

```
100 REM     CHARACTER DEFINER PROGRAM
110 MODE 6
120 PROCinit
130 REPEAT
140   choice=FNmenu
150   IF choice=1 THEN PROCload
160   IF choice=2 THEN PROCsave
```

```
 170  IF choice=3 THEN PROCdefine
 180 UNTIL choice=4
 190 PRINT''"Goodbye"
 200 END
 210
 220
1000 DEF PROCinit
1010  REM     Initialise
1020  REM     DIM a buffer for the character pattern
1030  DIM buff% 8
1040  osword=&FFF1
1070 ENDPROC
1080
2000 DEF PROCload
2010  REM     Load a character set
2020  CLS
2030  PRINT TAB(0,5);"Start Tape"
2040  *LOAD "CSET"
2050 ENDPROC
2060
3000 DEF PROCsave
3010  REM     Save a character set
3020  CLS
3030  PRINT TAB(0,5);
3040  *SAVE "CSET" 0C00 +0100
3050 ENDPROC
3060
4000 DEF PROCdefine
4010  REM     Define a character
4020  LOCAL  cx%,cy%,ch%,ended%
4030  CLS
4040  REPEAT
4050   INPUT TAB(0,5),"What character (224-255) ",ch%
4060  UNTIL ch%>=224 AND ch%<=255
4065  CLS
4070  REM     Define keys
4080  *FX4,1
4090  *KEY0 |!|L
4100  *KEY1 |!|M
4110  *KEY2 |!|N
4120  PRINT TAB(0,23);"f0: Reset point; f1: Set point"
4130  PRINT TAB(0,24);"f2: End; Cursor keys to move"
```

```
4140   VDU 28,0,21,39,0
4150   cx%=0: cy%=0: ?buff%=ch%
4160   A%=10: X%=buff% MOD 256: Y%=buff% DIV 256
4170   REPEAT
4180    PROCshow(ch%,cx%,cy%)
4190    PROCaction(ch%)
4200   UNTIL ended%
4210   *FX4,0
4215   VDU 26
4220 ENDPROC
4230
5000 DEF PROCshow(ch%,cx%,cy%)
5010   REM    Display pattern for CHR$(ch%)
5020   LOCAL x%, y%, byte%, f%
5030   CALL osword
5040   PRINT TAB(0,4);
5050   FOR y%=1 TO 8
5060    byte%=buff%?y%
5070    FOR x%=7 TO 0 STEP -1
5080     IF y%-1 = cy% AND cx%+x%=7 THEN COLOUR 129:COLOUR 0: f%=TRUE
5090     IF byte% AND &80 THEN PRINT"*"; ELSE PRINT" ";
5095     byte%=byte%*2
5100     IF f% THEN COLOUR 128:COLOUR 1: f%=FALSE
5110    NEXT x%
5120    PRINT SPC(y%);CHR$(ch%)
5130   NEXT y%
5140 ENDPROC
5150
6000 DEF PROCaction(ch%)
6010   REM     Redefine a character
6020   LOCAL byte%, in%, i%
6025   REPEAT
6030    PRINT TAB(0,15);"Command (f0-f2 or cursor keys) ? ";
6040    in%=GET-135
6045   UNTIL in%>0 AND in%<=7
6050   ON in% GOSUB 6100,6200,6300,6400,6500,6600,6700
6060   IF in%<>5 AND in%<>6 THEN ENDPROC
6070   VDU 23,ch%
6075   FOR i%=1 TO 8
6080    VDU buff%?i%
6085   NEXT i%
6090 ENDPROC
6100 REM    Cursor Left
```

```
6110  IF cx%>0 THEN cx%=cx%-1
6120 RETURN
6130
6200 REM     Cursor right
6210  IF cx%<7 THEN cx%=cx%+1
6220 RETURN
6230
6300 REM     Cursor down
6310  IF cy%<7 THEN cy%=cy%+1
6320 RETURN
6330
6400 REM     Cursor up
6410  IF cy%>0 THEN cy%=cy%-1
6420 RETURN
6430
6500 REM     Reset point
6510  byte%=buff%?(cy%+1)
6520  byte%=byte% AND NOT (2^(7-cx%))
6530  buff%?(cy%+1)=byte%
6540 RETURN
6550
6600 REM     Set point
6610  byte%=buff%?(cy%+1)
6620  byte%=byte% OR 2^(7-cx%)
6630  buff%?(cy%+1)=byte%
6640 RETURN
6650
6700 REM     End
6710  ended%=TRUE
6720 RETURN
6730
7000 DEF FNmenu
7010  REM get the user's choice
7020  LOCAL
7030  CLS
7040  PRINT TAB(0,5);"1. Load a character set"'
7050  PRINT"2. Save a character set"'
7060  PRINT"3. Amend a character pattern"'
7070  PRINT"4. Say goodbye"
7080  REPEAT
7090   INPUT TAB(0,15),"Which one (1-4) ",choice%
7100  UNTIL choice%>=1 AND choice%<=4
7110 =choice%
```

I have made the program as short as possible, so that it will fit into a 16K machine. Even so, it is still necessary to use MODE 6 in order to be able to run the program. This 40 column by 25 line mode is the most memory efficient of the soft modes, and there is about 1.5K left when the program is running. In view of this, better character-editing commands could be added; for example, one of the keys could be programmed to clear or set a whole row/column of dots, rather than just a single one. This could be extended to clearing, resetting or inverting (all zeroes become ones and vice versa) the whole character.

The load and save routines are not very good. They rely on the knowledge of where the character definitions for CHR$(224)-CHR$(255) are held. This is the page &0C00 (32 characters * 8 bytes/char = 256 bytes). The procedures PROCload and PROCsave use the MOS commands *LOAD and *SAVE to transfer this page of memory to and from the cassette tape. A much better method would be to use a proper BASIC data file in conjunction with VDU 23 and "osword" for the load and save operations respectively. This method uses only the MOS routines and should work on the "second processor". Unfortunately, this version will not fit in a 16K machine, even when using MODE 6, hence the "*LOAD" & "*SAVE" method. Owners of 32K machines might like to change PROCload and PROCsave so that the user can specify exactly which characters are to be saved, and give the file a distinctive name. The majority of the program is, of course, the character defining part. After setting up the function keys, the buffer array for the character definition and the A%, X% and Y% variables, the PROCdefine routine enters a loop of displaying the character and amending it in some way. The 256 dots are printed in a similar way to PROCdisp given earlier. The difference is that one of the dots is shown in inverse; this is the position of the cursor. It can be moved using the four arrowed keys. Also, a "life-size" version of the character is displayed to the right of the larger matrix. Apart from moving the cursor, the user can set the current point by pressing "f1" and reset it by pressing "f0". The character definition routine is exited by pressing "f2". The function keys are given ASCII codes which come just after the cursor keys, i.e. 140–142. This makes the ON ... GOSUB statement easier. You may notice that I used a REPEAT loop to get a correct key, rather than use the ELSE clause of the ON ... GOSUB. This is because there is a strange bug that causes an error to be printed at the next line. There is no text to the error, i.e. the program stops with "at line 6060". The function ERR returns 0. This is obviously something to be wary of when using the ELSE option in an ON statement. Line 6060 returns control back to PROCdefine if the action performed did not affect the character definition. If it did, the definition is updated using VDU 23, so that the change will be reflected when the shape is updated on the screen.

The routine that displays the shape is quite fast, but cannot keep up with rapid cursor movements. In fact, this is a good example where a section of BASIC could be improved using a machine code routine. A suitable replacement for PROC disp is given in Chapter five. It would, of course, be possible to convert the whole thing to machine code, though with little advantage. It is usually best to use BASIC for the things it is good at, such as routine input and output, and machine code where speed is the main concern.

The way in which user-defined characters are used obviously depends on the application. In games, figures such as the Enterprise given above can be combined with colour and possibly positional characters (i.e. CHR$(31)+ CHR$(x)+CHR$(y)) to provide dedicated graphics symbols. Another use is in providing the teletext mode characters in the soft modes. These are the arrows (left, right and up), the "divide" sign and the fractions. These characters are used for different symbols in the soft modes, and because they have ordinary codes (i.e. in the range 32 to 126), the patterns cannot be redefined using VDU 23. Instead, the characters have to be defined as CHR$(224), CHR$(225) and so on. To obtain a "three quarters" in a soft mode, you would have to use "VDU 224" or "PRINT CHR$(224);", assuming CHR$(224) has been thus defined. Another method is to "trap" the output from "oswrch" with an assembly language routine, and substitute the codes for the teletext characters with the appropriate user-defined ones. This technique is explained in Chapter five.

Below are the codes for various symbols found in the teletext character set that aren't normally available in the soft modes.

Character	ASCII	Pattern Bytes
Left arrow	91	&00,&30,&60,&FE,&60,&30,&00,&00
Right arrow	93	&00,&0C,&06,&7F,&06,&0C,&00,&00
Up arrow	94	&00,&18,&7E,&DB,&18,&18,&18,&00
1/2	92	&60,&60,&60,&6E,&66,&0C,&18,&1E
1/4	123	&60,&60,&60,&66,&6E,&16,&1E,&06
3/4	125	&60,&30,&60,&32,&66,&0A,&0E,&02
Divide	126	&18,&18,&00,&7E,&00,&18,&18,&00
Two bars	124	&66,&66,&66,&66,&66,&66,&66,&00

The characters look best in the 40 and 80 column modes. In the 20 column modes they are displayed big enough to show the limitations of the 8 × 8 matrix. Another application for user-defined characters is providing the letters of foreign alphabets. Greek letters are widely used in the sciences. If the BBC Computer's graphics are being used to show some scientific or mathematical image, the use of Greek where appropriate lends a professional air. There are 24 letters in the Greek alphabet. The provision of lower-case makes this 48. Since there are normally only 32 user-definable characters available, fitting in the whole alphabet would be a bit of a struggle. However, by using one of the many *FX calls, it is possible to allocate memory space for all the characters. If the command "*fx20,1" is executed (in MOS 1.0), six more pages are added to the area of RAM set aside for the soft characters. The way these pages are allocated is expounded on pp. 427–428 of the User Guide. Note though that after an "*fx20,1", the memory which was set aside for CHR$(224) to CHR$(255) is now used for the patterns of CHR$(128) to CHR$(159). Also, the rest of the characters' patterns are stored from OSHWM up. Since OSHWM is effectively PAGE at first, the character definitions for all the printable codes are stored where a BASIC program normally lives. Thus if you wish to define CHR$(160) (after executing *fx20,1), you must first move PAGE up by 256. Otherwise your program will suffer badly. Unfortunately, the keyboard characters CHR$(32) to CHR$(127) have their definitions well above PAGE (or OSHWM) so if you want to redefine them, you will need to lose between 1024 and 1536 bytes of program. Nice one Acorn.

The program below incorporates several of the topics mentioned in this chapter. Specifically, user-defined characters, colour-setting strings and "downwards scrolling" are used to animate a long and winding road. The road is drawn using sequences of three strings, straight$, left$ and right$. The string that is printed depends on the value of dx%, which is chosen to be −1, 0 or 1 with equal probability. The characters 224–228 are re-defined to represent the edge of the road. CHR$(224) is the "straight" part, which is just a solid blob of foreground colour. The two pairs CHR$(225), CHR$(226) and CHR$(227), CHR$(228) are used to give the sides of the road when turning left and right. They are the four triangular characters obtained by drawing the diagonals in the 8*8 character square. (Use the character re-definition program if you don't see what I mean.)

The strings red_bck$ and grn_bck$ are used to set the background colours in the road. The "outside" background colour is the usual colour zero, whose pallette entry is made green by the VDU 19 statement. In the road, the background colour is made red by inserting red_bck$ into the strings at the appropriate place. An interesting exercise is to convert the program for MODE 1, as the bends in the road look a little more subtle with 40 columns. The applications of the program include games such as "Wreckless Racing Car" and "Canoe Capers" (changing the road to a river by making it blue for the latter example).

```
100 REM    Road Program
110 MODE 5
120 PROCinit
130 x%=10
140 REPEAT
150    PROCprint(x%,0)
160    dx%=RND(3)-2
170    IF x%+dx%<0 OR x%+dx%>10 THEN dx%=0
180    x%=x%+dx%
210    PROCprint(x%,dx%)
230 UNTIL.
240
250
2000 DEF PROCprint(x%,dx%)
2010    REM  Prints right$, straight$, left$ for dx%=
2020    REM  -1, 0 1 resp. Then moves cursor up a line
2030    PRINT TAB(x%,0);
2040    ON dx%+2 GOSUB 2100,2200,2300
2050    PRINT up$;
2060 ENDPROC
2070
```

```
2100 PRINTright$; :RETURN
2200 PRINTstraight$; :RETURN
2300 PRINTleft$; :RETURN
2400
2410
10000 DEF PROCinit
10010    REM  Set up the strings for the "road"
10030    REM  Solid foreground colour
10040    VDU 23,  224,&FF,&FF,&FF,&FF,&FF,&FF,&FF,&FF
10050    REM  Triangular bits
10060    VDU 23,  225,&FF,&FE,&FC,&F8,&F0,&E0,&C0,&80
10070    VDU 23,  226,&01,&03,&07,&0F,&1F,&3F,&7F,&FF
10080    VDU 23,  227,&80,&C0,&E0,&F0,&F8,&FC,&FE,&FF
10090    VDU 23,  228,&FF,&7F,&3F,&1F,&0F,&07,&03,&01
10100    sp$="       ":  up$=CHR$(11)
10110    REM  Define colour code strings
10120    red_bck$=CHR$(17)+CHR$(129)
10130    grn_bck$=CHR$(17)+CHR$(128)
10140    REM Define the road sections
10150    straight$=" "+CHR$(224)+red_bck$+sp$+" "+CHR$(224)+grn_bck$
10160    left$=CHR$(226)+red_bck$+CHR$(225)+sp$+CHR$(226)+grn_bck$+CHR$(225)
10170    right$=" "+CHR$(228)+red_bck$+CHR$(227)+
         sp$+CHR$(228)+grn_bck$+CHR$(227)
10180    REM  Set the background colour to green
10190    VDU 19,0,2;0;
10200 ENDPROC
```

Chapter Four

BBC Graphics

The advanced graphics capability of the BBC Computer is one of its best known and least understood features. "Computer graphics" is a term used to describe a very wide range of computer-generated output, from pictures of naked women produced on teletype printers, to stunningly realistic scenes created in aircraft simulators. The subject of this chapter has more in common with the latter than the former. You cannot use the BBC Computer to provide fast-moving three-dimensional views of solid objects, but it is certainly capable of producing stunning colour displays. This chapter assumes that the reader has understood the sections on colour text and text windows of the last chapter. This knowledge is a good grounding for understanding some of the more complicated aspects of the BBC's graphics facilities.

4.1 Pixels and Co-ordinates

Whereas all the display modes can (naturally) show text, only some of them can display graphics as well. The modes that can produce graphics are the ones with 32 lines of text. (I do not propose to discuss the MODE 7 "graphics", as these have nothing in common with the proper, soft mode graphics.) The table below summarises the characteristics of these modes.

Mode	Format	Resolution	Colours	Memory
0	80 X 32	640 X 256	2	20K
1	40 X 32	320 X 256	4	20K
2	20 X 32	160 X 256	16	20K
4	40 X 32	320 X 256	2	10K
5	20 X 32	160 X 256	4	10K

The "Resolution" refers to the number of individual dots that can be controlled (set to a given colour) on the screen. In computer graphics, the dots are called "pixels", which is a shortening of "picture element". It is obvious that the resolution is connected with the text format. The number of pixels on one line is always eight times the number of text columns. Similarly, the number of vertical dots is always 256, eight times the 32 text lines. This relationship, a consequence of the way that each character is formed from a matrix of 8 × 8 dots, was discussed in Chapter 3. The entries in the "Colours" column are the same as those given in the table in that chapter. The "Memory" column gives the amount of memory taken

208

up by the different modes. This figure can be derived from the resolution and number of colours. For example, in MODE 0, there are 640*256, or 163840 pixels. Each pixel can be one of two colours. This means that there is one bit of storage per pixel. Eight pixel can therefore be squeezed into one byte. Thus the display requires 163840/8=20480 bytes. This is the same as 20K, as a big "K" means times 1024. Another example is MODE 2. This has 160*256 or 40960 pixels. In this mode, each pixels can be one of 16 colours. To store 16 quantities, four bits are needed. This means that only two pixels will fit into each byte. Again, then, the memory required is 40960/2 or 20480 bytes.

The way that the computer's memory is used to control the colour of each pixel individually has advantages and disadvantages. The good point is the flexibility gained; there is no restriction on which colour is assigned to each pixel, within the limitations of the mode in use. Many microcomputers' displays only enable control over a certain set of points. An example is the ZX Spectrum, whose colour control is restricted to each character position, as opposed to each pixel. This makes it very hard to move colour objects around the screen without the colours of surrounding objects changing too. The disadvantage of the BBC method is that it requires rather a lot of memory. The 20K needed by modes 0, 1 and 2 is nearly two thirds of the computer's total RAM. When you take into account the space needed by the operating system, there are only 8704 bytes left for the user's program and data. This is for a 32K machine – the 20K modes will not work at all on a 16K machine. On such a machine, the user is left with a mere 2560 bytes left when modes 4 or 5 are used. It is fortunate that MODE 7, which requires a measly 1024 bytes, is provided.

There are many parallels between printing text and plotting points and lines. Firstly, the need to specify the position where the action is to take place. This is done by the TAB(x,y,) modifier to the PRINT statement for text. The co-ordinates x and y specify the column and row respectively. A similar feat is performed using the "MOVE x,y" statement for graphics. This statement moves the position of the graphics cursor to the point specified. Unlike the text cursor, the graphics cursor is invisible, but it is always set to the most recent point "visited". You may remember from the last chapter that the number of columns and rows of text varies considerably from mode to mode, hence the action of TAB(x,y) varies as well. There is no such problem when using graphics. The screen can be likened to a sheet of graph paper (see Figure 4.1). No matter what mode is in use, the graph paper always has 1280 squares across by 1024 squares down.

The bottom left corner of the screen is given the co-ordinates "0,0", and is called the origin. The x and y co-ordinates increase to the right and in the up direction respectively. The top right-hand corner has the co-ordinates (1279, 1023). All graphics operations are expressed in terms of this co-ordinate system, and are therefore independent of the mode in use.

Two much-used graphics statements are MOVE and DRAW. MOVE, as mentioned above, positions the graphics cursor at the point specified. DRAW causes a line to be drawn from the current cursor position to the point given, and then updates the cursor position to the end of the line. Typing in the statements

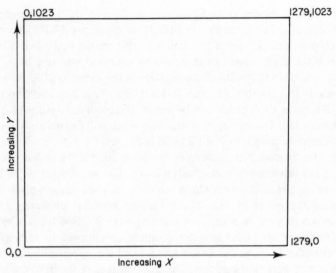

Figure 4.1 Co-ordinate System

below should illustrate these actions:

```
MODE 4:        REM  320 X 256 mode
MOVE 640,512:  REM  Move the cursor to the middle
DRAW 640,0:    REM  Draw vertical line to the bottom
DRAW 1279,1023:REM  Draw a diagonal line to the top-right.
MOVE 0,1023:   REM  Move to the top left
DRAW 0,0:      REM  Draw a line back to the origin
```

It doesn't matter what mode is used; the same line will be drawn regardless. The only thing that will change is the relative coarseness of the lines. Because the pixels in MODE 0 are much smaller than those in MODE 2, the lines will appear much smoother in the former mode. You may be wondering why the co-ordinate system has been defined as 1280 × 1024 instead of 640 × 256, which is the best resolution actually available. The main reason is for the ubiquitous "future expansion". It is just possible that some later version of the BBC Computer's video chip will have even higher resolution than at present. The limit to the physical resolution of modern monitors is about 1000 × 1000, so making provision for this order of resolution is quite sensible. A 1280 × 1024 display would need 160K of memory just for two colours, so such a capability is probably not planned for the immediate future.

Another good reason for using the 1280 × 1024 matrix is that the imaginary graph paper squares are almost exact squares. If the 640 × 256 system were used, the height of the "squares" would be over twice as large as their width. The result would be that when trying to draw circles, the programmer would obtain ellipses instead, unless he took precautions against it. Remember, though, that the 1280 × 1024 format is really illusory; there are only 160, 320 or 640 pixels per line, depending on the mode. This does have its disadvantages. There are more imaginary, or virtual pixels than real ones, so several virtual pixels correspond to one physical pixel on the screen. This relationship is shown in Figure 4.2 for the three different resolutions.

The result is that when plotting, the same pixels may be plotted many times. Obviously such duplication is a waste of time; once a pixel has been "lighted",

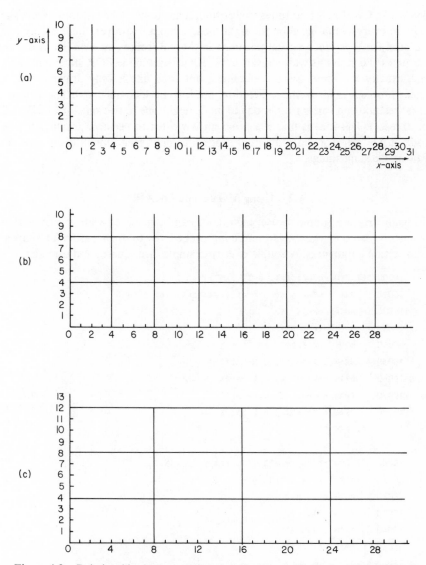

Figure 4.2   Relationship between Virtual and Actual Pixels for (a) MODE 0,
(b) MODES 1 and 4, and (c) MODES 2 and 5

plotting it again has no effect. Suppose it was necessary to plot the whole section of the screen below the bottom left to top right diagonal. One way (but not the best) of doing this is with a FOR. . .NEXT loop (assume we're in MODE 4):

```
100 FOR y%=0 TO 1023
110    MOVE 0,0
120    DRAW 1279, y%
130 NEXT y%
```

This works OK, but is four times slower than it has to be. A line is drawn from the origin to every virtual pixel on the right-most column. However, there is only one real pixel for every four virtual positions in the y direction, so each line is drawn four times. To stop this waste, insert a "STEP 4" part in the FOR statement. This time, exactly the same effect is obtained, but each line is only drawn once. A similar problem exists in the x direction, but it is more complicated. The virtual–actual relationship varies from mode to mode (eight:one to two:one for MODES 2 and 0 resp.). This means that if a program is written to perform graphics in one mode, it will still work in a different mode, but may spend much of its time re-drawing the same things.

4.2   Using MOVE and DRAW

Although they are simple to use, quite a lot can be achieved with just these two statements. A common use is in defining procedures to draw particular shapes, given certain parameters. A couple of easy examples are squares and triangles:

```
10000 DEF PROCsquare(cx%, cy%, len%)
10010    REM    Draw a square at (cx%, cy%), side len%
10020    LOCAL half%
10030    half%=len% DIV 2
10040    MOVE cx%-half%, cy%-half%
10050    DRAW cx%+half%, cy%-half%
10060    DRAW cx%+half%, cy%+half%
10070    DRAW cx%-half%, cy%+half%
10080    DRAW cx%-half%, cy%-half%
10090 ENDPROC


20000 DEF PROCtriangle(x1%,y1%, x2%,y2%, x3%,y3%)
20010    REM    Draw a triangle
20020    MOVE x1%, y1%
20030    DRAW x2%, y2%
20040    DRAW x3%, y3%
20050    DRAW x1%, y1%
20060 ENDPROC
```

The routines are fairly self-explanatory. The parameters for PROCsquare are the co-ordinates of the centre and the length of one side. The square is drawn in a clockwise fashion from the bottom left corner. The triangle procedure simply joins up the vertices (corners) whose co-ordinates are given as parameters. Recursion can often be illustrated well using graphics. Suppose PROCsquare is modified so that if the length of side is greater than some limit, it draws four more squares, half the size of the original, on the corners. If PROCsquare uses itself to draw squares, it must obviously be called recursively. If the lines:

```
10081    IF Len% <= Lim% THEN ENDPROC
10082    PROCsquare(cx%-half%,cy%-half%,half%,Lim%)
10083    PROCsquare(cx%+half%,cy%-half%,half%,Lim%)
10084    PROCsquare(cx%+half%,cy%+half%,half%,Lim%)
10085    PROCsquare(cx%-half%,cy%+half%,half%,Lim%)
```

are added, and the first line is changed to:

```
10000 DEF PROCsquare(cx%, cy%, Len%, Lim%)
```

then the call "PROCsquare(640,512,512,32)" provides quite a nice pattern in MODE 4. Reducing lim% to 16 produces a finer pattern; further reduction causes the squares to become too small before the recursion ends, so most of the screen is plotted white.

The examples above were simple, and didn't require very much calculation. A more complex shape is the circle. There are many ways of drawing circles, based on the various equations which exist. Two of the best known ones for a circle of radius R centred at (A,B) are:

$$(X-A)^2 + (Y-B)^2 = R^2$$
and $$X=A + R*COS(TH), \quad Y=B + R*SIN(TH), \quad 0<=TH<=2*PI$$

where X and Y are general points on the circle. Unfortunately, neither of these are particularly good for implementing on a computer. They both require a lot of calculation, and the first one doesn't even give evenly spaced values for X and Y. For illustration, I give the BBC BASIC version of the second form below:

```
10000 DEF PROCcircle(cx%, cy%, r%)
10010    REM    Draws a circle radius r% at (cx%,cy%)
10010    LOCAL th, step
10020    step=4/r%
10030    MOVE cx%+r%, cy%
10040    FOR th=step TO 2*PI+step*.1 STEP step
10050       DRAW cx%+r%*COS(th), cy%+r%*SIN(th)
10060    NEXT th
10070 ENDPROC
```

The step for the angle should actually be 1/r%, but since there are four virtual pixels to each actual pixel (in the 320 column modes), the multiplication by four ensures that each pixel is only plotted once. The addition of step*.1 to the FOR limit ensures that the circle meets at the start and end points. A way to speed the procedure up would be to increase the step, so that small lines are drawn instead of individual points. The problem is that the start and end points will rarely coincide, so there will be an ugly overlapping section. If the step is made large enough, the procedure degenerates into a polygon drawing routine. If the parameter "sides%" is added, and line 1020 changed to:

```
10020    step=2*PI/sides%
```

then the procedure will draw a polygon with sides% sides at (cx%,cy%). The small program below shows the modified procedure in use. It can be seen that sides% doesn't have to be very large for the "polygon" drawn to pass as a reasonable circle.

```
100 FOR s%=3 TO 40
110     PROCcircle(1000-s%*10, 512, s%*12, s%)
120 NEXT s%
130 END
```

Because working out sines and cosines is rarely a rapid operation on small computers, other ways of drawing circles have been invented. One such method is given below. Only one sine and one cosine are calculated for each circle. The next point is calculated from the present point, so a couple of variables are used to store these co-ordinates. The mathematical explanation of the procedure can be found in [Rogers].

```
1000 DEF PROCcircle(cx%, cy%, r%)
1010    REM    A more efficient circle routine
1020    LOCAL x, y, lx, ly, n%
1030    n%=32
1040    step=2*PI/n%
1050    cos=COS(step)
1060    sin=SIN(step)
1070    lx=r%: ly=0
1080    MOVE cx%+lx, cy%+ly
1090    FOR i%=1 TO n%
1100        x=lx*cos-ly*sin
1110        y=lx*sin+ly*cos
1120        DRAW cx%+x,cy%+y
1130        lx=x: ly=y
1140    NEXT i%
1150 ENDPROC
```

The variable n% holds the number of points on the circle. Ideally this should depend on the size of the circle, but this tends to make large circles very slow to draw. The value 32 is good enough for most sizes, and provides a reasonably fast routine.

As the modified square procedure showed, recursion is well illustrated by using graphics. The snowflake is a recursive object. It can be defined as "six arms, each of which may have smaller snowflake at the end". The criterion for deciding whether an arm has a small snowflake attached to it can be the same as that for PROCsquare; if the arm is greater than a certain limit it has a scaled-down flake drawn at the end:

```
1000 DEF PROCsnowflake(cx%,cy%,len%,lim%,fact)
1010    REM   Recursive routine to draw a snowflake
1020    LOCAL th%, x%, y%
1030    FOR th%=0 TO 300 STEP 60
1040       x%=cx%+len%*COS(RAD(th%))
1050       y%=cy%+len%*SIN(RAD(th%))
1060       MOVE cx%,cy%
1070       DRAW x%,y%
1080       IF len%>lim% THEN PROCsnowflake(x%,y%,len%*fact,lim%,fact)
1090    NEXT th%
1100 ENDPROC
```

Some interesting patterns are obtained by the calls:

```
PROCsnowflake(640, 512, 256, 32, 0.45)
PROCsnowflake(640, 512, 256, 16, 0.3)
PROCsnowflake(640, 512, 256, 16, 0.4)
PROCsnowflake(640, 512, 256, 64, 0.55)
PROCsnowflake(640, 512, 128, 90, 0.85)
```

If "fact" is made too large, the limit for FOR loops will be exceeded, and the procedure will halt with a "Too many FORs" error.

The binary tree was discussed in Chapter one. The procedure below draws complete binary trees (trees which have $2^n - 1$ nodes, where n is the level which the tree reaches). Like the snowflake program, it uses recursion to draw the nodes' children, if they are large enough:

```
1000 DEF PROCtree(x%, y%, len%,lim%, fact)
1010    REM   Draw a binary tree
1020    LOCAL dx%, dy%
1030    dx%=len%*1.25
1040    dy%=len%
1050    MOVE x%, y%
1060    DRAW x%-dx%, y%-dy%
1070    MOVE x%+dx%, y%-dy%
1080    DRAW x%, y%
1090    IF len% <= lim% THEN ENDPROC
1100    PROCtree(x%-dx%, y%-dy%, len%*fact, lim%, fact)
1110    PROCtree(x%+dx%, y%-dy%, len%*fact, lim%, fact)
1120 ENDPROC
```

The procedure works in much the same way as PROCsnowflake. The simplest tree is two lines emanating from (x%,y%). The variables dx% and dy% determine the size of each tree. If len% is greater than lim%, the two recursive children are drawn. A typical call would be:

```
PROCtree(640,1023,256,16,0.5)
```

though you can experiment of course. There is no limit on the depth of recursion except for the amount of RAM available.

4.3   Adding Colour

So far, all the plotting performed has been in black and white. This may not seem unusual if you are using a black and white display, but those with colour sets may suspect something has been missing. Also, there has been no way of erasing the lines made by DRAW, other than clearing the whole screen by a CLS or MODE, which is a little drastic if only one line needs to be erased. The subject of this section, GCOL, is the answer to these problems. The statement has the form:

```
GCOL mode, colour
```

The colour parameter has exactly the same meaning as the parameter after COLOUR, but it affects the graphics' foreground and background colours, and not the text. The mode parameter refers to the way the colour is actually placed on the screen. For now, only mode 0 will be used. This means that the colour specified by the second parameter is simply placed onto the screen whenever a DRAW is executed. The default graphics colours are the same as the default text colours, i.e. white foreground on a black background. The short program below draws four horizontal bars of colours 0, 1, 2 and 3 on the MODE 5 screen. These are black, red, yellow and white respectively, just as the text colours.

```
100 MODE 5
110 FOR y%=0 TO 1020 STEP 4
120    GCOL 0, y% DIV 256
130    MOVE 0, y%
140    DRAW 1279, y%
150 NEXT y%
160 END
```

The expression "y% DIV 256" gives 0 for y% in the range 0–255, 1 when y% is between 256 and 508, 2 for the range 512–764 and 3 for y% in the range 767–1020. After a GCOL, all subsequent DRAWing is performed in the colour specified. One way to erase lines on a black background is to set the graphics colour to black using GCOL 0,0, then redraw the lines. This method is used in the program below, which performs a moving "string-art" show. There are two moving points between which coloured lines are drawn. The co-ordinates of lines are stored in two arrays. When a certain number of lines have been drawn, the stored co-ordinates are used to erase the first lines. The arrays are used as "circular buffers"; as one item is removed (a line is deleted), a new item is entered (a new line drawn). When the array is full, it "wraps-round" to the beginning, hence the term circular.

```
100 REM String Art Program
110 MODE 4
120 PRINT TAB(0,10);"String Art"
130 MOVE 0,664:DRAW 320,664
140 REPEAT UNTIL INKEY(0)<>-1
150 PRINT TAB(0,12);"How many strings ";
160 INPUT str%
170 DIM x%(str%,1),y%(str%,1)
180 REM Initialise buffer pointer
190 ptr%=0
200 REM Set-up the initial points
210 x1%=RND(1279):y1%=RND(1023)
220 x2%=RND(1279):y2%=RND(1023)
230 REM Set-up the directions
240 dx1%=RND(51)-26:dy1%=RND(51)-26
250 dx2%=RND(51)-26:dy2%=RND(51)-26
260 MODE 5
270 REPEAT
280    REM Erase oldest line
290    GCOL 0,0
300    MOVE x%(ptr%,0),y%(ptr%,0)
310    DRAW x%(ptr%,1),y%(ptr%,1)
320    REM Draw new line
330    GCOL 0,RND(3)
340    MOVE x1%,y1%
350    DRAW x2%,y2%
360    x%(ptr%,0)=x1%
370    y%(ptr%,0)=y1%
380    x%(ptr%,1)=x2%
390    y%(ptr%,1)=y2%
400    REM Check for the boundary
410    IF x1%<0 OR x1%>1279 THEN dx1%=-dx1%
420    IF x2%<0 OR x2%>1279 THEN dx2%=-dx2%
430    IF y1%<0 OR y1%>1023 THEN dy1%=-dy1%
440    IF y2%<0 OR y2%>1023 THEN dy2%=-dy2%
450    x1%=x1%+dx1%
460    x2%=x2%+dx2%
470    y1%=y1%+dy1%
480    y2%=y2%+dy2%
```

```
490    ptr%=(ptr%+1) MOD str%
500 UNTIL INKEY(0)<>-1
510 REPEAT UNTIL INKEY(0)<>-1
520 MODE 4
530 PRINTTAB(0,10);"Another go ";
540 INPUT yn$
550 IF INSTR("Yn",yn$) AND yn$<>"" THEN RUN
560 PRINT''"See ya!"
570 END
```

The MOVE and DRAW at line 130 are used to underline the heading. Below is a procedure to print some underlined text anywhere on the screen. Because the number of text columns varies, while the number of graphics co-ordinates is constant for all modes, the procedure will only work for one text format. It has been written for forty column modes.

```
1000 DEF PROCunderline(text$)
1010    REM    Print text$ underlined
1020    LOCAL y%
1030    y%=994-32*VPOS
1040    MOVE 32*POS, y%
1050    PRINT text$;
1060    DRAW 32*POS-4, y%
1070 ENDPROC
```

For twenty column modes, the 32 in lines 1040 and 1060 should be changed to 64 and the 4 in line 1060 should be changed to 8. I leave it as an exercise to work-out the corresponding numbers for MODE 0. The text cursor is left immediately after the underlined text, so that normal text can be printed on the same line. The routine could obviously be extended to draw a whole box around the string. Remember that one character position is 64, 32 or 16 virtual pixels wide in 20, 40 and 80 column modes respectively, but always 32 pixels high.

There has not been much evidence of the graphics background colour in use yet. It is used by some of the PLOT options given later, and also by the CLG statement. Just as CLS fills the text window with the text background colour, CLG does the same thing for the graphics window. This defaults to the whole screen, and since the default graphics background colour is black, (colour zero), CLG seems to do exactly the same thing as CLS, albeit much slower. However, they are independent actions, and the text and graphics background colours are separate things. You can see this by typing in the following immediate statements:

```
MODE 4
GCOL 0,129 : REM  graphics background to white
CLG        : REM  fill the screen
PRINT "hello"
```

After the screen has been cleared to white, the prompt reappears as normal on a black background, and all subsequent printing is perfectly visible. If the "GCOL 0,129" had affected the text background, i.e. made it white as well, no output would be seen. The program below emulates the action of a simple Spirograph game, with a disc and a wheel of varying size. The user specifies how many teeth the wheel has, and the position of the pen (1 means on the circumference, 0 means in the middle). Because there is a lot of trigonometry, i.e. sines and cosines, the program is quite slow. I prefer to call it graceful. If you have a 32K machine, you could use MODE 1, and have the user specify which colour "pen" to use. You could then add a facility to move the wheel around, or change the number of teeth. This would enable you to build up proper Spirograph pictures, which you could then sell as Computer Art (after you've found a cheap way of getting the colour graphics screen onto paper). It is possible to use modes 5 or 2 for more colours, but the resolution leaves a bit to be desired.

```
100 REM Spirograph Program
110 MODE 4
120 PRINTTAB(0,10);"Spirograph"
130 MOVE 0,664:DRAW 320,664
140 REPEAT UNTIL INKEY(0)<>-1
150 PROCinit
160 REPEAT
170   INPUT'"Teeth on wheel ",teeth%
180   INPUT'"Pen position ",pen
190   PROCspiro(teeth%,pen)
200   INPUT'"Another one ",yn$
210 UNTIL INSTR("Yn",yn$)=0
220 MODE 4
230 PRINTTAB(0,10);"Bye Bye"
240 END
250
260
1000 DEFPROCinit
1010 wheel_rad%=416
1020 wheel_teeth%=144
1025 dth=4*PI/wheel_teeth%
1030 REM Move origin to centre
1040 VDU 29,640;192+wheel_rad%;
1050 REM Define text widow
1060 VDU 28,0,31,39,28
1080 ENDPROC
1090
1100
```

```
2000 DEFPROCspiro(teeth%,pen)
2010 LOCAL disc_rad%,ratio,th,th1
2015 LOCAL x%,y%
2020 disc_rad%=wheel_rad%*teeth% DIV wheel_teeth%
2030 ratio=-wheel_teeth%/teeth%
2040 GCOL 0,129: CLG
2045 GCOL 0,0
2050 MOVE wheel_rad%-(1-pen)*disc_rad%,0
2060 th=0
2080 REPEAT
2090   th=th+dth
2100   x%=(wheel_rad%-disc_rad%)*COS(th)
2110   y%=(wheel_rad%-disc_rad%)*SIN(th)
2120   th1=th*ratio
2130   x%=x%+pen*disc_rad%*COS(th1)
2140   y%=y%+pen*disc_rad%*SIN(th1)
2145   DRAW x%,y%
2150 UNTIL INKEY(0)<>-1
2160 ENDPROC
```

Simulating Spirograph in this way lets you try things that would be impossible in real life. For example, the disc could be made bigger than the wheel, or you could put the pen outside of the disc (pen > 1). If the minus sign is omitted from line 2030, the disc will be made to rotate in the same direction as it goes round the wheel, which is as if the disc were on the outside of the wheel instead of on the inside. For those interested, Figure 4.3 shows the geometry from which the program was derived.

So far only GCOL 0 has been mentioned. There are four more ways in which

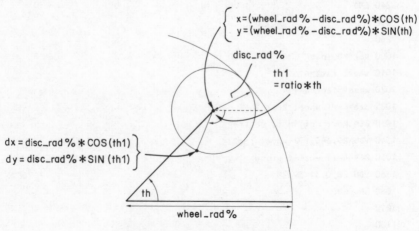

Figure 4.3   Geometry of Spirograph

the statement can be used, not surprisingly called GCOL 1 to GCOL 4. The table below summarises the meaning of all five GCOL modes.

GCOL mode	Meaning
0	Store colour specified
1	OR screen with colour specified
2	AND screen with colour specified
3	EOR screen with colour specified
4	NOT the screen

It is obvious that these operations are related to the BASIC logical operators OR, AND, EOR and NOT. The program below uses each combination of screen colour with GCOL colour to illustrate the effects obtained.

```
100 MODE 5
110 FOR y%=0 TO 1020 STEP 4
120     GCOL 0, y% DIV 256
130     MOVE 0, y%
140     DRAW 1276, y%
150 NEXT y%
160
170 FOR mode%=0 TO 4
180     start%=mode%*256
190     FOR x%=0 TO 248 STEP 8
200         GCOL mode%, x% DIV 64
210         MOVE start%+x%, 0
220         DRAW start%+x%, 1020
230     NEXT x%
240 NEXT mode%
250 END
```

The first part is the same as the program given earlier; it draws four bands of the MODE 5 colours black, red, yellow and white. The second part draws more bars of colour, this time vertical ones. The outer loop steps through all five GCOL modes. Within these five bands, the four colours are plotted. The effect is to obtain every combination of screen colour, plotting colour and plotting mode. For those who are too lazy to run the program, Figure 4.4 shows what the screen looks like when it has finished.

To understand what is happening, you have to think in terms of binary numbers. Since the MODE 5 display has four colours, each pixel must have two bits of memory to store its colour. These two bits can have the binary states 00, 01, 10, and 11, corresponding to that pixel being plotted in colour 0, 1, 2 and 3 respectively. The whole screen can be regarded as a large two-dimensional array of (in MODE 5) 256 rows of 160 pixels. The array is slightly unusual, since each element is only two bits wide, as opposed to BASIC integers' 32 bits. The analogy

SCREEN COLOUR	STORE				OR				AND				EOR				INVERT			
PLOT COLOUR →	0	1	2	3	0	1	2	3	0	1	2	3	0	1	2	3	0	1	2	3
0	0	1	2	3	0	1	2	3	0	0	0	0	0	1	2	3	3	2	1	0
1	0	1	2	3	1	1	3	3	0	1	0	1	1	0	3	2	3	2	1	0
2	0	1	2	3	2	3	2	3	0	0	2	2	2	3	0	1	3	2	1	0
3	0	1	2	3	3	3	3	3	0	1	2	3	3	2	1	0	3	2	1	0

PLOT MODE

0 = BLACK
1 = RED
2 = YELLOW
3 = WHITE

Figure 4.4   Effects of the various Plotting Modes

is still valid, though. If we call the array "screen()", any point can be set to the current graphics colour by the assignment "screen(x,y)=colour". This is exactly what the DRAWing routines in the MOS do when you draw a line after the statement "GCOL 0, colour". When the other GCOL modes are used, the assignment is performed in a slightly different way. After a "GCOL 1, colour" statement, points are plotted with the equivalent of "screen(x,y)=screen(x,y) OR colour". This means that the colour that finally appears depends not only on the value of "colour", but on the colour already on the screen. For example, suppose the statement "GCOL 1,1" was executed. This causes all subsequent plotting to be performed using the "OR with red" mode. If a line is drawn across the screen, the following effects would be achieved:

```
Old screen colour          New screen colour

  00 (Black)                 01 (Red)

  01 (Red)                   01 (Red)

  10 (Yellow)                11 (White)

  11 (White)                 11 (White)
```

This is confirmed by Figure 4.4 above (or by looking at the display if you have run the program). If you are not sure how the numbers were derived, look back at the truth tables for the logical operators in Chapter one. Remember that when two numbers are ORed, a one appears wherever a one occurred in either of the operands. The other three GCOL modes work in a similar way. The difference is that for GCOL 2 and GCOL 3, the AND and EOR functions are used, and for GCOL 4, the NOT function is used on the screen. In this case, the colour that is put on the screen is independent of the "colour" parameter of GCOL. The five modes are summarised in terms of the screen() array below.

```
GCOL statement            Effect of DRAWing

GCOL 0, colour            screen(x,y)=colour

GCOL 1, colour            screen(x,y)=screen(x,y) OR colour

GCOL 2, colour            screen(x,y)=screen(x,y) AND colour

GCOL 3, colour            screen(x,y)=screen(x,y) EOR colour

GCOL 4, colour            screen(x,y)=NOT screen(x,y)
```

The usefulness of the four new plotting modes may not be readily apparent. They have several uses, however, especially in the four and 16 colour modes. The EOR mode can be used where lines are to be drawn over a background, then erased again without affecting the background. This property stems from the equation "A EOR B EOR B = A". Translated into words this means that if you take the exclusive OR of two values, and then exclusive OR the result with the second value, the first value is the final result. A numerical example would be:

```
A=101, B=011  therefore  A EOR B = 110
110 EOR B is 110 EOR 011, which is 101, which is A
```

In the context of graphics, A represents the background on which a picture is drawn, and B represents the lines of the picture. By drawing the picture once in exclusive OR mode, it appears over the background. By re-drawing it in the same place, and in EOR mode, the picture is erased with no effect on the background. The program below draws a backdrop of squares in MODE 5. The GCOL 3 mode is used to obtain a patch-work effect. Then, a rotating square is continuously drawn, erased, moved and rotated, all without disturbing the background. This is also achieved using GCOL3. The colour plotted depends on the background colour. When the foreground is set to red (with the GCOL 3,1 at line 2130), the actual colour plotted will be "1 EOR background", i.e. red when the background is black, black when it is red, white when it is yellow and yellow when it is white. If the GCOL 3,1 is replaced with GCOL 3,3, the background colour will be inverted, i.e. the one bits become zeroes and vice versa. This is exactly the same as using GCOL 4,0 (or GCOL 4,1; the second digit is immaterial), as "inversion" can be regarded as "exclusive OR with all ones".

```
100 MODE 5
110 PROCinit
120 cx%=RND(1000)+100
130 dx%=RND(32)+16
140 cy%=RND(800)+100
150 dy%=RND(32)+16
160 rot=0
170 drot=RAD(RND(25)+10)
180 REPEAT
190   PROCsquare(cx%, cy%, 90, rot)
210   IF cx%<64 OR cx%>1216 THEN dx%=-dx%: drot=-drot
220   IF cy%<64 OR cy%>960 THEN dy%=-dy%: drot=-drot
230   PROCsquare(cx%, cy%, 90, rot)
240   cx%=cx%+dx%: cy%=cy%+dy%
250   rot=rot+drot
260 UNTIL INKEY(0)<>-1
270 END
280
290
1000 DEF PROCsquare(cx%, cy%, len%, rot)
1010   REM    Draw a square rotated by "rot"
1020   LOCAL sin%, cos%
1040   sin%=len%*SIN(rot)
1050   cos%=len%*COS(rot)
1060   MOVE cx%+cos%, cy%+sin%
1070   DRAW cx%-sin%, cy%+cos%
1080   DRAW cx%-cos%, cy%-sin%
1090   DRAW cx%+sin%, cy%-cos%
1100   DRAW cx%+cos%, cy%+sin%
```

```
1110 ENDPROC
1120
1130
1140
2000 DEF PROCinit
2010     REM Draw background and set colours
2020     LOCAL x%, y%
2030     FOR y%=0 TO 1020 STEP 4
2040        GCOL 0,y% DIV 128
2050        MOVE 0, y%
2060        DRAW 1272, y%
2070     NEXT y%
2080     FOR x%=0 TO 1272 STEP 8
2090        GCOL 3,x% DIV 128
2100        MOVE x%, 0
2110        DRAW x%, 1020
2120     NEXT x%
2130     GCOL 3,1
2140 ENDPROC
```

The square procedure is quite interesting on its own. The len% parameter is half the length of the diagonal of the square, so the side length is len%*SQR(2). The other parameter, rot, is the angle through which the square must be rotated. A value of zero gives a square whose diagonals are vertical and horizontal, i.e. rotated by 45 degrees to the position normally regarded as upright. As rot increases, the square turns in an anticlockwise direction. Below are some FOR ... NEXT loops that use PROCsquare to provide some nice patterns in MODE 4.

```
100 FOR i%=0 TO 90
110     PROCsquare(640, 512, i%*6, RAD(i%*4))
120 NEXT i%
130 a=GET: CLS
200 FOR i%=0 TO 45
210     PROCsquare(640, 512, i%*10, RAD(i%*4))
220 NEXT i%
230 a=GET: CLS
300 GCOL 3,1
310 FOR i%=0 TO 100
320     PROCsquare(640, 512, i%*5, RAD(i%*45))
330 NEXT i%
340 a=GET: CLS
400 FOR i%=0 TO 90
410     PROCsquare(640, 512, i%*6, RAD(i%))
420 NEXT i%
```

```
430 a=GET: CLS
500 GCOL 0,1
510 FOR i%=0 TO 100
520    PROCsquare(40+i%, 512, i%*4, RAD(i%*10))
530 NEXT i%
540 END
```

When using GCOL to set the background colour, the same plotting modes apply as with the foreground modes. For example, to invert the states of all the pixels on the screen, the two statements:

```
GCOL 4,128
CLG
```

can be used. The "4" specifies the invert mode, and the fact that the second parameter is greater than 127 causes the background colour to be set. Another example would be to OR the whole screen with red (in four or sixteen colour modes):

```
GCOL 1,129
CLG
```

All the black areas would be turned red; previously red areas would stay the same (and would thus be rendered invisible on a black background), and yellow and white regions would all be white after the CLG.

The CLG example above hints at the use of the OR and AND plotting modes. Instead of treating the MODE 5 display as an array of pixels, each of which can be one of four possible colours, it can be regarded as two separate pixel plains of one bit each. The higher bit of the colour number controls the first plane, which can be imagined to be positioned nearest the viewer's eyes. The lower bit represents a second plane which lies behind the first, and can be hidden by it. When both bits are zero, a third, unalterable background plane can be seen. The situation is shown in Figure 4.5.

By use of the AND and OR plotting modes, figures can be drawn on either plane without disturbing the other. For example, suppose we want a blue background, a red "middleground" and a white foreground. The four possible values of each pixel are:

Pixel value		Represents	VDU command
00	(0)	Background	VDU 19,0,4;0;
01	(1)	Middleground	VDU 19,1,1;0;
10	(2)	Foreground	VDU 19,2,7;0;
11	(3)	Foreground	VDU 19,3,7;0;

There are two possible versions of the foreground, both of which must be set to the same colour (white in this example). The "10" version is simply the foreground on its own. The "11" is when the middle ground colour has been drawn over the foreground. Because both colours two and three have been set to actual colour 7,

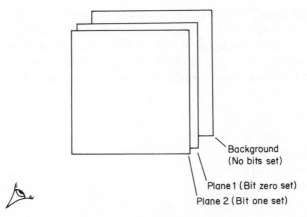

Figure 4.5   Colour Planes in MODE 5

the middle ground will not show up over the foreground. The table below summarises the GCOL commands for performing various actions on the two planes:

```
Action                      GCOL required

Draw the middleground       GCOL 1,1

Erase the middleground      GCOL 2,2

Draw the foreground         GCOL 1,2

Erase the foreground        GCOL 2,1

Erase both planes           GCOL 0,0
```

If you make the following amendments to the rotating square program given above, the square will move behind a white foreground, and in front of a blue background:

```
185     GCOL 1,1
225     GCOL 2,2
2040        GCOL 0,y% DIV 64 AND 2
2090        GCOL 3,x% DIV 64 AND 2
2130    VDU 19,0,4;0;
2132    VDU 19,1,1;0;
2134    VDU 19,2,7;0;
2136    VDU 19,3,7;0;
```

The meaning of lines 185 and 225 is given in the table above. Lines 2040 and 2090 set the display to a chequered pattern, alternating between colours zero and two (the "pure" foreground). The last four lines change the logical–actual colour relationships so that the background, middle-ground and foreground are blue, red and white. These do not look very stunning on a black and white display, so you could experiment to get a better effect. The only restriction on the colours is that two and three are identical, but different from zero and one (which are mutually different).

This "pixel plane" technique can naturally be applied to the sixteen colour MODE 2. This time there are four proper planes (corresponding to the four bits for each pixel) and the background plane. If the background is to be in "col0", the first foreground in "col1", up to "col4" for the foreground nearest the eye, the following VDU commands would be used to set up the logical–actual relationships:

```
1000 VDU 19,0,col0;0;
1010 VDU 19,1,col1;0;
1020 VDU 19,2,col2;0;
1030 VDU 19,3,col2;0;
1070 FOR i%=4 TO 7
1080     VDU 19,i%,col3;0;
1060 NEXT i%
1070 FOR i%=8 TO 15
1080     VDU 19,i%,col4;0;
1090 NEXT i%
```

The GCOL statements to draw and erase lines in the various levels are:

Action	GCOL required
Draw foreground 1	GCOL 1,1
Erase foreground 1	GCOL 2,14
Draw foreground 2	GCOL 1,2
Erase foreground 2	GCOL 2,13
Draw foreground 3	GCOL 1,4
Erase foreground 3	GCOL 2,11
Draw foreground 4	GCOL 1,8
Erase foreground 4	GCOL 2,7

These seemingly magic numbers can be explained in terms of the binary representations of 0–15. For example, to draw at the third foreground level, the third bit of the colour must be set, and the others must be left as they are. This implies an OR operation with binary 0100, hence the "GCOL 1,4" in the table. To erase a plane, the bit corresponding to that plane must be reset, while the others are untouched. This is achieved (for plane 3) by ANDing the current colour with binary 1011, hence "GCOL 2,11". The program below draws four square rings. Each of the rings is drawn on its own pixel plane. The ring on plane two is then moved across the screen to show the way the pixel planes may be protected by using the OR and AND modes. The two procedures PROCdraw and PROCerase join up the two points specified on the plane given, by drawing or erasing, as appropriate.

```
100 MODE 2
110 PROCinit
120 REM     Draw the four squares
```

```
130 FOR x%=0 TO 384 STEP 8
140    FOR plane%=1 TO 4
150        x1%=x%+(plane%-1)*256
160        y1%=128+plane%*128
170        PROCdraw(x1%,y1%, x1%,y1%+384, plane%)
175        IF x%>95 AND x%<288 THEN PROCerase(x1%,y1%+96, x1%,y1%+288, plane%)
180    NEXT plane%
190 NEXT x%
200 x%=640
210 REPEAT
220    PROCdraw(x% MOD 1280,384, x% MOD 1280,768, 2)
230    PROCdraw((x%-288) MOD 1280,480, (x%-288) MOD 1280,672, 2)
240    PROCerase((x%-384) MOD 1280,384, (x%-384) MOD 1280,768, 2)
250    PROCerase((x%-96) MOD 1280,480, (x%-96) MOD 1280,672, 2)
260    x%=x%+8
270 UNTIL INKEY(0)<>-1
280 END
290
300
310
1000 DEF PROCinit
1010    REM    Set up the colours
1020    LOCAL col0%, col1%, col2%, col3%, col4%, i%
1030    col0%=0
1040    col1%=1:  col2%=2
1050    col3%=3:  col4%=7
1060    VDU 19,0,col0%;0;
1070    VDU 19,1,col1%;0;
1080    VDU 19,2,col2%;0;
1090    VDU 19,3,col2%;0;
1100    FOR i%=4 TO 7
1110        VDU 19,i%,col3%;0;
1120    NEXT i%
1130    FOR i%=8 TO 15
1140        VDU 19,i%,col4%;0;
1150    NEXT i%
1170 ENDPROC
1180
1190
1200
2000 DEF PROCdraw(x1%,y1%, x2%,y2%, plane%)
2010    REM    Draw the line between (x1%,y1%) and (x2%,y2%)
```

```
2020      GCOL 1,2^(plane%-1)
2030      MOVE x1%,y1%
2040      DRAW x2%,y2%
2050 ENDPROC
2060
2070
2080
3000 DEF PROCerase(x1%,y1%, x2%,y2%, plane%)
3010      REM     Erase the line between (x1%,y1%) and (x2%,y2%)
3020      GCOL 2,15-2^(plane%-1)
3030      MOVE x1%,y1%
3040      DRAW x2%,y2%
3050 ENDPROC
```

The program can only be run on a 32K machine. When you get tired of seeing the ring move across the screen, press a key to stop the program. If you type in:

```
GCOL 1,136:CLG
```

the whole screen will turn white, the colour of plane 4. However, if you then try:

```
GCOL 2,135:CLG
```

planes one, two and three will re-appear, but not the white ring. This is because when the screen was flooded with colour 8 by the first CLG, all the information about the pixels lit in just plane 4 was lost. Hence, when the erasing CLG was executed, the whole plane was wiped out.

The colour planes technique just described obviously has many applications in games and other types of animation. In fact, some computer companies have been so impressed by the pseudo-three dimensional effect which can be obtained that they have designed special chips to implement it. These are the "sprite" graphics provided by the Texas TI 99/4 and the Commodore 64 computers. These objects are similar to user-defined characters, but are slightly larger (up to 32×32 pixels) and can be assigned to one of the 16 or 32 colour planes. The BBC method differs in that it is a software implementation. The disadvantage is that manipulating things in software (e.g. changing the pallette relationships) is slower than dedicated hardware which achieves the same effect. On the other hand, the programmer has potentially more versatility as the whole planes can be manipulated instead of limited-sized pre-defined objects. As an exercise to aid your understanding of the technique, change the string-art program so that, in MODE 2, the "strings" weave in and out of the four colour planes, enhancing the 3-D effect. For this you will need 32K. You can use PROCinit, PROCdraw and PROCerase from above (with a change to col0, col1 etc. if desired). Remember that to erase an old string you must save the plane in which it was drawn in addition to its end points' co-ordinates.

4.4 PLOT and POINT

Although the MOVE/DRAW combination is quite a powerful one, there is much more to graphics than plotting straight lines. These two statements are actually two particular versions of the more general PLOT statement (which in turn is one form of the VDU command). PLOT has the syntax:

```
PLOT option, x, y
```

The x and y parts are the familiar co-ordinates that are used in MOVE and DRAW. Option tells PLOT how to interpret the co-ordinates. Since it is treated as a one byte quantity, there are 256 possible options. Not all of these are implemented, though, with some of the options being reserved for the promised "curve plotting" ROM. The byte can be split into two main parts. The lower three bits tell PLOT whether to use relative or absolute co-ordinates, and whether to MOVE or DRAW. The other bits dictate whether lines, points or triangles are plotted. All these options are summarised by Figure 4.6. I will explain the meaning of the lower three bits first, then cover the effects of setting the higher bits. The three bits can have eight possible values. The actions of these first eight PLOT option codes (i.e. with all the other bits set to zero) are given below:

PLOT option	Action
0	MOVE the graphics cursor relative by (x,y)
1	DRAW a line in the foreground colour relative by (x,y)
2	DRAW a line in the inverse screen colour relative by (x,y)
3	DRAW a line in the background colour relative by (x,y)
4	MOVE the graphics cursor absolute to (x,y)
5	DRAW a line in the foreground colour absolute to (x,y)
6	DRAW a line in the inverse screen colour absolute to (x,y)
7	DRAW a line in the background colour absolute to (x,y)

The first notable thing is that the eight options can be divided into two sets of four

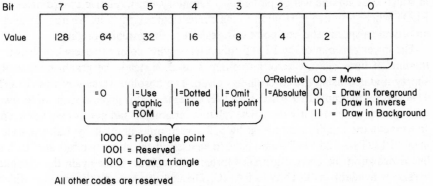

Figure 4.6   PLOT option fields

– the first four use relative co-ordinates, the latter four specify absolute co-ordinates. The difference between these two types is that relative co-ordinates specify a point in terms of the current cursor position, while absolute co-ordinates are always with respect to the graphics origin. Absolute is what we have been using with DRAW and MOVE. To illustrate relative co-ordinates, consider the piece of program below which draws a square, 128 screen units on a side, with the lower left-hand corner at (640,512), the middle of the screen:

```
100 MOVE 640,512
110 PLOT 1, 124, 0:    REM    124 units to the right, none up
120 PLOT 1, 0, 124:    REM    124 units up, none across
130 PLOT 1, -124,0:    REM    124 units to the left, none up
140 PLOT 1, 0,-124:    REM    124 units down, none across
```

Notice that once the start point has been reached, with the MOVE, there is no need for calculation to find the next point. Compare this example with PROCsquare given earlier, where there were a lot of +'s and –'s to find the co-ordinates of the next point from the current one. With relative co-ordinates, this calculation is done implicitly. The program below imitates a drunken snail on speed. The cursor is moved to the centre of the screen. Then a REPEAT loop draws short lines relative to the current position until the user presses a key.

```
100 MODE 4
110 MOVE 640,512
120 REPEAT
130    PLOT 1, RND(17)-9, RND(17)-9
140 UNTIL INKEY(0)<>-1
150 END
```

The "RND(17)–9" returns a value in the range 1–9 to 17–9, or –8 to 8. Therefore on each iteration of the loop, a short line at most two pixels long is drawn in one of the eight principal directions (unless both expressions yield numbers less than 4, in which case no line will be plotted). In summary, then, relative co-ordinates tell PLOT where to move in relation to the current cursor position, whereas absolute co-ordinates specify the new point with respect to the graphics origin.

The lower two bits of the PLOT option tell it what colour to use when drawing the line. If both bits are zero, no colour is used. Instead, the graphics cursor is simply updated using the co-ordinates given. The absolute version of this (PLOT 4) is exactly the same as BASIC's MOVE statement. It is given a name of its own because it is so commonly used. The relative version has not got its own keyword, so to move the graphics cursor up by 512 screen units and left by 128, the statement "PLOT 0,–128,512" would have to be used. If the lower two bits are "01", a line is drawn in the current graphics foreground colour. Once again the absolute version is available as DRAW in BASIC. The colour used and the mode in which the points are plotted (AND, EOR, etc.) are determined by the last GCOL statement to be executed.

If the lower two bits of the plot option are "10", inverse plotting is used. This is exactly the same as using "GCOL 4,colour". The colour placed on the screen is independent of the currently selected graphics foreground colour; it is merely the inverse of the colour already there.

When the lower two bits are "11", the current background colour is used to draw the line. This is obviously useful for erasing lines that have been drawn over a uniform background. Problems occur if a line has been drawn over several different background colours. When PLOT 3 or PLOT 7 is used to erase it, only the part of the line drawn across the most recently set background colour will be erased without a trace. Any line sections drawn over colours other than the current background colour will still show up, but in a different colour. Because of this, the previous PLOT option could prove more useful. As I mentioned earlier, inverting a number is equivalent to exclusive ORing each bit in the number's binary representation with a 1. The result is that drawing a line with PLOT 2 or PLOT 6 (the difference being the way the co-ordinates are interpreted) causes it to show up whatever the background is. What's more it can be erased without a trace simply by re-drawing it.

All of the codes given above are concerned with drawing lines (if you count a MOVE as drawing an invisible line). When various numbers are added to these options, the action of PLOT can be varied dramatically. Some of the variations are very useful, others less so. The numbers added to the 8 main codes for various effects are given below:

Number added to PLOT option	Effect
8	Omit the last point on the line
16	Draw a dotted line
24	Dotted line, last point omitted
64	Draw a single point only
80	Draw a triangle

All the other codes (there are 208 of them) are reserved for future expansion. The two really useful modifications are the single point and triangle ones. The others are less used, especially the "omit last point" ones. The dotted lines produced by PLOT 16 to PLOT 23 are a little unpredictable. The dotted effect is achieved by only plotting every other point on the line. The problem is that the exact points that are plotted varies with the length and direction of the lines. Try the small program below:

```
100 MODE 4
110 FOR th=0 TO 359.5 STEP .5
120    MOVE 640,512
130    PLOT 21, 1280*COS(RAD(th)), 1280*SIN(RAD(th))
140 NEXT th
150 END
```

The effect produced by this program is very uniform, the dots that are plotted and omitted in the various directions are clear from the square effect obtained.

However, if the 1280s in line 130 are changed to 512, a very different pattern appears. It is only uniform in the semicircle from north-west through north to south-east. In the other half, the "dottiness" of the lines seems almost random. This means that if you are using the dotted line option to achieve some particular effect, you must make sure that the lines are drawn in the correct direction.

The ability to plot individual points is obviously an important one. It is achieved in BBC BASIC by adding 64 to the basic 0–7 range of the PLOT option. The most commonly used variation is PLOT 69, which is the point equivalent to DRAW; it plots the point at the co-ordinates specified in the current graphics foreground colour. The program below draws a sine-wave using PLOT 69. Most graph routines have this sort of loop at their heart; a more general purpose graph plotter is given later, after graphics windows and origin translation have been covered.

```
100 MODE 4
110 FOR th=0 TO 359.5 STEP 0.5
120    PLOT 69, 1280*th/360, 512+512*SIN(RAD(th))
130 NEXT th
140 END
```

The fraction 1280/360 is given explicitly in line 120 as its meaning is clearer than simply putting th*3.5556. Dividing "th" by 360 gives a number in the range zero to just less than one. When multiplied by 1280, this yields a number from 0 to just less than 1280, so the whole width of the screen is used. Similarly, then SIN function returns a number between −1 and 1, so the last expression on line 120 gives a value in the range 0 to 1024. A function that is often used in conjunction with PLOT 64-71 is POINT. This returns the logical colour of a given pixel:

```
col%=POINT(x%, y%)
```

would put the colour value of the pixel (x%,y%) in the variable col%. The number returned is in the range 0 to N, where N is 1, 3 or 15 for 2, 4 and 16 colour modes respectively. If (x%,y%) is outside of the current graphics window, the function returns −1. The program below divides the MODE 4 screen into four quadrants. It copies the contents of the lower left-hand quadrant into the other four. The lower right and top left quadrants are inverted, i.e. pixels set to zero in the lower left quarter of the screen are copied as colour one, and pixels set to one are copied as colour zero.

```
100 MODE 4
110 FOR i%=1 TO 100
120    PRINT TAB(RND(20)-1, RND(16)+15);CHR$(RND(96)+31);
130 NEXT i%
140 FOR y%=0 TO 508 STEP 4
150    FOR x%=0 TO 636 STEP 4
160       col%=POINT(x%,y%)
170       GCOL 0, col%
```

```
180        PLOT 69, x%+640, y%+512
190        GCOL 0, 1-col%
200        PLOT 69, x%+640, y%
210        PLOT 69, x%, y%+512
220      NEXT x%
230 NEXT y%
240 END
```

The first FOR ... NEXT loop prints some characters in the bottom left corner to ensure that there is something to copy. The next two loops scan the screen from bottom to top, left to right. The program runs excruciatingly slowly. This is due to a combination of the large number of iterations of the loops (20480 in all), and the fact that POINT and PLOT 69 are not especially fast. They should be better on a 2MHz machine, though.

The program below plots Lissajous figures. These are the patterns that can be observed on an oscilloscope when two alternating voltages of different frequencies or phases are fed to the X- and Y-plates. The number of loops depends on the frequency relationship between the two voltages, while the phase relationship affects the size of the loops. The best patterns are obtained with small integer ratios of frequency, such as 1:2, 3:5, etc. (the lower frequency should be input first). The bulk of the work is done on lines 170 and 180. These work out the position of the dot on the oscilloscope at "time". Mathematically minded readers might recognise the two expressions as a pair of parametric equations in "time". The function FNhcf is the highest common factor function given earlier, altered to take real parameters. You should be careful when using real numbers here. The errors associated with the inexact storage of fractional numbers such as 2.4 means that the equality test may never be true, even though the two numbers are to all intents equal. It might be a good idea to change line 1050 to:

```
1050 UNTIL ABS(f1-f2)/f1 < 1E-3
```

or similar.

```
100 REM Lissajous Figures
110 MODE 4
120 INPUT TAB(0,5),"First frequency (Hz) ",f1
130 INPUT TAB(0,7),"Second frequency (Hz) ",f2
140 INPUT TAB(0,9),"Phase angle (degs.) ",phi
145 CLS
150 max_time=1/FNhcf(f1,f2)
160 FOR time=0 TO max_time STEP max_time/150/f2
170      x%=640+512*SIN(2*PI*time*f1+RAD(phi))
180      y%=512+512*SIN(2*PI*time*f2)
190      PLOT 69,x%,y%
200 NEXT time
210 END
```

```
 220
 230
 240
1000 DEF FNhcf(f1,f2)
1010     IF f1=f2 THEN =f1
1020     REPEAT
1030         IF f1>f2 THEN f1=f1-f2
1040         IF f2>f1 THEN f2=f2-f1
1050     UNTIL f1=f2
1060 =f1
```

The other useful variation on the PLOT theme cited above was the triangle drawing one. The option codes 80–87 allow triangles to be drawn on the screen very rapidly. These are solid triangles, rather than the outlines produced by things such as PROCtriangle given earlier. Actually, not all the eight option codes in the range 80–87 produce triangles; the codes 80 and 84 simply update the cursor position rather than plot anything, as the basic codes 0 and 4 are MOVE rather than DRAW options. Because a triangle needs three points to specify it uniquely, PLOT takes the last TWO points and the point specified after the option byte as the triangle's vertices. Again, the triangle equivalent to the DRAW statement, PLOT 85, is probably the most commonly used variation. The procedure listed below is an example of using relative co-ordinates with triangles. It draws a solid square at the given co-ordinates and of the given side.

```
1000 DEF PROCsquare(x%, y%, Len%)
1010     REM    Draws a square at (x%,y%), Len% Long
1020     MOVE x%,y%
1030     PLOT 0, Len%, 0
1040     PLOT 81, -Len%, Len%
1050     PLOT 81, Len%, 0
1060 ENDPROC
```

The MOVE puts the cursor at the bottom left-hand corner of the square. This is going to be used by PLOT 81 as one of the vertices. The PLOT 0, which is a relative MOVE, places the cursor len% screen units to the right. This will be the second vertex. Line 1040 draws the first triangle. The PLOT statement say "draw a triangle between the last two points visited and a point len% to the left and len% above the current one". This fills in the triangle below the top left to bottom right diagonal. It also updates the cursor position and last cursor position so that they are (x%,y%+len%) and (x%+len%,y%) respectively. The second PLOT 81 draws the triangle between those two points and the point (x%+len%,y%+len%), completing the square.

The above works fine if the graphics foreground colour mode is store, AND or OR. If, however, it is EOR or invert (e.g. the last GCOL was "GCOL 3,1"), a nasty side effect occurs. The problem is that the diagonal between the two triangles which form the square have a line in common, the one joining the top left and bottom right-hand corners of the square. This means that the first PLOT 81 draws this line, but the second one erases it again. The result is an unwanted diagonal line. The problem can be solved by erasing the line explicitly with a PLOT 1, then allowing the second PLOT 81 to re-draw it. This is done with the two changes:

```
1045    PLOT 1,len%, -len%
1050    PLOT 81, 0,len%
```

Just as DRAW can be used to plot polygon outlines, the triangle filling facility can be used to draw solid polygons. The procedure below does this, taking the centre co-ordinates, number of sides, side length and rotation as parameters.

```
1000 DEF PROCpoly(cx%, cy%, sides%, len%, rot)
1010    REM     Draws a "solid" polygon
1020    LOCAL int_ang, rad%, th
1030    REM     Work out the "radius"
1040    int_ang=2*PI/sides%
1050    rad%=len%*COS(int_ang*0.5)/SIN(int_ang)
1060    MOVE cx%,cy%
1070    MOVE cx%+rad%*COS(rot), cy%+rad%*SIN(rot)
1080    FOR th=int_ang TO 2*PI+int_ang*.1 STEP int_ang
1090       PLOT 85,cx%+rad%*COS(rot+th), cy%+rad%*SIN(rot+th)
1100       DRAW cx%, cy%
1110    NEXT th
1120 ENDPROC
```

The geometry of the polygon is shown in Figure 4.7.

The speed at which triangles are drawn means that it is usually better to use PLOT 85 rather than FOR ... NEXT loops containing MOVEs and DRAWs. You should be able to use this method to draw the squares in the moving ring program given earlier. It is still better to draw and erase lines when making the

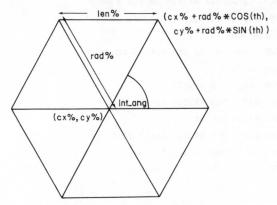

Figure 4.7   Geometry of a Polygon

ring move, though. The next program might be of interest to geography students. It draws a map of Antarctica using various projections. The island itself is drawn as a series of triangles around the South Pole. The data for the coastline is kept in DATA statements which hold the latitude of the intersections of the coast for incremental values of longitude. Unfortunately, this method is not readily extended to cover other areas.

```
100 REM      Antarctic Program
105 MODE 4
110 PROCinit
120 REPEAT
130    CLS
140    proj%=FNget_proj(num_proj%)
150    lo_lat=FNget_lo_lat
160    REM    Find scale factor, scale
170    scale=size% / FNproj(lo_lat, proj%)
180    REM    Draw the lines of lat. & long.
190    PROCgrid(lo_lat, proj%)
200    REM    Now draw the map
210    PROCmap(lo_lat, proj%)
220    INPUT "Another go (Y/N) ", yn$
230 UNTIL yn$="N" OR yn$="n"
240 END
250
260
270
1000 DEF PROCinit
1010    REM    Defines the projection equations,
1020    REM    sets up some constants
1030    LOCAL
1060    REM    graphics origin to the middle
1070    VDU 29, 640;512;
1080    size%=500
1090    REM    define the projection equations
1100    num_proj%=4
1110    DIM proj$(num_proj%)
1120    proj$(1)="SIN(RAD(co_lat))"
1130    proj$(2)="co_lat"
1140    proj$(3)="TAN(RAD(co_lat / 2))"
1150    proj$(4)="SQR(co_lat)"
1160 ENDPROC
1170
1180
```

```
1190
2000 DEF FNget_proj(num_proj%)
2010    REM    Returns the projection number to use
2020    REM    for this go
2030    LOCAL i%, proj%
2040    PRINT TAB(0,5);
2050    FOR i%=1 TO num_proj%
2060       PRINT ;i%;". ";proj$(i%)'
2080    NEXT i%
2090    REPEAT
2100       PRINT TAB(0,5+num_proj%*2);"Which one (1-";num_proj%;") ";
2110       INPUT proj%
2120    UNTIL proj% >= 1 AND proj% <= num_proj%
2130 =proj%
2140
2150
2160
3000 DEF FNget_lo_lat
3010    REM    Returns the lowest latitude to be mapped
3020    LOCAL lo
3030    CLS
3040    REPEAT
3050       INPUT TAB(0,5),"Lowest latitude to show (10-80) ", lo
3060    UNTIL lo >= 10 AND lo <= 80
3070 =lo
3080
3090
3100
4000 DEF FNproj(lat, proj%)
4010    REM    Returns the projection of lat
4020    REM    under projection proj%
4030    LOCAL co_lat
4040    co_lat=90-lat
4050 =EVAL(proj$(proj%))
4060
4070
4080
5000 DEF PROCgrid(lo_lat, proj%)
5010    REM    Draw the lines of latitude and longitude
5020    REM    under projection proj%
5030    LOCAL lat%, long%, rad%
5035    CLS
```

```
5040    REM    longitude first
5050    FOR long%=0 TO 350 STEP 10
5060       MOVE 0,0
5070       DRAW size%*SIN(RAD(long%)), size%*COS(RAD(long%))
5090    NEXT long%
5100    REM Now the circles
5110    FOR lat%=80 TO lo_lat STEP -10
5120       rad%=scale*FNproj(lat%, proj%)
5130       PROCcircle(rad%)
5140    NEXT lat%
5145    IF lo_lat MOD 10 = 0 THEN ENDPROC
5150    rad%=scale*FNproj(lo_lat, proj%)
5160    PROCcircle(rad%)
5170 ENDPROC
5180
5190
5200 DEF PROCcircle(rad%)
5210    LOCAL th%
5220    MOVE rad%, 0
5230    FOR th%=10 TO 360 STEP 10
5240       DRAW rad%*COS(RAD(th%)), rad%*SIN(RAD(th%))
5250    NEXT th%
5260 ENDPROC
5270
5280
5290
6000 DEF PROCmap(lo_lat, proj%)
6010    LOCAL n%, dth, lat, lat1, rad%
6020    RESTORE
6030    READ n%: dth=360/n%
6040    MOVE 0,0
6050    READ lat1
6060    MOVE 0,scale*FNproj(lat1, proj%)
6070    FOR i%=1 TO n%-1
6080       READ lat
6090       rad%=scale*FNproj(lat, proj%)
6100       PLOT 86, rad%*SIN(RAD(i%*dth)), rad%*COS(RAD(i%*dth))
6110       MOVE 0,0
6120    NEXT i%
6130    PLOT 86, 0,scale*FNproj(lat1, proj%)
6140 ENDPROC
6200 DATA 18: REM number of lats.
```

```
6210 DATA 71.3, 70.5, 69, 67.5, 68, 66.9
6220 DATA 66.9, 66.9, 69.4, 86, 84.5, 75.8
6230 DATA 73, 72, 73, 80, 80.5, 73
```

The program should be fairly self-explanatory. There are four projections provided, all of which provide a slightly different view of the Southern Hemisphere. There is nothing to stop you adding more; the only thing that needs changing is the variable "num_proj%" which is the number of projections held in proj$(). The triangle statement used is PLOT 86, the absolute inverting one. This enables the lines of latitude and longitude to remain visible under the map. The map is oriented so that 0 degrees longitude is at the top, with east to the right. This can be changed if desired by playing around with the SIN and COS functions in the plotting statements. There is a VDU 29 statement, which moves the origin to the centre of the screen. This is explained further in the next section.

4.5 The Graphics Origin, Window and Cursor

The first of this chapter's topics was mentioned in the last section. When a MODE statement is executed, the graphics origin is placed at the bottom left-hand corner of the screen. This in turn means that the right-hand column has an X co-ordinate of 1279, and the top row is at Y=1023. This arrangement is not always convenient, and lines' co-ordinates often have to be transposed (an offset added to the basic X and Y values) to place them correctly on the screen. A useful facility is one that lets us shift the position of the origin to a more convenient place. This often decreases the amount of calculation needed to draw complex figures. This transposition of the origin is achieved with a VDU command. It has the form:

```
VDU 29, X;Y;
```

The co-ordinates specify the position of the origin. This is always in relation to the default bottom left position. Notice the semicolons that follow X and Y. These tell BASIC to send the values as two-byte numbers, as required by the MOS "oswrch" routine. If you forget one of them, the origin is not moved until another byte is sent to "oswrch". This will lead to an unpredictable positioning of (0,0), so don't forget the semicolons! A common use of VDU 29 is to shift the origin to the middle of the screen. This is done with:

```
VDU 29, 640;512;
```

After the statement has been executed, co-ordinates of points on the screen will change so that X values are between −640 and 639 for the left-most and right-most columns respectively, and the Y values of the bottom and top rows are −512 and 511, also respectively. Figure 4.8 shows the "before and after" situations.

It is clear that the net effect of "VDU 29, x;y;" is to subtract x and y from the X and Y co-ordinates of all the points on the screen. Don't let presence of negative co-ordinates worry you; if anything, they should be more natural because there is more symmetry in the co-ordinate system.

242

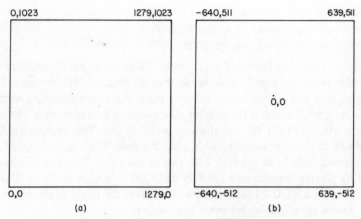

Figure 4.8   Before and After VDU 29,640;512;

The second subject discussed in this section is a distant cousin of the text windows covered in the last chapter. A graphics window, or clipping window, can be defined by yet another VDU statement. In the same way that text windows restrict the action of PRINT to a certain area on the screen, graphics windows limit the part of the display that can be PLOTted upon. Similarly, the default graphics window set to the whole screen by a MODE or VDU 26 statement. The graphics window-defining statement is VDU 24, as in:

```
VDU 24, x_left; y_bot; x_right; y_top;
```

Again, notice the semicolons implying 16 rather than eight bit quantities. There is a fine bit of logic in operation here. The VDU code for defining a text window is adjacent to that for moving the graphics origin, whereas the code for defining the graphics window is miles away. The word "clipping" was used above to describe the graphics window. This refers to the way lines that would appear outside of the window are dealt with. Almost without exception, BASICs that provide some graphics ability treat it as an error to plot outside the screen area. This is a very restrictive attitude, as graphics programs have to constantly check that no part of a (possibly moving) drawing will go off the screen. An exception to this rule is the BBC Computer. When you try to draw off the screen, or more precisely, outside of the current graphics window, lines are "clipped", so that only the portions that would be visible are drawn. The program below illustrates this by defining a clipping window a quarter of the normal full-screen one, and drawing lines at random all over the screen. The region of window is quite apparent from the section of lines actually displayed.

```
100 MODE 4
110 VDU 24, 320; 256; 960; 768;
120 FOR i%=1 TO 100
130     DRAW RND(1280), RND(1024)
140 NEXT i%
150 END
```

Up till now, it has been assumed that the total virtual graphics area is 1280 by 1024 points. This is not true; it so happens that the screen is configured to provide a maximum window into this size area. The true extent of the graphics area is dictated by the number of bits in each co-ordinate, 16. The legal range for both the X and Y co-ordinates is −32768 to 32768. Using VDU 29 and VDU 24 statements, any area of this total (up to the physical 1280 × 1024 restriction) can be used. Figure 4.9 shows the set-up when a MODE is first executed, and after the statement "VDU 29, -2560;1024;" has been executed.

The CLG statement affects only the current graphics window, just as CLS clears only those characters in the active text area. This provides a very simple way of drawing solid rectangular areas, viz.

```
1000 DEF PROCrect(x1%,y1%, x2%,y2%, col%)
1010    REM   Draws a rectangle with lower left and
1020    REM   upper right corners (x1%,y1%), (x2%,y2)
1030    REM   in colour col%
1040    VDU 24, x1%;y1%;x2%;y2%;
1050    GCOL 0, 128+col%
1060    CLG
1070    VDU 20, 26
1080 ENDPROC
```

The two windowing statements can be used to give a fair imitation of other computers' displays. For example,

```
100 VDU 24, 0;384;1279;1020;
110 VDU 28, 0,23,39,20
120 VDU 29, 0;384;
```

mimics an Apple][in "HGR" mode. Some things can't be emulated easily, such as the way Applesoft has the Y-axis upside-down, and the scaling factor on the BBC's co-ordinate system.

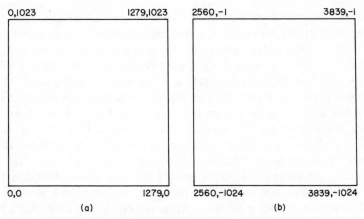

Figure 4.9   Before and After VDU 29,-2560;1024;

The last item in this section's title, the graphics cursor, relates not so much to the existence of such an object, which should by now be taken for granted, but to the ability to "join" it with the text cursor. Normally, the positions of the two cursors are quite distinct; the text cursor (whose position can be found by calls to POS and VPOS) is a flashing horizontal bar at the bottom of the position of the next character space to be written. The graphics cursor, on the other hand, is an invisible entity that remembers the last point visited on the graphics screen. No direct means exists to find the co-ordinates of the graphics cursor before MOS1.1, but this is offset by the provision of relative co-ordinates: if you can say "draw a line from here to a point 100 units across and 150 down", it doesn't really matter where "here" is.

The joining of the two cursors is initiated by the statement:

```
VDU 5
```

After such a statement, the text cursor as we know it disappears. Its position on the screen is remembered for posterity, or more accurately so that it can be replaced correctly when a VDU 4 statement is executed. However, from now on, all printing has its position determined by the location of the graphics cursor. This means that you are no longer limited to placing characters exactly in the eight by eight pixel boxes to where they are normally restricted. After VDU 5, printing can be performed at any addressable graphics point. Moreover, whenever a character is displayed, the graphics cursor position is shifted to the right, so that the next character is printed in the correct position. The program below prints 30 lines of text, each line being half a character space to the right of the one above it.

```
100 MODE 4
110 VDU 5
120 FOR i%=0 TO 29
130    MOVE i%*16, 1020-32*i%
140    PRINT "Hi Katrina!"
150 NEXT i%
160 END
```

The calculations need some explaining. The X co-ordinate isn't too hard to work out. The leftmost dot position in the character is printed at the current graphics cursor X co-ordinate. Since, in 40 column modes, each character cell is 32 screen units wide, TAB(0) is at X=0, TAB(1) is at X=32 and so on, up to TAB(39) at X=1248. The half-character positions are therefore at multiples of 16 screen units, hence the i%*16 at line 130. The character is drawn from the top to bottom. The top row is drawn at the current graphics cursor Y co-ordinate. Since the top graphics row is at virtual Y co-ordinate 1020 (in fact 1020 to 1023, as each real row is four virtual units high), positioning the graphics cursor here will cause characters to be printed at TAB Y=0. For each 32 (the height of a character in screen units) subtracted, the text is printed one row down. Although the text cursor is not visible, text can still be positioned with the TAB modifier to the PRINT statement, at least in MOS 0.1. Later versions ignore TAB after a VDU 5, apparently. Also VPOS and POS don't work after VDU 5; they return the cursor position before the cursors were joined.

There are several other noticeable results of typing VDU 5. Printing is visibly slower. Why this should be is not readily apparent without some appreciation of how characters are normally put on the screen. Basically, the screen memory is arranged so that the copying of the character patterns onto the screen, whether from the character set in ROM, or the user-defined ones in RAM, can be achieved very rapidly. In the two colour modes, it is simply a matter of transferring eight bytes of data (the character definition) from the character set area to eight consecutive locations in the display memory. There are very efficient ways of doing this, hence normal printing is fast. However, after a VDU 5, there is no guarantee that text will be put into these convenient cells. In fact, the very fact that a VDU 5 has been executed implies that programmer wants to disregard these text "boxes". This in turn means that the fast byte-copying routines cannot be used. In fact, each dot in the character must be plotted individually, more about which later.

Another trait of the joined cursors mode is the lack of scrolling. The reason behind this is the same as that for the slowness of printing. The scrolling mechanism of the BBC Micro works on units of one line. If the display scrolled while the cursors were joined, the chances are that there would be lines with only parts of characters on them, the result being a mess. Instead of scrolling, text simply "wraps-round" when it reaches the bottom (or top) of the screen. This has the unfortunate effect of overwriting what is already there. However, it does this is a different way to that which might be expected. This is another consequence of the way characters are printed. I mentioned above that each dot in the character is plotted. This is not quite true: all dots which are "on", i.e. have a one bit in the character's definition, are plotted in the current graphics foreground colour, and using the current graphics foreground colour plotting mode. "Off" dots are simply ignored; they are NOT plotted in the graphics background colour. Because plotting is used, the limit to text display is governed by the graphics window rather than the text one.

To leave the joined cursors mode, a statement such as "VDU 4", "PRINT CHR$(4);" or pressing CTRL-D will do the trick. After this, things revert to their previous state; the flashing text cursor appears in the position remembered by POS and VPOS. Also, scrolling and fast printing are restored. Although the principal use of joining the cursors is to enable labels to diagrams and graph axes to be positioned accurately, there are a couple of other possibilities that arise from the manner in which characters can be over-printed in a non-destructive fashion. Adding accents to foreign letters is an example. Underlining headings is another. I have already given a procedure that will underline some text on the screen, so won't give another one here. An interesting possibility is squeezing as many columns as possible out of the display. This is very important in the twenty column modes, where the width to height ratio of the normal characters makes them virtually illegible. The idea is to define a set of characters that are narrower than the ones provided, so that more can be fitted across the screen. By backspacing the graphics cursor after each character has been written, the gap between characters can be reduced. The best way to implement this is by intercepting the "oswrch" routine so that the characters to be printed in narrow mode can be "captured" automatically. Because such techniques are beyond the scope of this chapter, I will provide a BASIC PROC to print narrow-character strings. First, though, it is necessary to define the characters themselves. I will assume that only the upper case letters are to be used. These can be defined with the codes 224 to 249. Only half the width of the eight by eight matrix is used, giving a capacity for 40 characters per MODE 5 line. Since the "active" area of the character is only 3 by 7 dots, it is impossible to use the "vertical lines are double width" rule of the default character set. This should not prove too much of a problem in the 20 column modes, as the individual pixels are quite large. The VDU 23 statements for defining the narrow characters are given below.

```
VDU 23, 224, &E0, &A0, &A0, &E0, &A0, &A0, &A0, &00
VDU 23, 225, &C0, &A0, &A0, &C0, &A0, &A0, &C0, &00
VDU 23, 226, &E0, &80, &80, &80, &80, &80, &E0, &00
VDU 23, 227, &C0, &A0, &A0, &A0, &A0, &A0, &C0, &00
VDU 23, 228, &E0, &80, &80, &E0, &80, &80, &E0, &00
VDU 23, 229, &E0, &80, &80, &E0, &80, &80, &80, &00
VDU 23, 230, &E0, &80, &80, &A0, &A0, &A0, &E0, &00
VDU 23, 231, &A0, &A0, &A0, &E0, &A0, &A0, &A0, &00
VDU 23, 232, &E0, &40, &40, &40, &40, &40, &E0, &00
VDU 23, 233, &E0, &40, &40, &40, &40, &40, &C0, &00
VDU 23, 234, &A0, &A0, &C0, &C0, &C0, &A0, &A0, &00
VDU 23, 235, &80, &80, &80, &80, &80, &80, &E0, &00
VDU 23, 236, &A0, &E0, &E0, &A0, &A0, &A0, &A0, &00
VDU 23, 237, &20, &A0, &E0, &E0, &E0, &A0, &80, &00
VDU 23, 238, &E0, &A0, &A0, &A0, &A0, &A0, &E0, &00
VDU 23, 239, &E0, &A0, &A0, &E0, &80, &80, &80, &00
VDU 23, 240, &E0, &A0, &A0, &A0, &A0, &A0, &C0, &00
VDU 23, 241, &E0, &A0, &A0, &C0, &A0, &A0, &A0, &00
VDU 23, 242, &E0, &80, &80, &E0, &20, &20, &E0, &00
VDU 23, 243, &E0, &40, &40, &40, &40, &40, &40, &00
VDU 23, 244, &A0, &A0, &A0, &A0, &A0, &A0, &E0, &00
VDU 23, 245, &A0, &A0, &A0, &A0, &A0, &40, &40, &00
VDU 23, 246, &A0, &A0, &A0, &A0, &E0, &E0, &A0, &00
VDU 23, 247, &A0, &A0, &40, &40, &40, &A0, &A0, &00
VDU 23, 248, &A0, &A0, &A0, &A0, &40, &40, &40, &00
VDU 23, 249, &E0, &20, &20, &40, &80, &80, &E0, &00
```

The worst characters are the letters "N" and "Q". You could probably improve all the definitions by using a 4 × 7 matrix. This means the width of each character would be five dots, including the empty column to separate characters. This gives 32 columns in MODE 5 (or MODE 2). The procedure below prints out a string using these half-width characters.

```
1000 DEF PROCprint(text$)
1010    REM    Prints text$ in narrow characters
1020    LOCAL Len%, c$, i%
1030    Len%=LEN(text$)
1040    FOR i%=1 TO Len%
1050       c$=MID$(text$, i%, 1)
1060       IF c$<"A" OR c$>"Z" THEN PRINT c$;:GOTO 1090
1070          PRINT CHR$(ASC(c$)+159);
1080          PLOT 0, -32,0
1090    NEXT i%
1100 ENDPROC
```

The PLOT statement at line 1080 moves the cursor back half a character width. It should be changed to "PLOT 0, −16,0" for MODEs 4 or 1. I wouldn't exactly call this system a replacement for the existing character set, but it is certainly useful for cramming as much text as possible on the twenty columns screen. The procedure assumes that the cursors have already been joined by a VDU 5.

4.6   Graphs and Charts

The cliche says that a picture is worth a thousand words. It is therefore unsurprising that computer graphics are often used to show lists of figures in more easily understood pictorial forms. There are many ways of showing numerical data – as graphs, pie charts, histograms and even contour maps. The method used depends on the type of data being examined. The subject certainly warrants a book of its own, and indeed has one in the shape of [Harding].

As this is just one section of a single chapter, I can't hope to cover the subject in any depth. Instead, I present a few programs which, combined with the other methods and techniques discussed in this chapter, could act as blueprints for specific applications you may have. The first example is of a histogram. This is a familiar site to anyone who reads the adverts for graph plotters in Byte. The usual scenario is of a gleeful middle-manager showing his print-out to a impressed meeting of The Board. The caption reads something like "Isn't it about time you stepped up to a Jobniak Plotter?"

The histogram program is a slightly more "intelligent" version than the procedure given in Chapter 2. Firstly, the chart is scaled so that as much of the screen is used as possible. The area available depends not only on the number of values being plotted, but also on the size of the titles which label each "bar". Another enhancement is the provision of proper scale in the Y direction, rather than just a relative percentage. To keep flexible, the number of bars in the chart is only stored in one place: the variable n%. This is used to dimension the arrays tit$() and val() which store the titles and data values respectively. The value of n% is also used to determine the width of the bars.

The data acquisition procedure, PROCvalues, is a little artificial in the present program. It would be a poor program that took values from the user via DATA

248

statements. It is likely that in a real situation PROCvalues would take the value of n% and val() using INPUTs from the keyboard, or possibly from data that has already been prepared on a cassette or disc file. Another possibility is a "real-time" program that plots a histogram of the values on some external device (e.g. the analogue port) at specific time intervals. A purely graphical form would probably be superior in this case, though. The strings in tit$() could be used in prompts for the user, as in:

```
2100    FOR i%=1 TO n%
2110      PRINT TAB(0,i%);"Data for ";tit$(i%);" ";
2120      INPUT val(i%)
2130    NEXT i%
```

The bulk of the program is in PROCdraw. In fact, by changing this procedure, the characteristics of the program can be altered completely, as you will see in the next example. Much of PROCdraw is concerned with scaling the axes so that the histogram will look tidy for all possible values of n% and val() (within reason). The two devices that help in this task are being able to move the graphics origin to the corner of the graph itself, which simplifies many of the calculations, and the ability to print the scale labels are intermediate points, between the "official" display lines. Two subsidiary procedures are PROCbox and PROCy_scale. The former is responsible for drawing the vertical bars of the chart. It could be altered to, for example, draw them as outlines rather than solid blocks. The second procedure annotates the y-axis. This is a fairly tricky business, as if the value of "step" is chosen carelessly, the scale becomes cramped. The method employed here is to choose a basic step that is an order of magnitude less than the largest val(). For example, if maxval were 123.4, this is of the order of magnitude 100. The step would therefore be 10. If the initial value of step would give too many points on the y-axis, i.e. more points than the number of lines that can be printed in that space, step is doubled until it gives a more reasonable number of labels. For example, if maxval were 57.1, step would initially be 1. This gives 57 values on the y-axis, which would be a little cramped for the 20 or so lines available. Hence step is doubled; step=2 would still give 28 lines, so it is doubled again. This gives 14 readings of step 4, which is acceptable.

```
100 REM     Histogram Program
110 MODE 4
120 PROCinit
130 REPEAT
140     PROCvalues(n%)
150     PROCdraw(n%, fact%)
160     INPUT TAB(0,1),"Again (Y/N) ",yn$
170 UNTIL yn$="N" OR yn$="n"
180 MODE 4
190 END
200
```

```
 210
1000 DEF PROCinit
1010    REM     Set-up the display parameters etc.
1020    LOCAL i%
1030    REM     Number of items
1040    n%=12
1050    DIM val(n%), tit$(n%)
1060    REM     Read the titles
1070    FOR i%=1 TO n%
1080       READ tit$(i%)
1090    NEXT i%
1160    REM     Scale factor for this mode
1170    fact%=32: REM    or 64 or 16
1180 ENDPROC
1190
1500 DATA Jan, Feb, Mar, Apr, May, Jun
1510 DATA Jul, Aug, Sep, Oct, Nov, Dec
1520
1530
1540
2000 DEF PROCvalues(n%)
2010    REM     Reads n% value into val()
2020    REM     Amend for your application
2030    LOCAL i%
2040    RESTORE 2500
2050    FOR i%=1 TO n%
2060       READ val(i%)
2070    NEXT i%
2080 ENDPROC
2090
2500 DATA 12.5, 13.4, 15.9, 11, 9.5, 2.3
2510 DATA 4.5, 8.5, 12.1, 13.7, 14.1, 13
2520
2530
2540
3000 DEF PROCdraw(n%, fact%)
3010    REM     Draws a histogram of n% values from val()
3020    LOCAL long%, i%, maxval, height%, width%, scale
3030    REM     Find longest tit$() & maximum val()
3040    long%=LEN(tit$(1)): maxval=val(1)
3050    FOR i%=2 TO n%
3060       IF LEN(tit$(i%)) > long% TNEN long%=LEN(tit$(i))
3065       IF val(i%) > maxval THEN maxval=val(i%)
```

```
3070    NEXT i%
3090    REM     Work out size of chart
3100    height%=1024-32*(long%+5)
3110    width%=1280-fact%*10
3120    VDU 29, fact%*6; 32*(long%+1);
3125    VDU 5
3130    REM     Draw axes and titles
3140    MOVE 0, height%
3150    DRAW 0,0
3160    DRAW width%, 0
3165    bar_width%=width% DIV n%
3170    FOR i%=1 TO n%
3180       MOVE (i%-0.5)*bar_width%-fact% DIV 2,-8
3190       FOR j%=1 TO LEN(tit$(i%))
3200          PRINT MID$(tit$(i%), j%, 1);
3210          PLOT 0,-fact%, -32
3220       NEXT j%
3230    NEXT i%
3235    PROCy_scale(maxval, height%, fact%)
3240    REM     Now the data
3250    scale=height%/maxval
3260    FOR i%=1 TO n%
3270       PROCbox(bar_width%*(i%-1),0,  bar_width%-8,val(i%)*scale)
3280    NEXT i%
3290 ENDPROC
3300
3310
3320
4000 DEF PROCbox(x%,y%, width%,height%)
4010    REM     Draw a box with the above parameters
4020    MOVE x%,y%
4030    PLOT 0, width%,0
4040    PLOT 81, -width%, height%
4050    PLOT 81, width%,0
4070 ENDPROC
4080
4090
4100
5000 DEF PROCy_scale(maxval, height%, fact%)
5010    REM     Labels the Y axis
5020    LOCAL step, val
5030    step=10^(INT(LOG(maxval))-1)
```

```
5040     IF maxval/step <= height% DIV 32 THEN 5070
5050     REPEAT step=2*step
5060     UNTIL maxval/step <= height% DIV 32
5070     val=0
5090     REPEAT
5100       y%=val/maxval*height%
5110       MOVE 0,y%:  PLOT 1,  -fact%/2, 0
5120       text$=STR$(val)
5130       PLOT 0, -(LEN(text$) + .5)*fact%, 16
5140       PRINT text$
5150       val=val+step
5160     UNTIL val > maxval+step/5
5170 ENDPROC
```

As I mentioned above, the next example has a lot in common with the histogram program. In fact, the only difference is in PROCdraw. This means that it would be a simple matter to incorporate both the histogram and pie chart facility listed below into one program, giving the user the choice of how he wants to display the data. Fitting all the information onto the pie chart is a tricky operation in the forty columns modes, and almost impossible in MODEs 2 and 5. In the current program, the titles are displayed around the chart and the corresponding values printed inside the sectors. The positioning of the textual information is quite fiddly. Both the length of the text and its position around the circle have to be taken into account.

Once again, you will need to trim the program a little to make it run in a 16K machine. If you do have a 32K computer, MODE 1 is probably the best compromise between resolution and colour. Only line 110 needs be changed for this. If there are lots of data values (i.e. n% > 15), you will have to use MODE 0, as the text is much less obtrusive than in the forty columns modes. The procedure PROCdraw and its two subsidiaries, PROCcircle and PROCsector are given below. Of course, the program for the histogram (up to line 3000) must also be present to use the procedures.

```
3000 DEF PROCdraw(n%, fact%)
3010     REM    Draws a pie-chart of val()
3020     LOCAL i%, long%, th, th1, old_th, rad%, total, text$
3025     VDU 5, 29, 640;512;:REM   join cursors; centre origin
3030     REM    Find longest tit$() and total val()
3040     total=0
3050     long%=LEN(tit$(1))
3060     FOR i%=1 TO n%
3070       total=total+val(i%)
3080       IF LEN(tit$(i%)) > long% THEN long%=LEN(tit$(i%))
3090     NEXT i%
```

```
3100    rad%=512-long%*fact%
3115    PROCcircle(rad%)
3120    th=0
3125    REM    Draw the sectors
3130    FOR i%=1 TO n%
3140      old_th=th
3150      th=th + val(i%)*2*PI/total
3160      th1=old_th + val(i%)*PI/total
3165      GCOL 1,i%
3170      PROCsector(old_th, th, rad%)
3175      GCOL 0,15
3180      MOVE rad%*COS(th1)+fact%, rad%*SIN(th1)
3190      IF SIN(th1) > 0 THEN PLOT 0, 0,32
3200      IF COS(th1) < 0 THEN PLOT 0, -(LEN(tit$(i%))+2)*fact%,0
3210      PRINT tit$(i%)
3220      GCOL 4,0
3230      MOVE 0.8*rad%*COS(th1), 0.8*rad%*SIN(th1)
3240      text$=STR$(val(i%)): PLOT 0,-fact%*LEN(text$)/2,0
3245      PRINT text$
3250    NEXT i%
3260    MOVE 0,0
3270    PLOT 7, rad%,0
3280 ENDPROC
3290
3300
3310
4000 DEF PROCcircle(rad%)
4010    REM    Draws a circle of radius rad% about the origin
4020    LOCAL th
4030    MOVE rad%, 0
4040    FOR th=PI/18 TO 2.1*PI STEP PI/18
4050      DRAW rad%*COS(th), rad%*SIN(th)
4060    NEXT th
4070 ENDPROC
4080
4090
4100
5000 DEF PROCsector(th1, th2, rad%)
5010    REM    Draw a sector from th1 to th2
5020    LOCAL th, dth
5030    MOVE 0,0
5040    MOVE rad%*COS(th1), rad%*SIN(th1)
```

```
5050    dth=20/rad%
5060    FOR th=th1+dth TO th2 STEP dth
5070        PLOT 85, rad%*COS(th), rad%*SIN(th)
5080        MOVE 0,0
5090    NEXT th
5100    PLOT 85, rad%*COS(th2), rad%*SIN(th2)
5110 ENDPROC
```

The next program is one which performs linear regression. This means that a number of (x,y) pairs are given to the computer. It then works out the "best" straight line through the points. Usually, this is done by trial and error, by plotting the points on a sheet of graph paper and moving a ruler around to get the best looking line through them. However, there is an exact way to find this line. Straight lines have the equation:

$y=mx+c$

Where m, the slope of the line, and c, the y-intercept are both constants. The method of finding these two quantities is called linear regression. The expressions for m and c are shown in Figure 4.10.

Don't panic if these are meaningless to you, you can still use the program. That is, if you've got 32K of RAM, as the program is about 1.5K too big for a Model A. This is due to the number of instructions necessary to work out the formulae above. For those still with me, this is how to use the program. First, the computer asks for the number of points to be plotted. This could be anything from 2 (you can't describe a line with just one point) to an upper limit that is a function of your patience. Suppose you have been trying to find a simple formula for prime numbers. The (x,y) pairs would be n and the nth prime, where n is 1, 2, 3 ... Suppose you want to see if there is a straight line relationship between n and the nth prime, for n=1 to 10 (Hint: there isn't). In response to:

How many points?

$$
\boxed{
\begin{array}{l}
\text{EQUATION OF A LINE: } Y = mX + c \\[4pt]
\text{WHERE:} \\[8pt]
m = \dfrac{\sum\limits_{i=1}^{n}(x_i - \bar{x})(y_i - \bar{y})}{\sum\limits_{i=1}^{n}(x_i - \bar{x})^2} \\[20pt]
c = \bar{y} - m\bar{x} \\[8pt]
\bar{x} = \dfrac{1}{n}\sum\limits_{i=1}^{n} x_i, \quad \bar{y} = \dfrac{1}{n}\sum\limits_{i=1}^{n} y_i
\end{array}
}
$$

Figure 4.10   Linear Regression Equations

type "10". The program will then ask for the ten (x,y) pairs, verifying each pair. In the current example, these pairs would be (1,2), (2,3), (3,5), (4,7) . . . (10,29). The computer then works out the values of m and c, after which it asks if you want to give it the range for the x- and y-axes. There is no real need in this case, as the program makes a fairly sensible guess. Type "N". The graph is then drawn, crosses marking the points you typed in, and a straight line shows the regression line through them. The equation of the line is printed at the bottom. As for the program itself, there isn't really a great deal to explain. The procedure to find m and c will be understood by those who understand the notation above. It is, to coin a cliche, beyond the scope of this book to explain such things. After all, very few statistics books cover BBC BASIC programming. The procedures to draw the axes and scales are enhanced versions of those in the histogram program. The x-axis is much harder to label neatly than the y-axis, as there is less room to in which to fit the numbers. The current program will only work well for numbers of at most three digits along the x-axis. The minus signs are omitted to give more room for the digits; I assume you know that values to the left of the y-axis, and below the x-axis, are negative. Since the program won't fit in a 16K machine in a graphics mode, MODE 0 is used by default. This gives the best results, even though the crosses aren't particularly clear.

```
100 REM     Linear Regression Program
110 MODE 0
120 fact%=16
140 PROCdata
150 PROCplot
155 VDU 4
160 INPUT TAB(10,0),"Again ",yn$
170 IF yn$="Y" OR yn$="y" THEN RUN
180 MODE 4
190 END
200
1000 DEF PROCdata
1010    REM    Get the data points from the user
1020    LOCAL i%
1030    INPUT TAB(0,5),"How many points ",n%
1040    DIM x(n%), y(n%)
1050    FOR i%=1 TO n%
1060      REPEAT
1070        PRINT TAB(0,7);"x, y for point ";i%;SPC(15);STRING$(14,CHR$(8));
1080        INPUT x,y
1090        PRINT TAB(0,9);"Confirm x=";x;" and y=";y;"
                (Y/N)";SPC(9);STRING$(,CHR$(8));
1100        INPUT yn$
1110      UNTIL yn$="Y" OR yn$="y"
```

```
1120      x(i%)=x:   y(i%)=y
1130    NEXT i%
1140 ENDPROC
1150
1160
1170
2000 DEF PROCplot
2020    REM     Plots the points and regression line for x() and y()
2030    LOCAL yn$,i%, x%, y%, y
2040    REM     Do the numerical bits
2050    PROCstats
2060    INPUT TAB(0,11),"Do you want to give the limits of the graph (Y/N) ",y$
2070    IF yn$="N" OR yn$="n" THEN 2100
2080      INPUT TAB(0,13),"x low, x high ",xlo, xhi
2090      INPUT TAB(0,15),"y low, y high ",ylo, yhi
2100    PROCaxes(xlo,xhi, ylo,yhi)
2110    REM     Plot the points
2120    FOR i%=1 TO n%
2130      x%=FNx(x(i%))
2140      y%=FNy(y(i%))
2150      PROCcross(x%,y%)
2160    NEXT i%
2170    REM    Draw the regression line
2180    y=m*xlo+c
2190    MOVE FNx(xlo), FNy(y)
2200    y=m*xhi+c
2210    DRAW FNx(xhi), FNy(y)
2220 ENDPROC
2230
2240
2250
2500 DEF PROCcross(x%,y%)
2510    MOVE x%-8,y%
2520    PLOT 2,16,0
2530    PLOT 0,-8,-8
2540    PLOT 2,0,16
2550 ENDPROC
2560
2570
2580
3000 DEF PROCstats
3010    REM     Finds the slope and intercept of the
```

```
3020    REM    regression line. Also sets the default
3030    REM    xlo, xhi, yhi and ylo
3040    LOCAL i%, xi, yi, xsum, ysum , xmean, ymean, sum1, sum2
3050    REM    Find the means and limits
3060    xlo=x(1): xhi=x(1)
3070    ylo=y(1): yhi=y(1)
3080    xsum=x(1)
3090    ysum=y(1)
3100    FOR i%=2 TO n%
3110       xi=x(i%): yi=y(i%)
3120       ysum=ysum+yi
3130       xsum=xsum+xi
3140       IF xi < xlo THEN xlo=xi ELSE IF xi > xhi THEN xhi=xi
3150       IF yi < ylo THEN ylo=yi ELSE IF yi > yhi THEN yhi=yi
3160    NEXT i%
3170    REM    Make sure that the axes appear
3180    IF SGN(xlo)<>SGN(xhi) THEN 3200
3190       IF xhi<0 THEN xhi=0 ELSE xlo=0
3200    IF SGN(ylo)<>SGN(yhi) THEN 3220
3210       IF yhi<0 THEN yhi=0 ELSE ylo=0
3220    xmean=xsum/n%
3230    ymean=ysum/n%
3240    REM    Find the slope, m
3250    sum1=0: sum2=0
3260    FOR i%=1 TO n%
3270       sum1=sum1+(x(i%)-xmean)*(y(i%)-ymean)
3280       sum2=sum2+(x(i%)-xmean)*(x(i%)-xmean)
3290    NEXT i%
3300    m=sum1/sum2
3310    c=ymean-m*xmean
3320 ENDPROC
3330
3340
3350
4000 DEF PROCaxes(xlo,xhi, ylo,yhi)
4010    REM    Scale the graph and draw the axes
4020    LOCAL width%, height%, xrange, yrange, x%, y%, a%
4025    CLS: VDU 5
4030    width%=1280-5*fact%
4040    height%=1024-192
4050    xrange=xhi-xlo
4060    yrange=yhi-ylo
```

```
4070    xscale=width%/xrange
4080    yscale=height%/yrange
4090    REM   Set the origin
4100    VDU 29, -xlo*xscale+3*fact%; -ylo*yscale+128;
4110    y%=FNy(0)
4120    MOVE FNx(xlo),y%
4130    DRAW FNx(xhi),y%
4140    x%=FNx(0)
4150    MOVE x%,FNy(ylo)
4160    DRAW x%,FNy(yhi)
4170    PROCscales
4180    @%=&00000505
4190    PRINT TAB(10,31)"Graph of Y=";m;"X+";c;
4200 ENDPROC
4210
5000 DEF FNx(x)=xscale*x
5010 DEF FNy(y)=yscale*y
5020
5030
5040
6000 DEF PROCscales
6010    REM   Prints the scales on the axes
6020    LOCAL x,y,xstep,ystep,text$, odd%
6030    xstep=FNstep(xrange, width%/fact%/2.5)
6040    x=xstep*INT(xlo/xstep+.5)
6050    REPEAT
6055       IF ABS(x)<1E-2 THEN 6140
6060       MOVE FNx(x), 0
6070       PLOT 1,0,-16
6080       text$=STR$(ABS(x))
6090       PLOT 0,-fact%*LEN(text$)/2,-16
6100       PRINT text$
6140       x=x+xstep
6150    UNTIL x > xhi+xstep*.1
6160    ystep=FNstep(yrange, height%/64)
6170    y=ystep*INT(ylo/ystep+.5)
6180    REPEAT
6190       IF ABS(y)<1E-2 THEN 6250
6200       MOVE 0,FNy(y)
6210       PLOT 1,fact%/2,0
6220       text$=STR$(ABS(y))
6230       PLOT 0,fact%/2,16
```

```
6240        PRINT text$
6250        y=y+ystep
6260     UNTIL y > yhi+ystep*.1
6270 ENDPROC
6280
6290
6300
7000 DEF FNstep(range, max%)
7010     REM     Finds best step for range (see Histogram)
7020     LOCAL step
7030     step=10^INT(LOG(range)-1)
7040     IF range/step <= max% THEN =step
7050     REPEAT step=step*2
7060     UNTIL range/step <= max%
7070 =step
```

A simpler version of the linear regression program, but one with a more general use, is a simple cartesian graph plotter. "Cartesian" describes the type of co-ordinates used to expression functions. It is simply the usual (x,y) pairs with which most people are familiar. For example, the straight line has an equation of the form "y=mx+c". The equations gives the value up the y-axis for any number along the x-axis. Many equations that occur naturally have similar forms. For example, the distance travelled by a body moving with constant acceleration is given by:

```
s=ut+a(t^2)/2
```

where s is the distance, u is the initial velocity, t is the time and a the acceleration. Suppose you wanted to know how far a brick would travel in 5 seconds after you dropped it from the top of the Empire State Building. In this case, u is zero (you drop the brick rather than throw it down), t is 5s, a is 9.8m/s/s (the acceleration due to gravity). Doing the sum gives the answer 122.5 metres. This doesn't tell you much about how s varies with time, just what it is for this particular case. The program given lets you see this relationship graphically. First, it is necessary to put the equation into a suitable form. The equation is a function of t, as this is what varies, the other numbers being constants. The graph plotter program requires the equation given it to be in X, so it is re-written as "u*X+a*(X^2)/2". Since we know u and a, it can be further altered to "9.8*(X^2)/2". This is a form suitable for the computer, and can be given in response to the prompt:

```
"What function in X? Y="
```

though a more efficient way of expressing it is "4.9*X*X". The program also requires the user to type in a range for X (or t). The range 0 to 10 (seconds) seems as good as any, so this is typed in response to:

```
"What range for X (high, Low)"
```

After a short pause, the graph appears. To find the value of s (or Y as far as the program is concerned) corresponding to a particular t (or X), trace a vertical line from the place corresponding to t along the horizontal axis. Where this meets the curve, change direction by 90 degrees and trace a line horizontally to the y-axis. The value of s can then be read off. It is unlikely that the graph plotter will be used this way, as the precision is rather low. The main use is to see the shape of curves, rather than finding exact values.

The program itself has much in common with the last one. In fact it is somewhat shorter, as there is no need for PROCstats. Even so, I still had to cut out the REMs and most of the spaces to fit it into a 16K machine. The main new procedure is PROCy_range. This steps through all the possible values that the graph can take and finds the minimum and maximum Y. This y-range is used to scale the vertical axis, within the limitation that the x-axis will always appear. For example, if Y took values between 1 and 10, the lower limit would be reduced to 0 so that the x-axis fits on. A similar process occurs when finding the scaling factor (x-scale) for the x-axis. This is done in PROCaxes. Notice that only the local versions of xlo, xhi, ylo and yhi are changed when finding x-range, etc., so although the area covered by the graph may be larger than the x-range given, only this range is actually plotted. This leads to silly looking graphs when all of the important area is well away from the origin. For example, try "Y=X" for X=100 to 110.

The expression typed by the user is tested by trying a dummy assignment. This provides a check on the syntax of the expression, but there is no detection of errors caused by illegal values. For example, if "Y=1/X" and the x-range is 0 to 10, a "Division by zero" error will happen at line 3100 when the y-range is being found. There was no room left to include an ON ERROR for this case, so the program halts. This could be added to versions used on the larger memory machines.

The program is listed in its "suitable for a Model A" form below:

```
100 REM Graphs
110 MODE 4
120 fact%=32:points%=320
130 REPEAT
135   CLS
140   PROCparams
150   PROCplot
160   VDU 4:INPUT TAB(10,0), "Again ",yn$
170 UNTIL yn$="n" OR yn$="N"
180 MODE 4
190 END
1000 DEF PROCparams
1030   INPUT TAB(0,5),"What function in X? Y="f$
1040   ON ERROR PRINT"Sorry, that's wrong":in%=INKEY(300):RUN
```

```
1050   y=FNf(RND(1))
1060   ON ERROR OFF
1070   REPEAT INPUT TAB(0,7), "What range for X (low, hi) ",xlo, xhi
1080   UNTIL xlo < xhi
1130 ENDPROC
1500 DEF FNf(X)=EVAL(f$)
2000 DEF PROCplot
2040   PROCy_range(xlo, xhi)
2100   PROCaxes(xlo,xhi, ylo,yhi)
2110   REM   Plot the points
2130   MOVE FNx(xlo), FNy(FNf(xlo))
2140   FOR x=xlo+xinc TO xhi STEP xinc
2150     DRAW FNx(x), FNy(FNf(x))
2160   NEXT x
2220 ENDPROC
3000 DEF PROCy_range(xlo, xhi)
3070   xinc=(xhi-xlo)/points%
3080   ylo=FNf(xlo): yhi=ylo
3090   FOR x=xlo+xinc TO xhi STEP xinc
3100     y=FNf(x)
3110     IF y<ylo THEN ylo=y
3120     IF y>yhi THEN yhi=y
3130   NEXT x
3150 ENDPROC
4000 DEF PROCaxes(xlo,xhi, ylo,yhi)
4025   CLS: VDU 5
4030   width%=1280-fact%*5
4035   height%=832
4040   IF SGN(xlo)<>SGN(xhi) THEN 4050
4045     IF xhi<0 THEN xhi=0 ELSE xlo=0
4050   IF SGN(ylo)<>SGN(yhi) THEN 4060
4055     IF yhi<0 THEN yhi=0 ELSE ylo=0
4060   xrange=xhi-xlo
4065   yrange=yhi-ylo
4070   xscale=width%/xrange
4080   yscale=height%/yrange
4100   VDU 29, -xlo*xscale+3*fact%; -ylo*yscale+128;
4120   MOVE FNx(xlo),FNy(0)
4130   DRAW FNx(xhi),FNy(0)
4150   MOVE FNx(0),FNy(ylo)
4160   DRAW FNx(0),FNy(yhi)
4170   a%=&01000405
```

```
4180  PROCscales
4190  PRINT TAB(10,31)"Graph of Y=";f$
4200 ENDPROC
5000 DEF FNx(x)=xscale*x
5010 DEF FNy(y)=yscale*y
6000 DEF PROCscales
6030  xstep=FNstep(xrange, width%/fact%/2.5)
6040  x=xstep*INT(xlo/xstep+.9)
6050  REPEAT
6055   IF ABS(x)<1E-2 THEN 6140
6060   MOVE FNx(x), 0
6070   PLOT 1,0,-16
6080   text$=STR$(ABS(x))
6090   PLOT 0,-fact%*LEN(text$)/2,-16
6100   PRINT text$
6140   x=x+xstep
6150  UNTIL x > xhi+xstep*.1
6160  ystep=FNstep(yrange, height%/64)
6170  y=ystep*INT(ylo/ystep+.9)
6180  REPEAT
6190   IF ABS(y)<1E-2 THEN 6250
6200   MOVE 0,FNy(y)
6210   PLOT 1,fact%/2,0
6220   text$=STR$(ABS(y))
6230   PLOT 0,fact%/2,16
6240   PRINT text$
6250   y=y+ystep
6260  UNTIL y > yhi+ystep*.1
6270 ENDPROC
7000 DEF FNstep(range, max%)
7030  step=10^INT(LOG(range)-1)
7040  IF range/step <= max% THEN =step
7050  REPEAT step=step*2
7060  UNTIL range/step <= max%
7070  =step
```

4.7 Turtle Graphics

Some computer languages (notably UCSD Pascal and Logo) implement plotting in a slightly different way to that already discussed. They have a facility known as turtle graphics. The idea is that there is an imaginary turtle on the screen (corresponding to our graphics cursor). This turtle can be made to move, leaving a trail as it goes. Since real turtles don't actually leave any such trail, a better name would be "slug graphics", but since the former has become accepted, I will use it here. Special procedures can be used to tell the turtle to move, turn and change the colour of the trail it deposits on the screen. There are also functions to give the current position and direction in which it is heading. Another analogy to this type of graphics is the graph plotter. This mechanical device consists of a flat surface on which paper can be placed, and some pens which are held and moved around by a plotting arm. The plotter can be told to draw straight line, change pens, lift the pen off the paper, etc. The set of procedures presented in this section emulate the turtle graphics facilities of UCSD Pascal as implemented on the Apple][, with some changes that reflect the more sophisticated hardware of the BBC Machine.

First I will list the procedures' names along with their uses, after which the procedures themselves are listed.

PROCturtle. This sets up the turtle graphics by setting the colour relationships and windows to their default values. The turtle is also placed in the centre of the screen (640,512) facing east (zero degrees). The pen colour (i.e. the colour of the turtle's trail) is set to "none".

PROCviewport(left,right,bottom,top). This sets the graphics window using the parameters given. It is simply a VDU 24 call with the order of the parameters re-arranged, and is only included for completeness.

PROCpencolor(col). This is used to determine that colour of subsequent plotting. The parameter is the same as the second argument to GCOL. There are two additional possibilities: "none" cause no trail to be left; movement of the turtle is achieved using MOVEs rather than DRAWs. The argument "reverse" is used to obtain the inverse colour effect obtained by "PROCpenmode(4)".

PROCpenmode(mode). This is a special BBC turtle graphics command. It is used to set the plotting mode of subsequent drawing. The parameter has a meaning which is identical to the first argument of GCOL.

PROCfillscreen(col). This procedure clears the graphics window, as CLG, but does not affect the position or direction of the turtle.

PROCturnto(dir). This sets the direction of the turtle. "dir" is in degrees. A heading of 0 makes the turtle face due east, or right. Positive values of dir specify the angle in an anti-clockwise direction from east. For example, PROCturnto(90) will make the turtle point due north, or up the screen. Negative values imply angles in a clockwise direction; a call PROCturnto(−90) will point the turtle due south. In all cases the parameter is taken as MOD 360, so PROCturnto(370) is the same as PROCturnto(10).

PROCturn(dir). This is the relative version of PROCturnto. Instead of specifying the new direction, dir gives the number of degrees through which the turtle must turn. For example, if the current heading is 120, PROCturn(50) will make the new heading 170 degrees. Negative arguments make the turtle turn in a clockwise direction. Neither this nor the previous procedure has any effect on the screen, as the turtle is invisible.

PROCmoveto(x,y). This is the turtle graphics DRAW. The position of the turtle is

changed to (x,y). In moving, the turtle leaves his trail in the current colour and
mode. If the colour is "none", there is no visible effect, but the turtle's co-
ordinates are updated. This procedure does not alter the turtle's heading.

PROCmove(dist). This causes the turtle to move forward by dist screen units in
the current heading. The effects obtained are the same described above.

FNturtlex and FNturtley. These two functions return the current co-ordinates of
the turtle. They take no parameters.

FNturtleang. This function gives the turtle's current heading, in the range zero
(east) to 359.

FNscreenbit(x,y). This is a simplified POINT which returns TRUE if the pixel at
(x,y) is set, FALSE if is reset or off the screen.

The listings of all the turtle graphics procedures are given below. It is only
necessary to include those procedures and functions which are required in the
program, though PROCinitturtle should be present and called before any of the
others are used.

```
1000 DEF PROCinitturtle
1010     REM     Sets up turtle graphics system
1020     LOCAL
1030     VDU 20,26
1040     turt_ang%=0
1050     turt_x%=640
1060     turt_y%=512
1065     MOVE turt_x%, turt_y%
1070     none=-1
1080     reverse=-2
1090     mode%=0
1100     PROCpencolour(none)
1110 ENDPROC
1120
1130
2000 DEF PROCviewport(left%, right%, bottom%, top%)
2010     REM     Sets up the graphics window
2020     VDU 29,left%;bottom%;right%;top%;
2030 ENDPROC
2040
2050
3000 DEF PROCpencolour(c%)
3010     REM     Sets-up the plotting colour
3020     IF c% >= 0 THEN col%=c%
3030     IF c% = none THEN col%=none
3040     IF c% = reverse THEN mode%=4:col%=0
3050     GCOL mode%, col%
```

```
3060 ENDPROC
3070
3080
3500 DEF PROCpenmode(m%)
3510    REM    Sets-up the plotting mode
3520    mode%=m%
3530    GCOL mode%,col%
3540 ENDPROC
3550
3560
4000 DEF PROCfillscreen(c%)
4010    REM   Clear the graphics window with c%
4020    IF c% >= 0 THEN GCOL 0,128+c% ELSE IF c%=reverse THEN GCOL 4,128 ELSE
         IFc%=none THEN GCOL 1,128
4030    CLG
4040    MOVE turt_x%,turt_y%
4050 ENDPROC
4060
5000 DEF PROCturnto(ang%)
5010    REM    Change the turtle's heading
5020    turt_ang%=ang% MOD 360
5030 ENDPROC
5040
5050
6000 DEF PROCturn(ang%)
6010    REM    Change the turtle's heading
6020    turt_ang%=(turt_ang% + ang%) MOD 360
6030 ENDPROC
6040
6050
7000 DEF PROCmove(dist%)
7010    REM   Move the turtle by dist%
7020    LOCAL dx%, dy%
7030    dx%=dist%*COS(RAD(turt_ang%))
7040    dy%=dist%*SIN(RAD(turt_ang%))
7050    IF col%=none THEN PLOT 0,dx%,dy% ELSE PLOT 1,dx%, dy%
7060    turt_x%=turt_x%+dx%
7070    turt_y%=turt_y%+dy%
7080 ENDPROC
7090
7100
8000 DEF PROCmoveto(x%,y%)
```

```
8010    REM     Perform an absolute move
8020    IF col%=none THEN MOVE x%,y% ELSE DRAW x%,y%
8030    turt_x%=x%
8040    turt_y%=y%
8050 ENDPROC
8060
8070
9000 DEF FNturtlex=turt_x%
9010 DEF FNturtley=turt_y%
9020 DEF FNturtleang=turt_ang%
9030 DEF FNscreenbit(x%,y%)=POINT(x%,y) > 0
```

Most of the procedures are easy to understand. The only tricky one is PROC-move. This uses the polar to cartesian co-ordinate conversion equations that were given in Chapter two. The procedure must move the turtle forward by dist% screen units in the direction turt_ang%. To do this, we must convert this to a movement of so many units across and so many up. In mathematical terms, the task is to convert from the polar co-ordinates (r, theta) to the cartesian pair (x,y). The trigonometry of this is shown in Figure 4.11.

Once the x and y displacements have been found, they can be used by the relative plotting commands PLOT 0 or PLOT 1 to move the turtle or draw the line. The displacements are then added to turt_x% and turt_y% to update the position of the turtle.

It is natural to ask what can be done with these turtle graphics that can't be done normally. The answer is "not a lot", but there are several occasions when solutions can be expressed more naturally than with pure "cartesian" graphics. They can also be used to produce nice recursive patterns as well. Below is a procedure to draw an equilateral triangle:

```
10000 DEF PROCequi(x%, y%, len%)
```

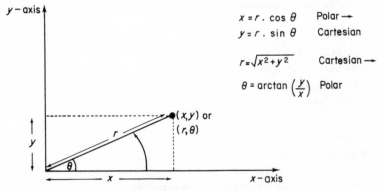

Figure 4.11   Polar to Cartesian Geometery

```
10010    PROCmoveto(x%,y%)
10020    PROCturnto(120)
10030    PROCmove(len%)
10040    PROCturn(60)
10050    PROCmove(len%)
10060    PROCturn(60)
10070    PROCmove(len%)
10080 ENDPROC
```

The program below produces pretty spiral patterns:

```
100 MODE 4
110 PROCinitturtle
120 PROCpencolour(1)
130 FOR L%=4 TO 512 STEP 4
140     PROCmove(L%)
150     PROCturn(91)
160 NEXT L%
170 END
```

The pattern of the spiral can be altered by changing the amount through which the turtle turns in line 150. Values near 180 are interesting, especially if line 120 is changed to "PROCpencolour(reverse)". A value of 90 in line 150 gives a "regular" square spiral.

The program shown below draws shapes known as Hilbert curves. The curves have a complexity which is determined by the order given as a parameter to PROChil. The curves for the first three orders are shown in Figure 4.12, for a constant len%. The derivation of the algorithm is given in [Bowles].

To fit the program into a 16K machine you will need to delete all the unused turtle routines, as well as most of the unnecessary spaces. If you experiment with different values for the ord% parameter, you will find that len% has to be reduced dramatically as ord% increases.

```
10 MODE 4
20 PROCinitturtle
30 PROCmoveto(0,0)
40 PROCpencolour(1)
50 len%=20
60 PROChil(5)
70 END
10000 DEF PROChil(ord%)
10010    LOCAL dir%, ord1%
10020    IF ord%=0 THEN PROCturn(180):ENDPROC
10030    IF ord%>0 THEN dir%=90:ord1%=ord%-1
```

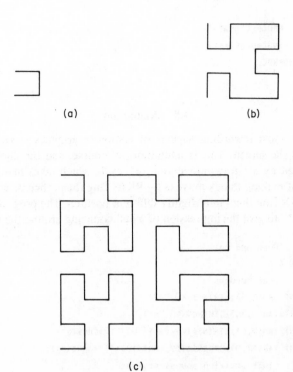

(a)

(b)

(c)

Figure 4.12   Hilbert Curves of Order 1, 2 and 3 (to scale)

```
10040      IF ord%<0 THEN dir%=-90:ord1%=ord%+1
10050      PROChi11
10060      PROChi12
10070      PROChi11
10080 ENDPROC
10090
10100
11000 DEF PROChi11
11010      PROCturn(dir%)
11020      PROChil(-ord1%)
11030      PROCturn(dir%)
11040 ENDPROC
11050
12000 DEF PROChi12
12010      PROCmove(len%)
12020      PROChil(ord1%)
12030      PROCturn(-dir%)
12040      PROCmove(len%)
12050      PROCturn(-dir%)
```

```
12060    PROChil(ord1%)
12070    PROCmove(len%)
12080 ENDPROC
```

4.8   Animation

One of the most rewarding aspects of computer graphics is seeing drawings move around the screen. This is animation, of course, and the illusion of movement is created by a "draw–move–redraw" cycle which takes many forms. The easiest way of making things move is by PRINTing them, then deleting them and finally re-PRINTing them in a slightly different position. The program below does this with an "*" to give the impression of a ball bouncing around the screen.

```
100 REM    Bouncing Ball
110 MODE 4
120 REM    Draw borders
130 PRINT TAB(0,0);STRING$(40,"=")
140 PRINT TAB(0,30);STRING$(40,"=");
150 PRINT TAB(0,0);STRING$(29,CHR$(10)+"|"+CHR$(8))
160 PRINT TAB(39,0);STRING$(29,CHR$(10)+"|"+CHR$(8));
170 REM    Init position and directions
180 ball_x%=RND(30)+5
190 ball_y%=RND(20)+5
200 REPEAT dx%=RND(3)-2 UNTIL dx%<>0
210 REPEAT dy%=RND(3)-2 UNTIL dy%<>0
212 REM    Remove the cursor
214 VDU 23,0,10,32;0;0;0
220 REM    Main loop
230 REPEAT
240     PRINT TAB(ball_x%, ball_y%);"*";
250     old_x%=ball_x%
260     old_y%=ball_y%
270     IF ball_x%<2 OR ball_x%>37 THEN dx%=-dx%:SOUND 1,-15,40,2
280     IF ball_y%<2 OR ball_y%>28 THEN dy%=-dy%:SOUND 1,-15,80,2
290     ball_x%=ball_x%+dx%
300     ball_y%=ball_y%+dy%
310     t%=TIME+4: REPEAT UNTIL TIME=t%
320     PRINT TAB(old_x%, old_y%);" ";
330 UNTIL FALSE
```

The interesting part is in the REPEAT loop at lines 230 to 330. The VDU statement at line 214 is used to turn the flashing cursor off, without having to enter the slow-printing VDU 5 mode. The statement is explained on page 385 of the User Guide.

Once the asterisk has been printed, the current ball position is stored in old_x% and old_y% for later use. The IF statements in lines 270 and 280 check that adding dx% and dy% will not make the ball go off the screen. If it will, dx% and/or dy% are negated to reverse the direction. After a small pause, the asterisk is erased and the cycle repeats until ESCAPE is pressed.

The order in which the statements appear is quite important. When objects are being repeatedly drawn and erased, it is important that they are present on the screen for longer periods than they are absent. With the arrangement above, the asterisk is PRINTed, and stays on the screen while ball_x%, etc. are updated, and for the duration of the delaying REPEAT loop. It is then instantaneously deleted with the space and redrawn very quickly (in the time in takes to jump back to the start of the REPEAT). This results in the asterisk being "on" for much longer than it is "off" so there is no flashing. It would be possible to get rid of old_x% and old_y% by PRINTing the "*" at TAB(ball_x%, ball_y%), then deleting it straight away and then updating the co-ordinates. This is a highly unsatisfactory approach, as the asterisk will hardly ever be on the screen. Introducing a delay between PRINTing it and erasing it wouldn't help much, as there would still be a comparatively long period when it was absent from the screen, while ball_x% etc. were being updated. (In this simple example old_x% and old_y% are not strictly necessary. The fact that the shape being drawn is only one character means that line 320 could be replaced by "PRINT CHR$(127);" to delete it. However, this is not the general case, and the equivalent to old_x% and old_y% will usually be required.)

Although PRINTing is very fast, it has the disadvantage that objects can only be placed at discrete character positions. Using VDU 5, they can be positioned anywhere on the screen, with a penalty of relatively slow speed at which characters can be drawn. The next program brings together several of the subjects already discussed – user-defined characters, exclusive-OR plotting and the concept of pixel planes. The object of the program is very simple. A car is shown to move across the screen behind a foreground of telephone boxes. Because MODE 5 is used, only two levels of "priority" are available, in addition to the background. Also, because it is necessary to draw the car in graphics plotting mode 3 (exclusive-OR), VDU 5 is used. This also enables the car to be moved in smaller increments than normal PRINTing would allow. The characters 224 to 227 are defined as the back and front of the car and the bottom and top of the 'phone box respectively. The two strings car$ and tel$ are assigned to simplify the PRINT statements.

The way the pallette (i.e. the logical–actual colour relationships) is set is as follows. The car, which is to be white, is drawn in the midground, and so is controlled by the first bit of the two-bit MODE 5 pixel. Thus colour 1 is set to 7. The telephone boxes, which are naturally red, occupy the foreground pixel plane, so colours 2 and 3 are set to 1. This is summarised below:

Logical Colour	Represents	So is set to
0	The background	Black (0)
1	The car	White (7)
2	The 'phone boxes	Red (1)
3	Both (1) & (2)	Red (1)

The program is listed below:

```
100 REM     Car Animation
110 MODE 5
120 REM Define the shapes
130 VDU 23,224,&3F,&52,&92,&FF,&FF,&CF,&30,&30
140 VDU 23,225,&80,&40,&20,&FE,&FF,&F3,&0C,&0C
150 VDU 23,226,&7C,&44,&44,&7C,&44,&44,&7C,&7C
160 VDU 23,227,&FE,&FE,&7C,&44,&44,&7C,&44,&44
170 tel$=CHR$(226)+CHR$(8)+CHR$(11)+CHR$(227)
180 car$=CHR$(224)+CHR$(225)
190 REM    Set up the pallette
200 VDU 19,1,7;0;: REM White car
210 VDU 19,2,1;0;: REM Red Phone box
220 VDU 19,3,1;0;
230 REM    The road & phone boxes
240 GCOL 0,2
250 MOVE 0,512: DRAW 1272,512
260 VDU 5
270 FOR x%=40 TO 1040 STEP 200
280    MOVE x%,544
290      PRINT tel$
300 NEXT x%
310 REM    Now the animation
320 car_x%=0: car_y%=544
330 GCOL 3,1
340 REPEAT
350    MOVE car_x%, car_y%
360    PRINT car$;
370    old_x%=car_x%
380    car_x%=(car_x%+16) MOD 1128
390    t%=TIME+6:REPEAT UNTIL TIME=t%
400    MOVE old_x%,car_y%
410    PRINT car$;
420 UNTIL FALSE
```

The general scheme of things is very similar to the last example. Since car_y% is a constant, there is no need to remember its value; only old_x% is needed. The

MOD in line 380 causes the car to reappear on the left hand of the screen before it disappears to the right. The way in which the car is drawn and deleted from its pixel plane is slightly different to the one discussed earlier. Using that method, there would be a GCOL 1,1 before line 360, to set the pixels in the car's plane, and a GCOL 2,2 just before line 410 to reset again. This method works perfectly well, but it introduces two unnecessary GCOL statements into the REPEAT loop. Instead, all PRINTing is performed under the influence of the single GCOL3,1 which is executed before the loop is entered. This is of course an "exclusive–OR with 01" mode. Consider the first time that car is PRINTed in the loop. Wherever the current colour is 0 (I'm talking about logical colours here), the new colour will be set to 1 (00 EOR 01 = 01), so the car will show up on the background. Wherever the colour is 2, i.e. the 'phone box, the new colour will be 3 (10 EOR 01 = 11), which means that part will stay red. When the second, erasing PRINT is executed, the white bits will turn back to black (01 EOR 01 = 00) and the red bits will stay red (11 EOR 01 = 10).

Despite the fact that the car is "erased" for a very short time compared to the period for which it is visible, there is still a fair amount of flashing. My untried theory of using an *FX19 to wait for the screen to be "blank" before the car is erased remains untried, as I still haven't got MOS 1.0. This means there is little one can do about the problem for now. Even using machine code would not help, as the "slow" part is the PRINTing, not the program itself.

So far I have only discussed animation using PRINT to draw solid shapes. Much the same principles apply to animating lines drawn with PLOT. A couple of examples have already be given (i.e. the rotating square and moving square rings). Because the time taken to draw lines can be much longer than that needed to PRINT characters, the flashing problem tends to be even worse. The root of the problem is that the viewer can see the shape while it is being drawn and erased. If you think about cartoons, the difference is very apparent; in the second case, the individual drawings are shown instantaneously: there is no pause while the artist draws the picture of Tom smashing Jerry over the head with a brick (or vice versa). There is a way to achieve this "instantaneous" effect by manipulating the pallette. This is quite involved, so as a gentle introduction I give a program that does the same thing as the "pallette" example later, but using the standard exclusive–OR erasing technique. MODE 5 is used as the pallette method can only be used when there are at least four colours available.

```
100 REM  Rotating Square - Normal method
110 MODE 5
120 rot%=0
130 GCOL 3,3
140 VDU 29,640;512;
150 REPEAT
160     PROCsquare(400,rot%)
170     t%=TIME+5: REPEAT UNTIL TIME=t%
180     rot%=rot%+10
```

```
190    PROCsquare(400, rot%-10)
200 UNTIL FALSE
210
220
1000 DEF PROCsquare(len%, rot%)
1010    REM    Draws a square rotated rot% about the origin
1020    LOCAL sin%,cos%
1030    sin%=len%*SIN(RAD(rot%))
1040    cos%=len%*COS(RAD(rot%))
1050    MOVE cos%,sin%
1060    DRAW -sin%,cos%
1070    DRAW -cos%,-sin%
1080    DRAW sin%,-cos%
1090    DRAW cos%,sin%
1100 ENDPROC
```

There is nothing new about the program above. It is a simple example of the "draw–wait–delete" cycle. Because it takes a while to draw the square, the periods when there is nothing on the screen are quite obvious. The way the pallette method improves this is as follows: while a square (or whatever) is being drawn, the current graphics foreground colour is set to black (i.e. the background colour), so it cannot be seen. When the drawing is completed, the actual colour for this logical colour is set to white to make it visible. Because this operation is instantaneous, the square appears immediately. Then, the foreground colour is changed and this colour is also set to black. The next square is drawn. When this is finished, the pallette is adjusted so that the previous square disappears and the new one appears very quickly. Then, the old square (which is now invisible) is erased. This colour is then used to draw the next square, which is made visible as the second one is made invisible. A look at the program might help to clarify things:

```
100 REM    Rotating Square - Better version
110 MODE 5
120 VDU 29,640;512;
130 REM    Colour 3 is always white
140 VDU 19,3,7;0;
150 REM    Draw first square
160 col%=1
170 GCOL 3,col%
180 rot%=0
190 PROCsquare(400,rot%)
200 REM    Make it visible
210 VDU 19,(3-col%),0;0;
220 VDU 19,col%,7;0;
```

```
230 col%=3-col%
240 GCOL 3,col%
250 REPEAT
260    REM     Draw the next square invisibly
270    rot%=rot%+5
280    PROCsquare(400,rot%)
290    REM    Make this one visible, hide the last one
300    VDU 19,(3-col%),0;0;
310    VDU 19,col%,7;0;
320    col%=3-col%
330    REM     Delete the last square
340    GCOL 3,col%
350    PROCsquare(400,rot%-5)
360 UNTIL FALSE
```

PROCsquare is assumed to exist in the program somewhere. The first half of the program is concerned with setting up the very first square, so that the first iteration of the REPEAT loop works properly, i.e. it has something to delete at line 350. All plotting is done in colour 1 or 2. At the time of plotting, the current actual colour of col% (the plotting colour) is black, so that the square is not immediately visible. When the square is finished, lines 300 to 320 change the pallette so that the square that is showing at the moment disappears, while the one that has just been drawn in black shows up. It is then necessary to delete the old square. Although the square is invisible, the pixels along the lines are still set to (3-col%), so they must be inverted to set them back to zero. Note that where the visible and invisible lines cross, the colour is set to 1 EOR 2 = 3. This means that colour 3 must also be white, which it is by default. The program sets it just in case. If the "visible" colour were changed to, say, yellow, the statement "VDU 19,3,3;0;" would need to be executed. A way of seeing what is going on is to make the "invisible" colour show. To do this, change line 300 to "VDU 19,(3-col%),1;0;" so the hidden bits actually appear in red.

The price paid for the improved performance of this type of animation is the number of colours available is reduced. This is because the two bits of the pixel are being treated as separate planes (much like the background–middleground–foreground scheme of earlier). Only one of the planes is "enabled" at once. In fact, by manipulating the pallette in the way just described, you can emulate the existence of up to four separate screens (in MODE 2), all of one bit per pixel. The screens can be switched "in" and "out" by use of VDU 19. The set of procedures below lets you do just this. The four screens are labelled 1 to 4 (if you use 0 to 3 instead, all the "$2^{(s\%-1)}$"s can be changed to "$2^{s\%}$"). All the screens have a common background which is logical colour zero. To use a screen, one of the procedures PROCset, PROCreset or PROCinvert must be used before any plotting or printing. Because the procedures use the AND, OR and EOR modes, text must be printed under VDU 5. For example, suppose you wish to plot on screen 2.

274

The call PROCset(2) will cause all subsequent plotting (and VDU 5 printing) to affect only screen 2. This does not mean that you will see it – to "enable" a screen, the pallette must be set up properly. The procedure PROCshow does this for you. PROCshow(2,7) will cause the set pixels in screen 2 to be shown in white. Reset pixels will always show up as logical colour zero, regardless of the screen being viewed. The normal CLG statement's action is a little drastic on its own; it would set all the screens to zero. To erase screens selectively, use PROCclg(screen). The procedures are given below with a short program that draws different sized circles on each screen, then cycles through them. By keeping a key pressed down it can be seen that the screens can be selected very quickly.

```
100 MODE 2
110 VDU 5,29,640;512;
120 FOR i%=1 TO 4
130    PROCshow(i%,i%)
140    PROCset (i%)
150    MOVE -640,502-32*i%: PRINT "Screen #"'i%
160    PROCcircle(i%*100)
170 NEXT i%
180 s%=1
190 REPEAT
200    PROCshow(s%,s%)
210    in%=INKEY(100)
220    s%=s% MOD 4 + 1
230 UNTIL FALSE
240
1000 DEF PROCset(s%)
1010    REM    Set pixels on screen s%
1020    GCOL 1,2^(s%-1)
1030 ENDPROC
1040
2000 DEF PROCreset(s%)
2010    REM    Reset pixels on screen s%
2020    GCOL 2,15-2^(s%-1)
2030 ENDPROC
2040
3000 DEF PROCinvert(s%)
3010    REM    Invert pixels on screen s%
3020    GCOL 3,2^(s%-1)
3030 ENDPROC
3040
4000 DEF PROCclg(s%)
4010    REM    Clear screen
```

```
4020      GCOL 2, 143-2^(s%-1)
4030      CLG
4040 ENDPROC
4050
5000 DEF PROCshow(s%,col%)
5010      REM   Show screen s% in col%
5020      LOCAL p%, q%, i%
5030      p%=2^(s%-1): q%=2*p%
5040      FOR i%=1 TO 15
5050         IF i% MOD q% >= p% THEN VDU 19,i%,col%;0; ELSE VDU 19,i%,0;0;
5060      NEXT i%
5070 ENDPROC
5080
9000 DEF PROCcircle(r%)
9010      LOCAL th, dth
9020      dth=PI/18
9030      MOVE 0,0
9040      MOVE r%,0
9050      FOR th=dth TO 2*PI+dth/2 STEP dth
9060         PLOT 85, r%*COS(th), r%*SIN(th)
9070         MOVE 0,0
9080      NEXT th
9090 ENDPROC
```

There is a number of ways in which the procedures can be altered. An obvious one is converting them to MODE 5, so that two one bit/pixel screens are available. This is easily done; simply restrict all the s% parameters to the range 1 to 2 (or 0 to 1 if you made the change suggested above). Also, if line 5040 is changed to "FOR i%=1 TO 3", the screen will be selected much quicker. The way this loop is used can be seen by considering the binary representations of the logical colour numbers. Suppose the call to the procedure is "PROCshow(2,4). This makes screen two show up in blue (colour 4). In this case, p% will be 2 and q% will equal 4. The IF in line 5050 will succeed for i%=2,3,6,7,10,11,14 and 15. Thus, the pallette will be set up as:

Logical colour	Actual colour	Why?
1 = 0001	0	1 MOD 4 (=1) < 2
2 = 0010	4	2 MOD 4 (=2) >= 2
3 = 0011	4	3 MOD 4 (=3) >= 2
4 = 0100	0	4 MOD 4 (=0) < 2
5 = 0101	0	5 MOD 4 (=1) < 2
6 = 0110	4	6 MOD 4 (=2) >= 2
7 = 0111	4	7 MOD 4 (=3) >= 2
8 = 1000	0	8 MOD 4 (=U) < 2

9 = 1001	0	9 MOD 4 (=1) < 2
10 = 1010	4	10 MOD 4 (=2) >= 2
11 = 1011	4	11 MOD 4 (=3) >= 2
12 = 1100	0	12 MOD 4 (=0) < 2
13 = 1101	0	13 MOD 4 (=1) < 2
14 = 1110	4	14 MOD 4 (=2) >= 2
15 = 1111	4	15 MOD 4 (=3) >= 2

Simply put, if the s%'th bit of i% is a 1, logical colour i% is set to col%, otherwise it is set to zero. Other schemes could implement 2 two bits per pixel screens in MODE 2, or even one of one bit and another of three bits. It might be instructive to see how the body of the rotating square program given earlier would be expressed in terms of these procedures.

```
100 MODE 5
110 VDU 5,29,640;512;
120 s%=1
130 PROCshow(3-s%,7)
140 PROCset(s%)
150 rot%=0
160 PROCsquare(400,rot%)
170 PROCshow(s%,7)
180 s%=3-s%
190 REPEAT
200    rot%=rot%+5
210    PROCset(s%)
220    PROCsquare(400,rot%)
230    PROCshow(s%,7)
240    s%=3-s%
250    PROCreset(s%)
260    PROCsquare(400,rot%-5)
270 UNTIL FALSE
```

The variable s% is used to keep track of the current screen and is flipped between 1 and 2 by subtracting the current value from 3. Notice that the procedures PROCset and PROCreset (which could be called PROCdraw and PROCerase) are used rather than the single PROCinvert. There is no practical difference; it just means that the REPEAT loop is a little longer and hence slower. This is hardly important in this case, as PROCsquare takes up the bulk of the processing. The "secret" deleting can be shown by setting the background colour to anything other than black. Note that if you set colour zero to a non-black colour and still want the hidden screens to stay hidden, you must change the ELSE part of line 5050 to "VDU 19,i%,bckgnd;0;", where bckgnd is the background colour used.

There is another way in which the pallette can be manipulated to achieve animation. This time, all the objects to be displayed are drawn before the animation begins, each in its own logical colour. This obviously sets a limit of three or fifteen objects for modes 5 and 2. All the objects' actual colours are set to the background colour initially. They are then set successively to other colours that show up. Only one colour is made visible at once, so the illusion of motion is achieved. A limitation of this method is that the objects may not overlap if they are to be shown in their entirety. The program below shows the method in action. Twelve numbers are arranged as on a clockface. They are then displayed successively, once a second.

```
100 REM      Animated Clockface
110 MODE 2
120 VDU 5,29,640;512;
130 FOR i%=1 TO 12
140    VDU 19,i%,0;0;
150    GCOL 0,i%
160    MOVE 400*COS(RAD(i%*30-90)), -400*SIN(RAD(i%*30-90))
170    PRINT STR$(i%)
180 NEXT i%
190 i%=0
200 REPEAT
210    VDU 19,(i%-1) MOD 12 + 1,0;0;
215    VDU 19,i% MOD 12 + 1,7;0;
220    REPEAT UNTIL TIME MOD 100 = 0
230    i%=i%+1
240 UNTIL FALSE
```

Of course, the second delay at line 220 is very long compared to the time it takes to update the pallette. Try decreasing it; you will find that the REPEAT loop can iterate faster than the 50 times a second that the TV picture is updated. As an exercise, you could try converting the car and 'phone box program to this method. The red parts could be colour 1, then colours 2 to 15 could be reserved for the car in various positions. It would be better to draw the cars first, then plot the red bits over them using GCOL 0.

4.9   Three Dimensional Graphics

One of the most interesting facets of computer graphics is the drawing of pictures in three dimensions. Of course, the screen is only two dimensional, so only an illusion of three dimensionality can be shown. A simple method of achieving such an effect is the prioritised bit planes discussed earlier. The two or four pixel planes can pass in front of or behind one another, which can give the illusion that the objects on the screen have some depth. More usually, though, people regard 3D displays as the perspective views of line drawings, or even solid objects. These types of display are frequently shown on programmes such as Horizon and Tomorrow's World. Unfortunately, the graphics devices discussed in such programmes are driven by very powerful computers which are still rather expensive. Moreover, computer "movies", such as the Jupiter fly-past one, are created in much the same way as animated cartoons: each picture "frame" is generated in a few seconds (or even longer for particularly complex scenes) and, when it is complete, recorded on film. The film is then shown at the normal 30 or 50 frames/second to create the illusion of continuous movement.

The reason that even large computers cannot draw complex 3D pictures in real time is the complex arithmetic that must be performed for each individual point. The computer must calculate the intensity of each point while considering the depth of the point into the screen, any light sources that are supposed to be present and shadows, among other things. Although such calculations are certainly within the capabilities of the BBC Computer (and any other microcomputer), the time required to perform them, and the limitation of the display, precludes their use. In the future, when the 32-bit second processor is available, such graphics may well become feasible.

In this section, then, I will concentrate on the simple 3D perspective drawings, using only line segments. As you will have gathered, 3D graphics is a highly mathematical subject. In particular, much use is made of matrix manipulation. This is arithmetic performed on whole arrays of numbers. Some BASICs have built-in facilities for performing such calculations. BBC BASIC is not one of them, so the calculations must be done with FOR . . . NEXT loops. This does not help to speed things up. Trigonometry is another device used in 3D graphics. Working out sines and cosines is not one of microcomputers' fortes, so this introduces more delays. The foregoing should dispel any final illusions you had about being able to write fast-moving 3D games in BASIC. However, if speed is not a major concern, there is still much that can be done with a few short procedures.

The crux of 3D graphics is converting the (x,y,z) co-ordinates of a point in three dimensional space to the (x,y) co-ordinates used on the screen. This is called a transformation. In particular, we want a perspective transformation, to get a perspective picture from the (x,y,z) co-ordinates. Figure 4.13 shows the situation. The three dimensional co-ordinate system is arranged so that its x and y axes are parallel to the screen's respective axes, and the z axis is into the screen. This is called a left-handed co-ordinate system.

The situation shown in Figure 4.13 is a very particular one; the viewing point is on the z-axis, and the projection plane is coincident with the computer's screen. This makes it very easy to perform calculations necessary to transform (x,y,z) to (X,Y). This is illustrated in Figure 4.14 for finding Y. The view is from a point on the positive half of the x-axis. It can be seen that, by similar triangles, $Y=y*dist/(dist+z)$. A similar calculation will give X. There is a restriction that z must be greater than $-dist$. If $z=-dist$, the denominator of the fraction will be zero, and an error will occur. If $z<-dist$, the point will be transformed to the wrong part of the screen. Since this point would be behind the viewer's eye, the program should ensure that such co-ordinates are never used. Just as the two dimensional plottings on the BBC's screen are clipped, there exist algorithms to

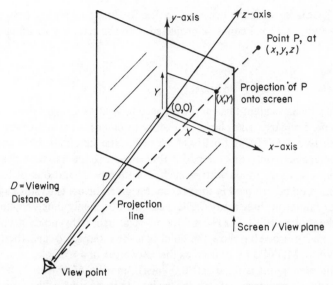

Figure 4.13   Perspective Projection onto the Screen

clip three dimensional lines. These are really beyond this book's scope. If you have at least an A-level in maths, or are very keen to learn, [Foley] is the definitive work for graphics. It goes into far greater detail than you will ever need for programming the BBC computer, but contains much that is applicable.

Now that we have a way of converting (x,y,z) to (X,Y), how do we use it? The obvious thing would be to define a function that could be used in MOVE, DRAW, etc. to draw three dimensional lines. For example, suppose FNx(x,z) gives the screen X co-ordinate for the point (x,y,z), and a similar function FNy(y,z) returns the screen Y co-ordinate for (x,y,z). (It is assumed that the viewing distance is held

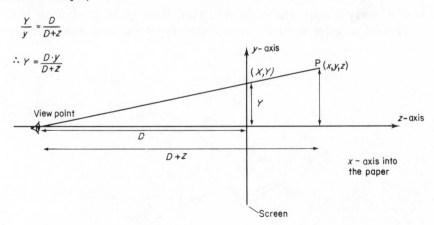

Figure 4.14   Perspective Projection Calculation

in a global variable which is accessed by the functions.) The line between points $(x1,y1,z1)$ and $(x2,y2,z2)$ could be projected onto the screen with statements such as:

```
100 MOVE FNx(x1,z1), FNy(y1,z1)
110 DRAW FNx(x2,z2), FNy(y2,z2)
```

This is possible as straight lines in the 3-space project as straight lines on the projection plane. Similarly, flat planes project onto planes, so that surfaces could be drawn with two MOVEs and a PLOT 85, using the functions FNx and FNy as above. The problem with this method is that once a shape has been drawn (e.g. a cube), it is hard to do much with it, such as rotation around one of the axes, or scaling. The method adopted in the procedures given below is to store a list of x, y and z co-ordinates in three arrays. These can then be manipulated en masse, using the aforementioned FOR ... NEXT loops. A fourth array holds a value which tells the drawing procedure how the point is to be interpreted, i.e. whether it is to be DRAWn to, MOVEd to, or used as the last vertex of a triangle.

Since the view point is fixed (at $(0,0,-dist)$), motion of objects is achieved by changing the co-ordinates of all the points that comprise the object. These changes are also known as transformations. There are several types – scaling, translation and rotation. Assume a shape array has been set-up in the format outlined above to represent a square plane, normal to the y-axis, 128 units on a side and 64 units above the x-z plane. This is shown in Figure 4.15. The array entries for this shape would be:

```
      x    y    z    m        Meaning
0)   63   64   63    4        Move to (63,64,63)
1)  -64   64   63    5        Draw to (-64,64,63)
2)  -64   64  -64    5        Draw to (-64,64,-64)
3)   63   64  -64    5        Draw to (63,64,-64)
4)   63   64   63    5        Draw to (63,64,63)
```

The "m" entry is simply the PLOT option used when drawing the shape. It must be an absolute option as relative co-ordinates do not transform from three to two

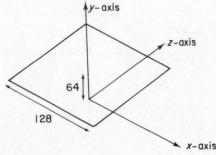

Figure 4.15   A 128*128 Plane with Centre (0,64,0)

dimensions without a scaling error. To plot a transformed triangle, for example, m would equal 85.

By performing various transformations on the co-ordinates, the image produced can be altered dramatically. The shape could be scaled, for example. In this case, the three co-ordinates of each point in the plane (or more precisely the entries in the array determining the plane) are each multiplied by a scaling factor. Each co-ordinate has its own scaling factor. Unless all three are equal, the object will change shape. If the three factors are 2, 1, and 0.5 for x, y and z respectively, the new co-ordinates for the shape above will be (126,64,31), (−128,64,31) and so on. When redrawn, the object would appear longer and shallower than before.

Another transformation is translation. This means moving. Again, each co-ordinate can be translated individually. To move the object under discussion back 100 units, and down 40, the translation (0,−40,100) would be used. Finally, there is rotation about an axis. This is where the use of trigonometry is necessary. The derivation of the equations used is not important, but those interested readers can refer to one of the books mentioned in the bibliography. When an object is rotated about an axis, all of its points are rotated by the same amount, so the shape is unaltered. The procedures to implement the facilities discussed so far are given below, along with some data for a cube shape, and a short demonstration program:

```
100 REM 3D Graphics
110 MODE 4
120 PROCinit
160 FOR i%=1 TO 10
170    PROCtrans(0,15,20,20,0)
175    GCOL0,1
180    PROCshow(0,15)
190    INPUT in%
195    GCOL0,0
200    PROCshow(0,15)
210 NEXT i%
220 FOR i%=1 TO 15
230    PROCtrans(0,15,0,0,100)
235    GCOL0,1
240    PROCshow(0,15)
250    INPUT in%
255    GCOL0,0
260    PROCshow(0,15)
270 NEXT i%
280 PROCreset(0,15)
290 PROCroty(0,15,30)
300 FOR i%=1 TO 36
310    GCOL 0,1
```

```
 320     PROCshow(0,15)
 330     INPUT in%
 340     GCOL 0,0
 350     PROCshow(0,15)
 360     PROCrotx(0,15,10)
 370 NEXT i%
 375 GCOL0,1
 380 PROCscale(0,15,2,2,2)
 390 FOR i%=1 TO 15
 400     PROCshow(0,15)
 410     PROCscale(0,15,.8,.8,.8)
 420 NEXT i%
 430 END
1000 DEF PROCinit
1010    REM  Set up tables and view parameter
1020    LOCAL i%
1023    VDU 24,0;224;1279;1023;
1024    VDU 28,0,31,39,25
1025    VDU 29,640;512;
1030    DIM x%(100), y%(100),z%(100), m% 100
1040    DIM xs%(100), ys%(100), zs%(100)
1060    d%=960
1075    READ n%
1080    FOR i%=0 TO n%-1
1090       READ x%(i%), y%(i%), z%(i%), m%?i%
1095       xs%(i%)=x%(i%): ys%(i%)=y%(i%): zs%(i%)=z%(i%)
1100    NEXT i%
1105    DATA 22
1110    DATA 160,-160,-160,4, 160,160,-160,5, -160,160,-160,5, -160,-160,-160,5
1120    DATA 160,-160,-160,5, 160,-160,160,5, 160,160,160,5, -160,160,160,5
1130    DATA -160,-160,160,5, 160,-160,160,5, 160,160,-160,4, 160,160,160,5
1140    DATA -160,160,-160,4, -160,160,160,5, -160,-160,-160,4, -160,-160,160,5
1145    DATA -200,0,0,4, 200,0,0,5, 0,-200,0,4, 0,200,0,5
1147    DATA 0,0,-200,4, 0,0,200,5
1148    PRINT"Hold on a sec."
1150    DIM sin% 359
1160    FOR th%=0 TO 359
1170       sin%?th%=127*(SIN(RAD(th%))+1)
1180    NEXT th%
1190 ENDPROC
1195
1200 DEF FNsin(th%)=sin%?(th% MOD 360)/127-1
```

```
1210 DEF FNcos(th%)=sin%?((th%+90) MOD 360)/127-1 1220
2000 DEF PROCtrans(lo%,hi%,tx%,ty%,tz%)
2010    REM    translate co-ordinates
2020    LOCAL i%
2030    FOR i%=lo% TO hi%
2040       xs%(i%)=xs%(i%)+tx%
2050       ys%(i%)=ys%(i%)+ty%
2060       zs%(i%)=zs%(i%)+tz%
2070    NEXT i%
2080 ENDPROC
2090
3000 DEF PROCrotx(lo%,hi%,rot%)
3010    REM   Rotate about the x-axis
3020    LOCAL s,c,i%,ys%
3030    s=FNsin(rot%)
3040    c=FNcos(rot%)
3050    FOR i%=lo% TO hi%
3055       ys%=ys%(i%)
3060       ys%(i%)=c*ys%(i%)-s*zs%(i%)
3070       zs%(i%)=s*ys%+c*zs%(i%)
3080    NEXT i%
3090 ENDPROC
3095
3100 DEF PROCroty(lo%,hi%,rot%)
3110    REM   Rotate about the y-axis
3120    LOCAL s,c,i%,xs%
3130    s=FNsin(rot%)
3140    c=FNcos(rot%)
3150    FOR i%=lo% TO hi%
3155       xs%=xs%(i%)
3160       xs%(i%)=c*xs%(i%)+s*zs%(i%)
3170       zs%(i%)=c*zs%(i%)-s*xs%
3180    NEXT i%
3190 ENDPROC
3195
3200 DEF PROCrotz(lo%,hi%,rot%)
3210    REM   Rotate about the z-axis
3220    LOCAL s,c,i%,xs%
3230    s=FNsin(rot%)
3240    c=FNcos(rot%)
3250    FOR i%=lo% TO hi%
3255       xs%=xs%(i%)
```

```
3260        xs%(i%)=c*xs%(i%)-s*ys%(i%)
3270        ys%(i%)=s*xs%+c*ys%(i%)
3280     NEXT i%
3290 ENDPROC
3295
4000 DEF PROCshow(lo%,hi%)
4010     REM  Display points
4020     LOCAL i%, f
4030     FOR i%=lo% TO hi%
4040        f=d%/(d%+zs%(i%))
4050        PLOT m%?i%, f*xs%(i%), f*ys%(i%)
4060     NEXT i%
4070 ENDPROC
4080
4100 DEF FNx(x%,z%)=x%*d%/(d%+z%)
4200 DEF FNy(y%,z%)=y%*d%/(d%+z%)
4210
50U0 DEF PROCreset(lo%,hi%)
5010     REM  Restore co-ordinates lo% to hi%
5020     LOCAL i%
5030     FOR i%=lo% TO hi%
5040        xs%(i%)=x%(i%)
5050        ys%(i%)=y%(i%)
5060        zs%(i%)=z%(i%)
5070     NEXT i%
5080 ENDPROC
5090
6000 DEF PROCscale(lo%,hi%,fx,fy,fz)
6020     REM Scale co-ordinates
6030     LOCAL i%
6040     FOR i%=lo% TO hi%
6050        xs%(i%)=xs%(i%)*fx
6060        ys%(i%)=ys%(i%)*fy
6070        zs%(i%)=zs%(i%)*fz
6080     NEXT i%
6090 ENDPROC
```

The action of the demonstration program is to draw a cube in the centre of the screen, move it up and to the right, then back into the screen. The cube then reappears in the centre, rotating about the x-axis. Finally, several scaled versions of the cube are drawn without being erased.

The first procedure, PROCinit, sets-up the arrays which are used by the rest of the program. It also initialises the value of d%, the distance of the imaginary eye from the projection plane (which is also the screen in this case). The shape data is held in the arrays x%(), y%(), z%() and xs%(), ys%(), zs%(). Additionally, the plotting option for each point is held in the byte array m%?. Initially, the co-ordinate triplets are read into both sets of arrays. However, whereas the contents of x%(), etc., are never altered, the other three (xs%() etc.) have their values changed by the various transformation procedures. The sole purpose of x%(), y%() and z%() is to save the original co-ordinates so that the other three arrays can be restored to these values if required. The final data structure is the array sin%?. This is another byte array. It is set-up with scaled values of the SIN function. There are 360 elements, for 0 to 359 degrees. The array is used by FNsin and FNcos to calculate those functions. Looking up the values in this way is faster than calling SIN or COS each time, which is why this method is used. Of course, there is the small matter of the 360 bytes of storage needed. By considering the SIN function, you could cut this down to 90 values, with an increase in the complexity of FNsin and FNcos. Also, the functions won't work with negative arguments. (FNcos works for −90 to 0, though). Rewrite the functions to incorporate these two improvements, and measure the difference in speed. As an aside, it is possible to show graphically the error introduced by storing the sine values as eight-bit quantities, within the resolution of the screen. Try the program below:

```
100 MODE 4
110 PROCinit
120 FOR i%=0 TO 319
130    PLOT 69, i%*4, 500+500*SIN(RAD(i%))
140    PLOT 70, i%*4, 500+500*FNsin(i%)
150 NEXT i%
160 END
```

In this case, PROCinit should only contain the set-up part for sin%?, not the window- and origin-changing statements. The point is plotted by the "official" sine function, then erased by the eight-bit version. Wherever there is no dot along the sine wave, FNsin is accurate to one part in 250. Numerically speaking, the greatest error occurs at 60 degrees, where FNsin is 0.90% out.

The remainder of the procedures are of similar form. They all take at least two parameters, lo% and hi%. Only the elements of xs%() etc. in the range (lo%) to (hi%) are affected by the procedure. This enables the arrays to be segregated into different objects that can be manipulated individually. In the DATA given in the program above, for example, the first 16 elements (that is, from 0 to 15) form the cube shape. The rest, from 16 to 21, draw three lines 400 units long along each of the axes. To rotate these lines about the y-axis, for example, the call:

```
PROCroty(16,21,30)
```

could be used. lo%=16, hi%=21 and the 30 is the number of degrees of rotation.

The first transformation procedure is PROCtrans. Apart from lo% and hi%, the parameters are the three amounts by which the elements are to be translated along the three axes. A value of zero implies no movement in that direction. To move the three lines back by 300 units, the call:

```
PROCtrans(16,21,0,0,300)
```

is used. The two zeroes are the x and y translations. The 300 means: "increase the z co-ordinate of these points by 300 units". Since the view on the screen is oriented so that the positive z-axis is into the TV set, increasing this co-ordinate's value will make a point recede. Similarly, decreasing z moves a point towards the viewpoint (remember that an object is displayed incorrectly if any part of it is behind the viewpoint, though). Notice that the translation values are relative quantities: the parameters tx%, ty% and tz% are added to the xs%(), ys%() and zs%() elements in the given range. It would, of course, be a simple matter to define an absolute version, say PROCmove(lo%,hi%,x%,y%,z%), which simply assigns the parameters given to xs%(), ys%() and zs%().

There are three separate rotation procedures, one for each axis. It takes 1 second to perform the call PROCrotx(0,100,45), and approximately proportional times for fewer elements (the actual times are slightly greater than a linear (hi%–lo%) to time relationship would suggest). Although this may seem like speedy work, it is slow compared to the speeds needed to produce smooth-looking animation. This is certainly one of the occasions where machine code could be used to speed things up (as suggested by the example of CALL on page 214 of the User Guide; shame they didn't include the program as well!). The third parameter of the rotation procedures is again relative; it gives the angle (in degrees) through which the points are to be rotated. Because of the limitations of FNsin and FNcos mentioned above, negative rotations have to be expressed as large positive ones. For example, to rotate by −30 degrees, 360−30=330 must be used. The direction of rotation can be worked out as follows: if you look down the axis in question from a positive value on that axis in the direction of the origin, positive rotations give a clockwise movement. Remember that the viewpoint is at z=−d%, so a positive rotation about the z-axis will appear an an anti-clockwise movement. Since PROCrotx, etc. rotate points about the axes, rotation of an object about its centre may require more than just a call to one of the rotation procedures if its centre is not on the required axis. If the centre of a cube is at (100,100,100), and it is desired to rotate the cube by 45 degrees about an axis parallel to the y-axis, but through the cube's centre, three transformations would be necessary:

```
PROCtrans(0,15,-100,0,-100): REM    Shift the cube to the y-axis
PROCroty(0,15,45):           REM    Rotate about y-axis
PROCtrans(0,15,100,0,100):   REM    Shift the cube back again
```

If the two PROCtrans were omitted, the cube would be rotated as a whole about the y-axis, changing the position of its centre to (141,100,0) − not the desired effect at all.

The last transformation procedure (or at least, the last one which actually alters the values in xs%(), ys%() and zs%()) is PROCscale, for scaling. The form is much the same as PROCtrans, with the first two parameters specifying the range of elements to be used and the last three giving the scale factors for the three co-ordinates. These latter parameters are real numbers, so objects can be diminished as well as magnified. For example, to halve the x co-ordinate of each point, the call PROCscale (0,15,.5,1,1) would be used. Note the "no effect" value is 1, not zero, which would reduce each point's co-ordinates to zero irretrievably. Also, since the co-ordinate arrays are integer ones, truncation errors can be caused by scaling with small factors. There is no reason why the co-ordinates shouldn't be held in real arrays, though speed and storage space would suffer by a factor of 20 or so percent. The method of scaling objects centred on arbitrary points is similar to that for rotation. To scale a cube which is defined by points 0 to 15 and whose centre is at (x%,y%,z%) by factors fx, fy and fz require the three calls:

```
PROCtrans(0,15,-x%,-y%,-z%)   : REM  Move to origin
PROCscale(0,15,fx,fy,fz)      : REM  Scale co-ordinates
PROCtrans(0,15,x%,y%,z%)      : REM  Move it back again
```

A special kind of scaling – reflection – can be obtained by giving the procedure negative factors. For example, PROCscale(0,15,–1,1,1) would "reflect" the cube about the y–z plane. The term "reflection" is simply explained. If, for this example, you imagine the y–z plane as being a mirror with its silvered surface pointing towards the cube, the cube's position after PROCscale(0,15,–1,1,1) is coincident with its reflection in the mirror. Similar scalings can yield reflections about x–y and x–z planes.

PROCreset is somewhat different from the previous procedures. It takes the usual lo%, hi% parameters, but the results of its action is independent of the previous contents of xs%() etc. What it does is to assign x%(i%) to xs%(i%), y%(i%) to ys%(i%) and z%(i%) to zs%(i%) for i% in the range lo% to hi%. in effect it restores the original co-ordinates of the points in the range given. The main use is to ensure that an object is where you think it is after many transformations. This is particularly important in view of the various sources of error in the procedures (rounding errors on scaling, FNsin errors, etc.).

The last procedure, PROCshow, is the only one that affects the display. Its action is very simple: for all elements between lo% and hi%, convert (xs%(),ys%(),zs%()) to screen co-ordinates and PLOT these as dictated by the value of m%?. The formula for perspective projection was given earlier. In PROCshow, the d%/(d%+zs%(i%)) part is calculated separately to save a little time. Notice that although d% is the distance of the viewpoint from the projection plane, the fact that the latter is fixed at z=0 means that increasing d% does not make the images smaller, as might be expected. In fact, if all the points being displayed have positive z co-ordinates, decreasing d% will increase the size of the drawing. You can see this by looking at Figure 4.14 and thinking hard at the same time. The main effect of changing d% is to alter the "perspectiveness" of the view. When d% is small (but –d% is still less than the smallest z co-ordinate being shown), the perspective effect is very noticeable. This is because lines near to the viewpoint subtend much larger angles than those further away. As d% increases, this disparity reduces, and the perspective effect becomes less pronounced. In the limit, as d% grows very large, the lines from the viewpoint to the displayed points are almost parallel. The expression for f then becomes $E/(E+zs\%(i\%))$, where E stands for "extremely large number". This simplifies to 1, so line 5050 could be rewritten:

```
5050        PLOT m%?i%, xs%(i%), ys%(i%)
```

and line 5040 deleted. What this has done is to change the projection from a perspective one to a parallel one (in particular, an orthographic projection, as the line of viewing is normal to the projection plane). The difference is that objects don't shrink as they move away from the viewer, and all lines which are parallel on the object are shown to be parallel on the screen, instead of converging. This type of projection finds use in drafting, as drawings projected thus can be used for taking measurements, something which is not possible on perspective diagrams.

Just after PROCshow there are one-line functions. These are the ones mentioned at the beginning of this section. FNx(x%,z%) returns the screen x co-ordinate of the point (x%,y%,z%) in 3-space and FNy(y%,z%) gives the screen y co-ordinate. These functions could be used in placing text on a three dimensional picture, as in:

```
120 MOVE FNx(0,0), FNy(-200,0)
130 DRAW FNx(0,0), FNy(200,0)
140 PRINT" y-axis"
```

assuming that VDU 5 is in force. Of course, if the co-ordinates in xs%() etc. have been transformed, the co-ordinates returned by FNx and FNy may not correspond to the same points on the picture. To alleviate this problem, a new m%? mode could be defined: values greater than 99 represent "text-moves". The co-ordinates given by xs%(), ys%() and zs%() are MOVEd to, then the string in an array text$() printed. The code to do this would be:

```
5045 IF m%?i% > 99 THEN MOVE f*xs%(i%),f*ys%(i%):PRINT text$(m%?i%-100):GOTO
5060
```

The array text$() could hold up to 156 strings (for values of m%? in the range 100 to 255).

The striking thing about the program above is the speed at which the cube isn't drawn. Obviously, the slowness is in proportion to n%, the number of co-ordinate entries, so things get pretty bad as the (arbitrary) limit of 101 is approached. Another point to note is that the exclusive–OR plot mode is not used. The reason is that whenever lines cross over the far one is "deleted" by the near one. With complex diagrams, this causes a great deal of confusion when the object is viewed from certain angles. Also, the object is in full view while it is being drawn and erased. This is quite distracting. This problem can be alleviated by using the "separate screens" technique of the last section. (The procedures of either that package or the current one will need to be renumbered, and one of the PROCshows will have to be re-named to avoid unpleasant clashes.) It is not compulsory to derive the shape's data from DATA statements; the program could generate them itself from some calculations, an example being a 3D graph plotter. The outline for such a program is given below:

```
100 MODE 4
110 PROCinit
120 i%=0
130 FOR x=xlo TO xhi STEP xstep
140     i%=i%+1
150     x%(i%)=fx*x: y%(i%)=fy*ylo
160     z%(i%)=fz*FNz(x,ylo): m%? i%=4
170     FOR y=ylo+ystep TO yhi STEP ystep
180         i%=i%+1
190         x%(i%)=fx*x: y%(i%)=fy*y
200         z%(i%)=fz*FNz(x,y): m%? i%=5
210     NEXT y
220 NEXT x
230 PROCreset(1,i%)
240 REM      Transformations to obtain the desired view
250 PROCshow(1,i%)
260 END
```

This is only a "bare-bones" outline. The factors fx, fy and fz convert the graph's co-ordinates into values suitable for obtaining good accuracy. For example, the function SIN(x)*COS(y) returns values between −0.5 and +0.5, which would not be stored very accurately in integer variables. Factor fz could be in the region of 256. The values such as xlo, xhi, etc. are assumed to be input from the user, as is the function to be plotted. FNz(x,y) returns the value of the function at (x,y). It would be defined something like:

```
20000 DEF FNz(x,y)=EVAL(f$)
```

where f$ is, for example, "x*SIN(y)". The arrays would need to be somewhat larger than the 101 elements indicated in the version of PROCinit above. 250 is about the lowest number that would be needed to provide a useful image.

The procedures and techniques described in this section cover a very small part of a very large (and expanding) subject. There is plenty of scope for experimentation, especially with the addition of second processors. Many computer graphics tasks require either lots of memory, or a lot of processing power (or both). With a 4Mhz Z-80 or 6502 second processor, or better still, the 16032, many of the techniques and algorithms described in [Foley], [Newman] and [Rogers] become usable on the BBC Machine. For now, though, I hope this chapter has given you something to think about.

Chapter Five

Using the Assembler

I was going to call this chapter "Assembly Language Programming", but that title implies a tutorial nature, which would be misleading. Just as the whole book does not set out to be a BASIC programming course, this chapter is concerned with using the built-in assembler, rather than teaching the reader assembly language. It would be arrogant for any book to claim to teach assembly language in a chapter, so I refer you to [Zaks] and [Leventhal] for a 6502 assembly language tutorial.

In spite of the comments above, even readers with relatively little experience of assembly language should learn something from the examples of this chapter. One of the most popular questions asked is "Why should I use assembly language?". There are several reasons, the most apparent is the speed of machine code (which is what the assembly language program ends up as). Because the simple instructions such as "LDA #&80" make up the "native tongue" of the computer, they are executed very rapidly. The times involved are measured in terms of clock cycles, where the clock cycle length is 0.5 microseconds. Instructions on the 6502 microprocessor take between 2 and 7 cycles. On the other hand, even simple statements in BASIC require thousands of cycles to interpret. The reason is that BASIC instructions tend to do a lot more than assembly language ones. For example, the most complex arithmetic that the 6502 can perform directly is addition and subtraction. The BASIC statement "PRINT SIN(RAD(x^1.5))" requires logarithms, multiplication and sines (which are worked out as sums of lots of powers of x – more multiplying). To express all this in terms of additions and subtractions is obviously a complex process in which many thousands of machine instructions are executed. This generation of many simple machine instructions during the execution of one BASIC statement is why machine code executes so much faster.

Another reason for using assembly language could be called "access to the machine". Because assembly language is essentially the computer's natural one, the programmer is able to access all the devices connected to it at the lowest level, which means he has more control over them than when he is "buffered" by a high-level language such as BASIC. This applies to things like the cassette interface chip, the printer/user port chip and the computer's keyboard. On the BBC computer this advantage is lessened by the presence of the powerful Machine Operating System. This is the program that looks after everything which is connected to the computer, and within it there are many routines provided to control the afore-mentioned devices. As most of these routines are callable from high-level languages, there is usually no need to resort to the lower-level assembly language. However, not all these MOS routines are suitable for use from BASIC, so that ability to get into the nitty-gritty which assembly language provides can still be necessary. A final advantage of assembly language is the size of the programs. This refers to the amount of space required by the final machine code and its data areas, rather than assembly source code (i.e. the mnemonics and operands and labels, etc.). Depending on what the program does, this memory requirement can be less than or greater than the equivalent BASIC program. In programs which require little complex arithmetic, assembly language versions can be made very compact. However, when there is much arithmetic or input/output, it may be wiser to use BASIC if program size is very important. BBC BASIC, like most other versions of the language, is tokenised. This means that all the keywords such as "PRINT", "LET" and "ENVELOPE" are converted into a special form that only takes one byte of storage. As a result, BASIC programs are stored very efficiently. If short variable names are used as well (not a procedure that can be recommended, as discussed in Chapter two), BASIC programs can usually be made smaller than their machine code counterparts.

Assembly language has its disadvantages as well, otherwise there would be no need for BASIC, Pascal and the other hundreds of computer languages. The most important of these is the relative slowness with which assembly language programs are developed (i.e. written and debugged) by humans. This stems from the simple nature of the language; each instruction only causes a very simple operation to take place, which implies that anything that is at all involved will take many instructions. Also, there are none of the advanced concepts that make high-level languages comparatively easy to use – no data structures (arrays, strings, etc.), no procedures (only a simple subroutine calling facility) and no structured flow control (only the equivalent of GOTO and IF ... GOTO). In fact, to paraphrase a well-known android, it gives humans a headache just thinking down to a 6502's level. The lack of structured constructs does not mean that it is impossible to write well-structured assembly language programs. The rules of program subdivision, intelligent naming and commenting apply equally to assembly programs, if not more so. They must be used to counteract the disadvantage of having to make explicit branches in the program to perform loops, complex IFs, etc. Another disadvantage which is particularly prevalent in eight-bit micros such as the BBC machine's 6502 is the limited word-length. This is the maximum amount of data that can be operated on in one go. This is a single byte on the 6502, so any operations on larger quantities require multiple assembly language instructions. The ability to say "a%=b%+c%" in BASIC is taken for granted. However, adding two 32-bit integers and storing their sum somewhere using assembly language takes a lot more work than that statement implies. If speed is the reason for using assembly language, the effort expended in writing the programs in the lower-level form will only be repaid if the calculations are simple ones, otherwise you might find that in the time it took to write and debug the assembly version, the slightly slower BASIC version could have been written and run.

Assembly language, then, has its advantages and disadvantages over higher level languages. The remainder of this chapter covers the BASIC assembler, the BASIC-machine code interface, and concludes with some examples of assembly language programs. As I mentioned above, it would be a fruitless exercise trying to teach the elements of assembly language programming in this chapter, so most of the programs are particular to the BBC machine rather than being of general application.

5.1 The BASIC Assembler

The ease at which assembly language routines can be intermixed with BASIC code is a feature unique to BBC BASIC (and its predecessor Atom BASIC). The facilities offered by the assembler are quite limited compared to some "custom-built" assemblers, though most of the more sophisticated facilities provided by the latter can be implemented by briefly returning to BASIC. These special features are the so-called pseudo operations which look like normal mnemonics but aren't translated as machine instructions. Instead, they cause the assembler to perform a special action, such as reserve some memory space in which tables, etc., can be placed.

The start of assembly code is marked by the [symbol. When the interpreter executes this "statement", the BASIC keywords such as "PRINT" are no longer recognised, except for the functions and operators used in expressions. The general form of an assembly line is:

```
1000 {label} {MNE {op}}
```

where "label" is a dot (period, fullstop) followed by a numeric variable name. Examples are ".ll", ".end%". A label is used to remember the address of the current instruction, so that it can be used by subsequent branch instructions. The "MNE" is a mnemonic, either a valid 6502 one (see pp. 508–509 of the User Guide) or the pseudo-operation "OPT". The "op" part, which is optional, but only allowed if there is a "MNE" part, is the operand for the instruction. The precise syntax depends on the addressing mode in use. For example, a # followed by an expression means immediate mode. "Implicit" instructions such as "TXA" have no operand field. The expressions used in the operand have the full generality of the expressions allowed in an EVAL string. In fact, the assembly language expression evaluator is even more general than EVAL; the latter does not recognise the pseudo-variables "TIME", "HIMEM", etc., so something like PRINT EVAL("TIME/100") would yield a "No such variable" error. On the other hand, it is perfectly all right to have assembly instructions such as LDA HIMEM, ADC #TIME MOD 100, etc. Of course, the values of the pseudo-variables are those returned when the program is assembled. If the code is executed under different conditions, e.g. in a different display mode, the program may not work properly.

Another possible operand is "A", which means accumulator addressing for those instructions where this applies. The presence of this symbol makes it wise to avoid using labels and other symbols in the assembly program that begin with capital A. The instruction:

```
ROL ADD
```

would be assembled as a "ROL A" instructions, even if the label ADD had already been defined in the program. The "DD" would just be ignored by the assembler.

It is sometimes nice to have the assembler ignore things, e.g. comments in the program. Strictly speaking, comments (the assembly language equivalent of REMs) are introduced by a / and terminated by a : or a new line. The colon marks the end of the current statement, and thus the start of the next statement. Thus assembly language programs can have several instructions on one line, even if a comment follows the first one:

```
1000 LDA &70 \Get flag: AND #&01 \Mask off the upper bits
```

Although this can be useful, the fact that assembly language is harder to follow than BASIC at the best of times dictates that there should only be one instruction per line, unless space is at an absolute premium. If you look at assembly listings such as those found in PCW Subset, it is clear that people take a lot more care about commenting on these than in BASIC. Also, the instructions are always indented by several spaces so that labels are shown clearly. You should aim to copy this style, rather than cramming as many instructions per line as possible. After all, once the program is assembled, the machine code is the same size, whether the source contained spaces and comments or not. If you have a BASIC program that contains assembly routines, it is pointless saving the program with the assembler source once it has been fully debugged. A better way is *LOAD the machine code from the program into some safe place, so that there is more room for BASIC's variables. "Safe" places are discussed later.

There is special variable connected with the assembly process – P%. This is normally just the same as the other 26 static variables. During assembly, however, it is used as the "program counter"; it contains the address where the next instruction's machine code will be stored. Before the program meets a "[", P% must be set to the address of the start of the machine code. This address depends on various things, such as the size of the assembly program. Short routines can usually be put in the page just below the start of BASIC program, i.e from &0D00 up. These locations are also used by the disc system, so cannot be used if you have floppy disc drives connected to your system. The most common method is to reserve space using the special form of the DIM statement. The statement:

```
200 DIM code% 100
```

will set aside 101 bytes of memory above the program (or more precisely above LOMEM. The default setting of LOMEM means that variables, including DIM arrays are stored just above the program area). The variable code% will contain the address of the first reserved byte. The general form of an assembly listing will thus be:

```
100 DIM code% 100
110 FOR i%=0 TO 2 STEP 2
120    PROCass(code%, i%)
130 NEXT i%
140 END
1000 DEF PROCass(addr%, opt%)
1010 P%=addr%
1020 [      OPT opt%
1030        LDA #&FF
1040        \ And so on ...
1100        RTS
1110 ]
1120 ENDPROC
```

The FOR ... NEXT loop performs the two passes necessary to resolve forward references, as explained on pages 314 and 450 of the User Guide. The reason for putting the assembly part in a procedure of its own (apart from the fact that is a separate section of the program and should therefore be set aside) is that labels can be made local to the procedure. Thus if your assembly program has a label ".fin", declaring it as LOCAL means that any global variable called "fin" will not be interfered with. It would also be possible to make P% the first formal parameter of PROCass and omit line 1010. This would make the program counter local to the procedure, thus protecting the value of the static global variable P%.

As mentioned above, most grown-up assemblers provide many more pseudo-operation than OPT (which they don't have as the two passes are performed automatically). I will mention some of these here, and give their BBC assembler equivalents so that you can convert programs for other machines more easily. First though, a couple of notes about the syntax differences between the BBC and more standard assemblers. The most noticeable one is the way labels are introduced. This is usually done by following the name with a colon, rather than preceding it with a dot:

```
Usual      Label:     JSR outch
BBC        .label     JSR oswrch
```

The BBC's method makes it easier for the assembler to recognise the label, as it gives "advanced warning". The first (and more usual) method can only recognise the label in hindsight after the colon has been encountered. Another difference is the way comments are introduced; 99% of all known assemblers use a semicolon for this purpose. Why the BBC BASIC assembler uses a backslash is anyone's guess. The only other places ; appears is in the PRINT and VDU statements. Since these are not allowed during assembly sections, I can't see that using ;

would have caused a difficulty. It's probably a carry-over from the Atom assembler; Atom BASIC uses a ; to separate statements rather than the more usual colon.

The way the location (program) counter is represented varies. The most popular method is to use a fullstop to denote the current location. The fact that P% is used in the BBC assembler is a result of the close interaction between the BASIC and the assembler. Many assemblers use the pseudo-operation (or pseudo-op or assembler directive) ORG. This gives the first location to be used:

```
Usual      ORG  D00H
BBC        P%=&D00
```

Notice the different methods for denoting hex notation. Other assemblers use "$" or "£" in place of the BBC's "&". The assignment to P% occurs outside the BBC assembly part, i.e. in BASIC, whereas the concept of being "outside" the assembly part does not appear in dedicated assemblers, so the ORG would just appear as the first assembly instruction.

Tables appear fairly frequently in assembly language programs. For example, to implement an ON ... GOTO facility, a table of addresses must be provided. The simplest method is to reserve some space in the listing (usually at the beginning or right at the end). A common directive for performing this is "RMB", or Reserve Memory Bytes. This just leaves a given number of bytes free for later use by the machine code program. It is usual to remember the address of the memory bytes by placing a label there, as in:

```
table:     RMB 10      ; Reserve 10 bytes
```

which would translate into:

```
1000 .table    \ table of ten bytes:]
1010 P%=P%+10
1020 [         OPT opt%
1020           \ and so on...
```

Note that it is necessary to leave the assembler, skip ten bytes by adding ten to the program counter, then re-enter the assembler. Note also that OPT must be set each time the assembler is entered. The method above does not actually set-up the table; it simply reserves space in the program for it. A directive to set up values at assembly time is "FCB", which stands for Form Constant Byte, or just BYTE. To make a table of the powers of two you might use:

```
twos:      FCB 1,2,4,8,16,32,64,128
```

This would set the memory location "twos" to 1, "twos+1" to 2 and so on. The table might be used in the program by instructions such as "LDA twos,X". The BBC version of this would be:

```
1000 .twos     \ table of powers:]
1010 !P%=&08040201
```

```
1020 P%!4=&80402010
1030 P%=P%+8
1040 [        OPT opt%
1050          \ and so on...
```

A table of addresses can be set up with the FDB (Form Double Byte) or WORD directives. For example:

```
actions:   FDB imp,rel,abs,abx,aby,ind
```

where imp, rel, etc., are labels whose values are placed into the table starting at "actions". To jump to one of these addresses, the code:

```
jump:      \ calculate X
           LDA actions,X
           STA addr
           LDA actions+1,X
           STA addr+1
           JMP (addr)
```

could be used, where "addr" is the address of a couple of bytes that have been reserved already.

The BBC version of setting-up this table is a little more involved. There is no way of dealing directly with 16-bit values in BBC BASIC, only eight and 32 bits. It is probably easier to use ! rather than ?, thus:

```
1000 .actions   \table of action addresses:]
1010 !P%=imp: P%!2=rel
1020 P%!4=abs: P%!6=abx
1030 P%!8=aby: P%!10=ind
1040 P%=P%+12
1050 [        OPT opt%
1060          \ and so on
```

There are a couple of things to note. First, ! alters the value of four bytes, not just the two affected by the FDB operation. This is unimportant in the example above, as the upper two bytes are subsequently overwritten by the next assignment. However, if you are changing two bytes of a table which has already been set-up, you must ensure that ! doesn't corrupt (set to zero) the two bytes after the value of interest. For example, suppose there is a table of two-byte values between addresses table and table+9 and you wish to change the entry at table+2 and table+3. The simple assignment:

```
table!2=value
```

where "value" is the new value of that element, will cause the entry at table+4 and table+5 to be set to zero. This is because those two bytes form the most significant two bytes of the four bytes making up table!2. To avoid this side effect, use one of the forms:

```
table?2=value MOD 256: table?3=value DIV 256
```
or   `table!2=table!2 AND &FFFF0000 OR value`

The other thing to remember about the BBC version of the table set-up is that accessing the variables ind, imp, etc., will cause a "No such variable" error if the corresponding labels have not already been encountered. There are several solutions. Make all label variables LOCAL so that their values are initialised to zero before they are assigned by the assembler. The table set-up part could be left till the end of the assembly instructions, so that all labels will have been encountered (thus created) by the assembler. Another type of table that is often embedded in machine code programs is a table of characters, or a string. These are used to send messages to the user, such as error messages and input prompts. This is performed using the ASCII or FCC (Form Constant Characters) directives in some assemblers. The method of inserting error messages into BBC assembly programs is explained on page 446 of the User Guide. The program listed therein uses the BBC BASIC error message-generating facility, as used by the interpreter to give messages such as "No such line". This enables you to insert meaningful errors in machine code programs, which can be trapped by ON ERROR, and REPORTed as usual. This is very useful, but only suitable for generating error messages, not general prompts, as the BRK instruction (which is used to generate the message) causes BBC BASIC to stop execution of the current program. For input prompts this is obviously undesirable, so the ASCII string has to be used in some other way. The program below shows how a small "print string" routine can be incorporated into a machine code routine without stopping the program:

```
1000 DEF PROCass(addr%, opt%)
1010 P%=addr%
1020 [ OPT opt%:  .prompt:]
1030 $P%="How many? "
1040 P%=P%+LEN($P%)
1050 [ OPT opt%:  BRK
1060               \ Some code
1070               LDX #prompt MOD 256
1080               LDY #prompt DIV 256
1090               JSR print
1100               \ Some more code
1110               RTS
1200    .print     \ Print a string at XY
1210               STX &70
1220               STY &71
1230               LDY #0
1240    .prloop    LDA (&70),Y
```

```
1250                BEQ prret
1260                JSR &FFE3
1270                INY
1280                BNE prloop
1290     .prret     RTS
1300 ]
1310 ENPROC
```

The routine "print" expects the address of the first character to be in the X and Y registers (low byte, high byte, as is standard in the MOS). It then outputs this string a character at a time until a zero byte is reached. This marks the end of the string. The routine at &FFE3 is known as osasci, and it prints the character whose ASCII code is in the accumulator on the screen. If the character is a carriage-return (ASCII &0D), a line-feed is also generated. The prompt generated by the example above will not do a new-line at the end, as the &0D character is over-written by the BRK instruction. This could be changed by making line 1040:

```
1040 P%=P%+LEN($P%)+1
```

which would cause the zero generated by the BRK to be placed just after the &0D of the string.

There are some constants used in the program that would be better as named quantities rather than simple numbers. For example, the output routine at &FFE3 has the name osasci, and the two locations &70 and &71 could be named strptr (string pointer) and strptr+1. The ability to name constants in this manner is done by way of the EQU directive in most assemblers, though some use the more obvious "=" sign. Of course, constants can simply be defined as normal (though unchanging) variables in BASIC. The lines:

```
cassbuff    EQU     1000H
bufflen     EQU     100H
```

would translate into the assignments:

```
1210 cassbuff=&1000
1220 bufflen=&100
```

in BBC BASIC, though they must naturally occur before the first use of the names in the assembly program. This use of variables to name important locations and values cannot be over-emphasised. Remember that the powers of expression of assembly is very much less than even BASIC, i.e. it is rarely apparent from raw, uncommented code what the programmer is doing. There should be as many aids to the reader as possible in an assembly program Ironically, most assembly language programmers recognise this need much quicker than people using BASIC, so their programs are more readable than the equivalents in the so-called high-level language.

Advanced assemblers offer several other facilities which might be useful in certain applications on the BBC machine. One example is conditional assembly.

This means that certain instructions are assembled only if a condition is true. This is easily accomplished using the BASIC IF statement. The "one line" restriction of this statement means that it is very desirable to make the conditional code into a procedure of its own. For example, suppose a program is being debugged. It might be necessary to include some trace information in the assembly code so that when it is executed the contents of the 6502's registers are displayed. This extra code could be assembled conditional on some flag called "trace".

```
1000 DEF PROCass(addr%,opt%)
1010    P%=addr%
1020 [          OPT opt%
1030            \ Some instructions
1040            \ Print status if wanted
1050 ]
1060 IF trace THEN [OPT opt%: JSR tracecd:]
1070 [          OPT opt%
1080            \ Some more instructions
1090            \ Some more status information
1100 ]
1110 IF trace THEN [OPT opt%: JSR tracecd:]
1120 [          OPTopt%
1125            RTS
1130 ]
1140 IF trace THEN PROCtrace
1150 ENDPROC
1160
1170
2000 DEF PROCtrace
200  REM    Print trace stuff
2020 [ .tracecd OPT opt%
2030            PHA         \ Save A
2040            LDA #ASC("A")
2060            JSR oswrch
2070            LDA #ASC("=")
2080            JSR oswrch
2090            PLA
2100            PHA
2110            JSR hexout \ Prints hex of A then a space
2120            LDA #ASC("X") \ Now X-reg.
2130            JSR oswrch
2140            LDA #ASC("=")
2150            JSR oswrch
2160            TXA
```

```
2170            JSR hexout
2180            \ Similar stuff for Y and S
2190            PLA \ Restore A
2200            RTS
2210 ]
2220 ENDPROC
```

The code of traced and the calls to it are only assembled if the flag trace is TRUE. There is no reason why the ELSE part could not be used as well, so one set of instructions is assembled if a condition is true, and another if the condition is false. For a program using a lot of conditional assembly, see [Johnson-Davies], pp. 96–108. Using procedures in the assembler is useful for another "advanced" assembler facility – that of macro definitions. The terms macro and macroprocessor are used to describe a wide variety of programs which process text, notably in the substitution of some symbols for others. In the context of assemblers, a macro capability is when the programmer can define his own operations in terms of several normal machine instructions. These new instructions can then be used in the assembly program as normal; the assembler substitutes the actual machine instructions in their place. For example, one 6502 assembler uses the pseudo-ops ".MACRO" and ".ENDM" to start and finish the definition. Suppose we found that an application requires the contents of the X and Y registers to be swapped fairly frequently. It would be possible to define a macro to do this, then call the macro whenever needed, thus:

```
        .MACRO SWAPXY
        PHA       ; Save A
        TXA       ; Get X-reg.
        PHA       ; Save it
        TYA       ; Put Y in X
        TAX
        PLA       ; Restore Y
        TAY
        PLA       ; Restore A
        .ENDM
START:  LDA #0FFH ; Do some stuff
        ; Some stuff
        SWAPXY    ; A call to the macro
        ; Some more stuff
        SWAPXY    ; Another call to the macro
        ; Finish off
```

The lines between the ".MACRO" and ".ENDM" are not assembled to begin with; they are ignored. Once all the macros have been defined, the assembler gets to work on the actual code, starting in this example with the line labelled "START:". Then, the macro is called, simply by including the instruction

SWAPXY. When this is encountered, the assembler looks for the definition of SWAPXY, which it duly finds. The instructions of that macro are then assembled into the code, just as if all those instructions had been inserted into the assembly listing. This happens each time the SWAPXY macro is called. You can see a certain similarity between this facility and the subroutine calling mechanism. There is a very important difference; the instructions of the macro definition are inserted each time it is called during the assembly. A subroutine, on the other hand, is a separate piece of code which only appears once in the program.

The BBC BASIC Assembler version of the macro example above should prove very easy to write. Instead of boring you with this, I shall give an example of a slightly more sophisticated form – one with parameters. The macro definition above simply created a new instruction of the implied addressing mode type. However, most instructions take an operand, for example an address or immediate data. The program below incorporates a macro definition of an instruction NEG, which negates the byte specified by its operand address. The macro is defined as a BBC BASIC procedure, and the operand is simply the procedure's parameter.

```
1000 DEF PROCass(addr%, opt%)
1010 P%=addr%
1020 [       OPT opt%
1030         \ Some code
1100 ]
1110 PROCneg(&70)
1120 PROCneg(&71)
1130 [       OPT opt%
1140         \ Some more code
1150         RTS
1160 ]
1170 ENDPROC
1180
2000 DEF PROCneg(addr%)
2010 [       OPT opt%
2020         DEC addr%
2030         PHA
2040         LDA addr%
2050         EOR #&FF
2060         STA addr%
2070         PLA
2080 ]
2090 ENDPROC
```

Negating a number involves decrementing it then complementing it (e.g. the negation of &10 is NOT (&10 − 1) = NOT &0F = &F0). This is exactly what the instructions of PROCneg do with the contents of location addr%. One of the weaknesses of the procedure is that the assembled listing which is produced when opt% is set to 1 or 3 will trace all the instructions which make up the macro instruction NEG. It is more usual for macro assemblers to list just the macro instruction. This can be achieved by amending the procedure with the changes:

```
2005 LOCAL p%
2007 p%=P%
2010 [          OPT opt% AND 2
2090 IF (opt% AND 1)=0 THEN ENDPROC
2100 A%=p% DIV 256: CALL &8570
2110 A%=p%: CALL &856A
2120 A%=addr%: CALL &856A
2130 IF addr% AND &FF00 THEN A%=addr% DIV 256:CALL &856A ELSE PRINT
     SPC(3);
2140 PRINT "   NEG &";~addr%
2150 ENDPROC
```

These additions to PROCneg cause it to perform listing if required. The OPT operand at line 2010 is changed so that the error reporting action is preserved, but the listing is disabled whether opt% has its "list" bit set or not. The instructions which make up the macro are then assembled as usual. After that, the opt% value is examined. If bit 0 is not set (no listing required), the procedure returns. Otherwise, the address and operand bytes are printed in the same format as used by the assembler, viz. address (high), address (low), space, operand (low), space, operand (high, if needed), 1/4 spaces, mnemonic, operand. The two routines used to print the hex are at &8570 and &856A. These are the very routines used by the assembler itself. They both print the contents of the accumulator as two hex digits, the second one follows this by a space. The method of CALLing machine code routines is explained in detail in the next section. The output produced by the procedure PROCneg merges naturally with the usual assembler listing, as if a new instruction has been added to the microprocessor's instruction set. This is the way a macro facility should behave. Just as libraries of useful procedures can be built-up, so a collection of often-used macros can be assembled. Remember though that inserting a macro call is more costly in terms of storage than a JSR to a common routine.

5.2   The Interface

With such a powerful assembler facility, it is important that BBC BASIC should have a good interface with machine code routines, i.e. it should be easy to pass values to machine code routines and get results back. This is indeed the case, and the machine code/BASIC interface is implemented with the CALL statement and the USR functions. These are similar in some ways, but have their distinct uses, so I will describe them separately.

The CALL statement has the syntax:

```
CALL addr [, param]*
```

where addr is the address of the machine code to be executed, and the part in square brackets indicates an optional list of parameters separated with commas. CALL isn't at all fussy about where the program that it executes is, so it is possible to CALL useful routines in the BASIC ROM and the operating system ROM, as well as routines that have been assembled from BASIC. An example of the first use was given above in the macro procedure. Before CALL passes control to the machine code routine at addr, it performs several initialisation actions. The first is to set up the 6502's registers as follows. The A, X and Y registers are set-up with the least significant bytes of the variables A%, X% and Y% respectively, and the carry flag is set to the value of the least significant bit of the variable C%. This is the simplest way of passing values to the machine code routine. As mentioned above, the routine at &856A prints the hex representation of the accumulator's contents followed by a space. The short program below proves that the LSB of A% is transferred to the accumulator by CALL:

```
100 FOR A%=0 TO 255
110     CALL &856A
120 NEXT A%
130 PRINT
140 END
```

Another routine in the BASIC ROM which uses the accumulator's value is located at &B53A. This routine is used to output characters onto the screen by calling oswrch. However, if the ASCII code in the accumulator is greater than 127, it is treated as a BASIC token, and is expanded into its text form. For a list of the token values, see page 483 of the User Guide. This routine is used by LIST to expand the compacted form of program lines to the format in which they were entered. The program below prints the list of tokens, together with their English words:

```
100 FOR A%=128 TO 255
110     PRINT ~A%;TAB(20);
120     CALL &B53A
130 NEXT A%
140 END
```

It's advisable to do a CTRL-N before running the program, so that the list doesn't scroll by too quickly.

The passing of parameters in the registers is not restricted to ROM routines, and programs created with the BASIC assembler can use the facility in the same way. The program below is a "hex dump" routine. It prints out the contents of a block of memory in hex. The address of the first byte is held in the X and Y registers, and the number of bytes to be "dumped" is passed in the accumulator.

```
100 FOR o%=0 TO 2 STEP 2
110 PROCass(&D00,o%)
120 NEXT o%
130 REPEAT
135     CLS
140     INPUT TAB(0,5),"Start Address &" sa$
150     IF LEFT$(sa$,1) <> "&" THEN sa$="&"+sa$
160     sa%=EVAL(sa$) AND &FFFF
170     INPUT TAB(0,7),"No. of bytes ", nb%
180     A%=nb%: X%=sa%: Y%=sa% DIV 256
190     CALL &D00
200     INPUT'"Again (Y/N) ",yn$
210 UNTIL yn$="N" OR yn$="n"
220 END
230
240
1000 DEF PROCass(addr%,opt%)
1010 P%=addr%
1020 pointer=&70: count=&72
1030 oswrch=&FFEE: osnewl=&FFE7
1035 hexout=&856A: hexout1=&8570
1040 [       OPT opt%
1050         STA count      \ Save count
1060         LDA #0         \ Set-up pointer
1070         STA pointer
1080         STY pointer+1
1090         TXA            \ Y-reg. = LSB of pointer
1100         TAY
1110         AND #&07       \ Need first address?
1120         BEQ loop       \ No
1130         JSR print_add
1140 .loop   TYA            \ Need address?
1150         AND #&07
1160         BNE f1         \ No
1170         JSR print_add
1180 .f1     LDA (pointer),Y  \Get the byte
1190         JSR hexout     \ Print it
1200         INY            \ Next address
1210         BNE f2
1220         INC pointer+1
1230 .f2     DEC count
```

```
1240                 BNE loop        \ More
1250                 JSR osnewl      \ New Line
1260                 RTS
1270
1280
1290 .print_add      JSR osnewl      \ New Line
1300                 LDA pointer+1   \ High byte
1310                 JSR hexout1
1320                 TYA             \ Low byte
1330                 JSR hexout
1340                 LDA #ASC("-")   \ Print a dash
1350                 JSR oswrch
1360                 LDA #ASC(" ")
1370                 JSR oswrch
1380                 RTS
1390 ]
1400 ENDPROC
```

The operation is fairly straightforward. First the pointer to the next byte is set-up. This pointer is a bit like PAGE, in that only the more significant byte is actually used. The byte within page is accessed by the Y register. The address of each eight bytes is printed at the beginning of the line. If the first address is multiple of eight (address AND 7 = 0), then there is no need to print the "FFFF —" part, as this will be produced on entering the main loop. Notice that if A% (hence the accumulator) is zero, then the loop will be executed 256 times, not zero. This is a result of the test being made at the end of one cycle, rather than at the beginning. This is equivalent to a REPEAT, rather than a WHILE. Once the assembly language part has been assembled, it can be saved on cassette (*SAVE "DUMP.OBJ" D00+FF). PROCass can then be deleted and the first three lines of the program replaced with *LOAD "DUMP.OBJ". This saves a lot of space; the machine code is only 67 bytes long, as opposed to about 1200 bytes of source listing. There are several improvements that can be made if an 80 column mode is used to display the data. If the "AND #&07"s are changed to "AND #&0F", 16 values will fit on each line rather than just eight. Alternatively, you could print the character represented by the (printable) ASCII codes just after the hex representation. You would have to test for the value lying in the range 32 to 255 (or 126, if we are talking strictly of ASCII printing characters).

Using A%, X%, etc., to pass information to machine code routines is a little limiting. Firstly, only 24 bits of data can be transferred (eight bits in each of X, Y and the accumulator), and secondly the flow of data is strictly one way; information can only be passed back to BASIC via a common area of memory known to both the machine code and BASIC programs. This restriction is alleviated by the provision of the CALL statement to take parameters. These parameters are similar to those of user-defined procedures and functions, in that they allow

BASIC quantities to be passed to machine code. However, they differ in a very significant way. Whereas PROC and FN parameters are "call by value", CALL parameters are "call by address". The way the actual parameters are passed in procedures was discussed in Chapter two. To recap, the expression(s) in the PROC statement are evaluated, and these values assigned to the variables which are the formal parameters of the DEF PROC. Hence calls of the form "PROCabc(1,2) are permissible. This is what is meant by "call by value". Call by address uses what Pascal calls "variable parameters". When the routine is called, the address of the actual parameter is passed, not the value. This clearly means that the actual parameter has to be a variable, not an expression. When the statement CALL &D00,left% is executed, the variable left% is the actual parameter (of which there may be several) and &D00 is the address of the machine code being called. The address of left% is passed to the machine code via an area of memory known as the parameter block. This is situated at &600, and has the format shown on page 214 of the User Guide (which is different from the incorrect version shown in the Provisional User Guide). The CALL just given would result in the following:

Address	Value	Why?
&600	&01	There's one parameter
&601	&30	LSB of the address of left%
&602	&0F	MSB of the address of left%
&603	&04	left% is an integer variable

The actual address (&0F30 in this example) will naturally depend on the size of the program, value of LOMEM and other things. It always gives the address of the value of the variable cited as an actual parameter, except where this is a string. In this case, the address points to the first byte of the string information block for that variable. The format of this is also explained in the User Guide, albeit not very well. There are four bytes in this block. The first two bytes give the address of first character of the string proper. This is initially immediately after the string information block, but if the string grows, it is moved about in memory. The next two bytes of the SIB are the number of bytes allocated to the string, and its current length. The latter quantity is what is returned by the LEN function. The "bytes allocated" takes a bit more explaining. If the initial length of the string (when it is assigned to for the first time) is less than eight bytes, then the bytes allocated is simply the length of the string. So A$="123" would cause both the length and bytes allocated parts of the SIB for A$ to be set to 3. However, if the length of A$ were initially greater than 7, then the bytes allocated would be set to eight greater than this initial length. This means that A$="12345678" would have the length set to 8, but the bytes allocated set to 16. The extra eight bytes are at the end of the string, and are present so that the string can grow a bit without BASIC having to move it to another part of the memory. This moving is necessary because the variables are stored end on end from LOMEM up. The two assignments A$="123" and A=1 would cause the three bytes of A$ to be followed immediately by entry for A. If A$ grows, it must be moved to after the A entry to avoid the latter being overwritten. The extra allocation of eight bytes for strings of eight or more characters means that this time consuming shifting of strings doesn't have to be carried out so often. As a general hint, if you envisage much appending of strings in the program, make the initial string lengths as long as possible.

The foregoing is quite complex, so some examples are in order. The one below simply prints all the information relating to the string given as a parameter when it is called.

```
100 REM    String Dump Program
110 FOR o%=0 TO 3 STEP 3
120     PROCass(&D00,o%)
130 NEXT o%
140 END
1000 DEF PROCass(addr%,opt%)
1010
1020 REM    Set-up the prompts
1030 P%=addr%
1040 p1=P%
1050 $P%="SIB at:    &"+CHR$(0)
1060 P%=P%+LEN($P%)
1070 p2=P%
1080 $P%="Text at:    &"+CHR$(0)
1090 P%=P%+LEN($P%)
1100 p3=P%
1110 $P%="Length is: &"+CHR$(0)
1120 P%=P%+LEN($P%)
1130 p4=P%
1140 $P%="Allocated: &"+CHR$(0)
1150 P%=P%+LEN($P%)
1160 p5=P%
1170 $P%="Text is:    "+CHR$(0)
1180 P%=P%+LEN($P%)
1190
1200 REM    Set-up various locations
1210 oswrch=&FFEE: osnewl=&FFE7: hexout=&8570
1220 par_blk=&600
1230 sib=&70: txt_add=&72: len=&74
1240 txt_ptr=&80
1250 [ .str       OPT opt%
1260               LDA par_blk
1270               CMP #1      \ One parameter?
```

```
1280               BEQ ok         \ Yes
1290    .err       BRK            \ No, print error
1300 ]
1310 ?P%=31: $(P%+1)="STR arguments"
1320 P%=P%+LEN($(P%+1))+1
1330 [ OPT opt%:   BRK
1340    .ok        LDA par_blk+3
1350               CMP #129       \ String parameter?
1360               BNE err        \ No
1370               LDA par_blk+1  \ Get SIB address
1380               STA sib
1390               LDA par_blk+2
1400               STA sib+1
1410               LDX #p1 MOD 256   \ Print first prompt
1420               LDY #p1 DIV 256
1430               JSR print
1440               LDA sib+1      \ Print SIB high
1450               JSR hexout
1460               LDA sib        \ Print SIB low
1470               JSR hexout
1480               JSR osnewl
1490               LDX #p2 MOD 256   \ Print second prompt
1500               LDY #p2 DIV 256
1510               JSR print
1520               LDY #1         \ Print text address
1530               LDA (sib),Y
1540               STA txt_add+1  \ Save for later
1550               JSR hexout
1560               DEY
1570               LDA (sib),Y
1580               STA txt_add
1590               JSR hexout
1600               JSR osnewl
1610               LDX #p3 MOD 256   \ Print third prompt
1620               LDY #p3 DIV 256
1630               JSR print
1640               LDY #3         \ Print string LEN
1650               LDA (sib),Y
1660               STA len        \ Save for later
1670               JSR hexout
1680               JSR osnewl
1690               LDX #p4 MOD 256   \ Print fourth prompt
```

```
1700              LDY #p4 DIV 256
1710              JSR print
1720              LDY #2          \ Print bytes allocated
1730              LDA (sib),Y
1740              JSR hexout
1750              JSR osnewl
1760              LDX #p5 MOD 256 \ Print fifth prompt
1770              LDY #p5 DIV 256
1780              JSR print
1785              JSR osnewl
1790              LDX len         \ Print the text
1800              BEQ ret
1810              LDY #0
1820  .loop       LDA (txt_add),Y
1830              JSR oswrch
1840              INY
1850              DEX
1860              BNE loop
1870              JSR osnewl
1880  .ret        RTS
1890
1900
1910  .print      STX txt_ptr \ Save prompt address
1920              STY txt_ptr+1
1930              LDY #0
1940  .prloop     LDA (txt_ptr),Y
1950              BEQ prret    \ End of string marker?
1960              JSR oswrch
1970              INY
1980              BNE prloop
1990  .prret      RTS
2000  ]
2010 ENDPROC
```

In BASIC, the program would just be a series of PRINT statements. However, before the information could be PRINTed, the SIB of the string in question would have to be found. This is done for us by BASIC when using CALL. First the parameter block is checked to see that there was only one parameter specified and that this was a string variable. The address of the SIB (held at locations parblk + 1 and parblk + 2) is transferred into a couple of zero page locations (sib and sib + 1) so that the indirect indexed addressing mode may be used to examine its contents. After that, the five messages are printed followed by the relevant information. Once again, the BASIC routine at &8570 is used to output the addresses in hex.

The only other subroutines used are the operating system calls oswrch and osnewl and the subroutine at "print" which has been described before. The whole program will just fit in 256 bytes, so I have used the spare page at &D00 to hold it. Once the routine has been assembled, it can be used with the call "CALL str,a$", where a$ naturally stands for any string variable name. To see the results of string assignments, you could define a function key as the string above (followed by |M), then assign the string a$. The effect of making it longer and shorter (using + and the functions such as MID$ respectively) can be seen by the changes in LEN, and possibly the text address and bytes allocated (if you make it longer than the current allocated length, the text will be moved and the allocated length changed to the new length plus eight).

Remember that the execution address of the code is not the same as the start address (&D00 above). It depends on the length of the prompt strings. The program as listed has the first four as 13 characters each and the fifth as 12 characters, giving a total of 64. This makes the start address (the value of str) &D40. You will need to remember this if str is deleted (by a NEW, CLEAR or amendment of the program). To obviate the necessity of remembering str, you could add the single instruction:

```
JMP str
```

at the very beginning, before the prompt strings are defined. This would of course be situated at &D00, so the CALL address would be easy to remember. Another alternative is to move the string assignments to the end of the code.

The next example shows how the argument variables specified in the CALL statement can be manipulated, i.e. changed, which is the thing that differentiates them from procedures' "value" parameters. It is possible to do all the manipulation of variables in situ, i.e. at the address given in the parameter block. However, this is inconvenient for string and real parameters, in the former case because of the need to reposition the string if its length is increased to greater than its current allocation, and in the latter because real variables are stored in a compact (five byte) form which is difficult to manipulate. The best way to deal with parameters is to transfer the values into "buffer" areas, where they can be handled conveniently, then replace them. Both these operations are carried out by a couple of BASIC interpreter routines which are called pack and unpack. Their use is summarised later for the various variable types, but by way of illustration the program below incorporates the unpacking of a string variable and the packing (assignment) of an integer. The program takes a string variable whose characters are all either "0" or "1". This is treated as a binary number, and its value is converted into a binary value. This is stored in the other parameter, which is an integer. The sequence below shows how the program would be CALLed:

```
10 A$="10101"
20 CALL btd,Q%,A$
30 PRINT A$;"=";Q%
40 END
```

"btd"stands for binary to decimal. The program above assumes the machine code has been assembled, and that the variable btd still exists. The listing is given below:

```
100 REM   Binary to Decimal
110 FOR o%=0 TO 2 STEP 2
120     PROCass(&D00,o%)
130 NEXT o%
140 END
150
1000
1010 DEF PROCass(addr%,opt%)
1020
1030 REM Set-up the locations
1040 par_blk=&600: iac=&2A
1050 int_ptr=&37: int_add=&70:sib_add=&72
1060 str_len=&74: type=&27
1070 unpack=&B35B: pack=&B4E3
1080 P%=addr%
1090 [       OPT opt%
1100 .btd    LDA par_blk    \ Check no. of parameters
1110         CMP #2
1120         BEQ ok
1130 .err    BRK
1140 ]
1150 ?P%=33: $(P%+1)="BTD arguments"
1160 P%=P%+LEN($(P%+1))+1
1170 [       OPT opt%
1180         BRK
1190 .ok     LDA par_blk+3  \ Check types
1200         CMP #4
1210         BNE err
1220         LDA par_blk+6
1230         CMP #129
1240         BNE err
1250         STA iac+2      \ Set-up string transfer
1260         LDA par_blk+4
1270         STA iac        \ Save string's address
1280         STA sib_add
1290         LDA par_blk+5
1300         STA iac+1
1310         STA sib_add+1
1320         LDA par_blk+1  \ Save integer's address
```

```
1330            STA int_add
1340            LDA par_blk+2
1350            STA int_add+1
1360            JSR unpack       \ Transfer string to &600
1370            LDY #3           \ Get string LEN
1380            LDA (sib_add),Y
1390            STA str_len
1400            LDY #0
1410            STY iac          \ Zero the result
1420            STY iac+1
1430            STY iac+2
1440            STY iac+3
1450 .loop      LDA par_blk,Y    \ Do conversion
1460            CMP #ASC("1")
1470            BEQ f1
1480            CMP #ASC("0")    \ Must be a 0 if not a 1
1490            BNE err1
1500            CLC
1510 .f1        ROL iac          \ Shift this bit in
1520            ROL iac+1
1530            ROL iac+2
1540            ROL iac+3
1550            INY
1560            CPY str_len
1570            BNE loop
1580            LDA int_add      \ Set-up integer packing
1590            STA int_ptr
1600            LDA int_add+1
1610            STA int_ptr+1
1620            LDA #4
1630            STA type
1640            STA int_ptr+2
1650            JSR pack         \ Save result
1660            RTS
1670
1680 .err1      BRK
1690 ]
1700 ?P%=28: $(P%+1)="Bad BINARY"
1710 P%=P%+LEN($(P%+1))+1
1720 [        OPT opt%
1730            BRK
```

```
1740 ]
1750 ENDPROC
```

There are four parts to the program. The first checks the parameter types, and that there are exactly two of them. Then the string has its text moved to the string buffer, which is located at &600. Since this is the same place as the parameter block, some of the parameter information has to be transferred to a safe place before it is overwritten by the string's characters. This includes the string's information block address, which is used to find the string's length, and the address of the integer, which is used later. When the important values at &600 have been saved, the routine to unpack the string there can be called. This needs some initialisation. The address of the SIB and string type must be stored in the first three bytes of BASIC's integer accumulator. This is a block of 32 bits stored at locations &2A to &2D which is used for almost anything concerning integers in BASIC. It is also used as the mini parameter block for the unpacking routine. Once it has been set-up, the routine, which is at &B35B, is called. This causes the text of the parameter string to be unpacked to &600 on, where it can be used as required.

Once the string is in place it can be used for processing. First, the numerical representation of the string, which is held in the four bytes of the integer accumulator (iac to iac+3) must be zeroed. The main loop of the program is very simple. Each character is checked, starting from the leftmost one, which is the most significant bit of the binary number. The character is first compared with "1". If it is equal, the carry bit will be set (this reflects the fact that no borrow was required in the imaginary subtraction which CMP performs). This is the desired state, so a branch is made directly to the shift part. If the character was not "1", it should be "0". This is checked by the second CMP. If it isn't a "0", the string contains an illegal character. This is duly reported by branching to the routine at err1. If the character was a "0", the carry will be set for the same reason given above. This is the opposite to what is required, so it is cleared by the CLC. The four ROL instructions shift the integer accumlator to the left by one bit. In the process, the current value of the carry flag is shifted into the lsb of the number. The Y register is incremented to point to the next character of the string, and then tested with the saved string length. If these are equal, all the characters have been used. (The string starts with Y at 0, so the last character is LEN−1.)

The fourth part is writing the value back to the integer variable. This is done with the pack procedure at &B4E3. Again, the procedure must be entered after some initialisation has been done. The address of the destination variable and its type are stored in the three locations &37 to &39. The value to be transferred must have its type stored in location &27. These are both "integer" in the current example, i.e. type 4. The JSR &B4E3 can then be made, and the contents of the integer accumulator are then transferred to the appropriate variable.

The pack and unpack operations have slight variations, depending on the types being moved. The unpack operation moves the contents of a variable to one of the accumulators (there is a floating-point accumulator as well) or the string buffer as appropriate. The entry conditions for the unpack routine and its effect is summarised below:

Type to unpack	&2A, &2B, &2C contain		Destination
String e.g. A$	Address,	129 (&81)	&600...
String e.g. $a%	Address,	128 (&80)	&600...
Integer e.g. a%	Address,	4 (&04)	&2A-2D
Byte e.g. ?a%	Address,	0 (&00)	&2A-2D
Real e.g. a	Address,	5 (&05)	&2E-&35

In all cases, the three bytes &2A–&2C are set to the three parameter block bytes, in the same order. Some notes on the destinations: for string variables (type 129), the bytes in the buffer are an exact copy of the current LEN bytes of the string, with no terminator. You must look at the SIB to find the string's length. For "byte strings" (type 128), the last character transferred is the &0D (RETURN) byte, so the end of the string can be detected by a CMP #&D. For integers, (a% or !a%, type 4), the integer accumulator is simply a direct copy of the variable's value bytes. &2A is the least significant byte, &2D the most significant. For bytes (type 0), only &2A is used, the other three bytes being set to zero. Real numbers have their own accumulator (two, in fact). When stored as variables, real numbers are five bytes longs. These are the exponent byte (similar to the number after the E in 12.34E11, except in binary), and four mantissa bytes (the 12.34 part). When unpacked, the representation is changed to an eight-byte one, to facilitate the various operations that can be performed on reals. The unpacking routine puts this representation in the first floating-point (real) accumulator, fac1, which is at &2E to &35. Since performing operations on floating point numbers is a tedious business, I give a list of useful routines in the BASIC ROM. This should be sufficient for most purposes. The first group acts on either one or both of the floating point accumulators, so these routines do not require any setting-up before being called. The secondary floating point accumulator lives at locations &3B to &42.

Routines which act on fac1 and/or fac2

Operation	Address
fac1=10*fac1	&A1E5
fac1=fac1/10	&A23E
fac1=0	&A691
fac1=1	&A6A4
fac1=1/fac1	&A6B0
fac1=-fac1	&ADA0
fac1=VAL($&600) &36 holds the string LEN	&AC5A
Set status flags to sign of fac1	&A1CB
Normalise fac1	&A2F4
Round fac1	&A3D8

```
Test fac1 for over/undeflow                              &A68B
fac1=SQR(fac1)                                           &A7B7
fac1=ABS(fac1) LDA #&FF before call                      &AD90
fac1=ASN(fac1)                                           &A8CF
fac1=ATN(fac1)                                           &A90A
fac1=COS(fac1)                                           &A98C
fac1=SIN(fac1)                                           &A997
fac1=TAN(fac1)                                           &A6CC
fac1=DEG(fac1)                                           &ABEA
fac1=RAD(fac1)                                           &ABD9
fac1=EVAL($&600) if Acc.<0 on exit. &36 = LEN            &AC17
fac1=EXP(fac1)                                           &AAB7
fac1=LN(fac1)                                            &A807
fac1=PI                                                  &ABF0
```

The three routines which normalise, round and test fac1 should always be called (in that order) before the assignment is made to a variable. The reason the accumulator must be loaded with &FF before ABS is called is to tell BASIC to expect the argument of the function in fac1, rather than iac. &FF is used for real, &40 for integer and &00 for string values. Some functions (e.g. EVAL) exit with the accumulator set to one of these values to tell the calling routine where the result is located. The table below gives the addresses of some routines which pack and unpack real variables into the floating point accumulators, and also some arithmetic ones. In all case, the address of the variable involved must be placed in the bytes &4B and &4C.

```
Operation                                   Address

fac1=var                                    &A3A6
fac2=var                                    &A33F
var=fac1                                    &A37E
Swap var and fac1                           &A4DE
fac1=var/fac1                               &A6B8
fac1=fac1/var                               &A6F2
```

The next set of routines works on one or both of fac1 and iac.

```
Operation                                   Address

iac=INT(fac1)                               &ACA5
iac=FALSE (zero)                            &AEF9
iac=TRUE  (-1)                              &ACEA
iac=NOT iac                                 &ACFA
iac=-iac                                    &ADB5
iac=&000000ac, ac=contents of accumulator   &AF07
```

```
iac=&0000yrac, yr=contents of Y register              &AF19
fac1=iac                                              &A2AF
Print iac AND &FFFF  (Print width zero, five)         &98F1, &98F5
Assign value to integer variable:
     &37,&38 = Address of var. &39=&04
     &27=&FF to save fac1, &40 to save iac.    JSR  &B4E3
Assign value to real variable:
     &37,&38 = Address of var. &39=&05
     &27=&FF to save fac1, &40 to save iac.    JSR  &B4E3
Assign value to string variable:
     &2A,&2B = Address of SIB. &36 = LEN of string
                                               JSR  &8BD3
```

The lists above should be sufficient for most people's needs. You can examine the routines in detail by using the disassembler which is listed later. When compiling the list, I noticed something about the code for STR$ which I've never seen documented. If the function name is followed immediately by "~", the string returned is in hex, e.g. A$=STR$~(1234) would set A$ to "4D2".

To conclude this section on CALL parameters, I give another example which uses some of BASIC's internal routines. The program is a string finding program; it is CALLed with a single string parameter containing the string to be looked for. The program text is searched, and wherever the string is encountered, the line number is printed. To understand how the program works, it is necessary to know the way in which programs are stored inside the computer. The format is shown in Figure 5.1.

All the reserved words are stored in a tokenised form, i.e. compacted into a one-byte representation. This means that the search program cannot find reserved words, only things such as variable and procedure names, literal strings and

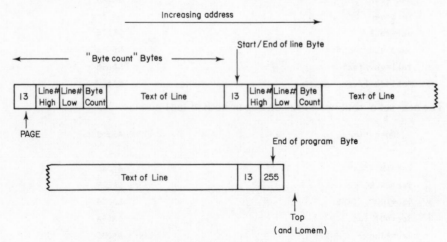

Figure 5.1   Internal Representation of a BASIC Program

numeric constants, and assembly language mnemonics. The search starts from the location pointed to by PAGE. This is always a &0D byte. There are three information bytes, consisting of the line number (stored, unusually in high- then low-byte format) and the length of the line. All of these are used by FIND. The line number is stored in the lower two bytes of iac, where it is used by outline. This routine is the one used by LIST. It precedes the line number proper by enough spaces to make the total number of characters 5. After the main loop has checked for the &FF byte which follows the last end of line marker, and reset the found flag, the inner loop is entered. This consists of checking at each character in the line to see if the string can be matched. This matching is performed by the subroutine cmp. It returns with the zero flag set if a match was made, reset otherwise. If there is a match, the line number is printed if it is the first time for the present line. When six line numbers have been printed, a new line is generated. Notice that all the output from the program is done via BASIC's own routines. These update COUNT automatically. If the BASIC routines were not used, the same effect could be achieved by finding the horizontal cursor position with an osbyte call (see later). At the end of each line, txt_ptr is updated to point to the start of the next line. A branch is then made to the beginning of the main loop. At the last line, a new-line is printed to ensure that the program stops on a fresh line.

After the program has been assembled (into the usual &D00 location), *KEY9 is defined to make its use a little easier. While having "address" parameters is useful, it is tedious to always have to define a variable before the routine can be called. That is, it would be nice to be able to say 'CALL &D00,"Fred"', rather than 'A$="Fred":CALL & D00,A$'. Defining a function key in the manner shown in the program, the drudgery is taken out of using CALLs in immediate mode. A final BASIC routine worthy of note is ESCAPE detection one at &9834. When called, this looks to see if the user has pressed ESCAPE. If he has, the program aborts with the usual message (or is trapped by an ON ERROR statement). Otherwise, the routine returns to the calling program with registers intact. The program is listed below.

```
100 FOR o%=0 TO 2 STEP 2
110    PROCass(&D00, o%)
120 NEXT o%
130 *KEY9INPUT'''"Find ",f$:CALL &D00,f$|M
140 END
150
160
1000 DEF PROCass(addr%,opt%)
1010 REM BASIC routines used
1020 outline=&98F5: unpack=&B35B
1030 outspace=&B57B: newl=&BC42
1040 escape=&9834
1050 REM BASIC variables used
```

```
1060 page=&18: count=&1E
1070 par_blk=&600: iac=&2A
1080 REM Zero page locations
1090 txt_ptr=&70: str_len=&72
1100 flag=&73: lin_len=&74
1110 P%=addr%
1120 [         OPT opt%
1130 .find     DEC par_blk    \ Check the parameter
1140           BEQ ok
1150 .err      BRK
1160 ]
1170 ?P%=33: $(P%+1)="FIND arguments"
1180 P%=P%+LEN($(P%+1))+1
1190 [         OPT opt%
1200           BRK
1210 .ok       LDA par_blk+3
1220           CMP #129       \ Make sure its a string
1230           BNE err
1240           STA iac+2       \ Save type for unpacking
1250           LDA par_blk+1  \ Save SIB address
1260           STA iac
1270           LDA par_blk+2
1280           STA iac+1
1290           LDY #3
1300           LDA (iac),Y     \ Get LEN from SIB
1310           STA str_len
1320           JSR unpack
1330           LDY #0          \ Set pointer to PAGE
1340           STY txt_ptr
1350           LDY page
1360           STY txt_ptr+1
1370 .line     JSR escape      \ Main loop; check for ESCAPE
1380           LDY #0
1390           STY flag        \ Already found flag
1400           INY
1410           LDA (txt_ptr),Y \ Get hi byte of line number
1420           BMI ret         \ &FF if lst line of program
1430           STA iac+1       \ Save line number for outline in iac
1440           INY
1450           LDA (txt_ptr),Y
1460           STA iac
1470           INY
```

```
1480              LDA (txt_ptr),Y    \ Get length of this line
1490              STA lin_len
1500              INY
1510 .loop        JSR cmp            \ Loop for each line; compare strings
1520              BNE next
1530              INC flag           \ See if it's already been found on this line
1540              BEQ done
1550              DEC flag           \ No. Set the flag
1560              JSR outline        \ Print the line number
1570              JSR outspace
1580              LDA count          \ Need a new line?
1590              CMP #35
1600              BCC done
1610              JSR newl
1620 .done        DEC flag
1630 .next        INY               \ Move onto the next byte
1640              CPY lin_len        \ End of this line?
1650              BNE loop           \ No, keep on trying
1660              CLC                \ Update pointer to new line
1670              LDA txt_ptr
1680              ADC lin_len
1690              STA txt_ptr
1700              BCC line           \ And do it all again
1710              INC txt_ptr+1
1720              BCS line
1730 .ret         JSR newl           \ Get onto a new line
1740              RTS
1750
1760
1770 .cmp         LDX #0             \ Match parameter string with line
1780              TYA
1790              PHA
1800 .cmplp       LDA par_blk,X
1810              CMP (txt_ptr),Y
1820              BNE cmpret         \ No match, so return
1830              INY
1840              INX
1850              CPX str_len        \ End of match string?
1860              BNE cmplp          \ No, carry on
1870              PLA                \ Got a match. Return with zero set
1880              DEY
1890              LDA #0
```

```
1900           RTS
1910 .cmpret   PLA              \ Unsuccessful try. Zero flag reset
1920           TAY
1930           RTS
1940 ]
1950 ENDPROC
```

The other way of accessing machine code from BASIC mentioned above was USR. This is a function and therefore returns a value. The value is an integer and is formed from the contents of the 6502's registers when the RTS handing control back to BASIC was executed. There are no parameters for USR; it has the form

```
10 var%=USR(addr%)
```

As usual the brackets are optional, but it is good style to include them. The values of A%, X%, Y% and C% are used to initialise the registers in a manner identical to that when CALL is used. The value returned by USR is arranged thus:

```
Byte 0 (LSB)   Accumulator
Byte 1         X register
Byte 2         Y register
Byte 4         Processor status
```

These four bytes can be "masked-off" by use of the AND statement and the divide operator. An example of this is shown on page 432 of the User Guide. USR is of limited utility because of its lack of parameters. The use given in the Guide of reading the results of osbyte calls seems to be the most important one. For completeness I include a program here that might be useful in some circumstances. It returns in XY the address of the first occurrence in memory of a particular value. The start address of the search is specified by XY on entry, and the byte to look for is in the accumulator.

```
100 FOR o%=0 TO 2 STEP 2
110     PROCass(&D00,o%)
120 NEXT o%
130 addr%=PAGE
140 A%=13
150 REPEAT
160     X%=addr% MOD 256
170     Y%=addr% DIV 256
180     new_addr%=(USR(&D00) AND &FFFF00) DIV 256 + 1
190     PRINT new_addr%-addr%;
200     addr%=new_addr%
210 UNTIL ?addr%=&FF
220 PRINT
```

```
 230 END
 240
 250
1000 DEF PROCass(addr%,opt%)
1010 ptr=&70
1020 P%=addr%
1030 [       OPT opt%
1040         STY ptr+1     \ Save high address
1050         PHA           \ Remember search byte
1060         TXA           \ Low address in Y reg.
1070         TAY
1080         LDA #0        \ Low ptr is always zero
1090         STA ptr
1100         PLA           \ Retrieve search byte
1110 .loop   CMP (ptr),Y   \ Found it?
1120         BEQ ret       \ Yes
1130         INY           \ No; try next byte
1140         BNE loop
1150         INC ptr+1
1160         BNE loop
1170         BEQ loop      \ Wraps round at &FFFF
1180 .ret    TYA           \ Address low in X reg
1190         TAX
1200         LDY ptr+1     \ Address high in Y reg
1210         RTS
1220 ]
1230 ENDPROC
```

The program uses the function to calculate the length of each line in the BASIC program. Starting from PAGE, the function finds the next occurrence of the end of line character (13 or &D). The start address is then updated to the byte after the &D one. If this is &FF, the last line has been reached and the program ends. Notice that the &D byte at PAGE is effectively a null line which is always present, even after a NEW. This enables REPEAT to be used (whose equivalent in machine code is shorter then a WHILE loop).

Another use for the routine above would be to look for particular machine code instructions. For example, JSR is the byte &20. A program could be written using the USR function just described to list the addresses of all suspected JSRs in a piece of machine code. They would have to be "suspected", as some of the &20 values might be data, as in "LDA &20".

The next section in this chapter is a collection of programs which use most of the points already mentioned, and introduce some other ideas, e.g. interaction with the MOS at machine code level.

5.3   Some Egg Samples

The previous section discussed CALL and USR with a few example programs. The diversity of uses of machine code sections in BASIC makes it impossible to catalogue each one individually. Instead, I give a few more examples in this section which should serve to illustrate some of the possibilities. The examples of the last section contained references to BASIC internal routines, and also accessed the i/o processor's (i.e. the BBC Computer's) memory directly. Both these would be regarded as bad practice by purists, as such programs would not work on second processors connected via the Tube. I am unrepentant, though, as MOS 0.1 (which I am currently restricted to using) does not support the Read/Write i/o processor memory options of osword. Accessing the computer's memory directly (whether it be by the ? and ! operators of BASIC, or assembly language instructions such as LDA) should cause no real problems if the locations accessed are either used solely by the user's program (such as the locations &70–&8F used for storing temporary values and addresses), or you are absolutely sure the program will never be used outside of the BBC Computer proper

All programs should take advantage of the MOS routines which are provided (if they have been implemented on your version). They save a lot of effort for the machine code programmer who wants to use the graphics capabilities of the machine from assembly programs. There are also many other useful routines, such as inputting a whole line of text from the keyboard, and reading/writing the built-in clock. All these routines are well documented in the User Guide, so I will not repeat the explanations here. The most useful of the MOS routines are oswrch, osrdch (which BASIC calls VDU and GET), osbyte (*FX to BASIC) and osword (no direct access is provided from BASIC, but it is used by TIME, POINT & others). The filing commands are less likely to be used from machine code, unless the machine code program happens to be a high level language or similar program which requires its own set of filing commands. Oscli would find similar uses. The four main routines mentioned above are all illustrated below. In addition to using the MOS routines, it is also possible to "intercept" them. This is a result of the way MOS keeps the addresses of the routines in RAM so that they can be changed by the user. This is quite a powerful facility. For example, if you are unhappy with the way the MOS draws lines, or clips them against the graphics window, it is possible to redirect the oswrch routine so that you can check for the PLOT command (VDU 25). When such a command is executed, if the PLOT option which follows is a line drawing one, you could stop the command reaching the MOS, and invoke your own plotting routine. It is highly unlikely that anyone would be so disgusted with the (rather inefficient) clipping routine in the MOS that they substituted it with their own. Nevertheless, oswrch is the most likely routine whose calls will be intercepted. This is a pity, as it is also the hardest to intercept due to the way many of the control codes are followed by parameter bytes (again, PLOT is a good example. The command code 25 is followed by five parameter bytes). The presence of these extra bytes means that the user's oswrch program must keep track of how many control bytes are needed to complete the current command. If it doesn't, it may detect spurious characters which are actually part of control code sequences (see page 457 of the User Guide).

The first example was promised in Chapter three. It is a machine code version of the routine to print character definitions as very large characters. It uses MOS routines oswrch, osnewl and osword. Oswrch is, as mentioned before, the routine used by VDU, and ultimately all other commands affecting the screen. The BASIC statements "PRINT CHR$(c%);" and "VDU c%" translate into the instructions "LDA #c%: JSR oswrch", where "oswrch" has been set to &FFEE. Similarly, "VDU d%;" becomes the sequence:

```
LDA #d% MOD 256
JSR oswrch
LDA #d% DIV 256
JSR oswrch
```

Since the graphics commands are simply forms of VDU, they can be translated with similar ease. The relevant example here is COLOUR c%, which in its VDU form is VDU 17,c%. The variable c% represents the foreground or background colour, depending on whether its value is less than or greater/equal to 128. The assembly language version of COLOUR is therefore:

```
LDA #17    \ COLOUR
JSR oswrch
LDA #c%    \ parameter
JSR oswrch
```

The osword call is used to obtain the character pattern. In order that the routine can be used as a direct replacement for PROCshow given earlier, the meanings of the static variables A%, X% and Y% have been kept the same, i.e. A% must be 10 and X%+256*Y% must be the address of the nine-byte buffer when the routine is called. This way, the machine code can be used with a minimum of alterations to the BASIC. In particular, PROCshow can be deleted (lines 5000–5150) and line 4180 changed to "CALL &D00, cx%,cy%". It is obviously wasteful to have the source program below in the character definer, so once it has been run, save the machine code with '*SAVE "show" D00 + 100'. It can then be loaded from the BASIC program by '*LOAD "show"'

```
100 FOR o%=0 TO 2 STEP 2
110     PROCass(&D00,o%)
120 NEXT o%
130 REM  Set-up registers for osword
140 A%=10:  X%=P% MOD 256:  Y%=P% DIV 256
150 REM  Cursor address
160 cx%=4:  cy%=4
170 REPEAT
180     ?P%=GET
```

```
 190    CALL &D00, cx%, cy%
 200 UNTIL FALSE
 210 END
 220
 230
1000 DEF PROCass(addr%, opt%)
1010 REM   Assembly language character printer
1020 REM   Define the important addresses
1030 oswrch=&FFEE: osword=&FFF1: osnewl=&FFE7
1040 par_blk=&600
1050 colour=17: set_cols=20: home=30
1060 cx=&70: cy=&71: cx_ptr=&72: cy_ptr=&74
1070 inv_flg=&76: byte=&77: buff=&78
1080 P%=addr%
1090 [        OPT opt%
1100          \   Assumes A, X and Y set-up for osword
1110          \   See page 462 of User Guide
1120          STX buff            \ Save buffer address
1130          STY buff+1
1140          JSR osword          \ Get the character definition
1150          JSR params          \ Get cx and cy
1160          LDA #home           \ Move cursor to top of page
1170          JSR oswrch
1180          JSR osnewl          \ Then two lines down
1190          JSR osnewl
1200          LDY #1              \ FOR row=1 TO 8
1210 .rowloop LDA #0              \ Reset Inverse flag
1220          STA inv_flg
1230          LDA (buff),Y        \ Get this row's byte
1240          STA byte
1250          LDX #0              \ FOR column=0 TO 7
1260 .colloop CPX cx             \ Check cursor position
1270          BNE f1
1280          CPY cy
1290          BNE f1
1300          JSR inv             \ We're at the cursor. Inverse text
1310 .f1      ROL byte            \ Get this column's bit
1320          LDA #ASC(" ")       \ Get space char.
1330          BCC f3              \ 0 bit; keep as a space
1340          ADC #ASC("*")-ASC(" ")-1 \ Convert to a *
1350 .f3      JSR oswrch          \ Print the character
1360          BIT inv_flg         \ Are we at the cursor?
```

```
1370              BPL f2                  \ No
1380              JSR norm                \ Yes. Normal text & reset the flag
1390 .f2          INX                     \ Next column
1400              CPX #8
1410              BNE colloop
1420              JSR osnewl              \ End of column. Newline & check row
1430              INY
1440              CPY #9
1450              BNE rowloop
1460              RTS                     \ All done
1470
1480
1490 .inv         LDA #colour             \ Invert text colours
1500              JSR oswrch
1510              LDA #129
1520              JSR oswrch
1530              LDA #colour
1540              JSR oswrch
1550              LDA #0
1560              JSR oswrch
1570              DEC inv_flg             \ And set inverse flag
1580              RTS
1590
1600 .norm        LDA #set_cols           \ Normal colours
1610              JSR oswrch
1620              INC inv_flg             \ And reset flag
1630              RTS
1640
1650
1660 .params      LDA par_blk             \ Check the parameters
1670              CMP #2
1680              BEQ show_ok
1690 .show_err    BRK                     \ Parameter error
1700 ]
1710 ?P%=&FF: $(P%+1)="SHOW parameters"
1720 P%=P%+LEN($(P%+1))+1
1730 [            OPT opt%
1740              BRK
1750 .show_ok     LDA #4                  \ Check they're integers
1760              CMP par_blk+3
1770              BNE show_err
1780              CMP par_blk+6
```

```
1790          BNE show_err
1800          LDA par_blk+1          \ Get address of cursor x
1810          STA cx_ptr
1820          LDA par_blk+2
1830          STA cx_ptr+1
1840          LDA par_blk+4          \ Get address of cursor y
1850          STA cy_ptr
1860          LDA par_blk+5
1870          STA cy_ptr+1
1880          LDY #0                 \ Now get cx% and cy% themselves
1890          LDA (cx_ptr),Y
1900          STA cx
1910          LDA (cy_ptr),Y
1920          STA cy
1930          INC cy                 \ Put in range 1-8 (from 0-7)
1940          RTS
1950 ]
1960 ENDPROC
```

When I first wrote the routine, inv_flag didn't exist. Instead, the subroutine "norm" was called each time through the loop. I was a little disappointed at the speed of the routine, which was only about four times faster than the BASIC version listed in Chapter three. As an experiment, I changed it to the form given above, so that "norm" is only called when "inv_flg" has been set. This speeded up the routine considerably. It came as a bit of a surprise, as I assumed changing the colours would be a very rapid operation, even if it is performed 64 times for each character. The moral is, of course, that even in machine code it is sometimes necessary to optimise the inner loops (those which are executed many times) if efficiency is very important.

The routine is less than 200 bytes, so it fits comfortably into page &D00. However, the need to check the parameters is probably not that great, as the program will only ever be used in the character definer program. As a general rule, it is a good idea to include checks when developing a machine code routine, but when it is installed in the BASIC program these can be removed to decrease the size a little. Always keep a well-commented version of the source though, just in case it needs to be altered. The REPEAT loop after the assembly bit in the listing above simply sets-up A%, X% and Y% as required (the buffer being immediately after the assembled machine code) and then calls the routine to display characters entered at the keyboard.

The next program is not written in assembly language itself, but should prove useful for assembly language programmers. It is a 6502 disassembler written in BASIC. The program takes a pair of addresses from the user and disassembles the machine code program which lies between them. The output is very similar to that provided by the BBC BASIC assembler after an OPT 3. The main difference is that after the one, two or three bytes of data, the CHR$s of those bytes are displayed, if the ASCII code is a printable one. This is useful for detecting strings of text embedded in the program. It is usually easy to spot these, as they include illegal 6502 instructions, which are disassembled as "???" by the program. The program also assumes that whenever a BRK instruction is encountered, it is followed by an error message of the standard format. This message is printed on a separate line to make it easier to read.

Although the program is in BASIC, it is fast enough for casual viewing on the screen, and is probably fast enough to outrun most printers. The main loop is very simple: print the current address; get a byte; if it's a BRK, print the message otherwise do PROCrest to process the rest of the instruction. Repeat that until the program counter (p%) is greater than e%, the end address. PROCrest is principally an ON . . . GOSUB. The branch taken depends solely on the addressing mode of the instruction, which is found from the table at M%. The two procedures PROC1byte and PROC2bytes get the one or two operand bytes, again depending on the addressing mode, and print them with the ASCII data and instruction's mnemonic. The way the mnemonics and addressing modes are found is a brute force one. The data for all possible instructions (1 to 255, 0 is the special case BRK) is held in tables. These are O%? and M%?. O%?i% contains the index for the mnemonic whose instruction code is i%. This is an index into $S%, which contains the string "ADCANDASLBCC......TXATXSTYA???". M%?i% contains the addressing mode for the instruction code i%. There are thirteen modes. The first four (absolute; abs,X; abs,Y; indirect) require two-byte operands Modes 5 to 11 need one-byte operands and the last two (accumulator and implied) require no operand. It would be possible to set-up these tables by reading them from DATA statements. However, this is very wasteful of space since in addition to the DIM space for the tables, the DATA statements would take up about 1.5K. Instead, the tables' data is read from a data file. This obviously needs to be set-up, and the program to do this is given later. The only other notable point is the way LOMEM is altered at the start of the program. When the program is first run, L% will contain some number which is very unlikely to be TOP+169. Thus the IF at line 1000 calls PROCinit. This sets paging mode and reads the arrays from cassette. It also makes L% 169 greater than S%, which is the first byte above the data tables. The program then runs normally. Now, if the user were to ESCAPE from the program, perhaps to examine some memory locations' hex data with hex dump (see earlier), he would have to remember to use GOTO to restart the program, rather than RUN. RUN, of course, destroys any variables, which in this case would include the assembler tables. The addition of line 1000 obviates the necessity to use GOTO; the program can be restarted using RUN. The second time round, L% will equal TOP+169 so PROCinit is not executed. In addition, LOMEM is set to L% to protect the tables from having new variables assigned on top of them. This process is akin the warm and cold starts of the machine, the former being a less drastic version of the latter.

```
100 REM Disassembler
1000 IF L%=S%+169 THEN LOMEM=L% ELSE PROCinit
1010 REPEAT
1020   CLS:INPUT''"Start, End ",s$,e$
1030   s%=EVAL(s$): e%=EVAL(e$)
1040   p%=s%
1050   REPEAT
1060     PRINT FNaddr(p%);" ";
1070     byte%=?p%
1080     PRINT FNhex(byte%);" ";
1090     IF byte%=0 THEN PROCbrk ELSE PROCrest(byte%)
1095     PRINT
1100     p%=p%+1
1110   UNTIL p%>e%
1120   in%=GET
1130 INPUT''"Again ",yn$
1140 UNTIL LEFT$(yn$,1)="N"
1150 END
1997
1998
1999
2000 DEF PROCinit
2005   REM   Read the assembler tables from tape
2010   DIM O% 255, M% 255, S% 168
2015   L%=S%+169
2020   VDU 14: REM   Paging ON
2030   LOCAL i%
2050   ch%=OPENIN("dis.data")
2060   FOR i%=0 TO 167
2070     S%?i%=BGET#ch%
2080   NEXT i%
2085   S%?168=13
2090   FOR i%=1 TO 255
2100     O%?i%=BGET#ch%
2110   NEXT i%
2120   FOR i%=1 TO 255
2130     M%?i%=BGET#ch%
2140   NEXT i%
2150   CLOSE#ch%
2180 ENDPROC
2997
2998
3000 DEF FNaddr(x%)=RIGHT$("0000"+STR$~(x%),4)
```

```
3100 DEF FNhex(x%)=RIGHT$("00"+STR$~(x%),2)
3110
3200 DEF FNch(b%)
3210 IF b%<32 OR b%>126 THEN =" " ELSE =CHR$(b%)
3220
3300 DEF FNmnem(b%)=MID$($S%,0%?b%,3)+" "
3997
4000 DEF PROCbrk
4005   REM    Process a BRK message
4010   PRINTSPC(12);"BRK"'
4020   p%=p%+1
4030   REPEAT
4040    A%=?p%: CALL &B53A: REM   Out the character
4050     p%=p%+1
4060   UNTIL ?p%=0
4080   PRINT
4090 ENDPROC
4997
4998
4999
5000 DEF PROCrest(b%)
5005   REM    Get operand bytes and mnemonics
5010   LOCAL mo%,b1%,b2%
5020   mo%=M%?b%
5025   IF mo%<5 THEN PROC2bytes ELSE IF mo%<12 THEN PROC1byte
5030   ON mo% GOSUB
     5100,5200,5300,5400,5500,5600,5700,5800,5900,6000,6100,6200,6300
5040 ENDPROC
5050
5100 REM Absolute
5150 PRINT"&";FNaddr(b1%);
5160 RETURN
5170
5200 REM Abs,X
5250 PRINT"&";FNaddr(b1%);",X";
5260 RETURN
5270
5300 REM Abs,Y
5350 PRINT"&";FNaddr(b1%);",Y";
5360 RETURN
5370
5400 REM Indirect
5450 PRINT"(&";FNaddr(b1%);")";
```

```
5460 RETURN
5470
5500 REM Immediate
5530 PRINT"#&";FNhex(b1%);
5540 RETURN
5550
5600 REM Pre-indexed
5630 PRINT"(&";FNhex(b1%);",X)";
5640 RETURN
5650
5700 REM Post-indexed
5730 PRINT"(&";FNhex(b1%);"),Y";
5740 RETURN
5750
5800 REM Relative
5830 PRINT"&";
5840 IF b1% AND &80 THEN PRINT FNaddr(p%+b1%-255); ELSE PRINT FNaddr(p%+1+b1%);
5850 RETURN
5860
5900 REM Zero page
5930 PRINT"&";FNhex(b1%);
5940 RETURN
5950
6000 REM Zero page,X
6030 PRINT"&";FNhex(b1%);",X";
6040 RETURN
6050
6100 REM Zero page,Y
6130 PRINT"&";FNhex(b1%);",Y";
6140 RETURN
6150
6200 REM Accumulator
6220 PRINTSPC(7);FNch(b%);SPC(4);
6230 PRINT FNmnem(b%);"A";
6240 RETURN
6250
6300 REM Implied
6320 PRINTSPC(7);FNch(b%);SPC(4);
6330 PRINT FNmnem(b%);
6340 RETURN
7997
7998
```

```
8000 DEF PROC2bytes
8010   b1%=p%?1:b2%=p%?2
8020   p%=p%+2
8030   PRINT FNhex(b1%);" ";
8040   PRINT FNhex(b2%);SPC(2);
8045   PRINT FNch(b%);FNch(b1%);FNch(b2%);SPC(2);
8050   PRINT FNmnem(b%);
8060   b1%=b1%+256*b2%
8070 ENDPROC
8998
8999
9000 DEF PROC1byte
9010   b1%=p%?1: p%=p%+1
9020   PRINT FNhex(b1%);SPC(5);
9025   PRINT FNch(b%);FNch(b1%);SPC(3);
9030   PRINTFNmnem(b%);
9040 ENDPROC
```

The data statements for the assembler are given below. Before committing the values to tape, it is wise to check them. The program given with the data does this. It checks the sum and exclusive–OR of the three sets of values. Unfortunately, the error is only pin-pointed to the accuracy of one of these blocks, so you will need to do some careful scanning of the program if an error does occur.

```
100 REM Check the DATA is correct
110 tot%=0: eor%=0
120 FOR i%=1 TO 56
130    READ mn$
140    FOR j%=1 TO 3
150       tot%=tot%+ASC(MID$(mn$,j%,1))
160       eor%=eor% EOR ASC(MID$(mn$,j%,1))
170    NEXT j%
180 NEXT i%
190 IF tot%<>&31BC OR eor%<>&70 THEN PRINT"ERROR between lines 1000 and
    1600":END
200 tot%=0: eor%=0
210 FOR i%=1 TO 255
220    READ x%
230    tot%=tot%+x%
240    eor%=eor% EOR x%
250 NEXT i%
260 IF tot%<>&71C7 OR eor%<>&89 THEN PRINT"ERROR between lines 1700 and
    4300":END
270 tot%=0: eor%=0
```

```
280 FOR i%=1 TO 255
290    READ x%
300    tot%=tot%+x%
310    eor%=eor% EOR x%
320 NEXT i%
330 IF tot%<>8963 OR eor%<>85 THEN PRINT"ERROR between lines 4400 and
    6300":END
340 PRINT "OK"
350 END
1000 DATA ADC,AND,ASL,BCC,BCS,BEQ,BIT,BMI
1100 DATA BNE,BPL,BVC,BVS,CLC,CLD,CLI,CLV
1200 DATA CMP,CPX,CPY,DEC,DEX,DEY,EOR,INC
1300 DATA INX,INY,JMP,JSR,LDA,LDX,LDY,LSR
1400 DATA NOP,ORA,PHA,PHP,PLA,PLP,ROL,ROR
1500 DATA RTI,RTS,SBC,SEC,SED,SEI,STA,STX
1600 DATA STY,TAX,TAY,TSX,TXA,TXS,TYA,???
1700 DATA 100,166,166,166,100,7,166,106,100
1800 DATA 7,166,166,100,7,166,28,100,166,166
1900 DATA 166,100,7,166,37,100,166,166,166
2000 DATA 100,7,166,82,4,166,166,19,4,115
2100 DATA 166,112,4,115,166,19,4,115,166,22
2200 DATA 4,166,166,166,4,115,166,130,4,166
2300 DATA 166,166,4,115,166,121,67,166,166
2400 DATA 166,67,94,166,103,67,94,166,79,67
2500 DATA 94,166,31,67,166,166,166,67,94,166
2600 DATA 43,67,166,166,166,67,94,166,124
2700 DATA 1,166,166,166,1,118,166,109,1,118
2800 DATA 166,79,1,118,166,34,1,166,166,166
2900 DATA 1,118,166,136,1,166,166,166,1,118
3000 DATA 166,166,139,166,166,145,139,142
3100 DATA 166,64,166,157,166,145,139,142,166
3200 DATA 10,139,166,166,145,139,142,166,163
3300 DATA 139,160,166,166,139,166,166,91,85
3400 DATA 88,166,91,85,88,166,151,85,148,166
3500 DATA 91,85,88,166,13,85,166,166,91,85
3600 DATA 88,166,46,85,154,166,91,85,88,166
3700 DATA 55,49,166,166,55,49,58,166,76,49
3800 DATA 61,166,55,49,58,166,25,49,166,166
3900 DATA 166,49,58,166,40,49,166,166,166
4000 DATA 49,58,166,52,127,166,166,52,127
4100 DATA 70,166,73,127,97,166,52,127,70,166
4200 DATA 16,127,166,166,166,127,70,166,133
```

```
4300 DATA 127,166,166,166,127,70,166
4400 DATA 6,13,13,13,9,9,13,13,5,12,13,13
4500 DATA 1,1,13,8,7,13,13,13,10,10,13,13
4600 DATA 3,13,13,13,2,2,13,1,6,13,13,9,9
4700 DATA 9,13,13,5,12,13,1,1,1,13,8,7,13
4800 DATA 13,13,10,10,13,13,3,13,13,13,2,2
4900 DATA 13,13,6,13,13,13,9,9,13,13,5,12
5000 DATA 13,1,1,1,13,8,7,13,13,13,10,10,13
5100 DATA 13,3,13,13,13,2,2,13,13,6,13,13
5200 DATA 13,9,9,13,13,5,12,13,4,1,1,13,8
5300 DATA 7,13,13,13,10,10,13,13,3,13,13,13
5400 DATA 2,2,13,13,6,13,13,9,9,9,13,13,13
5500 DATA 13,13,1,1,1,13,8,7,13,13,10,10,11
5600 DATA 13,13,3,13,13,13,2,13,13,5,6,5,13
5700 DATA 9,9,9,13,13,5,13,13,1,1,1,13,8,7
5800 DATA 13,13,10,10,11,13,13,3,13,13,2,2
5900 DATA 3,13,5,6,13,13,9,9,9,13,13,5,13
6000 DATA 13,1,1,1,13,8,7,13,13,13,10,10,13
6100 DATA 13,3,13,13,13,2,2,13,5,6,13,13,9
6200 DATA 9,9,13,13,5,13,13,1,1,1,13,8,7,13
6300 DATA 13,13,10,10,13,13,3,13,13,13,2,2,13
```

Once you are happy that the DATA statements are correct, change the program to that given below (keeping the DATA part of course). This will create the file "dis.data" which can then be read in by the disassembler.

```
100 REM Data set-up for disassembler
110 ch%=OPENOUT("dis.data")
120 FOR i%=1 TO 56
130    READ mn$
140      FOR j%=1 TO 3
150         BPUT#ch%,ASC(MID$(mn$,j%,1))
160      NEXT j%
170 NEXT i%
190 FOR i%=1 TO 510
200      READ x%
220      BPUT#ch%,x%
230 NEXT i%
240 CLOSE#ch%
250 END
260
270
280
```

The method for setting up the disassembler on the tape is a follows. First type in and save the program itself. Stop the tape at the end. Then type in the DATA program, using the first listing to verify the data is correct. Then change the program's body to that shown above and run the program. This will create the data file immediately after the disassembler, so that the tables can be read in immediately. After running the data creation program, save it somewhere, just in case "dis.data" becomes corrupt. It would also be useful for later, when you might try to re-write the disassembler in assembly language. If you are unfortunate enough to still be using MOS 0.1, it is wise to check that the "dis.data" file has been written correctly, using *CAT. The file is nearly three blocks long, so *CAT should indicate that it has read blocks 00, 01 then 02, finishing with 02A6.

The use of the disassembler is in examining other people's programs rather than your own. When using the BASIC assembler, you should naturally save the source (the BASIC program), even if you only actually use the object code (with *LOAD or *RUN). That way it is easy to come back and change the program when necessary. Two programs of great interest are BBC BASIC and the MOS. The former is probably more interesting, as it is easy to see what is going on by the numerous error messages scattered throughout. The interpreter was well mapped out by David Christensen in the July 1982 issue of Personal Computer World, though there are many gaps which can be filled in by careful examination of the disassembled listing. Another target for the disassembler is in machine code games. If you have the patience, getting a listing of Acornsoft Defender or Snapper would prove enlightening. The disassembler would have to be relocated somewhere above the program itself. For example, Defender is loaded at &E00 and is about 8.5K long, so PAGE would have to be changed to about &3200 before loading the disassembler.

As mentioned above, all the important MOS routines are called indirectly (or are vectored) via RAM locations. This enables things like osbyte and oswrch calls to be intercepted by the user's own routines, so that he can cause certain codes to be interpreted in a different way to the default one. It also means that it is very easy to change the filing system from cassette to ROM or disc, as all the filing calls are vectored too. The following program shows the general form of a vector interception program. Most people will use the indirection property to trap selected options of a call, such as all osbytes with the accumulator set to &89 (*FX137), rather than to completely replace an operating system routine. This may be necessary sometimes, though. The filing system was just given as an example. Another might be where a company produces a very high resolution display board for the computer. It would be desirable to send all oswrch calls to this, rather than simply intercept certain options.

The first example does the *FX137 (*MOTOR) trap just mentioned. It says in the User Guide (page 433) that by intercepting this call, it would be a simple matter to implement a dual cassette system, one for reading and one for writing. The normal cassette (which plugs into the back of the computer) would be used for all read operations and another one which would be activated by the user's own hardware used for writing. This is possible because MOS 1.0 (but not 0.1) sets the Y register to zero when the motor is activated for writing and to one for reads. The user's program would first check that a MOTOR function is required, by comparing the accumulator with &89. If it isn't equal, control is passed to the normal osbyte routine, whose address is held at &20A,B. If a MOTOR is required, Y is examined to see if a read or write operation is being started. If it is the former, control is again passed to the default program to allow the internal relay to be activated. Otherwise, it is time for the user's program to actually do something. Exactly what depends on the X register. If it contains a 0, the external cassette must be disabled. A 1 in the X register means the cassette must be started, preferably with a prompt from the computer to the user. The hardware used to achieve the switching depends on the user. I will assume that the user port is being used to drive a relay. This requires a knowledge of the 6522 VIA. If you don't possess this, see [Leventhal]. Control is via CB2, which is one of the i/o handshake lines on side B of the 6522 located at location &FE60. To activate the external cassette this line is made high (5 volts). To turn the motor off the line is set to low (zero volts). Control of the line is simply achieved via the Peripheral Control register. Setting this register (at location &FE6C) controls the state of this line easily. The program is given below.

```
100 FOR o%=0 TO 3 STEP 3
110    PROCass(&D00,o%)
120 NEXT o%
130 ?&20A=osbyte1 MOD 256
140 ?&20B=osbyte1 DIV 256
150 END
160
170
1000 DEF PROCass(addr%,opt%)
1010 osbyte=!&20A AND &FFFF
1020 osrdch=&FFE0: oswrch=&FFEE: ptr=&70
1030 P%=addr%
1040 mesg=P%
1050 $(P%)="Cassette #2 "
1060 P%=P%+LEN($(P%))
1070 [        OPT opt%
1080          BRK
1090 .osbyte1 CMP #&89   \ Is it a MOTOR ?
1100          BEQ motor  \ Yes
1110 .exit    JMP osbyte \ No; pass control to the usual routine
1120 .motor   CPY #0     \ Is it a write ?
1130          BNE exit   \ No; pass control to the usual routine
1140          TXA        \ Is it an OFF ?
1150          BEQ off    \ Yes
1160 .on      LDX #mesg MOD 256   \ Display message
```

```
1170            LDY #mesg DIV 256
1180            JSR print
1190            LDA #1        \ It's an ON
1200 .off       PHA           \ Save A
1210            LDA #&96      \ Read from Sheila
1220            LDX #&6C      \ Offset of PCR in Sheila
1230            JSR osbyte    \ Get value in X
1240            PLA           \ Restore A
1250            BEQ off1      \ Make CB2 zero
1260 .on1       TYA           \ Make CB2 one
1270            ORA #&E0
1280            BNE write     \ Put it in the PCR
1290 .off1      TYA           \ Make CB2 zero
1300            AND #&DF
1310 .write     TAY           \ Value to write in Y
1320            LDA #&97      \ Write to Sheila
1330            LDX #&6C      \ Offset of PCR
1340            JSR osbyte
1350            RTS
1360
1370 .print     STY ptr+1     \ Same old routine
1380            STX ptr
1390            LDY #0
1400 .prloop    LDA (ptr),Y
1410            BEQ prret
1420            JSR oswrch
1430            INY
1440            BNE prloop
1450 .prret     RTS
1460 ]
1470 ENDPROC
```

Before the assembly part is entered, the value of osbyte is found. This is the address of the default osbyte routine in the MOS ROM. As mentioned above, the address is located at the vector address, &20A,B. It is required by the program above so that non-MOTOR calls to osbyte can be passed directly to the ROM routine. In fact, the intercepting program itself uses the proper osbyte program to access the 6522. The label osbyte1 gives the address of the first location of the intercepting program. Once this has been assembled, the vector at &20A,B is set to "point" to it. Figure 5.2 shows the paths taken by the processor after a "JSR &FFF4" before and after the program above has been run.

After the "Cassette #2" prompt has been printed for a write operation (this comes immediately before the "RECORD then RETURN" generated by the

(a)   (b)

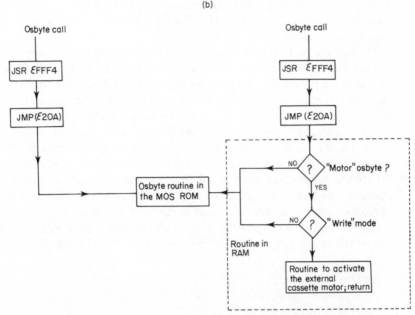

Figure 5.2   Result of Re-vectoring the Osbyte Routine

filing system software), all that needs to be done is set CB2 via the 6522's Peripheral Control Register (PCR). First, the current status is obtained by reading the
value at &FE6C. It would be possible to set the PCR without first reading it, but
this would affect all the bits, not just the three which control CB2. Since the PCR
also controls the A side of 6522, which is used for the Centronics (R) interface,
this could affect the printer. Instead, the value is read, the relevant bits (5, 6 and 7)
adjusted, then it is written back. To turn CB2 on, these three bits are all one, so
the value read must be ORed with binary 11100000, or &E0. To set CB2 to low,
the three high bits must be 110. This implies that the current value must be
ANDed with 11011111, or &DF.

The comparatively straightforward process of reading, masking and writing
just described is clouded in the program by the use of more osbyte calls to access
the 6522. Acorn are very keen on people writing programs which will work
outside of the BBC Computer, i.e. across the Tube interface. To this end, they
have supplied many routines which obviate the need to access the BBC Computer's "special" locations directly. Programs which do this will not work in a
second processor, as location &FE6C (say) in the second processor will not be the
6522 PCR which lives in the i/o processor. Whether you stick to this philosophy
of using only MOS routines is a matter for you to decide. On the one hand, adopting it means that all your programs will work on Tube processors, even if they are
longer to write. On the other hand, many of the important osbyte and osword
calls are not implemented on MOS 0.1. This stops the first 30,000 (at least) BBC
users from adopting the "good habits" that Acorn insist they should. The example

here is by way of illustration. By the time this book is published I should have been able to test it. (The availability of MOS 1.0 is "four to five weeks", irrespective of the date at which the enquiry is made.)

The two osbyte calls with the accumulator set to &96 and &97 enable the user to read and write respectively the devices on page &FE00, or Sheila as she is known to her friends. On this page are located all the "on board" devices, such as the A/D converter and, of current interest, the i/o 6522 (there is another one used to read the keyboard). This occupies the sixteen Sheila addresses &FE60 to &FE6F. To read a device on page &FE00, a call is made to osbyte with the accumulator set to &96. The X register must contain the offset into Sheila. This is simply the lower byte of the address in question, &6C for the 6522 PCR. When the routine returns, the value at the location given is in the Y register, though deducing this from the User Guide is almost impossible. Similarly, to write to a Sheila location, the accumulator is set to &97, the X register to the offset, and the Y register to the value to be written. For those wishing to rebel against the system, and be able to run programs on MOS 0.1 machines, lines 1200 to 1340 should be:

```
1200 .off   LDX &FE6C
1210        TAY
1230        BEQ off1
1240 .on1   TXA
1250        ORA #&E0
1260        BNE write
1270 .off1  TXA
1280        AND #&DF
1290 .write STA &FE6C
1300        RTS
```

Calls to the operating system can be traced by intercepting them. Before control is passed to the default ROM routine, the contents of the important registers can be printed on the screen using oswrch. The program below traces calls to osbyte and osword. Osbytes are traced in the form "*FX A,X,Y" and oswords become "*word A,X,Y". Osword calls perform miscellaneous operations which require more parameters than can be passed in the X and Y registers. For example, the BASIC POINT function is an osword call since the two co-ordinates require a total of four bytes. In all osword calls the X and Y registers are used to "point" to a parameter block which contains the information for the function, and where the osword routine deposits its results. The accumulator specifies the particular osword required.

```
100 FOR o%=0 TO 2 STEP 2
110     PROCass(&D00, o%)
120 NEXT o%
130 !&20A=osbyte1+&10000*osword1
140 END
150
```

```
 160
1000 DEF PROCass(addr%,opt%)
1010 osword=!&20C AND &FFFF
1020 osbyte=!&20A AND &FFFF
1030 osnewl=&FFE7: oswrch=&FFEE
1040 hexout=&8570
1050 acc=&70: xreg=&71:yreg=&72
1060 ptr=&74
1070 P%=addr%
1080 fx=P%
1090 $fx="*FX "
1100 P%=P%+LEN($fx)+1
1110 P%?-1=0
1120 word=P%
1130 $word="*word "
1140 P%=P%+LEN($word)
1150 [          OPT opt%
1160            BRK
1170 .osbyte1   CMP #&7E       \ Don't trace this one
1180            BEQ jmpbyte
1190            JSR save        \ Save the registers
1200            JSR osnewl
1210            LDX #fx MOD 256 \ Print "*fx "
1220            LDY #fx DIV 256
1230            JSR print
1240            JSR params      \ Print & restore the registers
1250 .jmpbyte   JMP osbyte      \ Perform the call
1260
1270 .osword1   CMP #0          \ Don't trace this one
1280            BEQ jmpword
1290            JSR save        \ Save A, X and Y
1300            JSR osnewl
1310            LDX #word MOD 256 \ Print "*word "
1320            LDY #word DIV 256
1330            JSR print
1340            JSR params      \ Print & restore the registers
1350 .jmpword   JMP osword      \ Go to the default routine
1360
1370 .save      STA acc
1380            STY yreg
1390            STX xreg
1430            RTS
```

```
1440
1450 .print       STX ptr
1460              STY ptr+1
1470              LDY #0
1480 .prloop      LDA (ptr),Y
1490              BEQ prret
1500              JSR oswrch
1510              INY
1520              BNE prloop
1530 .prret       RTS
1540
1550 .params      LDA #ASC("&")  \ Print the parameters
1560              JSR oswrch
1570              LDA acc
1580              JSR hexout
1590              LDA #ASC(",")
1600              JSR oswrch
1610              LDA #ASC("&")
1620              JSR oswrch
1630              LDA xreg
1640              JSR hexout
1650              LDA #ASC(",")
1660              JSR oswrch
1670              LDA #ASC("&")
1680              JSR oswrch
1690              LDA yreg
1700              JSR hexout
1710              JSR osnewl
1750              LDA acc          \ Restore the registers
1760              LDX xreg
1770              LDY yreg
1780              RTS
1790 ]
1800 ENDPROC
```

The two intercepting routines are very similar. The only differences between them is that osbyte1 prints the string "*FX" and osword1 prints "*word", and of course the final destinations are different. The two vectors which are replaced are bytev at &20A,B and wordv at &20C,D. These are altered to point to osbyte1 and osword1 respectively. Both routines ignore (i.e. don't trace) one of their options. Osbyte &7E (*FX126) is not traced as this is called once every line by BASIC. Similarly, osword &00 is passed straight to the MOS routine. This is the "get a line of input" call, which is also used frequently by BASIC. Both these ignored options can be traced by deleting the CMP and BEQ instructions at the beginning of the respective routines. The other notable thing is that the numbers A, X and Y in the line "*FX A,X,Y" are in hexadecimal. The reason is that the hexout routine does not affect any memory locations, whereas the decimal number output routine (at &98F1) does. These locations could be important to the program which is calling osbyte/osword. Changing them would cause an unwanted side effect. This is an important point for all interception programs; they should leave all the registers intact and any memory locations used should be isolated ones (e.g. use the spare 32 bytes at &70 to &8F). The effect of the trace can be seen by typing a statement which needs to use osbyte or osword. For example:

```
A=OPENIN("data"):      REM Uses *FX137,1
c%=POINT(100,100):     REM Uses *word 9
SOUND 1,-15,20,20:     REM Uses *word 7
```

The most interesting MOS call to "trap" is oswrch, the character output one. Unfortunately, as I mentioned earlier, it is also the hardest. Whereas all the other "os" calls are specified by one single JSR, with the option required in the accumulator, many graphics commands require several successive calls to specify their parameters. For example, calling the oswrch routine with &12 in the accumulator tells the MOS that the user wants to define a graphics colour. The MOS then expects to receive two more parameter bytes, again via oswrch. So, to perform the command GCOL 0,1 in machine code, the following is required:

```
LDA #&12    \ GCOL
JSR oswrch
LDA #0      \ Plot mode 0
JSR oswrch
LDA #1      \ Colour 1
JSR oswrch
```

Because of this method of passing parameters, trapping oswrch calls is made considerably more involved, unless you can be absolutely certain that multi-byte calls (i.e. PLOTting, changing MODE, changing colours, changing windows, etc.) will not be used. This is very unlikely. To see why the difficulty arises, suppose we want to trap the BELL command, which is an oswrch with the accumulator set to 7 (or VDU 7 in BASIC). Using the previous trapping examples as a model, this would be:

```
.oswrch1  CMP #7       \ Is it a "bell"
          BEQ bell     \ Yes, branch
          JMP oswrch   \ No, goto default routine
.bell     \ instructions to do a special "bell"
```

If no multi-bytes calls are used this will work OK. Suppose, though, that we now move the cursor to (0,7) by a VDU 31,0,7 (or PRINT TAB(0,7);). This will generate three calls to oswrch. The first, oswrch 31, will tell the routine to expect two more bytes specifying the co-ordinates. The first of these, oswrch 0, gets through the intercepting routine with no bother (the CMP #7 fails, so the JMP oswrch is made). However, then the second co-ordinate is sent, which is oswrch 7. This is duly intercepted and treated as a bell character. This is obviously not what is wanted; we only want to trap bona fide bell calls, not other commands which happen to contain 7s in their parameter bytes. This problem will occur with 11 of the 32 control codes. Since almost every program will use at least one of them (and programs which use graphics will use several), some way must be found of ignoring bytes in control characters' parameter sequences.

The next program illustrates a way of doing this. The bell example is used for simplicity. A table is set up which contains the number of bytes which must be sent to oswrch without interception for each control character. The table is located at cnt_tab, so the number of bytes to ignore for the PLOT command, for example, would be found at cnt_tab?25, as PLOT is VDU 25. A single routine, "check", and a counting location are used to keep track of the parameter bytes. Before testing for the character(s) to be trapped, oswrch1 calls check. This has the following effect. If the output routine is in the middle of receiving parameter bytes, the carry flag is set and the routine returns immediately. The test is made by decrementing the location cnt, which holds the number of parameter bytes which are pending. If this is not zero, the DEC will not cause it to become minus, hence the jump to "clear" will not be made. If cnt is currently zero, i.e. there are no parameter bytes pending, the byte to be output must be checked to see if it will require subsequent parameter bytes. Only control codes (values less than 32) do, so all others can be eliminated immediately by the BCS. If the character is a control code, the number of parameter bytes is stored in cnt for subsequent calls to examine. Note that any routine intercepting oswrch must preserve the registers, as most calling routines will assume this is done.

When "check" returns, control must be passed directly to oswrch if the carry flag is set. If it isn't set, the bell character can be trapped as it is certain that the character in the accumulator is a proper character, rather than a parameter byte. All the present program does is to substitute the beep of the normal bell with a printed exclamation mark. The program is listed below.

```
100 FOR o%=0 TO 3 STEP 3
110     PROCass(&D00,o%)
120 NEXT
130 ?&20E=oswrch1 MOD 256: ?&20F=oswrch1 DIV 256
140 END
1000 DEF PROCass(addr%,opt%)
1010
1020 bell=7
1030 oswrch=!&20E AND &FFFF
1040 cnt=&70: xreg=&71
1050 cnt_tab=addr%: ?cnt=0
```

```
1060 !cnt_tab=&00000100: cnt_tab!4=&0
1070 cnt_tab!8=0:cnt_tab!12=0
1080 cnt_tab!16=&05020100: cnt_tab!20=&09010000
1090 cnt_tab!24=&00000508: cnt_tab!28=&02000404
1110 P%=cnt_tab+32
1120 [        OPT opt%
1130 .oswrch1 JSR check    \ Check control codes
1140          BCC ok       \ We're not in a control sequence
1150 .jmpwrch JMP oswrch   \ Yes we are; goto the default routine
1160 .ok      CMP #bell     \ Is it a bell?
1170          BNE jmpwrch \ No. Goto default routine
1180          LDA #ASC("!") \ Do our own bell; print a !
1190          BNE jmpwrch
1200
1210 .check   DEC cnt       \ Are we in a control sequence?
1220          BMI clear     \ No
1230          SEC           \ Yes, set carry
1240          RTS           \ And return
1250 .clear   INC cnt       \ Restore count
1260          CMP #32       \ Is this a control code?
1270          BCS noctrl    \ No
1280          STX xreg      \ Yes, get byte count
1290          PHA           \ Preserve A and X
1300          TAX
1310          LDA cnt_tab,X
1320          STA cnt       \ Save it
1330          PLA           \ Restore and return
1340          LDX xreg
1350 .noctrl  CLC
1370          RTS
1380 ]
1400 ENDPROC
```

A slightly better use of the "intercepting oswrch" routine is given next. It was mentioned in Chapter three that by using VDU 23 to redefine some of the character set, different alphabets could be used on the soft displays (all except MODE 7). It is possible to redefine the characters "A"–"Z", whose ASCII codes are 65 to 90 respectively. However, this requires PAGE to be moved to &1400 to make room for the new patterns (see page 427 of the User Guide). The method presented here uses the permanently redefinable characters with codes 224–255. The new alphabet is the upper case version of the Greek alphabet. It occupies the codes 225 to 248 (there are 24 letters). The Greek letters are obtained in the following way. All output is sent to the screen as normal, until a "{" is encountered. This acts as a "start of Greek" character. After it has been sent, the letters "A" to "X" are intercepted. Before they are sent to oswrch, 160 is added to their ASCII codes to give the required 225 to 248. Thus after a "{" most of the upper case Roman alphabet is unavailable. To retrieve it, the character "}" must be output. This acts as a "stop Greek" code, and stops the normal characters from being intercepted and changed. As given, the program does not echo the "{" and "}". This is desirable, as they would not usually be required adjacent to Greek letters. If it is absolutely vital to have them, the codes 249 and 250 can be used.

Before the characters can be intercepted it is wise to define the Greek alphabet in the codes mentioned above. My version of these letters is given below. I am no graphics designer, and anyone with even a marginally artistic bent should be able to improve on them. They are given as the normal VDU 23 statements. However, if you intend to use them a lot, it would be better to save the character definitions along with the program: "*SAVE "Greek" C00 +200".

```
VDU 23,225,&3C,&66,&66,&7E,&66,&66,&66,&00: REM alpha
VDU 23,226,&7C,&66,&66,&7C,&66,&66,&7C,&00: REM beta
VDU 23,227,&7F,&31,&30,&30,&30,&30,&30,&00: REM gamma
VDU 23,228,&18,&3C,&66,&66,&66,&66,&7E,&00: REM delta
VDU 23,229,&7E,&60,&60,&7C,&60,&60,&7E,&00: REM epsilon
VDU 23,230,&7E,&06,&0C,&18,&30,&60,&7E,&00: REM zeta
VDU 23,231,&66,&66,&66,&7E,&66,&66,&66,&00: REM eta
VDU 23,232,&3C,&66,&66,&7E,&66,&66,&3C,&00: REM theta
VDU 23,233,&7E,&18,&18,&18,&18,&18,&7E,&00: REM iota
VDU 23,234,&66,&6C,&78,&70,&78,&6C,&66,&00: REM kappa
VDU 23,235,&18,&3C,&66,&66,&66,&66,&66,&00: REM lambda
VDU 23,236,&63,&77,&7F,&6B,&6B,&63,&63,&00: REM mu
VDU 23,237,&66,&66,&76,&7E,&6E,&66,&66,&00: REM nu
VDU 23,238,&7E,&66,&5A,&18,&5A,&66,&7E,&00: REM xi
VDU 23,239,&3C,&66,&66,&66,&66,&66,&3C,&00: REM omicron
VDU 23,240,&7F,&36,&36,&36,&36,&36,&36,&00: REM pi
VDU 23,241,&7C,&66,&66,&7C,&60,&60,&60,&00: REM rho
VDU 23,242,&7F,&61,&30,&18,&30,&61,&7F,&00: REM sigma
VDU 23,243,&7E,&18,&18,&18,&18,&18,&18,&00: REM tau
VDU 23,244,&67,&6E,&6C,&18,&18,&18,&18,&00: REM upsilon
VDU 23,245,&08,&3E,&6B,&6B,&6B,&3E,&08,&00: REM phi
VDU 23,246,&66,&66,&3C,&18,&3C,&66,&66,&00: REM chi
VDU 23,247,&6B,&6B,&6B,&3E,&08,&08,&08,&00: REM psi
VDU 23,248,&3E,&63,&63,&77,&36,&55,&77,&00: REM omega
VDU 23,249,&0C,&18,&18,&70,&18,&18,&0C,&00: REM {
VDU 23,250,&30,&18,&18,&0E,&18,&18,&30,&00: REM }
```

Before I give the program itself, here is an example of the way it would be used from BASIC. In addition to the usual oswrch1 routine, there are two others. The subroutine at "on" enables oswrch1 by setting the appropriate vector (wrchv, which is at &20E,F) to point to oswrch1. It also zeroes "gk" which is a flag. It is set after a "{" is encountered and reset after a "}". The other routine, "off", redirects wrchv to the default routine in ROM. This prevents a "{" from entering Greek mode when this isn't wanted.

```
100 REM  Greek Letters e.g.
110 on=&D20:  REM might need to be altered if you
120 off=&D2F: REM change the program
130 CALL on:  REM Enable oswrch1
140 P."Roman: ABCDEFGHIJKLMNOPQRSTUVWX"
150 VDU 123:  REM Turn on Greek
160 P."Greek: ABCDEFGHIJKLMNOPQRSTUVWX"
170 VDU 125:  REM Turn off Greek
180 CALL off: REM Disable oswrch1
190 END
```

The assembly language program is listed below.

```
100 REM Greek Letters
110 FOR o%=0 TO 2 STEP 2
120    PROCass(&D00,o%)
130 NEXT o%
140 END
150
160
1000 DEF PROCass(addr%,opt%)
1010
1020 gk=&80
1030 wrchv=&20E
1040 oswrch=!wrchv AND &FFFF
1050 cnt=&70: xreg=&71
1060 cnt_tab=addr%
1070 !cnt_tab=&00000100: cnt_tab!4=&0
1080 cnt_tab!8=0:cnt_tab!12=0
1090 cnt_tab!16=&05020100: cnt_tab!20=&09010000
1100 cnt_tab!24=&00000508: cnt_tab!28=&02000404
1110 P%=cnt_tab+32
1120 [        OPT opt%
1130 .on      LDA #oswrch1 MOD 256    \ Enable intercepting program
1140          STA wrchv
1150          LDA #oswrch1 DIV 256
1160          STA wrchv+1
1170          LDA #0                  \ Reset "in Greek" flag
```

```
1180            STA gk
1190            RTS
1200
1210
1220 .off       LDA #oswrch MOD 256     \ Disable intercepting program
1230            STA wrchv
1240            LDA #oswrch DIV 256
1250            STA wrchv+1
1260            RTS
1270
1280
1290 .oswrch1 JSR check       \ Check control codes
1300            BCC ok          \ We're not in a control sequence
1310 .jmpwrch JMP oswrch       \ Yes we are; goto the default routine
1320 .ok       INC gk          \ Are we in Greek mode?
1330            DEC gk
1340            BNE ingk        \ Yes
1350            CMP #ASC("{")   \ No. Is this a Greek start char.?
1360            BNE jmpwrch     \ No. Goto the default routine
1370            INC gk          \ Set the Greek flag
1380            RTS             \ Don't echo the "{"
1390 .ingk     CMP #ASC("}")   \ Is this a Greek stop char.?
1400            BNE ingk1       \ No
1410            DEC gk          \ Yes. Reset the flag
1420            RTS             \ But don't echo it
1430 .ingk1    CMP #ASC("A")   \ Is it an upper case letter?
1440            BCC jmpwrch     \ No
1450            CMP #ASC("Y")
1460            BCS jmpwrch     \ No
1470            ADC #&A0        \ Yes, convert to 225-248
1480            BNE jmpwrch     \ and print it
1490
1500 .check    DEC cnt         \ Are we in a control sequence?
1510            BMI clear       \ No
1520            SEC             \ Yes, set carry
1530            RTS             \ And return
1540 .clear    INC cnt         \ Restore count
1550            CMP #32         \ Is this a control code?
1560            BCS noctrl      \ No
1570            STX xreg        \ Yes, get byte count
1580            PHA
1590            TAX
```

```
1600              LDA cnt_tab,X
1610              STA cnt     \ Save it
1620              PLA         \ Restore and return
1630              LDX xreg
1640 .noctrl      CLC
1650              RTS
1660 ]
1670 ENDPROC
```

Although the PLOT command in BASIC is a powerful one, it is only capable of drawing one line at a time. Many graphics micros have statements which enable you to draw shapes or line drawings. Examples are the shape tables of Applesoft BASIC and the DRAW command of Microsoft extended colour BASIC. The latter is of interest here, as the next program emulates it. Computers such as the Dragon 32 and the TRS-80 colour computer use this BASIC. The DRAW command has a very simple syntax:

```
DRAW string
```

where "string" is any string expression. The syntax of the text in the string is not so simple. It is of the form [command]*, where command is any of the following:

Command	Meaning
U n	Draw a line Up n co-ordinates
D n	Draw a line Down n co-ordinates
L n	Draw a line Left n co-ordinates
R n	Draw a line Right n co-ordinates
E n	Draw a line North-East n co-ordinates
F n	Draw a line South-East n co-ordinates
G n	Draw a line South-West n co-ordinates
H n	Draw a line North-West n co-ordinates
M x,y	Draw a line to co-ordinates (x,y)
B	Prefixes any of above to make a move instead of draw
A n	Rotate the drawing by n right-angles
X s$	Execute the string s$
C r	Set the scale to r (a real quantity)

"n" is an integer and "s$" is a string variable name. The command C is set-off from the rest as it is not in the standard version of the DRAW statement; I added it here for extra versatility. Also, in the original, all the numbers "n", "x", etc. had to be constants, so command strings looked like "BM500,500U100L100D100R100" which would draw a square whose bottom right-hand corner is at (500,500). The "B" before the move to (500,500) ensures that no line is drawn: it is a BASIC MOVE. The version of DRAW presented here is far more powerful.

By tokenising the string and using BASIC's own expression evaluator routine, the parameters can be arbitrary (numeric) expressions, such as "BMx,y U100*SIN(th)D100*COS(th)" and so on. This enhances its usefulness quite a lot. The scale command, C, takes a real number as its parameter, whereas the others all have integers (real expressions are truncated by INT). This enables the scaling factor to be fractional, as in "C0.5". ("C.5" is illegal, as the "C." would become "COLOUR".) The rotation is a little less finely controlled. Following the A command is an expression which is treated as an integer MOD 4. This gives a rotation of 0,1,2 or 3 right-angles in the clockwise direction. The diagonal line commands, E to H, actually draw lines longer than "n", the parameter. For example, E100 draws a line which is 100 right and 100 above the current position (as would PLOT 1,100,100). This gives the line an actual length of $100*SQR(2)$ (from Pythagoras' theorem). In the original version of the program I took this into account and shortened diagonal lines by a factor of $SQR(2)$. This made diagonal squares (e.g. E100F100G100H100) the same size as the upright ones. However, such compensation does not seem to exist in the original (see Personal Computer World, August 1982. The Dragon review has some examples of DRAW). The version presented here therefore draws diagonal lines longer than other ones.

The X command is very useful. It is possible to execute one string from inside another, much as a program would call a subroutine. Consider the BASIC program below:

```
100 A$="U100 R100 D100 L100"
110 B$="BM640,512 A0 XA$ A1 XA$ A2 XA$ A3 XA$"
120 C$="C0.5 XB$ C1 XA$ C2 XA$"
130 CALL draw,C$
140 END
```

First some points. The "CALL draw,C$" is the BBC version of the DRAW string command. Colour BASIC uses simply "DRAW C$". Also, in the latter C$ may be a constant – DRAW "BM100,100L10" is possible. The equivalent of this in BBC BASIC 'CALL draw,"BM100,100L10"' is illegal as the parameters of CALL have to be variables, not expressions. The spaces in the strings are mostly unnecessary; they just make the strings look nicer. However, spaces are needed sometimes "L100E10" would be treated as a left draw 100E10 points. This would give a "Too big" error. To avoid it, make the "E" lower case, which would be acceptable to the draw line interpreter, or insert a space – "L100 E10". Also there should be a space between a command letter and a reserved word – "A SINth" not "ASINth", as the latter would prevent SIN from being tokenised, resulting in a "No such variable" error when BASIC tried to look for the variable SINth. Finally, there should be a space between a variable and the next command, "AX BM100,100", not "AXBM100,100". In the second one, the parameter of A would be taken as "XBM100", rather than the simple X.

The way the call works is as follows. When C$ is executed, the command C0.5, which sets the scale to a half normal size is executed. The next command X is met. This should be followed by the name of a string variable, and indeed is in this case. If it weren't, either a "No such variable" or "DRAW: Parameters" would be given, depending on whether the erroneous parameter was an existing variable or not. Assuming all is well, DRAW (my DRAW, not BBC BASIC's DRAW) remembers its position in the current string and goes off to execute the named "subroutine" string. This is B$ in the current example. The two commands "BM640,512" (move to the middle of the screen) and "A0" (set rotation to zero) are obeyed. Then, another X is encountered: XA$. The computer once more remembers where it is in B$ and starts to execute A$. This draws a square of side 50 units (remember the scale is 0.5). When A$ has finished, DRAW restarts with B$. After B$ is completed (via three more calls to A$), C$ is restarted. This finishes after it has used B$ twice more. It should be noted that the scale and rotation are global values. Once they are changed, this affects all subsequent drawing, not just the drawing in the string being executed. The X command is slightly "dangerous". For example:

```
100 MODE 4
110 A$="U12 R12 XA$"
120 CALL draw,A$
```

Executing the above would result in a "No room" error. This is because DRAW gets into an infinite loop of executing A$, which calls itself. Since each X requires three bytes of storage on the 6502's stack (to remember the return address & current position), a maximum of about 84 Xs are possible at any time. This shouldn't usually be a problem. Before the DRAW program is given, another "usage" example is listed below.

```
100 REM DRAW demo
110 draw=&C00: REM or wherever DRAW is on your machine
120 main$="BMx,y Xsquare$"
130 wind$="C0.25 BELen/2 Xsquare$ BRLen*2 Xsquare$"
140 wind$=wind$+"BULen*2 Xsquare$ BLLen*2 Xsquare$"
150 roof$="BULen*1.5 BLLen*1.5 C1 RLen*1.5 HLen/4 LLen GLen/4"
160 square$="RLen ULen LLen DLen"
170 house$=main$+wind$+roof$
180 FOR Len=32 TO 512 STEP 32
190    x=640-Len/2: y=512-Len/2
200    CALL draw,house$
210 NEXT Len
220 END
```

The program is quite large. The text is about 12K, though this only becomes 700 odd bytes when assembled. It makes great use of BASIC's sub-routines, especially evaluating expressions and searching for variables. Because the program won't fit

350

conveniently into page &D00, some other home must be found for it. In the listing
below, an array is dimensioned and the object code placed in there. This is not
very useful if the interpreter is to be used in other programs. The best way to
assemble the program would be to make PAGE equal to &1000, then load the
source. Instead of dimensioning code%, set addr% to &D00 as usual, then save it
with *SAVE "Draw" D00 +300. Whenever the program is to be used, set PAGE
to &1000 first then simply *LOAD it. The listing is given below.

```
100 REM   Graphics string interprete
110 DIM code% 700
120 FOR o%=0 TO 2 STEP 2
130    PROCass(code%,o%)
140 NEXT o%
150 END
160
170
1000 DEF PROCass(addr%,opt%)
1010 REM        Routines used in the BASIC ROM
1020 crnch=&88D3:   REM  Tokenise text pointed to by (&37)
1030 getch=&8A13:   REM  Get a character from the line
1040 neg =&ADB5:    REM  iac=-iac
1050 fmult=&A61E:   REM  fac1=fac1*fac2
1060 unpack=&B35B:  REM  Unpack string into &600 on
1070 oswrch=&FFEE:  REM  Output a character
1080 no_such=&AE72:REM  No such variable error
1090 get_flp=&A33F:REM  fac2=var pointed to by (&4B,&4C)
1100 get_var=&95A0:REM  Gets address and type of var in iac
1110 st_flp=&A37E:  REM  Store fac1 in var pointed to by (&4B,&4C)
1120 st_acc=&AF07:  REM  Store acc in iac (zero the three MSB)
1130 st_AY=&AF19:   REM  Store acc and Y in iac (zero the two MSB)
1140 stk_iac=&BDAC:REM  Save iac on stack
1150 stk_str=&BDCA:REM  Save str on stack
1160 uns_iac=&BE02:REM  Restore iac from stack
1170 uns_str=&BDE3:REM  Restore str from stack
1180 chk_com=&8A35:REM  Check  that the next non-space is a comma
1190 typ_err=&8B7E:REM  Do a "Type mismatch" error
1200 rm_err=&8C4B: REM  Do a "No room" error
1210 getexpr=&9B03:REM  Evaluate an expression and return type
1220 expr=&928C:   REM  Evaluate an expression and return type
1230 f_to_int=&A3F2:REM  iac=INT(fac1)
1240 int_to_f=&A2AF:REM  fac1=FLOAT(iac)
1250
1260 REM     BASIC Values used
```

```
1270 iac=&2A:      REM   Integer accumulator
1280 crn_ptr=&37:  REM   Pointer used by tokenisation routine
1290 flp_ptr=&4B:  REM   Pointer to variable
1300 str_len=&36:  REM   String length for stacking
1310 txt_ptr=&19:  REM   Points to text at &600
1320 par_blk=&600: REM   Parameter block and string buffer
1330 txt_index=&1B:REM   Offset from (txt_ptr)
1340
1350 REM     Zero page values
1360 mode=&70:     REM   Plotting option to be used
1370 rot=&71:      REM   Current rotation (0-3 * 90 degrees)
1380 scale=&72:    REM   Current scale factor
1390 act_ptr=&77:  REM   Action address for commands
1400 dx=&79:       REM   X distance
1410 dy=&7B:       REM   Y distance
1420 P%=addr%
1430 [         OPT opt%
1440 .draw     JSR init      \ Set-up pointers and other things
1450 .recurse  JSR string    \ Get string
1460           JSR crunch    \ Crunch string
1470 .loop     LDA #1        \ Main loop
1480           STA mode      \ Set to "draw" mode
1490           LDA #0
1500           STA dx        \ Set distances to zero
1510           STA dx+1
1520           STA dy
1530           STA dy+1
1540 .loop1    JSR getch     \ Get a character
1550           AND #&DF      \ To upper case
1560           CMP #&0D      \ End of line?
1570           BNE f1
1580           RTS           \ Yes. Return
1590 .f1       CMP #ASC("B") \ Special case for "blank"
1600           BNE f2
1610           LDA #0
1620           STA mode
1630           BEQ loop1     \ DON'T reset "draw"
1640 .f2       SEC           \ Convert to 0-25
1650           SBC #ASC("A")
1660           BCC err       \ ERROR if out of range
1670           CMP #26
1680           BCS err
```

```
1690              ASL A          \ Get "action address"
1700              TAX
1710              LDA actions,X
1720              STA act_ptr
1730              LDA actions+1,X
1740              STA act_ptr+1
1750              JSR act         \ Perform the action
1760              JMP loop        \ Next instruction
1770
1780 .act         JMP (act_ptr)   \ Indirect "action" jump
1790
1800 .err         BRK             \ Illegal command error
1810 ]
1820 ?P%=&FF: $(P%+1)="DRAW: Illegal Command"
1830 P%=P%+LEN($(P%+1))+1
1840
1850 [            OPT opt%
1860              BRK
1870 .init        LDA #0          \ Initialise. Set-up text pointer
1880              STA scale+1
1890              STA scale+2
1900              STA scale+3
1910              STA scale+4
1920              STA txt_ptr
1930              STA rot         \ and rotation
1940              LDA #&6         \ txt_ptr is &600
1950              STA txt_ptr+1
1960              LDA #&81        \ &000081 is 1 in floating point
1970              STA scale
1980              RTS
1990
2000 .A           JSR expr        \ Set rotation. Get expression
2010              LDA iac
2020              AND #3          \ 0-3 multiples of 90 degrees
2030              STA rot
2040              RTS
2050
2060 .B           \ Blank is a special case
2070
2080 .C           JSR getexpr     \ Set scale. Get real expression
2090              BMI Cf1         \ It's real already.
2100              BNE Cf2         \ Integer; convert to real
```

```
2110              JMP typ_err     \ A string. Give an error
2120 .Cf2         JSR int_to_f
2130 .Cf1         LDA #scale MOD 256 \ Save fac1 in scale
2140              STA flp_ptr
2150              LDA #scale DIV 256
2160              STA flp_ptr+1
2170              JSR st_flp      \ Save it
2180              RTS
2190
2200 .D           JSR expr        \ Move down. Get distance
2210              JSR neg         \ Negate for -Y movement
2220              JSR stdy        \ Store in dy
2230              JMP plot        \ Plot the line
2240
2250 .E           JSR expr        \ Draw at 45 degrees. Get distance
2260              JSR stdx        \ Store in dx and dy
2270              JSR stdy
2280              JMP plot        \ Plot the line
2290              RTS
2300
2310 .F           JSR expr        \ Draw at 135 degrees. Get distance
2320              JSR stdx        \ Store in dx
2330              JSR neg         \ Store -dist. in dy
2340              JSR stdy
2350              JMP plot        \ Plot the line
2360
2370 .G           JSR expr        \ Draw at 225 degrees. Get distance
2380              JSR neg         \ Store -dist. in dx and dy
2390              JSR stdx
2400              JSR stdy
2410              JMP plot        \ Plot the line
2420
2430 .H           JSR expr        \ Draw at 315 degrees. Get distance
2440              JSR stdy        \ Store in dy
2450              JSR neg         \ Store -dist. in dx
2460              JSR stdx
2470              JMP plot        \ Plot the line
2480
2490 .L           JSR expr        \ Draw left. Get distance
2500              JSR neg         \ Store -dist. in dx
2510              JSR stdx
2520              JMP plot        \ Plot the line
```

```
2530
2540 .M          JSR expr        \ Draw to (X,Y). get X
2550             JSR stdx
2560             JSR chk_com     \ Check for a comma
2570             JSR expr        \ Get Y
2580             JSR stdy
2590             LDA mode        \ Make plot mode absolute
2600             ORA #4
2610             STA mode
2620             JMP plot        \ Plot the line
2630
2640 .R          JSR expr        \ Draw right. Get distance
2650             JSR stdx        \ Store dist. in dx
2660             JMP plot        \ Plot the line
2670
2680 .U          JSR expr        \ Draw up. Get distance
2690             JSR stdy        \ Store dist. in dy
2700             JMP plot        \ Plot the line
2710
2720 .X          JSR get_var     \ Execute a string. Look it up
2730             BNE Xf1
2740             JMP no_such     \ Not found. Give error
2750 .Xf1        LDA txt_index   \ Save position in text on 6502 stack
2760             PHA
2770             TSX             \ Check for stack overflow
2780             BNE Xok
2790             JMP rm_err      \ Oh dear. Give a message
2800 .Xok        JSR stk_str     \ Then save the string itself
2810             LDA #1          \ Set-up par_blk. 1 parameter
2820             STA par_blk
2830             LDA iac
2840             STA par_blk+1   \ Address low
2850             LDA iac+1
2860             STA par_blk+2   \ Address high
2870             LDA iac+2
2880             STA par_blk+3   \ Type
2890             JSR recurse     \ Recursive call
2900             JSR uns_str     \ Get string back
2910             PLA             \ Restore index into text
2920             TAY
2930             STY txt_index
2940             RTS
```

```
2950
2960 .plot      LDA mode        \ Draw the line. Is it absolute?
2970            AND #4
2980            BNE plf1        \ Yes. No scaling or rotation
2990            JSR rotn
3000            JSR scaling
3010 .plf1      LDA #25         \ Do the plot
3020            JSR oswrch
3030            LDA mode
3040            JSR oswrch
3050            LDA dx
3060            JSR oswrch
3070            LDA dx+1
3080            JSR oswrch
3090            LDA dy
3100            JSR oswrch
3110            LDA dy+1
3120            JSR oswrch
3130            RTS
3140
3150 .rotn      LDA rot         \ Get rotation
3160            BEQ rof3        \ Zero rotation
3170            TAX             \ Save Acc for later
3180            AND #2          \ Negate Y?
3190            BEQ rof1        \ No
3200            JSR lddy        \ Yes
3210            JSR neg
3220            JSR stdy
3230 .rof1      TXA
3240            CMP #3          \ Negate X?
3250            BCS rof2        \ No
3260            JSR lddx        \ Yes
3270            JSR neg
3280            JSR stdx
3290 .rof2      TXA
3300            AND #1          \ Swap X and Y?
3310            BEQ rof3        \ No
3320            JSR lddx        \ Yes    iac=dx
3330            JSR stk_iac     \        t=dx
3340            JSR lddy        \        iac=dy
3350            JSR stdx        \        dx=iac(=dy)
3360            JSR uns_iac     \        iac=dx
```

```
3370              JSR stdy         \          dy=iac(=dx)
3380 .rof3        RTS
3390
3400 .scaling     JSR lddx         \ Scale the X and Y distances
3410              JSR scal1        \ Scale it
3420              JSR stdx
3430              JSR lddy
3440              JSR scal1
3450              JSR stdy
3460              RTS
3470
3480 .scal1       LDA #scale MOD 256  \ Get address of scale factor
3490              LDX #scale DIV 256
3500 .mult        STA flp_ptr      \ Multiply iac by var at (AX). Get var
3510              STX flp_ptr+1
3520              JSR get_flp      \ Get variable in fac2
3530              JSR int_to_f     \ fac1=iac
3540              JSR fmult        \ fac1=fac1*fac2
3550              JSR f_to_int     \ Put product in iac
3560              RTS
3570
3580 .stdx        LDA iac          \ Save iac in dx
3590              STA dx
3600              LDA iac+1
3610              STA dx+1
3620              RTS
3630
3640 .stdy        LDA iac          \ Save iac in dy
3650              STA dy
3660              LDA iac+1
3670              STA dy+1
3680              RTS
3690
3700 .lddx        LDA dx           \ Load iac with dx
3710              LDY dx+1
3720              JMP ldiac
3730
3740 .lddy        LDA dy           \ Load iac with dy
3750              LDY dy+1
3760 .ldiac       JSR st_AY
3770              TYA              \ Extend sign if minus
3780              BPL lddyf1
```

```
3790            DEC iac+2
3800            DEC iac+3
3810 .lddyf1    LDY txt_index
3820            RTS
3830
3840 .string    DEC par_blk    \ Check parameter and unpack it
3850            BEQ parok
3860 .parerr    BRK
3870 ]
3880 ?P%=&FE: $(P%+1)="DRAW: Parameters"
3890 P%=P%+LEN($(P%+1))+1
3900 [          OPT opt%
3910            BRK
3920 .parok     LDA par_blk+3
3930            CMP #129
3940            BNE parerr
3950            STA iac+2      \ Save type for unpack
3960            LDA par_blk+1  \ Get SIB address
3970            STA iac
3980            LDA par_blk+2
3990            STA iac+1
4000            LDY #3         \ Get string length
4010            LDA (iac),Y
4020            TAY            \ Store a &D at the end of the string
4030            LDA #&0D
4040            STA par_blk,Y
4050            JSR unpack
4060            RTS
4070
4080
4090 .crunch    LDA #0         \ Tokenise string so that expressions work
4100            STA txt_index  \ Set up pointer to string
4110            TAY
4120            STA crn_ptr    \ Store address of string buffer
4130            LDA #&06
4140            STA crn_ptr+1
4150            JSR crnch
4160            LDY crn_ptr    \ Save length for stacking
4170            STY str_len
4180            RTS
4190 ]
4200 REM Set up the action address table
```

```
4210 actions=P%
4220 !actions=A:   actions!2=B
4230 actions!4=C:  actions!6=D
4240 actions!8=E:  actions!10=F
4250 actions!12=G:actions!14=H
4260 FOR i%=16 TO 50 STEP 2
4270   actions!i%=err
4280 NEXT i%
4290 actions!22=L
4300 actions!24=M
4310 actions!34=R
4320 actions!40=U
4330 actions!46=X
4340 P%=actions+52
4350 ENDPROC
```

As the program is rather long, I have tried to make the REMs and comments as lucid as possible. In particular, the use of many BASIC routines means that a knowledge of the interpreter's internal working would be helpful. Almost all of BASIC's routines use the text pointer. This consists of three locations: &19 and &1A are used to point to the beginning of the current "block" of text, and &1B (and usually the Y register) is used to move about within that block, with instructions such as "LDA (&19),Y". The routine "getch" returns the next character in the accumulator and increments the text pointer.

The "crunch" routine converts the text (pointed to by &37,&38) into its tokenised form, i.e. all reserved words such as SIN and ABS are converted to their one-byte form. This enables the use of BASIC's expression evaluator routine. This routine is at &9B03. It evaluates an expression (starting at the current text pointer position) and puts the result in the integer accumulator, the floating point accumulator or the string buffer as appropriate. Just before it returns, the routine sets the flags depending on the type of result: zero for strings, positive but non-zero for integers and negative for reals. This enables detection of "Type mismatch" errors. For example, none of the graphics commands require a string argument (X needs a string variable name, not an expression), so if &9B03 ever returns with the zero flag set, a "Type mismatch" error is generated. In fact, almost all the commands (with the exception of C) want integers expressions. The routine at &928C uses &9B03 to obtain an expression and converts it into an integer if necessary, or gives an error if the result was a string. A strange thing is that EVAL uses the same technique of tokenising the string and evaluating it. However, "EVAL("PAGE")" gives a "No such variable" error, whereas "M PAGE,PAGE" works fine in the current program.

The main loop of the program is a simple "get a command, if it's legal and not &0D, execute it. Otherwise end or give an error as appropriate". An erroneous command is a character which lies outside the range "A" to "Z" after it has been forced into upper case. The way commands are executed has a lot in common with the way BASIC execute commands. For each command there is an "action address". This is the address of the main part of each of the commands' code. The addresses are held in a table called "actions". For example, the address of the "A" command is held at actions+0 and actions+1. Once this address has been fetched and stored in the indirection vector act_ptr, all that is required is a JSR (act_ptr). Since no such command exists on the 6502, a JSR is made to a one-line routine which then does a JMP (act_ptr). The effect is the same. As not all of the letters represent legal commands, many of the addresses in actions send control to the "Illegal command" error routine.

The only command which isn't processed as described above is "B", which converts the next draw into a move. This is treated as a special case as it returns to a point just after all the others. If it didn't, it would be ineffectual as the plot mode is set to "draw" at the beginning of each loop. By returning from "B" to just after this point, the blanking action affects only the next command, not all subsequent commands.

The main routines are described now, albeit in little detail. The set-up routine, init, initialises the values which need to be assigned at the beginning of each CALL draw, but not each recursive call. These are the scale, which is set to 1, the rotation, whose initial value is zero, and the base value of the text pointer, &0600. As the scale is held in floating point form, it occupies five bytes. One is represented as &0000000081. Where this comes from is unimportant, but for those who understand such things: the first byte is the exponent in excess 128 form, the MS bit of the second byte is the mantissa sign, and the first bit of the mantissa is assumed to be 1. This gives "+0.100000... *2^(129-128)", which is 2 times 0.1, which is 1. (Forgive the mixing of binary fractions and decimal integers.)

After "init" comes the routine "string" at the label "recurse". This is the entry point for recursive calls caused by an X command (see later). The string routine does the necessary parameter checking and, if all is well, unpacks the string into the buffer at &600. It also puts a "&D" at the end. This is used by the tokenisation routine, which routine is called from "crunch". It is very easy to use: set the pointer at &37,&38 to the start of the routine and ensure that the last character is a "&D". Then call "crnch" at &88D3. The routine exits with the text tokenised (as it would be stored in a BASIC program). Also, &37,&38 points to the last character in the transformed string. As our example starts on a page boundary, this can be used as the length of the tokenised form. It is stored in str_len, and used later by the "push string on the BASIC stack" routine.

The actions routines, at labels A, B, etc. are mostly self-explanatory. All the line drawing ones are of the form "get the distance; set-up the plot co-ordinates dx and dy as appropriate; jump to plot". The exceptions are M, A and X. M needs two co-ordinates, which it obtains with two calls to the integer expression routine. These are separated by a call to chk_com, a BASIC routine which checks the presence of a comma and moves the text pointer to it. A "Missing comma" error is given if the next non-space character is not a comma. As M causes an absolute move, the current plot mode is ORed with &4 to force this. Then the normal jump to plot is made. The A and C commands obtain integer and real expressions respectively and store the results in rot and scale, also respectively.

The most interesting command is X. It is (in my humble opinion) a fine example of recursion in machine code. (For other fine examples see the expression evaluator in BASIC.) Since the command has the form "Xs$", the first thing to do is find the string given. This is done with a call to "get_var". This BASIC routine scans the text for any variable name. This could be "A$", "!23", "A(12,32)" and so on. If no variable name is present, the routine returns with the zero flag set. Otherwise, the zero flag is reset and the address and type of the variable are stored (in parameter block format) at iac to iac+2. If a variable is found, X sets-up the parameter block in the same way as CALL (but not before saving the current string, which also lives at par_blk, on the BASIC stack). Notice that no attempt is made to check the type of the variable – this will be done by "string". The other item which needs to be saved is the current text pointer. This is saved on the 6502 stack, as it only requires one byte. The stack is checked for overflow before the recursive call is made. Upon return from the call to "recurse", the stored information is pulled from the stacks, and the text pointer reset. Life then carries on as normal with an RTS.

The other routines are fairly simple. Rotation works out the co-ordinates with respect to the value of rot. If the rotation is zero, or the plot absolute, no rotation is necessary. Otherwise, dx and dy are transformed depending on the value of rot. I leave it as an exercise to work out how the tests and assignments correspond to the transformed co-ordinates. (Hint: (x,y) becomes (x,y), (y,–x), (–x,–y), (–y,x) for rot=0,1,2,3 respectively.) Another exercise is to go back to "find" presented earlier and incorporate a call to crnch, so that you can find things like "FOR I". It only takes about eight extra instructions.

After the code, the jump table is set-up. This uses the values of the labels A, B, X, etc. to determine the command addresses, and err to give the default error command. As already mentioned, the program is very large. It won't fit in a 16K machine (even in MODE 7) unless you delete the REMs and comments, and probably most of the spaces as well. Nevertheless, there are many improvements to be made. The rotation factor could be expressed in degrees. To rotate (x,y) by th degrees in a clockwise direction, use xrot = x*COS(RAD(th)) + y*SIN(RAD(th)), yrot = y*COS(RAD(th)) – x*SIN(RAD(th)). There are many cases of the form "JSR label:RTS" in the program. These could be replaced by "JMP label", to save a few bytes. The saving is at the expense of some readability. Using the action address table, it is a simple matter to add new commands, such as one to change the graphics colour from within a string. This should be very easy: "JSR gcol:RTS", but you'd have to check (with a disassembler) that the code at gcol (&932F) uses the same text pointers and returns with an RTS. If not, you will have to re-write the code.

Here is a moral tale. I wrote the main part of draw, except for X command in one evening (where an evening is from 6 p.m. to 4 a.m. the next morning). The next day, I started on X. This alone took another three days to get working. The reason is that (as a matter of course) I inserted some trace commands of the form "TYA: JSR hexout:JMP osnewl" so that I could check what was going on during the recursion. However, there was no way that I could get the X command to work. Finally, I realised that my flash "hexout" was changing the value of Y register, which proved fatal. When I removed the "debugging" routines, the X command worked fine. The moral? Make sure the bloody debugging routines are debugged!

The shortcomings of the built-in LIST command were mentioned earlier. To recap, the indentation produced by LISTO 2 and LISTO 4 for FOR and REPEAT loops is not very well done, as the loop terminating statements do not appear under their respective FOR/REPEAT. As the whole idea of indenting a program is to show clearly which statements are affected by which constructs, the LISTO statement is self-defeating in this respect. Writing a LIST program which indents properly is not very hard. The only extra work required is the "look ahead" at the beginning of each line to see if there is a loop terminator as the first statement. If there is, the space count for indentation is decremented before the word is printed instead of after.

The list program given below indents procedures/functions in addition to FORs and REPEATs, and also treats IFs in a special way if required. The LISTO options are as follows:

```
LISTO option          Action
     1                Print a space after the line number
     2                Print three spaces in FOR loops
     4                Print three spaces in REPEAT loops
     8                Print three spaces in PROC/FNs
    16                Print the ELSE clause on a newline
```

The LISTO command is used in exactly the same way, so to list a program with all of the options given above, you would say:

```
LISTO 31
CALL list
```

The program below is listed with LISTO 0 then LISTO 31 in effect.

```
100FOR i%=1 TO 100
110PRINT i%/100;
120IF i% AND 1 THEN PRINT i%*100 ELSE PROCa(i%)
130t%=TIME+20
140REPEAT UNTIL TIME=t%
150NEXTi%
160END
170
180DEFPROCa(i%)
190REM a procedure
```

```
200IF i% THEN PROCa(i%-1) ELSE IF TIME<200 THEN PROCa(i%+1) ELSE ENDPROC
210ENDPROC

100 FOR i%=1 TO 100
110    PRINT i%/100;
120    IF i% AND 1 THEN PRINT i%*100
                    ELSE PROCa(i%)
130    t%=TIME+20
140    REPEAT UNTIL TIME=t%
150 NEXTi%
160 END
170
180 DEFPROCa(i%)
190    REM a procedure
200    IF i% THEN PROCa(i%-1)
            ELSE IF TIME<200 THEN PROCa(i%+1)
                         ELSE ENDPROC
210 ENDPROC
```

Note that the "program" doesn't do much! Any of the five formatting options can be disabled by choosing the appropriate LISTO. For example, if you want indenting of loops and procedures, but not a space after the line number or formatted IFs, use LISTO 2+4+8, or LISTO 14. There is only one undesirable "feature" of the list program given, which is the behaviour of FNs. If the "indent DEFs" bit of LISTO is set, three is added to the space count whenever the word DEF is encountered in the BASIC text. The count is decreased again when an ENDPROC or "=" is reached. However, "=" crops up a lot more often than just the =expression form of functions, e.g. in assignments and FOR lines. It is very hard to distinguish between these different occurrences. Because of this, the space count is only decremented when "=" is the first non-space on a line. The result is that:

```
100 DEF FNA=1000
110 DEF PROCA
120 REM statements
130 ENDPROC
```

becomes:

```
100 DEF FNA=1000
110    DEF PROCA
120       REM statements
130    ENDPROC
```

To indent functions properly, there should be an =expression at the beginning of the last line of the function.

As the example above suggested, the list program is used via a CALL. It is placed at &C00, so you can't use the user-defined characters 224 to 255. Since the program's main use would be to get nicely formatted listings on a printer this should not be a problem. The BASIC LIST command is quite versatile: "LIST" lists the whole program, "LIST line" lists just one line, "LIST line," lists from the line specified to the end and "LIST ,line" lists from the beginning to the line specified. To incorporate most of these possibilities in a CALL statement requires the provision of a variable number of parameters, zero, one or two. This makes the parameter-checking part of the program quite long. It could be shortened if just (for example) the ability to list the whole program is required. The way the parameters are interpreted is as follows. If there aren't any, all the program is listed. If there is one parameter, the action depends on its sign. The statement "CALL list,n%", where n% is positive is equivalent to "LIST n%," (except that n% would have to be a constant for LIST). If n% is negative, "CALL list,n%" acts as "LIST ,n%". When there are two parameters, a% and b%, the action is the same as "LIST a%,b%". The only way to list just one line is "CALL list,a%,a%", so you might as well use LIST for that.

The speed of the program is quite good. It's about 3% slower than the built-in command. This is mainly due to the extra checking (for THEN, etc.) that must be performed. When the "added extras" are removed, it runs at about 99.7% of the speed of BASIC's LIST. This is because I am only 99.7% the programmer that Roger Wilson is, if that. The program is given below:

```
100 code%=&C00
110 FOR o%=0 TO 2 STEP 2
120    PROCass(code%,o%)
130 NEXT o%
140 *KEY9INPUT''''"LIST "A%,B%:CALL &C00,A%,B%|M
150 END
160
170
1000 DEF PROCass(addr%, opt%)
1010 REM   BASIC Routines used
1020 chk_esc=&9834: out_lin=&98F5: out_num=&98F1
1030 out_spc=&B57B: newl=&BC42
1040 outch=&B53A: abs=&AD94
1050 search=&9942: unpack=&B35B
1060 REM   BASIC variables used
1070 count=&1E: page=&18
1080 listo=&1F: txt_ptr=&19
1090 txt_index=&1B: iac=&2A
1100 ind_cnt=&3B: par_blk=&600
1110 REM   Constants used
1120 for=&E3:  next=&ED
```

```
1130 def=&DD:   endproc=&E1
1140 repeat=&F5:   until=&FD
1150 then=&8C:  else=&8B
1160 REM    Zero-page locations
1170 then_flg=&70:  tmp=&71
1180 last=&72:  first=&74
1190 P%=addr%
1200 [           OPT opt%
1210 .list       JSR init         \ Get parameter(s) & init. pointer etc.
1220 .line       JSR chk_esc      \ Check for Escape key pressed
1230             JSR tst_lin      \ Check for last line or end of prog.
1240             BCS end_list     \ Yes, we're at the end
1250             JSR getch        \ Skip byte count byte
1260             JSR lin_num      \ Print line number
1270             JSR chk_ends     \ Check for Until, Next etc.
1280             JSR indent       \ Print indentation spaces
1290             JSR rest         \ Do the rest of the line
1300             CLC              \ Update txt_ptr
1310             LDA txt_index
1320             LDY #0
1330             STY txt_index
1340             ADC txt_ptr
1350             STA txt_ptr
1360             BCC line
1370             INC txt_ptr+1
1380             BCS line
1390 .end_list   RTS
1400
1410
1420 .tst_lin    JSR getch        \ Get line no. high byte
1430             CMP #&FF         \ &FF marks end of program
1440             BEQ tst_ret
1450             STA iac+1        \ Save it for printing
1460             CMP last+1       \ Greater than limit?
1470             BCC tstf1        \ Less than
1480             BNE tst_ret      \ Greater than. Return with carry set
1490             JSR getch        \ Equal. Get low byte
1500             CMP last         \ Greater than limit?
1510             BCC tstf2        \ Less than or equal is ok
1520             BEQ tstf2
1530             BNE tst_ret      \ Greater than. Return with carry set
1540 .tstf1      JSR getch        \ Get LSB
```

```
1550 .tstf2      STA iac          \ Save for printing
1560             CLC              \ Not at end so carry clear
1570 .tst_ret    RTS
1580
1590
1600 .lin_num    JSR out_lin      \ Print line no. and a space if required
1610             LDA listo        \ Get option
1620             ROR A            \ Get bit 0 in carry
1630             BCC lin_ret      \ No space needed
1640             JSR out_spc      \ Print the space
1650 .lin_ret    RTS
1660
1670
1680 .chk_ends   LDY txt_index    \ Look ahead for Next, Until etc.
1690 .ends_loop  LDA (txt_ptr),Y
1700             CMP #&20
1710             BNE endsf0
1720             INY
1730             BNE ends_loop
1740 .endsf0     TAX              \ Save it in X
1750             LDA #8           \ Check for an "=" at the start of the line
1760             BIT listo
1770             BEQ chk_ends1    \ We're not indenting Defs
1780             CPX #ASC("=")     \ Yes we are. Is it an "=" then?
1790             BEQ dec_cnt      \ Yes. Decrement count
1800 .chk_ends1  LDA listo        \ Get LISTO option
1810             ROR A            \ Ignore "space" bit
1820             ROR A            \ Get FOR...NEXT bit
1830             BCC endsf1       \ We're not indenting For loops
1840             CPX #next
1850             BEQ dec_cnt      \ Yes, decrement indent count
1860 .endsf1     ROR A            \ Look for Until?
1870             BCC endsf2
1880             CPX #until       \ Yes; got an Until?
1890             BEQ dec_cnt      \ Yes; decrement indentation
1900 .endsf2     ROR A            \ Look for Endproc
1910             BCC ends_ret     \ No; go home
1920             CPX #endproc
1930             BNE ends_ret
1940 .dec_cnt    DEC ind_cnt      \ Decrement count
1950             BPL ends_ret     \ Still positive
1960             INC ind_cnt      \ Gone negative; make zero
```

```
1970 .ends_ret  RTS
1980
1990
2000 .indent    LDX ind_cnt        \ Print indentation spaces
2010            BEQ indentf1       \ No indentation to do
2020 .indentlp  JSR out_spc        \ Print 3 spaces
2030            JSR out_spc
2040            JSR out_spc
2050            DEX
2060            BNE indentlp
2070 .indentf1  JSR getch          \ Now do the spaces in the text
2080            CMP #ASC(" ")
2090            BNE indentf2       \ Finished with spaces
2100            JSR outch          \ Print it
2110            JMP indentf1
2120 .indentf2  RTS                \ Return with char. in Acc. for "rest"
2130
2140
2150 .rest      LDX #0             \ Do rest of line. Reset "THEN" flag
2160            STX then_flg
2170            INX                \ Set "first token" flag
2180            STX first
2190 .restloop  CMP #&0D           \ End of line?
2200            BEQ restf1         \ Yes.
2210            CMP #&8D           \ Line number follows?
2220            BNE restf2         \ No.
2230            JSR decode         \ Convert to binary in iac
2240            JSR out_num        \ and print it
2250            JSR getch          \ Get next char
2260            BNE restloop       \ Always taken
2270 .restf2    TAX                \ Save it
2280            DEC first          \ First token?
2290            BEQ restf3         \ Yes, don't do "end" checks again
2300            JSR chk_ends1
2310 .restf3    JSR chk_strts
2320            JSR chk_then
2330            JSR chk_else
2340            TXA                \ Restore character and print it
2350            JSR outch
2360            JSR getch
2370            BNE restloop       \ Always taken
2380 .restf1    JSR newl           \ Do a newline
```

```
2390              RTS
2400
2410
2420 .decode      JSR getch          \ Convert 3 bytes after &8D into binary no.
2430              ASL A
2440              ASL A
2450              TAX
2460              AND #&C0
2470              INY
2480              EOR (txt_ptr),Y
2490              STA iac
2500              TXA
2510              ASL A
2520              ASL A
2530              INY
2540              EOR (txt_ptr),Y
2550              STA iac+1
2560              INY
2570              STY txt_index      \ Update txt_index
2580              RTS
2590
2600 .chk_strts LDA listo            \ Do checks for For, Repeat and Def
2610              ROR A              \ Ignore "space" bit
2620              ROR A              \ Get "FOR" bit
2630              BCC strtsf1
2640              CPX #for
2650              BEQ inc_cnt
2660 .strtsf1     ROR A              \ Check Repeat?
2670              BCC strtsf2
2680              CPX #repeat
2690              BEQ inc_cnt
2700 .strtsf2     ROR A              \ Check Def?
2710              BCC strts_ret
2720              CPX #def
2730              BNE strts_ret
2740 .inc_cnt     INC ind_cnt        \ Incrememt indent count
2750 .strts_ret RTS
2760
2770
2780 .chk_then    LDA #16            \ Check for then (if LISTO 16)
2790              BIT listo
2800              BEQ then_ret
```

```
2810            CPX #then        \ Is it a Then, then?
2820            BNE then_ret
2830            LDA count        \ Remember count for Else
2840            STA then_flg
2850 .then_ret  RTS
2860
2870
2880 .chk_else  LDA #16          \ Check for then (if LISTO 16)
2890            BIT listo
2900            BEQ else_ret
2910            CPX #else        \ Is it an Else, then?
2920            BNE else_ret
2930            LDA then_flg
2940            BEQ else_ret     \ Only do a newline if there's been a Then
2950            JSR newl         \ Do a newline
2960 .elseloop  JSR out_spc      \ Print enough spaces to align the ELSE
2970            DEC then_flg
2980            BNE elseloop
2990 .else_ret  RTS
3000
3010
3020 .getch     LDY txt_index    \ Get a character from (txt_ptr), txt_index
3030            LDA (txt_ptr),Y
3040            INC txt_index
3050 .getchf1   RTS
3060
3070
3080 .init      LDY #1           \ Get parameters. Set default start and ends
3090            STY txt_ptr      \ to PAGE+1 and line &7FFF resp.
3100            DEY              \ Y=0
3110            STY txt_index    \ Displacement within current line
3120            STY ind_cnt      \ "Indentation count"
3130            DEY
3140            STY last         \ Low byte of &7FFF for last line
3150            LDY #&7F         \ High byte of &7FFF for last line
3160            STY last+1
3170            LDY page         \ PAGE+1 is first byte of first line
3180            STY txt_ptr+1
3190            LDY par_blk      \ Modify those defaults with params.
3200            BEQ init_ret     \ No parameters, nothing to change
3210            DEY
3220            BEQ initf1       \ One parameter. Might change first or last
```

```
3230              DEY
3240              BEQ initf2         \ Two parameters give new first and last
3250 .init_err    BRK                \ Parameter error
3260 ]
3270 ?P%=&FF: $(P%+1)="LIST: Parameters"
3280 P%=P%+LEN($(P%+1))+1
3290 [          OPT opt%
3300              BRK
3310 .initf2      LDA #4             \ Check types
3320              AND par_blk+3
3330              AND par_blk+6
3340              BEQ init_err
3350              LDA #0             \ Get param #1 in iac
3360              JSR param
3370              JSR set_low        \ Set pointers to low line given
3380              LDA #1             \ Get param #2 in iac
3390              JSR param
3400              JSR set_high
3410 .init_ret    RTS                \ and return
3420 .initf1      LDA par_blk+3      \ Check type
3430              CMP #4
3440              BNE init_err
3450              LDA #0             \ Get the parameter
3460              JSR param
3470              BIT iac+3          \ If negative, change high line number
3480              BMI initf3
3490              JSR set_low        \ Set pointers to low line given
3500              RTS
3510 .initf3      JSR abs            \ Make iac postive
3520              JSR set_high
3530              RTS
3540
3550
3560 .param       STA tmp            \ Get parameter #(Acc+1)
3570              ASL A
3580              CLC
3590              ADC tmp            \ Acc=3*Acc
3600              TAX
3610              LDA par_blk+1,X    \ Set-up for unpack
3620              STA iac
3630              LDA par_blk+2,X
3640              STA iac+1
```

```
3650            LDA par_blk+3,X
3660            STA iac+2
3670            JSR unpack
3680            RTS
3690
3700
3710 .set_low   JSR search      \ Look for the line number
3720            BCS lowf1       \ Not found.
3730            SEC             \ First byte of line at (&3D,&3E)-2
3740            LDA &3D
3750            SBC #2
3760            STA txt_ptr
3770            BCS lowf2
3780            DEC &3E
3790 .lowf2     LDA &3E
3800            STA txt_ptr+1
3810            RTS
3820 .lowf1     INC &3D         \ Not found. Line is at (&3D,&3E)+1
3830            LDA &3D
3840            STA txt_ptr
3850            BNE lowf2
3860            INC &3E
3870            BNE lowf2
3880
3890
3900 .set_high  LDA iac         \ Set high line #. Just copy from iac
3910            STA last
3920            LDA iac+1
3930            STA last+1
3940            RTS
3950 ]
3960 ENDPROC
```

Though shorter than the DRAW program, LIST is probably harder to follow. I hope the comments help a little. Once the parameters have been decoded, the program enters a loop of "check for the end, if not there list the line". Before describing the program proper, I will give brief details of the BASIC routines used. I mentioned "outch" earlier. This routine works like oswrch, and indeed uses that call. The difference is in the way that characters with codes above &80 are handled. These are not proper ASCII codes, as only the lower seven bits (codes 0–127) of a byte are used for ASCII. The top 128 codes are used by BASIC as tokens for the reserved words of the language. What happens is that when a line of BASIC is typed in, it is scanned for any occurrences of reserved (or key) words such as "PRINT" and "REPEAT". When these are detected, the characters of the word are replaced by the single character in the range 128 to 255. This saves a lot of space in programs, especially with long words like "ENVELOPE". There is a list of the token values on pp. 483–484 of the User Guide.

When the outch routine is called with a token value in the accumulator, it is expanded to the reserved word for which it stands (see the example using CALL earlier). Other characters (i.e. in the range 0–127) are sent straight to oswrch, so are printed normally. Obviously outch is a routine central to any list program, as it enables the tokenised form to be expanded into the original "English". The routines out_lin and out_num are really the same one. They print the contents of the two least significant bytes of iac as a decimal number in the range 0–65535. The print width is set by the contents of &14. The difference between the two calls is that out_lin sets &14 to 5 (hence all line numbers are right-justified to exactly 5 print positions) and out_num sets &14 to 0 (numbers are printed left-justified). The first form is used to print line numbers at the start of the line, the second for GOTO, GOSUB, etc. destination line numbers.

The "search" routine looks through the current program for a line number equal to that in (iac,iac+1). If it finds such a line number, the routine returns with the carry flag cleared. The line is pointed to by (&3D,&3E). These two bytes hold the location of the line-length byte of the line in question. Since this is the third byte of a line, the address required by LIST is actually (&3D,&3E)–2. If the line is not found, the carry flag is set upon return to the calling program. This time, (&3D,&3E) contains the address of the last byte of the highest line less than the one required. For example, if a program contained the lines 30 and 50, and line 40 was sought, (&3D,&3E) would point to the &0D character at the end of line 30. Since LIST would start at line 50 in this example, the address is simply incremented by one to get the first byte of line 50.

The main loop of the program starts by testing for the ESCAPE key. The necessary action is performed by BASIC if ESCAPE has been pressed. Otherwise, control returns immediately to list. Next, the present line is tested. At this point, the text pointer will always point to the first byte in the line, which is the high byte of the line number. This is set to &FF at the end of the program. The routine tst_lin checks for this end-of-program byte, and also for the current line number exceeding the limit held in "last". In either case the routine returns with the carry set. It is cleared otherwise. Assuming the end has not been reached, the line number (which tst_lin placed in the iac) is printed, along with any extra space which the current LIST option requires. Next, the program takes a quick look to see if the first non-space character on the line is one of the "end" tokens, NEXT, UNTIL, "=" or ENDPROC. If so, the count of indenting spaces is decremented so that the end-loop token will not be indented. If inc_cnt becomes less than zero (because there are more UNTILs than REPEATs for example), it is set to zero.

After chk_ends, the indentation for this line can be printed. This comes from the spaces present between the line number and the first token, and also the spaces produced by ind_cnt. If you wanted to be forceful, you could ignore the spaces already present. This would simplify the program slightly. After "indent" comes "rest", which lives up to its name by listing the remainder of the line. First, the "then_flg" is reset. This flag is set if a THEN is encountered and bit 4 (counting from zero) of listo is also set. The loop of "rest" has the form: "check this token for being &0D. If it is, do a new-line and return. Otherwise, save the character in X and do the various tests on it. Then print the token and get the next one. Jump back to test_loop". The exception to this is when the token is &8D. This token means "a line number comes next". The line number is the destination of a GOTO, GOSUB, etc. It is not held as a normal 16-bit number (or even a reversed bytes 16-bit number as initial line numbers are). Rather, it is a strange manipulation of the binary form. Before it can be printed by out_num it must be converted into binary. This is done by "decode".

The four test routines check the LIST option determined by bits 1,2,3 and 4 for listo. Bit 1 is the "indent FOR loops", bit 2 "indent REPEAT loops", bit 3 "indent procedures/functions" and bit 4 "format IF ... THEN ... ELSE". The last is most interesting. When a THEN is encountered, the then_flg is set by storing COUNT in it. This is effectively the present horizontal tab position, as all LIST output is via BASIC routines which update COUNT at each character. When an ELSE is subsequently met, the flag then_flg is tested. You may think that if we are at an ELSE then logically we must have passed a THEN. Not so as:

```
100 IF A=B PRINT "HELLO" ELSE PRINT "GOODBYE"
```

is legal, if hard to read. Assuming the three conditions 1) the relevant listo bit is set; 2) we have an ELSE and 3) there has been a THEN are met, then the ELSE is printed on the next line, under the THEN. This is achieved by printing "then_flg" spaces. It could be achieved with an oswrch 31, but this might not work if a printer were being used.

The init routine is fairly straightforward. It must cater for 0, 1 or 2 parameters as mentioned above. The "search" routine is used to set the initial address when a lower line limit is specified, and "last" is altered from its default value if specified by the parameters. The two values default to PAGE+1 for the initial line pointer and 32767 for the highest line. "Param" puts the address of the accumulator+1th parameter in iac, and is of general application.

If you didn't know assembly language before you started this chapter you are probably even more confused by now. However, you should still be able to use the complete programs from the descriptions given, even if you don't understand them. There is an awful lot more that can be done with 32K of ROM routines than I can mention here. In my next book (which is provisionally entitled "How to Cook Peking Roast Duck on a BBC Computer, with a foreword by Vincent Price") I am planning to delve into far greater detail on the BASIC ROM.

Annotated Bibliography

The following is a list of the books which have been mentioned in the text, or which I thought of just after finishing the book. Since I've restricted the list to those which I have read, it isn't particularly long, but should provide many a starting point for further investigation.

Beech: Graham Beech, *Successful Software for Small Computers*. Sigma Technical Press, 1980. Many of the subjects mentioned in the text are covered in more detail in this book. The technique of designing programs using a Program Description Language is introduced, then converting PDL to BASIC. The same technique can be applied to BBC BASIC, though much more easily as this is considerably more like PDL than the TRS-80 version used in the book. It was £5.50 when I bought it.

Bowles: Kenneth Bowles, *Microcomputer Problem Solving Using Pascal*. Springer-Verlag, 1977. Another structured programming book, this time with reference to Pascal. The actual version used is UCSD Pascal, which was designed by the author and is implemented on many micros (probably not the BBC Micro, though). It's of particular interest as UCSD Pascal supports turtle graphics, and this is used to illustrate several points, such as recursion. It should be fairly easy to convert some of the Pascal programs to BASIC using the turtle procedures of Chapter four.

Brown: Peter John Brown, *Pascal from BASIC*. Addison-Wesley, 1982. The reason for including this book is not that its author played an important part in making the current work possible, but because he gave me a fiver for mentioning it, which was a waste of money as I was going to include it here anyway. The book assumes the reader has a knowledge of BASIC, and builds on this to turn him into a reasonably competent Pascal programmer. It's useful for the way in which BASIC's shortcomings are pointed out, and like all good Pascal books it contains many useful programming techniques. Shame about the cover art though.

Cownie: John Cownie, *Creative Graphics*. Acornsoft Ltd., 1982. This wasn't mentioned in the text as I received my copy too late. (What's six months between friends?) The book is of the standard one comes to expect from Acornsoft. It contains many good examples of using the BBC's graphics, especially pallette manipulation. It's well illustrated, with colour plates, but £7.50 for 108 pages seems a trifle dear.

Cryer: Neil & Pat Cryer, *BASIC Programming on the BBC Microcomputer*. Prentice-Hall, 1982. This book was absolutely essential reading when the BBC Micros were still supplied with the Provisional User Guide. The new User Guide tends to render some of the introductory material in Cryer and Cryer unnecessary, but the book is still about the best intro. to BBC BASIC. I would expect readers of the present book to have at least covered the material in Cryer and Cryer. £5.95 for 208 paperbound pages.

Dijkstra: O.-J. Dahl, E. W. Dijkstra, C. A. R. Hoare, *Structured Programming*. Academic Press, 1972. The standard reference on structured programming. It provides a very good insight into the methodology of structuring programs and data, but can only really be recommended to people with a fairly mathematical background, as many of the examples include set theory etc. At £7.50 for 200 odd pages (hardbound, 1981 price) it's a very good buy.

Foley: J. D. Foley and A. Van Dam, *Fundamentals of Computer Graphics*. Addison-Wesley, 1982. Like most books with "fundamentals" or "principles" in the title, this is a very thorough work. It covers pretty well everything you would want to know about computer graphics (though how long this will be true in this fast-moving field is not certain). Again, a mathematical bent would be a distinct advantage to get the most from the book. At £15.95 for 660 hardbound pages in 1982, it's a bargain.

Gardner: Martin Gardner, *Mathematical Puzzles and Diversions, More Mathematical Puzzles and Diversion, Mathematical Circus*. Pelican Books, 1959, 1961 and 1979 resp. These three books provide much entertainment for anyone who finds fascination in playing with numbers and shapes. They contain much material which should make you say "I wonder if I could do that on the computer?". The last title is my favourite, as it's a little more modern than the others, though mathematics isn't really a subject which ages greatly. Prices were £1.25, £1.50 and £1.95 in 1982.

Goodman: S. E. Goodman and S. T. Hedetniemi, *Introduction to the Design and Analysis of Algorithms*. McGraw-Hill, 1977. An understanding of using and designing algorithms is just as important as knowing how to "code" in a given language, if not more so. This book provides a good basis for this understanding, and also provides many exercises for the reader to try. The example algorithms are given in a pseudo-language which is a bit tiresome to read; a revised edition would be much more useful if Pascal, for example, were used. £4.95 (paperback, 1980), so not a bad buy.

Grogono: Peter Grogono, *Programming in Pascal*. Addison-Wesley, 1980 (Revised Edition.) This is my favourite Pascal book. It's very comprehensive in its coverage of the language, and contains some decidedly non-trivial problems and example programs. Two bugbears: the first edition has lots of mistakes in it, and he spells PASCAL IN CAPITAL LETTERS ALL THE TIME. It cost £5.95 in 1980.

Harding: Robert D. Harding, *Graphs and Charts*. Acornsoft Ltd., 1982. Although half of this book's 104 pages are taken up by solid program listings, I can't really see it being used as a source of much inspiration for programmers. In order to fit the programs into the limited memory of the computer, they have been made very compressed, with hardly any indentation or spacing. The book will probably serve better as a guide for people who have bought the tape of the book, which means half of it is irrelevant to them. £7.50 again.

Horowitz: E. Horowitz and S. Sahni, *Fundamentals of Data Structures*. Pitman, 1977. Another comprehensive, if heavy-going, book which covers in great detail all sorts of things mentioned in the text (searching, sorting, hashing, arrays etc.). It uses a language called Sparks for illustration. Why don't these people ever use real languages? Luckily Sparks isn't very complex, so most of the algorithms will translate directly into BBC BASIC. £9.95 for the paperback edition in 1981. Not bad for such a thick book.

Jennings: A. Jennings, *Matrix Computation for Engineers and Scientists*. John Wiley, 1977. To be honest, I haven't read this one. Graham Beech recommends it for matrices though, and that's good enough for me. Also, it's published by Wiley's so it must be good.

Johnson-Davies: David Johnson-Davies, *Practical Programs for the BBC Computer and Acorn Atom*. Sigma, 1982. As you can tell from the title, it's only half applicable to us at best. Still, the fact that it has a compiler, with lots of BBC Assembler bits in it, makes it a worthwhile purchase. Some entertaining graphics programs are also included. At £5.95, a good buy. Can I have a job now, please, sir?

Kernighan: Brian Kernighan and P. J. Plauger, *Software Tools*. Addison-Wesley, 1976. The title says it all really. It's a collection of useful programming tools, such as sorting, searching, editing and formatting. The average micro owner will benefit from the discussions of style, rather than being able to use the programs themselves, though some may be directly translatable. This is the original version, which was geared towards the mainframe user. The successor, *Software Tools in Pascal*, is probably a better buy nowadays. I haven't read it but my friend Pete says its OK, which is good enough for me. Used to be £7.95.

Leventhal: Lance A. Leventhal, *6502 Assembly Language Programming*. Osborne/ McGraw-Hill, 1979. I use my copy so much, the front cover's come off. A great reference manual, not only for the 6502, but also the peripheral chips such as the 6522 VIA. Contains many good examples of 6502 assembly language (see also **Saville**), and explains all about interrupts. They've changed the format to larger size now, so it's probably quite expensive.

Liffick: Blaise Liffick (Editor), *Programming Techniques*. Byte Books, 1980. This is a collection of reprints from Byte Magazine which were concerned with various programming techniques (hence its title). I like it particularly for the articles on Warnier-Orr diagrams, and because it saves you from having to wade through hundreds of pages of American Adverts. The other books in the series, *Simulation*, and *Numbers in Theory and Practice* are also worth reading.

Nevison: John M. Nevison, *The Little Book of BASIC Style*. Addison-Wesley, 1978. A smashing book, this. It expounds all the things about program layout and structuring which I've tried to illustrate throughout the text. Of necessity, it covers only minimal BASIC, but the extensions to the techniques Nevison presents when using BBC BASIC should be clear. It says $5.95 on my copy, so the English price can't be much more than £5.95.

Newman: William Newman and Robert Sproull, *Principles of Interactive Computer Graphics*. McGraw-Hill, 1979 (2nd. Edition). Another very comprehensive graphics book. Its advantages over **Foley** are an appendix on the use of matrices in computer graphics, and the cheaper price (£8.75, 1979 paperback). I find Foley a bit easier to follow, though. All the examples are in a Pascal extension (hurrah!).

Nobbs: David Nobbs, *The Fall and Rise of Reginald Perrin, The Return of Reginald Perrin, The Better World of Reginald Perrin*. Penguin, 1976, 1977, 1979. These three should be in everyone's book case. In case you're looking for a computer connection, Reggie says to Bill, "I've got a PXL 2, double checked through the computer" on page 161 of the first book. Cheap at twice the price (especially when compared to computing books). They *were* 95p each.

Page: E. S. Page and L. B. Wilson, *Information Representation and Manipulation in a Computer*. Cambridge, 1978 (2nd. Ed.). If you can get past the title you're doing well. This is a good introduction to data structures, searching and sorting. It is aimed (like most computing books of its ilk) at undergraduate students, so your maths should be at least CSE grade three. There are a lot of exercises, though these are mostly of a theoretical nature as they come from past University exams. Each chapter has a fair number of references, which are useful if you live near a University library. It cost £4.75 in 1980, though I doubt if it still does.

Pan: *The Universal Encyclopaedia Of Mathematics*. Pan Reference Books, 1964. This is the cheapest and probably most widely available of the maths reference/formulae books. It is also more useful than many as, in addition to the lists of all sorts of formulae, the body of the book is arranged in the form of an illustrated dictionary of mathematics. It's very handy for looking up strange maths terms which appear in computing books, and only cost £1.50 in 1979.

Richards: Martin Richards and Colin Whitby Strevens, *BCPL – the language and its compiler*. Cambridge, 1980. There are a couple of good reasons for reading this book. Firstly, the source of many of BBC BASIC's novel features is revealed. As was mentioned in Chapter one, the indirection operators are found in BCPL, and several other ideas such as the static variables are also recognisable in this book. The book is also a must if you are going to buy BBC BCPL, and it contains a part of the listing of a real compiler, which should be of use to anyone trying to struggle through one of the more theoretical compiler books. The paper back edition is £4.95.

Rogers: David Rogers and J.A. Adams, *Mathematical Elements of Computer Graphics*. McGraw-Hill, 1976. As its title implies, the scope of this book is much narrower than **Newman** or **Foley**. It concentrates on the algorithms which are used in computer graphics, and supports this practical approach by including many BASIC listings in the appendix. Once the matrix operations have been converted, most of these programs can be used on the BBC machine. £10.45 for 236 pages may seem dear, but they're fairly action-packed pages.

Saville: Lance Leventhal and W. Saville, *6502 Assembly Language Routines*. Osborne Books, 1982. This book contains a multitude of useful techniques for 6502 assembly language programmers. These are presented in the form of 350 pages of program listings preceded by 150 pages of general advice and discussion of the 6502 instruction set. The programs are very well documented which means that it is easy to extract the lines relevant to your application without fear of something important being omitted. £9.50 for 550 pages.

Wilson: I. R. Wilson and A. M. Addyman, *A Practical Introduction to Pascal*. Macmillan, 1978. This little book is a nice, quick introduction to Pascal, with an emphasis on practical applications, as you may have inferred from the title. Its greatest virtue as a first Pascal book is the incredibly low price of £3.95. The original text has now been superseded by a second edition (which includes a copy of the BSI Pascal standard, for better or for worse), and also by books such as **Brown**, which are aimed more specifically at BASIC programmers.

Zaks: Rodnay Zaks, *Programming the 6502*. Sybex Books. This is an alternative to **Leventhal**. It is probably better as a first read, as it has more English and less reference data.

Index